An Evening With Jehan Sadat

Monday, April 14, 2003
Mondavi Center, Jackson Hall
University of California, Davis
A Western Health Advantage Distinguished Speakers Series Event

MONDAVI CENTER
UCDAVIS

Jehan Sadat

Middle East scholar and peace activist

Proponent of international peace, children's welfare reform, and women's equality and education, Jehan Sadat has devoted her life to activism while also maintaining the legacy of her late husband, Anwar Sadat, former President of Egypt. Today she is an associate research scholar at the University of Maryland, a position from which she supports economic development, human rights, ethics, and religious tolerance. She has also been an associate at the Center for International Development and Conflict Management since 1988.

Dr. Sadat has been involved in social work and women's movements in the Middle East since she was a young woman. Several years before she met her husband, she had initiated a women's emancipation movement in her home village of Talla. Since 1972, she has devoted much of her time to the establishment of the Wafa Wa Amal (Faith and Hope) Society in Egypt, which has constructed and now operates a fully integrated city for handicapped war veterans and civilians, complete with clinics, rehabilitation centers, national training programs, and recreation areas.

In 1977, Sadat initiated SOS Children's Villages in Egypt, offering needy orphans opportunities to lead normal family lives. She is a long-time national and international advocate of legal reform on the behalf of family affairs and women's equality, and has founded or headed many organizations and charitable associations, including the Egyptian Blood Bank and the Egyptian Society for Cancer Patients.

At the age of 40, Sadat entered Cairo University, earning her BA in Arabic literature four years later graduating at the top of her class. She has since earned both an MA (1980) and a PhD (1986) from Cairo University. Dr. Sadat has received 18 honorary doctoral degrees and a number of prestigious international awards, including the Eleanor Roosevelt Award from the United Nations Association of San Francisco and UNICEF's Children's Champion Award.

A Western Health Advantange Distinguished Speakers Series Event
Additional support provided by American Airlines

WESTERN
HEALTH
ADVANTAGE

AmericanAirlines

A Woman of Egypt

Jehan Sadat

SIMON AND SCHUSTER
New York

Simon & Schuster
Rockefeller Center
1230 Avenue of the Americas
New York, NY 10020

Designed by Levavi & Levavi
Manufactured in the United States of America

10 9 8 7 6 5 4 3 2 1

Library of Congress Cataloging-In-Publication Data
Sādāt, Jīhān, 1933-
        A woman of Egypt.

Includes index.
        1. Sādāt, Jīhān, 1933-   . 2. Sadatm Anwar, 1918-1981
        —Family.   3. Egypt—Presidents—Wives—Biography.   I. Title.
        DT107.828S24A3   1987   962'.054'0924   [B]   87-12697
        ISBN: 0-7432-3708-0

For information regarding the special discounts for bulk purchases, please contact Simon &
Schuster Special Sales at 1-800-456-6798 or business@simonandschuster.com

I could not have written this book without the help of Linda Bird Francke. From our first meeting in Giza in 1985 to the conclusion of the writing in Virginia in 1987, Linda has supported and encouraged me. She helped me with my English, for it is a second language to me, and guided me in shaping the book for Western readers. Through it all, she has remained a dear and loyal friend. For all her efforts and her concern, I wish to give her special thanks.

Acknowledgments

When I set out to write this book several years ago, I envisioned a short book about my husband and our life together. But the more I traveled, and the more I talked with people outside of Egypt, the more I realized how misunderstood Egyptian culture was. Many Westerners think of us still as riding on camels, hidden behind veils. But that is the story of Lawrence of Arabia, not of modern Egypt.

And so the book grew to include the history of Egypt from the time of the Revolution in 1952 through my husband's historic journey to Jerusalem in 1977, our peace with Israel in 1979, and finally Anwar's assassination in 1981. It grew to include an explanation of our religion of Islam, of our many traditions that play so large a part in Egyptian life, of our family-centered society. It grew bigger than my capacity to remember every detail, and so I turned to the excellent histories of modern Egypt written by P. J. Vatikiotis, professor of politics at the University of London, and John Waterbury, professor of politics at the Woodrow Wilson School at Princeton University.

I read and reread my friend Mousa Sabri's book *Sadat: The Truth, the Legend* as well as two of my husband's books, *In Search of Identity,* published in 1977, and *Those I Have Known,* published posthumously in 1984. My living room floor became piled with research papers and clips from Egyptian magazines and newspapers.

Alice Mayhew, my editor at Simon and Schuster, supported me throughout the growing pains of the book, as did Daniel Wolfe who helped so much with the research and revisions. In Cairo, my son-in-law, Hassan Mare'i, read the manuscript and made valuable suggestions. I thank them all.

Finally now, the book is finished. It is no longer mine, but

yours. I hope that when you finish it, you will better understand our beautiful area of the world and come visit us. Egypt
is a land of civilization both ancient and modern, a contrast of
wind-swept desert and fertile green fields, a rich oasis stretch-
ing the length of the Nile and bound together by Islam. Let this
book be a bridge between my culture and yours. Let it be a
book of hope. Let it be a book of peace.

To the proud memory of my husband, Anwar el-Sadat, and to our children, Loubna, Gamal, Noha and Jehan, who have suffered as I have suffered, loved as I have loved

Contents

mawt zawji
1. The Death of My Husband   13

el-tufula fil qahira
2. Growing Up in Cairo   34

el-tha'ir wal taliba
3. The Revolutionary and the School Girl   71

tahrir misr
4. The Liberating of Egypt   108

fatret abdel nasser
5. The Time of Nasser   133

el-hayah fil qura
6. Life in the Villages   181

awga' misr
7. The Agony of Egypt   210

el-khiyana wal ghadr
8. Treachery and Traitors   251

damm ibrahim
9. The Blood of Abraham   272

maktab el-sayyida el-'ula
10. The Office of the First Lady   299

el-mar'a fil islam
11. *Women in Islam* 326

el-tariq ilal salaam
12. *The Road to Peace* 367

bismallah
13. *In the Name of God* 410

el-huzn bila nihayya
14. *Sorrow Unending* 444

Epilogue 461

Index 467

Chapter 1

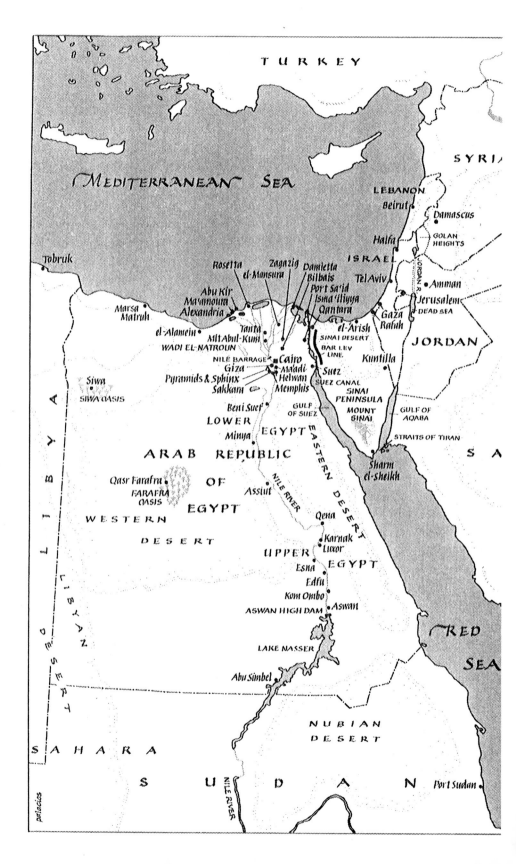

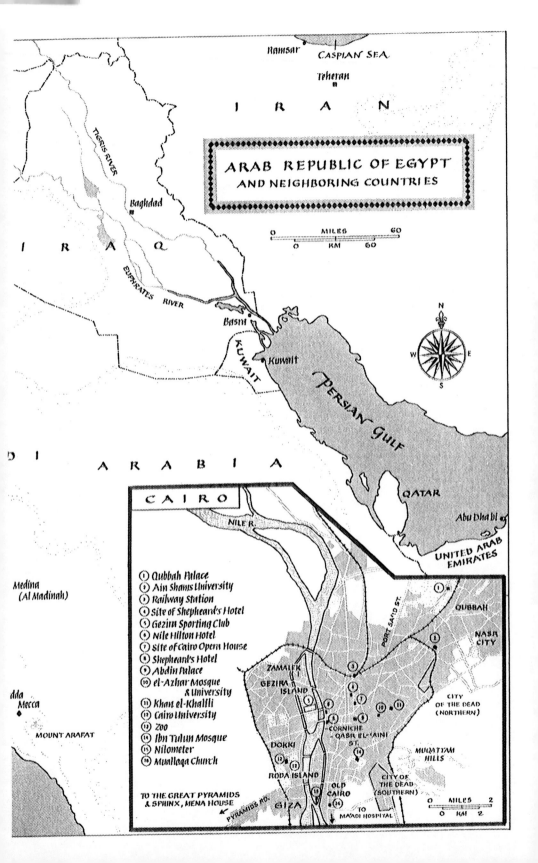

mawt zawji

The Death of My Husband

October 6, 1981, was one of the few days out of thousands that I didn't fear for my husband's life. October 6 had become one of Egypt's proudest anniversaries, the annual celebration of the moment in 1973 when our soldiers had crossed the Suez Canal to reclaim the land taken from us by Israel. Domestic quarrels were forgotten on that day. So were religious differences, political differences, class differences. All Egypt was one every October 6, and, as one, acclaimed my husband, Anwar el-Sadat, who had led our country out of humiliation to the beginnings of justice. So sure was I that Anwar on this special day faced no danger that I almost did not attend the traditional military review in Nasr City, on the outskirts of Cairo. Instead, with Anwar's blessing, I planned to watch the parade on television with my three daughters and work on my Ph.D. dissertation on poetic criticism at Cairo University. Our son, Gamal, was traveling in America.

Am I thankful that at the last minute my security officer so chided me for even considering not sharing this celebration with Anwar that I changed my mind and went? I am not sure. For the rest of my life I will hear the automatic gunfire that ripped the life out of my husband and nine others, see Anwar's blood spilled over the scattered wooden chairs on the reviewing stand, cry at the memory of my little grandchildren screaming in terror as bullets shattered the windows above the reviewing stands and thudded into the cement wall we were crouching behind. It would take my grandchildren five years to be able to sleep without nightmares. I will never know a restful night's sleep again.

How handsome my husband always looked in the special uniforms he had had designed just to wear for the military review on October 6. This year he had a new one, and like his others it was very tight, styled after the German uniforms he admired so much. In other years, my daughters and I would tease him about this vanity as we tugged and tugged at his boots, helping him to pull them up over his long britches. "Don't you think the uniform should be a little looser?" I'd chide him as he struggled into it. "Oh, Jehan, don't say that," he'd say with pretend impatience. "You know nothing about the military."

He cared very much about how he looked this day. To stress the pride and importance he had always felt serving as an officer in the Egyptian Army, he would finish out his appearance by carrying a field marshal's baton under his arm, an affectation which I did not like. "People will think you are showing off, and you are not a show-off," I would protest. But, insisting that his stick represented "the true style of military life," he always carried it anyway. Except for that last October 6. Did he forget it? Or did he not take it out of deference to me? I will never know.

For everything was different on this October 6. Every other year I had dressed early myself, then helped my husband into his uniform. While he finished dressing, I would go downstairs to greet the Vice-President and the Minister of Defense, who came early to our home in Giza overlooking the Nile to accompany my husband to the parade grounds. Together we would greet Anwar as he came down the stairs ready to go. I couldn't tease him in front of these government officials, of course, so I would offer more formal congratulations. "Many happy returns of this day," I would say. "God bless all of you." Then they would set out in one car for a preliminary meeting at the Defense Ministry, and twenty minutes later I would leave for the parade grounds in another.

But on this October 6, because I decided to go at the last minute, I had to rush to get dressed myself, to call quickly for the hairdresser, and I missed Anwar's departure altogether. In the early morning I had woken him as usual and given him the newspapers to read. Because this was a special day I had also put our two-year-old granddaughter, my son's daughter Yasmin, in his bed, and he had laughed as she tried to pull his mustache, laughed again when she wouldn't kiss his lathered cheek while he was shaving.

"Jehan, be sure to bring Sherif with you in his uniform," Anwar said to me about our five-year-old grandson. "He's grown-up now. I want him to watch the parade."

"Of course," I replied.

Anwar had treated our own son, Gamal, the same way when he was young, dressing him up in a military uniform, expecting him to attend official functions, to learn his responsibilities as a man. Always when he traveled, Anwar would say to him, even when Gamal was five years old, "Gamal, you are responsible for your three sisters. You are the man of this home. I trust you to be good to them and to take care of them." Gamal had taken his duty very seriously. "Loubna, where are you going?" he would say sternly to even his older sister when she went out. And though it irritated the girls, they would have to answer him.

Now Anwar was beginning to make a man out of Sherif. But I had no intention of putting the boy into the heavy uniform Anwar had had copied from his own. Sherif had asthma, it was a warm day, and I was afraid he would get overheated. I would take him in light clothes, I decided, and explain to Anwar later. But if I didn't hurry, I wouldn't be able to take Sherif at all. My last memory of my husband at home is in his bathroom shaving. I didn't even have time for our ritual parting downstairs. I didn't say goodbye. I didn't kiss him. I didn't see him at all. Through my bedroom window I heard his car pull out through the gates.

But no matter, I thought then. I would see him soon enough at the parade grounds and then we would return to a victory celebration at the house. As always on this day, I would greet him at the door with the sound of the *zaghreet*, the trilling ululation that Egyptian women make by rippling their tongues on the roofs of their mouths. All our neighbors would come out on the balconies of their apartment houses at his return, and the women would perform the *zaghreet* with me, filling the air with excitement and congratulations. I could count on all this ahead of me, as well as the family photo taken every year on this day in our walled garden.

The photographer had in fact been at our home the day before, taking pictures of Anwar and Yasmin in the garden. I had watched Anwar sitting so quietly reading while our granddaughter crawled all over him. "Come for a photo, Mrs. Sadat," the photographer had called. But I was on my way to a meeting. "Let it keep till tomorrow," I told him. "I'm busy now." I couldn't know that not only my husband but the photographer too would be killed in the carnage just hours away.

"Granny, Granny, we want to go. Please take us with you," my granddaughters cry when I prepare to leave for the parade grounds with Sherif. Why not take all of them? I think to myself. This is a special day for their grandfather, for our country. If they get tired or restless watching the military review, the nanny can bring them home in the car. And so we all go together.

God must have meant to bring this last moment of happiness on earth to Anwar. Never will I forget the smile on his face when he entered the reviewing stands amidst a swell of applause and looked to the top of the stands to see his four grandchildren standing there with me. His face, usually quiet and thoughtful, was suddenly filled with the warmth of the sun as he waved up at us. "What a smile," whispers my friend and a member of Parliament Dr. Zeinab el-Sobky, in my ear. She was right. It was not just any smile. It was the smile of a man who loved his country especially on this day, who loved his family more than his own life. Always now in my mind, I see the beauty of that last smile, remember the happiness his face was radiating.

"What is this delay?" I say to Suzanne Mubarak, the wife of Vice-President Husni Mubarak as we sit together at the review. A motorcycle has broken down. But there are more delays to come.

"Now we are going to see our courageous guerilla forces," comes the voice over the loudspeaker. Two or three minutes go by with no one marching. The parade isn't as perfect as it was in other years when it was under the control of former Minister of Defense Gamasi. Then there hadn't been a moment wasted.

"This parade is not well organized," I complain to Mrs. Mubarak before stopping myself. Why am I criticizing something this woman has had nothing to do with? I must say only good things and not reflect my true feelings on others.

And then the Air Force planes come in formation, Phantom jets doing aerobatics and leaving plumes of brightly colored smoke behind them. The sky is crisscrossed with ribbons of red and blue and green as the jets thunder around and around.

"This is the best of all," laughs Mrs. Mubarak, whose husband, sitting just beside Anwar, has been an Air Force pilot himself.

I laugh with her in the excitement and all the noise, though I am worried for the pilots. How Anwar must be enjoying this. I look down at him through the large glass windows on the balconies at the top of the stands. Like everyone else he is looking up at the spectacle in the sky, his hat on the railing in front of him.

But what is this? What is this army truck suddenly pulling out of the line of artillery vehicles and stopping in front of the reviewing stands? Three army men are running toward the stands with machine guns. Instantaneously I hear the explosion of a grenade, almost lost in the roar of the jets overhead. Smoke fills the air. Immediately I look to Anwar, who is standing up now, pointing to his bodyguards as if to say, "Go and stop this." It is the last sight I have of my husband.

Cries. Screaming. Bullets smash the glass window through which he have been watching the parade. I try to rush toward my husband, but my bodyguard blocks my way.

"Madam, I beg you not to leave your place," he says. But I must get to Anwar.

"Keep your distance," I say to my bodyguard.

But he is stronger and pulls me in such a severe way to the

ground that for two weeks my arm is purple. All around me is chaos. My grandchildren are crying, crying as another grenade explodes, and the sound of bullets fills our ears. What is this screaming?

"Stop that!" I shout at the wife of one of our ministers who is huddled in the hallway along with the wives of the generals and the wives of the government officials seated below us in the open. Beside me sitting on the floor is Mrs. Mubarak, as well as my secretary. "It is the Muslim fanatics," I tell her.

For months now, Egypt has been wracked by religious violence. Tensions between religious extremists have pitted Muslims against our ancient community of Coptic Christians for the first time in Egypt's history. Many lives have been lost, and much blood spilled in an escalating siege of violence that had threatened the stability of the country. With the greatest reluctance, Anwar had had to temporarily detain over a thousand religious and political extremists in September. The final phase of the return of the Sinai, Egyptian land occupied by the Israelis since the '67 war, was soon to take place and Anwar could not risk any civil unrest.

The religious strife had fanned other minority opposition to Anwar's leadership. For his peace with Israel, Anwar was being called a traitor by Islamic fundamentalists and by some leaders of the Arab countries. For his dream of bringing harmony to the followers of Christianity, Judaism and Islam, he had been branded an infidel. For his economic policy of *infitah,* the opening of Egypt to foreign investments, he was being called a puppet of the West. I too had been denounced by the religious extremists, for my encouragement of Muslim women, for choosing not to cover my head in a veil. During this critical period in the summer and fall of 1981, I had feared greatly for my husband's life. In the escalating tension of the last few weeks there had not been one morning when I said goodbye to him and blessed him that I did not expect him to be dead by evening. Except for this one day.

The barrage of bullets continues at the parade grounds and becomes even more. Crouched in a windowless passageway, we can see nothing, but I am sure the shooting we are hearing is from our own security guards finishing whatever trouble there has been. "Be calm," I keep saying to the women. And, remarkably, I feel myself very calm. I am not weeping. I am not frightened. I do not even fear for my husband's life. I still believe that the members of the Army cannot harm him. He thinks of them as his children, calls them his "sons." And they in turn love their Commander in Chief.

In a surprise attack in 1973, Egyptian forces had stormed across the Suez Canal and the Bar Lev Line, the earthen barrier forty-seven feet tall that the Israelis had claimed was impenetrable. By defeating the Israelis for the first time in twenty-five years, giving us a victory over them after three humiliating defeats, Anwar had restored our pride in Egypt's military. For this, soldiers and civilians alike referred to him as *batal el-'ubur,* the Hero of the Crossing.

"Mr. Atherton! Mr. Atherton!" I call down to the ambassador from the United States, the first person I see when the firing is finished. But he does not hear me. Everywhere there are chairs overturned, people lying on the ground, being put into ambulances. Others who are not wounded are just standing and staring, as if they are knocked out but still upright. I look to my husband, but he is not there. Slowly and carefully I walk down into the stands. I do not want to appear hysterical at this moment, to show fear for my husband or my country.

"Where is President Sadat?" I say to one of his Presidential Guard, trying not to notice the blood staining his white uniform.

"He is all right, I swear it, Mrs. Sadat," he tells me. "I carried him to the helicopter myself to take him to Ma'adi Hospital. It seems only his hand is wounded."

"Let us go to the hospital," I say calmly to my bodyguard. But there are so many things I do not know. Is a takeover of the country in progress? Are my daughters safe at home? And what of my husband? I see Fawzi Abdel Hafez, Anwar's secretary, being carried away on a stretcher badly wounded and remember he was sitting just behind my husband. But still I cannot believe that my husband has come to harm. Vice-President Mubarak, I know, is all right. While we were still crouched behind the wall in the stands, one of his bodyguards came to whisper in Mrs. Mubarak's ear that her husband was safe.

Quickly I gather my grandchildren into the car to drive us to the helicopter waiting at the nearby Qubbah Palace to fly us to the hospital. The children are almost hysterical with fear, and I spend my time in the car trying to quiet them. I decide to ask the helicopter pilot to put down at our home to leave the grandchildren. I will complete the journey to the hospital by car. The landing pad at the hospital is far from the front door and I am worried that there will not be a car to meet me, that we will waste too much time making the last part of the journey by foot. I look for Mrs. Mubarak, to take her with us, but I cannot find her.

Dr. el-Sobky is still right beside me. "I will not leave you," says this good and dear friend.

I do not understand at the hospital why everyone is just staring at me in a frozen way and not speaking to me. I know all of the doctors and nurses I see in the hall, having spent so much time in the hospital with the wounded from the '67 war and the '73 war.

A man very distracted rushes up to me and starts asking me questions in French about the condition of Ambassador Ruelle of Belgium. "I'm so sorry, Mrs. Sadat," he says when he finally recognizes me. It is the French ambassador. Ambassador Ruelle, I find out later, has been severely wounded, but he survives.

Now I am more concerned for my husband, for I am told that he is in the operating theater. The corridors have never seemed so long as I hurry toward the room where other government officials and my family are waiting for me. Thank God my daughters are all right. And here. Of course, I remember, as I walk and walk, they were watching the parade on television. Finally I find the room where they are waiting along with their husbands and the government ministers who have survived the attack. Mr. Mubarak, whose hand had been grazed by a bullet, has already had his wound bandaged.

There is such a silence in that room. I join them and say nothing. Instead, I wait for a doctor to come and tell me not to worry, that my husband is all right. But no one comes. My son-in-law Hassan Mare'i takes a call from my twenty-five-year-old son Gamal in California, where he has learned of the attack on his father. The wound, American television has reported, is in Anwar's chest beside his heart. Gamal tells Hassan that our embassy in Washington has arranged for a plane to bring him home quickly. For further medical insurance, Gamal has also called our ambassador in London, Hassan Abu Seda, to arrange to pick up Dr. Magdi Yacoub, a world-famous Egyptian heart specialist, on his way to Egypt. Dr. Yacoub is in fact in the middle of an operation but turns his duties over to another doctor, leaving immediately for the airport with all his instruments and equipment.

In Ma'adi Hospital, we wait and wait. But still, even after half an hour, no doctor comes to the room where we are sitting in silence. And though I do not want to know the truth, I feel it. I have to do my duty. Taking a deep breath, I stand up and turn to Mr. Mubarak.

"It seems that Sadat is gone," I say calmly to him, "It is your turn to lead the country now. Please, Mr. Mubarak, take care of Egypt." He looks at me numbly.

"Don't say that, Mrs. Sadat. Don't say that!" I hear someone shouting. I turn toward the voice to see Anis Mansour, the editor of *October* magazine, a friend who met with Anwar every week for an interview. But I don't answer him at all. I have to go to my husband.

No one stops me as I walk down the hall alone toward the room where Anwar lies. In the hallway I pass the chief surgeon, who had lost his son in the '67 war. Often I had sat with him in the hospital and consoled him. Now he is leaning against the wall, as if he cannot stand up alone. Why is he not inside the operating room trying to save my husband?

"I cannot bear to see him," he says to me, his eyes overflowing with tears.

I already feel the truth. And now I know it. "I understand, Doctor," I say to him. "Thank you for all that you have done."

I push open the doors to the operating room, still hoping against hope. But there is none. Anwar is lying on a bed, still dressed in his new military uniform. The sleeve has been ripped open so that the doctors could quickly start blood transfusions. But there was nothing they could do. I rush to my husband, throwing myself in tears on his chest. I am so lost in my grief that it is minutes before I notice the doctors and nurses standing around the room, their own tears pouring down their faces. Already they have closed his eyes and wrapped a cloth around his head, binding his jaw shut.

It is such a moment that I cannot explain. To see a man who was so much alive, who just a few hours before had smiled at me with the light of a thousand candles, to see him lying there so still. My tears come pouring, but with no sound. I have to be cautious. Officially no one knows yet that Sadat has passed away. And no one must know until we are sure the country is secure. I smooth his hair, kiss his face and his hands. How can he be dead? I can see no wounds, hardly any blood on his suit. I want so much to wake him from his sleep. But I cannot.

Through my tears I see one of my sons-in-law come into the room. "Hassan," I say to him quietly. "Bring my children."

"No! No!" he protests, not wanting to believe what he sees.

"Hassan," I say more firmly, "please bring my children to say goodbye to their father."

And they come, my daughters with their husbands, into the operating room. Over and over they kiss their father on the forehead and on his hands, their tears falling on his body. Like me, they loved him very, very much and cannot stop their grief. Together we recite the traditional Muslim prayer to the dead: "*Inna li Allah, wa inna ilayhi raji'un. La illaha ila Allah, wa Muhammad rasul Allah.* To God we belong, and to Him we must return. There is no God but Allah, and Muhammad is His Prophet."

"Let us go," I say to my children after a few minutes. I turn to the doctors. "Thank you for all that you have done for my husband. Now I have one last favor. I don't want anyone to enter this room. I don't want people to come just to look at him. Please give my husband his privacy."

They nod in agreement.

The government ministers have to know. Mubarak has to know. For eleven years, my husband has been president of Egypt. Now the responsibility will be passed to Mubarak.

"Mr. President," I say to him back in the waiting room, "Anwar Sadat is gone. He is not living anymore. This is God's will. But Egypt is still living and is in mortal danger. Now it is you who must lead us." But still he sits there, not moving. "I have one favor," I go on. "Please do not announce that Sadat has passed away until you know what the situation is in the country and how you can control it."

Immediately the ministers file out of the room to hold an emergency meeting. But still Mubarak sits. One of the ministers returns to get him, but it is as if he cannot hear him.

"I will not leave the hospital until you go to the meeting," I tell Mubarak. "Go away from this place now. Your duty is to save Egypt." And finally Mubarak stands.

The rumor persisted that Sadat had only been wounded in the hand. But all those in the hospital knew the truth. As my daughters and I walked back down those long corridors, doctors, nurses, even our bodyguards cried in very loud voices. I tried to remain composed, hiding my eyes with dark glasses, but it was very hard. One of the head nurses, whom I had come to know well, threw her arms around me and we cried together, but silently.

Outside the hospital there were many other people, even members of Parliament, just standing and wailing. In a mourning ritual that had been passed down from the days of the pharaohs, the Minister of Social Affairs was sitting on the ground, beating her chest with her arms and crying out to God. The sadness at my husband's passing was very, very deep, and all the way home my driver cried louder and louder. The mourning intensified when we entered our home. The staff still believed that Anwar had only been wounded, that the President would be all right. But when they saw the driver and my family, they knew.

I could not talk with them right away. Immediately I went upstairs with my daughters to the balcony outside Anwar's room where often he sat and thought while looking over the Nile. Finally, then, I could cry freely for the man who had been my husband for thirty-one years, whose vision of peace and democracy had cost him his life. I could hear the sound of wailing spreading through the house. My granddaughter's nanny started tearing her clothes, jumping up and down and shrieking in the tradition of the villages. "Stop that," I begged her, worried that she would harm herself.

The phone rang. It was Gamal calling from the airport in the United States. "Mummy, I am on my way to pick up Dr. Yacoub," he told me.

I took a deep breath. The phone line we were talking on was not secure. "Come home directly, Gamal," I told him quietly. "There is no need for another doctor."

There was a terrible pause. "I understand, Mummy," he finally said. "I'll phone the ambassador in London and tell him there are doctors enough in Cairo and they don't need Dr. Yacoub anymore."

"Are you all right?" I asked him.

"Yes, Mummy," he told me. "The doctor here in our embassy has given me a Valium to stay calm."

"Be brave," I said to our son. "Be as your father would want you."

How my heart went out at that moment to Gamal. He had been close, very close, to his father. Every day his father would walk for at least an hour in our garden, and often Gamal would join him. Anwar wanted his son to understand his responsibilities toward Egypt and also toward his family. In Egypt, the oldest son in any family is considered the next head of the household and responsible for the well-being and support of his mother and sisters. As Gamal was our only son, Anwar had spent much time preparing him for that moment when his father would be gone. And now that moment had come.

But nobody in Egypt yet knew the truth. As soon as the firing had begun at the parade ground, television coverage had been stopped. That had prompted speculation. Rumors flew that a full-fledged revolution was under way. The Muslim fanatics were trying to take over the radio station to mobilize the masses in the name of Islam, ran one such rumor. Another suggested that the assassins had escaped and fled to Assiut University, a fundamentalist center, where they had taken over the campus and were killing all who opposed them. There was conjecture, too, about the fate of the President. He was unharmed and trying to quell the insurrection. The President was dead.

In the late afternoon an inscription from the Quran suddenly appeared on the television screen: "Nothing will befall us except what Allah has ordained. He is our Guardian. In Allah let the faithful put their trust." Taking this as a sign of the worst, people began to gather on the street in front of our house, wailing and lamenting the attack on their leader. The phones in our home were ringing and ringing, but the staff protected me, saying the doctor had given me a sedative and put me to sleep. Even Jimmy Carter, the former President of the United States who had been so instrumental in the peace between Egypt and Israel, was not allowed to speak to me. I could not come to the phone. I could not talk to the people. My children and I were too stunned.

It was not until 8 P.M., seven hours after the attack on my husband, that Mubarak came on television to announce my husband's death. "God has ordained that Sadat should die on a day which itself is symbolic of him, among his soldiers, heroes and people proudly celebrating the anniversary of the day on which the Arab nation regained its dignity," Mubarak said solemnly. Afterward, I was told, the Voice of America, which many Egyptians listen to, played Chopin's Funeral March, interrupting it often to announce in Arabic that Anwar el-Sadat, President of the Arab Republic of Egypt, was dead.

How could members of the Army have killed him? Who was responsible for the lack of security at the parade grounds? Gamal arrived late that night as my daughters and I tried to control our tears and look for answers. And there were some. Anwar himself had asked his personal bodyguard not to stand between him and the armed forces, believing not only that he did not need protection from his own Army, but that such a show of security would signal vulnerability. On this special day, even the President's special security force had been standing on the far side of the reviewing stands, out of sight.

But many questions remained. Every other year a regiment of guerilla forces had led the parade, then taken up position between the President and the rest of the troops. This year they had not. Every other year there had been government marksmen on the roofs of surrounding buildings to keep a good eye on potential saboteurs. This year there had been no marksmen at all. Each army vehicle and each gun was supposed to have been checked several times at various checkpoints before reaching the reviewing stand, to make sure no one carried live ammunition. But somehow those three men, an officer and two enlisted men, had managed to arrive in front of my husband with live ammunition.

Was it a bigger plot? Everyone in the reviewing stands had thought so. Hearing the grenades and the automatic gunfire at the same time as the jets were flying overhead, most people had thought we were being bombed. They had crouched instinctively, hands over their ears, and thought everything was finished. No one believed that the attack on the President of Egypt could be the act of a few rather than the plot of many.

Hours passed in this way. Everyone in Egypt was blaming everybody. The Presidential Guard was blaming the Army Guards and vice versa. And both were putting the blame on the President's special security men. Meanwhile, the wailing on our street grew louder and louder.

My tears dried into suspicion, suspicion of everyone. Had there been a stranger in the reviewing stands, someone we didn't know? The next day, while I was receiving the sympathies of the foreign ambassadors in my living room, Prime Minister Fuad Muhi el-Din called to ask my permission to remove the one bullet which had lodged in Anwar's body as part of the investigation into his assassination. I readily agreed. But with one condition. I would be present, I told the Prime Minister, as would my son Gamal. After all, I told him, God would wish that Gamal have the opportunity to say farewell to his father who had died in his absence.

I did not tell him the real reason. Gamal was a member of the Shooting Club in Cairo and had often gone duck hunting with his father. He knew a great deal about guns and ammunition, and could see whether the bullet in his father's body came from the machine guns of the terrorists or from some other guns, even from a pistol. Perhaps my husband had been shot from the back by someone in the stands sympathetic to the Muslim fanatics, or even by a member of the guards, at the same time the assassins were shooting from the front. I trusted no one.

Prime Minister Muhi el-Din was shocked when I insisted on being present with Gamal. "It will be too hard on you to watch this," he protested.

"I will be there," I insisted.

On the way to the hospital I was more worried about Gamal seeing his father's body than I was for myself. With all the shooting, I felt sure his body must have been torn apart. To prepare Gamal, I reminded him of our belief that though the flesh of his father was destined to be mortal, his father's soul would live forever in Paradise. Anwar had been very religious, even mystical toward the end, fasting when there was no need, praying more often than the five required prayers a day. His soul would certainly enter heaven, I told Gamal, and be rewarded with the supreme spiritual honor: to behold the face of God.

"Do not be upset by what you see, but be glad that he will be in heaven," I said to Gamal. "I am his wife, you are his son. Because we are still of this earth, it is our duty to honor his remains. He cannot be operated on alone. We have to be beside him." And I shared my suspicions with him. "Look carefully at the bullet to see what kind it is," I told him very quietly.

"You know about these things and I don't. If the bullet comes from a different kind of gun than those used by the assassins, then we will know if more people were involved."

At the hospital, it was the Surgeon General's turn to try to spare me the ordeal. "You will always remember this last sight of your husband, and the memory will come into your life to disturb you," he tried gently to dissuade me.

"I will stand by my husband," I insisted. "Please don't argue. I am not going to give my permission to operate on my husband unless we stand beside him."

But still he resisted. Gamal then called President Mubarak. "I cannot prevent her," Mubarak told Gamal. "He was her husband. I can't tell her no." And he ordered the doctors to admit me to the autopsy.

Anwar's body was wheeled in on a tray from the hospital's morgue, covered by a sheet. I sucked in my breath with shock. How could this be? I had never seen him look so relaxed and happy, a smile on his lips. Every morning I had wakened him from his sleep at nine o'clock. "I will just sleep ten minutes longer," he would often say, his eyes puffy from his not having slept well. In his eternal sleep now, he looked better, more serene, than he had ever looked. A light seemed to radiate from him, and if his eyes had not been closed I would have expected him to speak to me.

Even his body looked perfect. His body had not been torn apart by bullets. On the contrary, when the sheet was removed I could see only three tiny holes, one in his leg and two in the chest just beside the heart. They looked more like little bruises than they did mortal wounds, far too insignificant to have felled such a man. I reached out to touch him because he looked so alive. But where my hand felt his body, it was freezing. There was no life. I kissed him for the last time on his forehead. He was like ice.

Gamal could not hold back his tears at this last sight of his father. Wiping his eyes, he stood very close while the surgeon sliced open Anwar's shoulder, put in his finger and pulled out the bullet. Gamal took it from the doctor and studied it carefully. It was the same type as those fired from the terrorists' machine guns. No one else had fired on my husband.

"We can leave now," I said to Gamal. And we returned home while the doctors completed the official autopsy.

Martial law was declared immediately after the attack on my husband, and a curfew imposed. Already the military police were rounding up hundreds of religious extremists and searching their houses, finding not only huge caches of weapons but a detailed plan for the takeover of the country. Why hadn't our security forces known about this beforehand?

Negligence killed my husband. Carelessness killed my husband. Anwar's own affection for the armed forces, his belief that they could not be infiltrated by the Muslim fanatics, helped kill my husband. And we had all stood by and watched. "This is inconceivable," were Anwar's last words to Husni Mubarak as the members of his own Army ran toward him, their machine guns spitting death.

Anwar was buried in a tomb shaped like a small pyramid, right across from the parade grounds in Nasr City where he was gunned down. This was my decision, not his. He and I had often talked of where he would be buried, especially in the last months when he had felt his death approaching. I had made light of these conversations, trying to deflect the premonition he felt so strongly. But persistently he had continued to speak about his death and his desire to be buried in his beloved childhood village of Mit Abul-Kum in the Nile Delta. "Oh, Anwar, it will take the children and me an hour and a half to go visit you there," I would tease him, trying to get him off the subject.

But he would not be diverted. "If not Mit Abul-Kum, then at the foot of Mount Sinai by St. Catharine's Monastery, where we will be building a mosque and a synagogue," he said to me several times as we walked in the garden. "If I am buried there, it will tell people that all religions are the same, that God is one for all of us." That was a lovely idea, of course. Anwar's fervent dream was that Jews, Christians and Muslims would live together in harmony. And the Sinai was important to all of us. It was in the Sinai that the prophet Moses had received the Ten Commandments from God and seen the burning bush. And it was through the Sinai that the prophet Jesus had traveled when he and his family were fleeing from King Herod in Palestine.

To be buried in the Sinai was symbolically important to Anwar as well. He had dedicated himself to regaining this land taken from us by the Israelis in Nasser's time. That my husband had succeeded in his mission through peaceful means had ironically proved to be his death sentence. His burial there would have been fitting, yes. But still I had tried to tease Anwar out of planning the site of this own tomb. If Mit Abul-Kum was inconvenient to visit, I told him, Mount Sinai would be far worse. "It will take a plane and a car to get there, Anwar," I protested. "I could come visit you only once or twice a year. Better to be buried in Mit Abul-Kum."

But the time for teasing was over. Anwar's premonitions had been right. And when President Mubarak asked me where to bury Anwar, I decided to override my husband's wishes. This was a great man, I thought, not an ordinary man. Why bury him where it will be difficult for people to visit him? Why not bury him where he died, a military place of which he was very proud? How he enjoyed every year going to light the flame at the Tomb of the Unknown Soldier, listening to the lovely music that was played there every Sixth of October, reviewing the troops who had served Egypt with such bravery. Burying him there would remind everyone of all he had done for our country. And each year at the Sixth of October parade, every soldier and every officer would pass by his tomb and know that Sadat was there and salute him.

I did not know then that Mubarak would cancel any further military reviews on the Sixth of October, rightly avoiding putting himself in the same dangerous position as his predecessor. I also did not know that for the next two years Mubarak would declare October 5 to be the official day of mourning for Sadat while keeping the Sixth a day of celebration for victory over Israel. Anwar would not have liked that. He liked to combine extremes. He had chosen the fifth of June, the anniversary of our humiliating defeat by Israel in the Six-Day War in '67, to joyfully reopen the Suez Canal in 1975, turning what had been a day of national shame into a day of national celebration.

But Mubarak did not think in such contrasts and seeming contradictions. "Please," I would say to him. "Sadat belongs to the Sixth of October. You cannot take it away from him." But for two years he replied that he feared celebrating victory on the same day as my husband was killed would make me bitter. "I am bitter from other things," I would argue gently. Finally he must have believed me. Now there is a single bittersweet day of mourning and celebration on the Sixth of October. And no matter where I am in the world, I return to Cairo to honor my husband and visit his grave.

On the day of the funeral I sat in the same chair that Anwar had, in the same reviewing stands. I felt as if I were in a drama, not knowing exactly what was real and what was fantasy. He was shot in this seat, I kept thinking to myself. Just a few days ago he was sitting here in this exact place, full of energy, full of life, full of love for his country. Now he is coming here again, but it is just his body. Just a few days changed completely our lives and our future.

Very few people were on the streets of Cairo to watch the funeral procession. In the state of emergency declared after my husband's death, groups larger than five were forbidden to gather in public. Instead the people watched the funeral at home on television. Before the funeral, a documentary of his life was played: Anwar going to the front in the '73 war despite the danger, Anwar praying at el-Aqsa Mosque in Jerusalem in '77 during his daring peace mission to Israel, Anwar addressing the Knesset. My husband was not a victim of war. He was a victim of peace.

As is our tradition, only men marched in the funeral procession, among them Jimmy Carter, Richard Nixon and Gerald Ford, all former Presidents of the United States, Prince Charles of England, King Baudouin of Belgium, Grand Duke Jean of Luxembourg, Chancellor Helmut Schmidt of West Germany, President François Mitterrand of France and former President Valéry Giscard d'Estaing, leaders from the Soviet Union and from Africa. Hundreds of foreign dignitaries came to honor my husband, as well as the most controversial, Prime Minister Begin of Israel. My dear friend Farah Diba, the former Empress of Iran, joined me in the reviewing stands, as did Rosalynn Carter, U.S. Ambassador to the United Nations Jeane Kirkpatrick, and Bouthaina el-Numeiry, wife of the President of the Sudan.

I was shocked and saddened that no Arab leaders save President Numeiry of the Sudan and President Siad el-Bery of Somalia came to pay their respects to their fallen brother. Yes, there had been differences between Egypt and the Arab countries when Anwar made peace with Israel. After the signing of the Camp David Peace Accords, every Arab country, state or kingdom except the Sudan, Oman and Somalia had severed diplomatic relations with Egypt. But Islam says that any quarrels we might have with one another in this life are settled by death. The duty of these Arab leaders as good Muslims was to honor the passing of one of their own. But they did not. Why, I would ask some of the Arab leaders later. "Because Begin attended, and I would not walk in the same funeral procession as the Prime Minister of Israel," came one of their replies. But I knew that this was just an excuse. Their absence hurt me deeply.

The motorcade escorting Anwar's body drew near, a police car in front of the horse-drawn caisson, another behind, two motorcycles on each side. I shook my head in disbelief. With my children, I walked across the street to the tomb to join President Mubarak and President Numeiry. The coffin containing Anwar's remains was wrapped in an Egyptian flag. His nostrils had been stuffed with perfumed tufts of cotton, his ankles bound together and his arms placed on his breast. His body had been completely washed, sprinkled with rose water and wrapped in seven white shrouds. Hassan Mare'i, my son-in-law, and Talaat, Anwar's brother, had stayed with the body while it was being washed, but Gamal had had to leave he was so overcome by his grief.

I could not stop my tears as the coffin was taken down into the tomb. Standing as composed as I could, I watched Gamal, my sons-in-law and Anwar's brothers go down into the tomb to perform the last funeral rituals and say their final farewells. As a woman, it was not traditional for me to follow my husband's body into the tomb, but I knew what would happen there. The portion of the coffin over Anwar's face would be opened and the coffin laid in the sand facing Mecca. Over it the men would recite verses from the Quran. "Who is thy God?" "Allah." "What is thy religion?" "Islam." "Who is its Prophet?" "Muhammad," Gamal and the others would whisper to Anwar, reminding him of the answers he would have to give to the angels Naaker and Nakeer to ensure his passage to Paradise.

We come from dust and we return to dust. Waiting before the open door of the tomb, I fought for control as I listened to the funeral music being played by the military orchestra, the sole trumpet playing "Taps." The flag had been taken off the coffin. And when a few minutes later the men emerged and the tomb door was sealed, I knew that Anwar's body was also wrapped in the flag of the country he had loved so deeply, the country for which he had given his life. For Egypt.

Anwar! Can this be? I am sleeping in his bed after the funeral. Suddenly I feel him there beside me, *see* him there beside me, sleeping. Is it a dream? No, I am awake. And he is here, beside me. He turns to me, opens his eyes and smiles. I dare not move, praying he will not leave me again. There is his shape in the bed. I reach out slowly to touch him. He is still smiling. And then he is gone.

"Mummy!" I hear Gamal's voice, high with excitement. "Pappi was in my room. He spoke to me." I have tears in my eyes as I see Gamal's eyes stretched wide in wonder. "I was in bed reading when suddenly I heard his voice. 'Gamal, I am happy and at peace,' he said to me. 'Tell your mother and your sisters not to worry. I am well.' I jumped out of bed to look for him, looked even in the living room. But I could not see him."

Forty days after my husband's death, I joined more than fifty of his relatives, his brothers, sisters, nephews, nieces and cousins, his three daughters from his first marriage, beside his tomb for the *Arba'in*. Together my children and I wept while we listened to a sheikh, a Muslim holy man, read passages from the Quran. I could not drive from my mind what Anwar's secretary, Fawzi Abdel Hafez, had told me earlier. Lying wounded beside Anwar just after the shooting, he had seen my husband's eyes open and look up at the balcony where I had been standing. My husband could not speak and knew he was dying. But his eyes were talking. "Look after my family. Take care of them, Fawzi," his eyes were telling his loyal friend. And Fawzi would remain one of our most faithful friends, coming to see us often and crying with us.

I go now to visit Anwar's tomb alone, standing and reading from the Quran. And whenever I arrive, in the morning, the afternoon, sometimes late at night when I have trouble sleeping, always there are people there. After the Pyramids and the Sphinx, I have been told, Anwar's tomb is the most frequently visited place in Cairo.

Still my tears come when I think of my husband. But from the beginning I knew I had to accept his death, to go on. I had to face his loss courageously for my family—and for Egypt. It was not easy to learn to live with such grief and sadness. It was not easy after thirty-one years with such a man, who loved me as I loved him. We were two partners completing each other, not like any ordinary husband and wife. We understood each other completely. We respected each other completely. He was my strength. I was his light. This was something very hard for me to lose.

I try now to stop my tears. Instead of crying, I think of how he would like to see me. If he saw me in my grief, he would not be satisfied. He thought of me as a fighter and was always proud of me. I have to continue as he wished me to continue. Always his expectations are on my mind, and when I feel I am going to lose myself in grief or to be weak, immediately I say to myself: Don't be like that. Sadat doesn't want you to be that way. Anwar wants to see you as strong as you always were. Because of this image of him I carry always, I have conquered my difficulties. Even with all that I have seen.

el-tufula fil qahira

Growing Up in Cairo

i did not know until I was eleven that my name was Jehan, a Persian name picked out by my father which means "the world." My mother, who was English, had nicknamed me Jean, and that was what I was called by my father, an employee at the Ministry of Health, by my teachers at the Christian missionary school I attended, and by my friends. It was not at all strange for me or my classmates to have European names. I had friends named Mimi and Fifi, Helen and Betty. Egyptians had greatly admired European ways since our leader Muhammad Ali had opened Egypt to foreign influence one hundred years before, believing the Europeans to be much more advanced. But it was strange that I did not even know my proper name until I received my primary-school certificate before moving on to secondary school.

"Who is Jehan?" I asked the teacher, seeing it written on my certificate over my address.

"You," she told me.

I ran home to my mother. "What is my name?" I asked her.

"In school now you are Jehan," she told me. "In our family you are Jean." And to this day that is what my sister and brothers call me.

I was born on Roda Island, one of two islands in the Nile linked by bridges to Cairo in the east and Giza to the west. My island of Roda was a lovely area of gardens and gracious peach limestone villas populated by middle-class Egyptian families. The neighboring island of Zamalek was fancier, home to many British families and those of the Egyptian upper class. The Gezira Sporting Club on Zamalek, to which my family did not belong, boasted cricket pitches and polo fields, tennis courts and swimming pools, and a bar at which liquor was served. The Gezira Club was in another world to me as a child, and to many other Egyptians as well. King Farouk was a member there, as were many of the foreign families, but there was a membership quota for Egyptians.

I was the third of four children in my family, and the first girl. A great space of age spread between my brothers and me. Magdi was ten years older, Ali seven. My mother, I was told, had yearned to have a girl, to comb a daughter's hair and embroider her dresses. The day of my birth was a cause of great celebration in our house, compounded by an *'allawa,* a raise in pay my father took that very same day from his government job. From the beginning, I was considered by my parents to be a good omen. Twenty-one months later, my sister Dalia was born and our family was complete.

We were all very light-skinned, a legacy not only from my English mother but on my father's side as well. My father's father was a Sa'idi, an Upper Egyptian from the tall, usually dark-skinned tribe descended from pure Pharaonic stock. Yet my grandfather too had been fair with blue eyes. His children —my father, my uncle and my two Egyptian aunts—were also fair, and, like all Egyptian families, we were all very close.

When I was a baby we lived with our relatives in one house, splitting up when I was five years old. But no one moved very far away. My bachelor Uncle Mustafa lived just one house away with his divorced sister, 'Aziza, it being his responsibility as a brother to look after her and her young daughter, 'Aida. I visited my Auntie 'Aziza, or Auntie Zouzou as she was nicknamed, every afternoon, and often she came to our home in the evenings. She was my favorite aunt and my Egyptian mother, showering me with affection and spoiling me.

After my Uncle Mustafa finally married at thirty-eight, Aunt Zouzou continued to live with him and his new wife, for it was improper then for a woman to live alone. I'm sure she was very lonely, but she continued to refuse many offers of marriage, fearing that her daughter might be mistreated by a stepfather.

My other aunt, Fatima, whom we fondly called Auntie Batta —Auntie "Duck"—lived just outside Cairo on the Pyramids Road. She was not as affectionate as Auntie Zouzou, but she was a very strong woman. After my grandmother died, Auntie Batta effectively took her place. It was to Auntie Batta's house that the whole family went to break the fast on the first day of Ramadan, and to her that they went to seek advice. Auntie Batta was married to Husni Abu Zaid, an official in the Wafd nationalist party who had served as governor of both Munufiyya province and Minia province. Uncle Husni had a government car, quite a symbol of prosperity at the time, and I loved to drive with him around Cairo. With its official license plate and the flag of Munufiyya fluttering on the fender, the car prompted all the soldiers who saw it to salute. As a little girl, I liked to imagine they were saluting me.

"The mother of the world," the historian Ibn el-Khaldun had called Cairo in the fourteenth century. As a child growing up in Roda, it was easy to see why. Everywhere were the signs of Cairo's rich past. Directly across the Nile to the east was Coptic Cairo, which for more than fifteen hundred years had been the center of Egyptian Christian art and religion. On my way to school I could see the spires of the fourth-century Abu Serga Church, built on the spot where it is believed the family of Jesus stayed during their flight into Egypt. Beyond Abu Serga, I could sometimes make out the thin Ottoman minarets of the Alabaster Mosque, built by Muhammad 'Ali in the nineteenth century. Still farther along was the Old City founded by the Fatimids in 973, and el-Azhar Mosque and

University. El-Azhar is the oldest university in the world, and attracts more than 100,000 students from countries as far away as Mauritania and Indonesia. All who come are students of Islam, for though el-Azhar is old, our religion is still young and growing.

From the other side of Roda, I could look across the Nile to the west and see the river gardens of the rich merchants who lived in Giza, beyond to the campus of Cairo University, and to the Pyramids Road, which, if followed to the end, terminated at the Farafra Oasis in the Libyan Desert. On a clear day when no dust or sand blew, I could make out the tips of the Great Pyramids themselves. And always in the air, five times a day, I could hear the beautiful voices of the muezzins high up in the minarets of Cairo's thousands of mosques, calling the believers in Islam to prayer.

How lovely and quiet Roda Island was during my childhood. Everyone had green gardens, and between the villas on both sides of the island you could always see the Nile passing. In 1933, the population of Egypt was around 15 million, and the population of Cairo less than one million.

My mother must have been very brave to leave her native land of England to come live in Egypt. My father must have been brave also to have married a foreigner. Such a marriage was not against our religion of Islam, for the children of a Muslim man will always themselves be Muslim. It was forbidden only for a Muslim woman to marry into another religion, for her children would have to bear the religion of their father. No. My grandparents' objection to their marriage was not religious, but one of family tradition.

My father, Safwat Raouf, had met my mother, Gladys Charles Cotrell, in 1923 in Sheffield, England, where he was studying medicine at the University of Sheffield and she was a music teacher. Their love was very strong from the beginning. It had to be, for a marriage had already been arranged in Cairo between my father and his cousin. "No one in our family has ever married a foreigner," my grandfather wrote to my father in England. "I will not give you permission to marry this Englishwoman."

My grandparents were well used to the British, of course, for there were many, many British in Egypt at that time. Since the 1880s more than ten thousand British troops had been stationed in Egypt to "protect" our government. The British High Commissioner, Lord Cromer, was effectively ruling the country. Britain and France controlled Egypt's finances. Even Egypt's shares in the Suez Canal, completed in 1869, had had to be sold to the British by our then debt-ridden Khedive Isma'il. It was certainly not uncommon to see the British and many other foreigners in Cairo. But it was difficult for my conservative grandparents to adjust to new ways.

"If you do not allow this marriage, I will not eat until I am dead," my father wrote back to my grandfather. My grandfather was just as stubborn. "I will not give my permission," he replied. And back and forth the letters went until my grandmother grew worried that my father really might harm himself or, just as bad, not come back to Egypt at all. "You must give your permission," she told my grandfather. "Is it not better to welcome our son and his wife home to Egypt than to force him to live in a country foreign to our ways?"

Reluctantly my grandfather had agreed, and my grandmother had sent my mother the traditional Egyptian engagement present of jewelry, in this case a diamond ring and a diamond-and-sapphire necklace she had inherited from her grandfather, along with money for a honeymoon. My mother and father were married in a civil ceremony in England, and when my father returned home with my mother three years later it was with my brother, who had been born in Liverpool. As was the custom then, my parents moved into my grandparents' house on Roda Island. Quickly, my grandparents grew to love my mother, though it must not have been easy for any of them. Our society was more conservative then. And my mother's ways, indeed, were strange.

She never ate Egyptian food, but insisted on the Sudanese cook making a separate meal for her of boiled meat, boiled vegetables, boiled everything. The rest of the family ate the usual Egyptian fare: grilled pigeon; grilled fish; lamb kebab and *kufta*, spiced patties of minced lamb; *wara einab*, grape leaves stuffed with rice and minced meat; *molokhia*, a thick soup made of a minced green leaf and chicken stock; *bamia*, okra sautéed with butter, onion, garlic and tomato paste in broth, served almost always with rice, and different kinds of beans and salads. But my mother would eat boiled mutton and potatoes with mint sauce.

Breakfast was different for us also. In the morning, and indeed for all meals, Egyptians traditionally eat *ful medammes*—fava beans boiled into a thick paste with spices and topped with a fried egg. At our house we had cornflakes, boiled eggs, and thinly sliced toast instead of *'aish,* our flat, unleavened bread, along with jam my mother had made. Tea every afternoon at four was sacred, and she would serve us English tea instead of the sweet mint tea Egyptians drink, and wonderful British cakes, biscuits and sweets she'd made for us to eat. They were delicious, really, especially the lemon curd preserve which we didn't have in Egypt at all.

We shared our house with another family who lived in an apartment upstairs, and, to their wonder and the wonder of our other neighbors, my mother would bring a lovely pine tree into the house at Christmas and decorate it with shiny stars and balls, topping it off with a figure of Father Christmas. Nadia and Tahani, the children who lived upstairs, as well as other children in the neighborhood would rush to see our tree, because very few Egyptian families celebrated Christmas and none had ever seen a Christmas tree. Our friends envied us not only because of our tree and the delicious Christmas pudding my mother made, but because we received gifts as well.

It was difficult for my mother to live so far away from her country. During World War II all communication was cut off between England and Egypt. She heard no news from her family at all and was very worried. One day I found her crying in her room when I returned from school.

"What is wrong with Mummy?" I asked Betty, a friend of my mother's who had been visiting.

"She has just learned her father passed away," Betty told me. "Her family has sent her some money and his watch." A few months later she lost her mother as well.

I felt so sorry for her. I would never have wanted to be away so long from my family. But she did not want to leave her children or her husband to go for a visit. For thirty years she did not return to England, and when she did she could not recognize the streets or even find her family house in Sheffield. To locate her family, my mother put a notice in the local newspaper, saying what hotel she was staying in. That afternoon her only living sister and other relatives rushed to see her. It was a very moving meeting after such a long separation, and the newspaper in Sheffield published a story about it.

My mother did not raise us to be British. Not at all. At home we all spoke Arabic, which she had learned to speak as well. She was not a proselytizer, so she did not influence us in any way from our Muslim traditions. But still it was a little bit confusing to me as a small child. My mother kept a crucifix of the prophet Jesus over her bed, and sometimes I would see her kneeling before it in prayer, her hands clasped together in the Christian manner. Though as small children we did not yet pray, I knew that the Muslims prayed differently, standing with the arms outstretched and prostrating themselves on the ground. I was confused by this difference between my mother and the rest of the family.

"Why are you Christian while we are all Muslim?" I asked her one afternoon after a classmate questioned me about it.

"Nobody chooses their religion," she explained to me in a very sweet way. "We are all what we are born to be. The important thing to remember is that all religions have just one God. It does not matter how we worship Him so long as we have faith."

But still it bothered me. My mother's Christian ways made me think more deeply about our Muslim traditions which others just took for granted. At the Coptic missionary school that all the children attended, the only primary school on Roda, the Christian teacher read stories to us several times a week from the Bible, stories about all the prophets and about Jesus Christ. Every morning before classes began there was a Christian prayer service, which the teacher had told us we did not have to attend if we did not want to. So I didn't, staying at my desk in the classroom while all the other students went to the service, including my sister, who was too young to understand.

"Why don't you come with me?" my sister said.

"It is for the Christians and we are Muslim," I told her.

"But you will make the teacher angry," she said.

I didn't care. "I am not going to go listen to a priest just to please the teacher," I insisted.

But my sister was right. The teacher became cruel toward me, making me stand in the corner with my face to the wall every day during our recreational period.

"Your sister comes to prayers. So do the other students, both of whose parents are Muslim," the teacher said to me. "Why must you be different?"

"I am not a Christian," I would reply. And back I would go into the corner.

I was only eight at the time, and after three weeks of this I told my father how cruelly I felt the teacher was treating me. The next morning he came to see the British headmistress.

"I do not want either of my daughters to attend the Christian prayer service," he told her. "That is not their religion and the teacher is pressuring them."

The headmisttress was evidently shocked when my father told her how severely I was being treated. She must have spoken to my teacher, because after my father's visit she treated me very kindly. From then on both Dalia and I stayed at our desks while the others went to chapel.

My mother never converted to Islam, though many of her British friends who were married to Egyptians did. Conversion was very simple, requiring registration as a Muslim at el-Azhar Mosque with two people as witnesses, and the recitation five times of the profession of faith: "I testify that there is no god but God, and Muhammad is His messenger." Her reluctance to convert perplexed my aunts and uncle. "Why doesn't Gladys change her religion?" my father's family and friends used to ask. But my father loved my mother very much and never wanted to pressure her. Instead, we would follow our traditions and holidays with my father's family. And my mother would share somewhat, even fasting a few days during Ramadan to encourage us. We were a Muslim family with a Christian mother.

She was not a typical Egyptian mother, protectively hovering over her children. Not at all. When we fell playing games in the garden, our aunts would always rush to pick us up. "Let them get up by themselves," my mother would say. Unlike many Egyptian mothers, who, after washing their children's hair, for example, made their children stay inside until their hair was dry, my mother would say, "Nonsense. Go outside and let the wind and sun dry it."

Many Egyptian mothers sat at night with their children until they fell asleep, then left a light burning for them so that they would not be frightened if they awoke. My mother disapproved of that, thinking it made the children dependent and soft. Instead she went in quite the other direction. Every night before we went to bed she made us go out into the black, black garden alone and find our way around it three times in the dark.

That way, she said, we would learn not to be afraid of being alone and not be afraid of the dark. And she was right.

Our home had a very warm, loving atmosphere. Every day my father returned from his office at two, the time all government offices closed for the day, with packets of chocolates, a new French cheese or a present of smoked tongue for us. Our main meal was at midday, after which all Cairenes including us, took naps until four or five. After his nap, my father never went out again the way many other Egyptian men did—going to the cafés to drink coffee, play backgammon or smoke the nargilehs or water pipes. Either we all went out together or he stayed home.

Sometimes on Friday, our Sabbath day, my father would take us to the Old City, marked by the Bab el-Metwalli, or Gate of the Holy Man, named after the Sufi sheikh who reportedly sat there centuries before, performing miracles for passersby. For all that Cairo was my hometown, I never ceased to marvel at the sights and the exotic history that made up my city. The streets of the Old City, far too narrow for automobiles, were choked instead with the traffic of horses, donkeys and even people laden down with loads of fresh vegetables, firesticks, vases of copper and brass to be sold in the bustling Khan el-Khalili bazaar. Cairo had been the greatest trading center in the world for centuries, and it was here in the caravanserai of the Khan el-Khalili that medieval traders from all over the Arab world had unloaded their camel trains. It was near here also that the Fatimid sultans had kept a zoo for the giraffes, ostriches and elephants sent to them as tribute from kingdoms in Africa.

The twelve thousand shops of the Khan el-Khalili were filled with remnants of the past being used in the present. My parents often took us through the dark, winding streets to the silver and gold market, located in the very heart of the bazaar so as to protect it from invaders. There my sister and I could buy silver bracelets for ten cents. While my mother stopped by the spice market to buy mint, thyme and sage for her British sauces, we children would strain to hear the clanking finger cymbals of the roving juice seller as children had for centuries, then pester our father to buy us glasses of the cold black syrupy sweet juice of the *tamarhindy*.

Not far from Khan el-Khalili was the eleventh-century mosque of el-Hakim, the legendary Fatimid Sultan whose mind had been quite disordered. El-Hakim had tried to force women to stay inside their houses by forbidding cobblers to make shoes for them and had ordered every dog in the city killed. He was also fond of riding about in the dark on his ass, inspecting the behavior of his subjects. Those who incurred his disfavor were killed. Such wanton killings had made el-Hakim an object of considerable hatred, and few mourned when one night in 1020 he rode his donkey into the Muqattam Hills and disappeared forever. But like all the Fatimids who had swept over Egypt in the tenth century from North Africa, el-Hakim was a Shiite Muslim. In Egypt now we were Sunni Muslims, as were 90 percent of the 800 million Muslims throughout the Islamic world.

As a child, I knew no Shiites, the excitable and sometimes violent minority Muslim sect centered in Iran. Though both Sunnis and Shiites followed the Prophet Muhammad, a quarrel about the rightful heirs to the Prophet's leadership had divided the believers since the Prophet's death in 632 without male heirs. Most Muslims believed that the Prophet's father-in-law, Abu Bakr, was their rightful leader. But a passionate few believed that leadership belonged to Ali, the Prophet's nephew, and his successors. While the former became known as Sunni Muslims, those in opposition formed the Shi'at Ali, the Party of Ali, and were known as Shiites. In the seventh century, Sunni forces ambushed and murdered the leader of the Shiites, Ali's son Hussein. From that moment began the Shiitte tradition of rebelliousness against authority and the glorification of martyrdom which would dominate Iran 350 years later.

The difference between the moderate Sunnis and the more radical Shiites was most obvious in our separate celebrations honoring Hussein, the Prophet's grandson. Hussein's *mulid,* his birthday, was a week-long celebration in Egypt which I loved. Once a year my family and most of Cairo crowded into the mosque named after Hussein in the Old City, then enjoyed the familiar and beautiful *tawashih,* religious poems performed by musicians and singers in tents set up in the square outside the mosque. Sweets, nuts and small toys were sold from peddlers' carts in the streets, and children rode on the swings and carousels set up on this special occasion. In Iran and other Shiite communities they also commemorated Hussein's birth, but even more significant to the Shiites was the anniversary of his death.

Driven by the guilt of not having saved Hussein's life, the

most zealous Shiites on this day beat their heads and bare chests with chains and whips to punish themselves and share Hussein's agony. I had never seen this ritual of self-flagellation in person, but even hearing about it made me feel quite ill. I preferred the gentleness and joy of the Sunni traditions during the *mulid* celebrations of Hussein, especially the *zikr,* the recitation that the Sufis, Muslim mystics, performed in their brightly colored tents.

Dancing to drums, cymbals and the beautiful chanting of a sheikh, the Sufis would swing their shoulders to the right and the left, shouting out "Allah!" each time they turned. Gradually the music would pick up speed, the dancers whirling faster and faster as they shouted out the name of God. So hypnotic is this ritual that many Sufis claim to join with God while taking part in it, leaving the physical world behind. To demonstrate the power of the *zikr* during the *mulid,* some Sufi groups would lie down and let horsemen ride across their backs, or swallow snakes, or put live coals into their mouths. These things would hurt or maybe even kill ordinary men, but somehow the Sufis always seemed to remain unharmed.

Later I would come to admire, even envy, the intimate relationship the Sufis had with God. Unlike the religious fanatics who obeyed mechanically the rules and regulations of Islam, the Sufis looked on God with love and emotion. They were always gentle, requiring few worldly pleasures for themselves and respecting all God's creatures, often writing beautiful poems and songs to the birds and other animals. Even now in Egypt when we find a snake living in a house or office building, we call a Rifa'i Sufi to come and charm the snake out of his hole. By playing his beautiful music, the Sufi is always able to take the snake away without harming it.

Even when there was not a *mulid* celebration, a walk through the Old City was fascinating. As we passed the houses of the medieval Mameluke sultans, built always with separate harems for their wives and female relatives, we could smell onions frying and hear the squawks of geese belonging to the poor families who now lived in them. Often my sister and I would gaze up at the *mashrabiyya,* the ornately carved wooden windows of the harems which would allow the women to look out but no one to look in. My sister and I would jump with fright when occasionally we would catch the eye of someone peering down at us. In my imagination, it was the eye of a ghost. I could not imagine being hidden away as so many of my sex had been. Nor could I imagine my mother, now strolling arm in arm with my father, to ever be so subservient as had been the invisible women in the harems. Thank heavens, I said to myself, that those days were gone. But I soon discovered they weren't.

At the age of eight or so I visited one of my neighborhood friends and saw her mother waiting only on her husband, preparing his food and presenting it to him, not eating herself until he was completely satisfied. I was shocked. Never did she sit with him, not deeming herself worthy. Rarely did she leave the house, and then only to shop for her husband's favorite food. As soon as he was through eating, he would go out with his friends, leaving her behind. Once when I was there, a man came to the house to walk with the husband to the café. After admitting him into the house, the wife ran into another room so that she would not be seen. My father laughed when I told him about it. "They are old-fashioned," he said.

It was never like that at our house. Often in the evenings my father's sisters and brother or my mother's friends, most of whom were British women married to Egyptian men, would come to the house to visit. They would sit together, men and women, in the salon, and we children would sometimes sit with them, listening to their talk. This was natural for us, but not for many Egyptian families, where the sexes entertained separately. Anwar himself would be shocked after we married when I would admit male friends of his to the house, offering them tea in our sitting room and inquiring about their families while they waited for Anwar to appear. "Jehan, how can you do this? You barely know them," Anwar would say furiously to me later. But we had been brought up differently. "I am the hostess in this house," I would reply to Anwar. "Whether a man or a woman comes to call makes no difference." But it made a difference to Anwar, and for the first years of our marriage he struggled with my more modern ways.

In Cairo my family was not poor, not rich, but middle class. There were very few members of the middle class at that time, mostly employees of the government. Unlike other countries, where the middle class was defined by income, in Egypt government employees made up a class of their own. Like my father, most wore Western suits, had educations, spoke Arabic, but did not earn much money—only fifteen Egyptian pounds or so a month, the equivalent then of fifteen dollars. The rest of Egypt under King Farouk was divided into two classes: the very rich, who numbered few, owned vast areas of land and spoke only French, and the very poor, who numbered in the millions, could not read or write and who earned maybe fifty dollars a year. Most of the poor were fellaheen, meaning literally "tillers of the soil," those who farmed the estates of the rich. The fellaheen had always been the backbone of Egypt.

Then, of course, there was the foreign colony. Egypt had long been an international crossroads, with more than 300,000 Greeks, 100,000 Italians, 50,000 stateless Jews and thousands more who carried French and British passports settling in Cairo and Alexandria after World War I. Many Cypriots, Maltese and North African Arabs had also made their homes in Egypt. World War II had brought even more refugees, as well as thousands of soldiers who came under the British flag: Englishmen, Indians, Australians, and Africans from the British colonies. In Cairo, a high wall and barbed wire surrounded the encampment of the British troops, which stretched from Tahrir Square, the site of the present Nile Hilton Hotel, all the way to the banks of the Nile. The Cairo of my childhood was two different cities, its center modern and Western, the outlying areas ancient and traditionally Egyptian.

I used to watch the British officers ride by in horse-drawn carriages, the taxis of the city, on their way to visit friends in the tall, immaculate apartment buildings with roof gardens or to the cosmopolitan Shepheard's Hotel, the Ritz, the Cecil and the other famous downtown restaurants. At night the British officers went also to the Cairo Opera House, built for the opening of the Suez Canal and the first performance of Verdi's *Aida*. They always looked quite peculiar to me, their faces as red as the tarbushes, or fezzes, they wore on their heads to blend in with the natives. But they also looked very content. The sun shone in Egypt. Labor was cheap. And Cairo offered them everything Paris did—at one third the price.

In the forties, life in Cairo was just as pleasant for us. The war had drawn hundreds of thousands of fellaheen from the villages to work for the British, and there was no limit to the labor pool. In our house on Roda we had six servants—a Sudanese cook, Osman, who would move with me years later into the presidential villa, one gardener, one driver, three women to clean the room and do the laundry. This was not unusual. All middle-class families had servants, because the wage was low then, two to three pounds a month. My family's income was also enhanced by the land my father and his brothers and sisters had inherited from their father, over 120 acres in Buhayra which were farmed by the fellaheen. The income from the land put us on the edge of privilege. Often my father would take us for drives out of Cairo into the countryside, to the Pyramids just ten minutes away in the Sahara, or to celebrate our many religious rituals and secular holidays.

Ramadan, the celebration of the month in which the Quran was revealed to our Prophet Muhammad, was one of my favorite religious holidays as a child. For thirty days we fasted from sunrise to sunset, forbidden by the Quran to eat even a crumb or to drink even a drop of water. There was to be no smoking of cigarettes or pipes during the days of Ramadan, no intimacy between husband and wife, no cursing or quarreling from dawn to dusk. All thoughts of earthly concerns were to be replaced by spiritual thoughts. It was said that even a single lie or a glance of passion could ruin the day's fast.

Ramadan always came at different times of year, eleven or twelve days earlier than the year before, for the Muslim calendar is based on the lunar month and not the solar cycles of the Western calendar. The month of fasting was more difficult when it fell in the heat of the summer. But its spiritual message was always the same. To learn self-discipline and identify with the poor, all Muslims were to deprive themselves of worldly pleasures.

The anticipation would build for several days before Ramadan began, for no one knew exactly when the sheikhs would sight the new moon of the ninth month. "Ramadan will probably start tomorrow," the radio would broadcast. "The new moon was not sighted this morning." Finally the evening news would declare the beginning of Ramadan, the holiday fast to begin at the first rays of dawn the next morning, at that moment when a white thread held against the sky could be distinguished from a black thread. Though as children we were not obliged by the Quran to fast until the age of puberty, like most others we were encouraged by our family to try fasting for at least a day or two when we reached the age of eleven or twelve. From the age of eleven I always tried to fast for the entire month, but I didn't achieve such self-discipline until I was thirteen.

The days were not too different during Ramadan. Most businesses and offices remained open, though they opened later in the day to allow those who had stayed up most of the night to sleep later in the mornings. But at dusk, when the time approached for the *iftar,* or breaking of the fast, the atmosphere would change completely. The streets of Roda and even Cairo would suddenly be empty and quiet, not a shop open, not a car or bus in sight. Everyone, including the bus drivers, had rushed home to prepare for the moment when eating and drinking would again be permitted.

Eagerly we would all wait to hear the cannons that were fired in every neighborhood at the instant the sun went down. As one, all the mosques in our city would turn on the bright lights strung up and around their minarets. As one, my family, along with millions of others, would celebrate the moment by quenching our thirst with a special drink called *qamar el-din* made from the syrup of apricots. And as one, all over Egypt, Muslims would begin their evening feast.

For all its deprivation, Ramadan was—and is—the most joyous and social month of the year. Our family never ate the evening meal alone during Ramadan, gathering instead with as many as twenty of our relatives at their various homes. And never has food looked so good, smelled so good, tasted so good. As children we would circle the table just before sunset, staring hungrily at the special dishes prepared just for Ramadan: *qat'aif,* a pastry stuffed with pistachios, almonds and raisins and drenched in a syrup of lemon and sugar; *kunafa,* a dessert spun out of angel hair and topped with raisins, nuts and cream; *kushaf,* a compote of stewed apricots, figs, prunes and raisins. At the shot of the cannon, we would stuff ourselves, then sit at the table for hours telling stories and exchanging jokes.

I loved every minute of Ramadan, the commonplace suddenly becoming special. Night was turned into day, making life seem longer. We children ran from house to house, knocking on the doors and asking for sweets. The streets of Cairo were filled with people until well after two in the morning, for everyone went out to visit friends after sitting with their families. *"Ramadan karim,"* all would greet one another in the streets: "Ramadan is kind to us." To light the way of the adults, we each carried a *fanuz,* a special stained-glass lantern in the shape of a mosque, while larger, more elaborate lanterns were hung from poles on every street corner. Sheikhs recited the Quran all night long in colorful tents set up in Hussein Square and in village squares all over Egypt. Between the opening and closing readings of the Quran in Cairo, often singers and folk dancers performed.

I stayed up very late during Ramadan—and woke up very early. Just when my sister and I had gone to sleep, it seemed, we would be awakened by the beautiful voice of our neighborhood *misaharati,* the man responsible for waking the believers before dawn. Chanting a song to the accompaniment of his little drum, the *misaharati* would stop before each house and call out a special verse to the children sleeping there: "Wake up, Jehan. Wake up, Dalia. Wake up, Nadia. Wake up, Tahani. Fasting is better than sleep. Wake up to praise the Everlasting." On the first day of the feast at the end of Ramadan, the *misaharati* would come to collect his *'aidiyya,* a small present of money. To thank him for his lovely songs, we would sometimes wrap a few piaster coins in a paper, set fire to it so he could see where it landed, and throw it out the window. But I hated getting up at 3A.M. to eat *suhur,* the pre-dawn meal. "I don't want to eat," I would say to my mother when she came to get me. "Let me sleep." But she always insisted I get up, just as I would do with my own children in spite of their identical protests. One meal a day wasn't enough for their bodies while they were growing.

Not every Muslim was required to fast during Ramadan. Besides children, the Quran specifically spared those who were traveling, who were fighting in a holy war, or who were ill. Muslims who suffered perhaps from kidney trouble or diabetes which required them to regularly drink or eat were excused from fasting, though they had to compensate by feeding the poor. Women who were pregnant or nursing their babies were also excused, as were those having their time of the month. There was no fasting or even praying for any woman whose body was not clean.

At the end of Ramadan we had another religious holiday, the

three-day feast of 'Aid el-Saghir. This holiday, however, was entirely the opposite. Just as God forbade us to eat during Ramadan, on 'Aid el-Saghir it was unlawful *not* to eat. And everyone participated. Businesses, schools, factories and offices closed. Beggars and the homeless were given alms. Servants were given large bonuses or gifts of clothing from their employers. Children were given new clothes and new shoes. No one was to be deprived at the conclusion of Ramadan. And life returned to normal.

One of my favorite secular holidays as a child was Shamm el-Nessim, the Smelling of the Breezes. The first day of spring, it fell every year on the Monday following the Coptic Christian observance of Easter. All Cairenes who could go to the countryside did so, for tradition held that during the early morning of this day the wind had particularly beneficial effects. Like many of our traditions, Shamm el-Nessim had been celebrated since the time of the pharaohs.

Many of the rituals of Shamm el-Nessim had been handed down intact. Though our family did not observe them all, our servants did, either sleeping with an onion under their pillows or starting the day by breaking an onion and smelling it. That way, tradition had it, the nose would then be better able to absorb the good from the winds later on. For us, however, Shamm el-Nessim was a lovely spring day to spend with our friends and relatives in the country.

The preparation was great fun. My sister and I would color boiled eggs red, yellow or blue, drawing designs on them with a wax pencil. If we were lucky, my parents had also taken us to Groppi, the famous downtown tea salon and chocolatier, to pick out baskets filled with chocolate rabbits and eggs. Early in the morning we would set out to my Auntie Batta's house, which overlooked a branch of the Nile, to the Pyramids, to the lovely public gardens at the Nile Barrage, or to Giza, though the zoo there was always too crowded.

The roads were jammed, as were the banks of the Nile. But nobody cared. All the children had new and bright clothes to wear on this day, and the ground was crowded with families having picnics. Flower vendors would wander through the parks, selling strings of jasmine flowers and freshly cut roses. Often my father rented a felucca, the single-sail Nile River boat unchanged from Pharaonic times, and we would cut back and forth across the strong currents of the Nile, smelling the freshest of breezes.

Sometimes my father took us to a brunch at the Mena House, a lovely old hotel near the Pyramids built originally as a royal hunting lodge for Khedive Isma'il, then converted in 1869 into a guest house for the festivities surrounding the opening of the Suez Canal. We would have cold drinks on the terrace by the swimming pool and eat the traditional foods that symbolized the new life of spring—boiled eggs, fresh onions and lettuce, and *fisikh,* pungent salted fish which had had been buried in the sand to ripen. The fish smelled awful, but tasted delicious. Not surprisingly my mother always refused to eat it, ordering eggs and cheese instead.

My mother especially loved Mena House. Many Cairenes regularly took their tea on the terrace there, in the shadow of the Pyramid of Cheops. Later, my husband and I would bring our own children to brunch at Mena House on Shamm el-Nessim. It would be at Mena House also that Anwar would meet with President Jimmy Carter to negotiate peace with Israel.

If Shamm el-Nessim was my favorite secular holiday in the spring, Wafa' el-Nil, Abundance of the Nile, was my favorite of late summer. On this day in August the barrage just south of Cairo would be cut, and the Nile, swollen with water and rich silt from its origins in Uganda and Ethiopia, would begin the annual two-month-long fall flood.

The best part of Wafa' el-Nil was that the festivities happened right on Roda Island. For days before, the *munadi el-Nil,* the crier of the Nile, had marched around our neighborhood, calling out the height the river had reached on the eighth-century Nilometer at the southern foot of our island, built on the spot where the infant Moses is believed to have been found in the bulrushes. Every day the crier in our district would proclaim the level of the Nile closer to the sixteenth cubit on the Nilometer, a rise of over twenty feet from its normal level.

What a celebration took place on the day the Nile finally reached flood level. We knew it was time when we saw that the crier was accompanied by small boys banging on little drums and bearing brightly colored flags. "The river has given abundance and completed its measure," the crier would call out, to which the boys would reply, "God has given abundance!" They continued their call in front of each house until they were given a small present of money. And the festival began.

Feluccas, their riggings outlined in lights and dressed with colorful streamers and pennants, crowded into the Nile just off the shores of Roda. Lights were strung on the shore as well. Some boats had musicians aboard, and from the shore we could hear the sounds of different songs echoing across the river. Gunboats fired salvos every quarter of an hour all day until 9 P.M., summoning all to the banks of the Nile.

It was a lovely sight—and, to me, very romantic. Tied to the pier at the foot of our island was a brightly painted boat bearing a large decorated statue of a girl known as the Bride of the Nile. When the flood started, the "bride" was thrown into the Nile at sunset to join her "bridegroom," thus ensuring a good harvest year. On the shore we all clapped and cheered and gave tongue in the *zaghreet* while fireworks were shot into the air. I loved the romance of their watery union, but was thankful that the "bride" was a statue now and not the young virgin that legend held Egyptians used to sacrifice annually years before.

When the completion of the High Dam in Aswan would eliminate the annual flood in 1964, I would be very sad that we stopped celebrating the Wafa' el-Nil. Its colorful traditions had already been eroded, the crier of the Nile having been replaced by flood-level updates on Cairo radio. But some of the legend of Wafa' el-Nil, at least, continues. Lotuses, the beautiful flowers that bloom in the calm backwaters of our river, are still called "Brides of the Nile."

In my childhood before the High Dam was built, the normally gentle flow of the Nile moved swiftly, even treacherously north toward the Mediterranean for the two months of the flood. Every morning we would walk to school beside the river, and during the flood the water rose to six feet from the road. My parents would always warn us not to go too close to the banks. But we were children and did not pay enough attention.

One day when I was eight and my sister six, I saw a black cat stranded on a felucca bobbing near the steps down to the Nile. "We must rescue that cat!" I said to my sister. "Otherwise it will drown." But it was my sister who almost drowned.

While I watched in horror, she slipped on the bottom step and fell in. Immediately she disappeared into a whirlpool, sucked down by the quick currents of the river. "Help! Help!" I called to my brothers who were following us, rushing back to find them. Both dove into the water after her, my brother Ali getting caught in the whirlpool himself.

I cried and cried on the riverbank as I watched my oldest brother, Magdi, struggle to rescue both my sister and Ali. Miraculously Magdi got them both ashore, where he collapsed in exhaustion. A crowd had gathered, and several people immediately came forward to give my sister artificial respiration. I was terrified. Her stomach was swollen with water, her face bright red. They turned her over, face down, and held her legs up while thumping on her back. Never have I felt so guilty. I had been looking after the cat on the boat and not my own sister. Finally Dalia started to choke and to breathe again. My parents, who had been summoned, rushed to the Nile and took us all home. For the first and only time in my life, I was severely punished. Both my mother and my father shouted at me for my irresponsibility. My father then locked me in my room, where he beat my legs and smacked my face. I did not resist at all, believing I deserved the punishment.

Always in my family, I was considered the leader of the children. I do not know why, really, my brothers being so much older than I. Perhaps it was the way I felt about myself, as if I knew that my life would be special. I often dreamed that people were paying me great respect, and I would tell these dreams to my mother, to my father, to my Auntie Zouzou.

"I am going to do something special when I grow up," I told them all, a boastful prophecy which frightened Auntie Zouzou.

"Don't say that," she told me, appalled by my brashness and fearful that I would bring bad luck on myself.

"Don't worry," I'd reassure her, reminding her of the story in the Quran of the prophet Joseph, who after becoming powerful had forgiven his brothers for selling him into slavery. "When the day comes, I will be good to you and do my best for all my family just as Joseph did." My aunt laughed, but still she urged me to keep my dreams to myself.

I do not know where such dreams came from, for we were very sheltered, very protected, as children in Roda. I thought all families lived in comfort and peace as we did. We did not see the poverty that affected so many Egyptians. I did not even visit a village until I was thirteen and went with my father to see his family's land. But the problems of the greater world had to intrude at some point. And my education began with an old lady who lived in the hollowed-out trunk of a tree.

A school friend told me about this woman one day, and immediately after school I went to see this mystery. And it was true. She had no children, the old woman told me, no one to take care of her. I felt very sad and determined, at the age of ten, to take care of her myself. I visited her every day before school and on the way home, giving her what pocket money I had, bringing her the sandwich meant for my lunch. I told no one about her, not even my mother. She was my secret, and my friend.

"Would you like to come live in my home?" I asked her, a little worried that my mother might be furious if she accepted my offer.

"I like it here," the old woman said, nestled in the tree. "Just keep coming to visit me."

I worried about her eyes, seeing her wiping them often. I started packing eyedrops and ointment into my school bag and put them gently on her eyes. She never stopped me.

After a week of coming home late from school, I was questioned by my mother. And I broke down and told her my secret. She was shocked and immediately sent a doctor to at least look after the old woman's eyes. It was then I discovered she was blind, probably from "river blindness," a common eye disease carried by flies. But my secret was out and I decided to share with my friends my time with the old woman. "You don't have children of your own," I told her, introducing my friends to her. "Now we are your children."

For months we visited her after school, bringing her presents of food and clothing. Then one day, the tree was empty.

"Where is she?" I asked the man on the corner who sold sweets.

"She passed away early in the morning," he told me. "The police came and took her body away."

I was heartbroken, for I had imagined that I could keep her alive with my attention. And I never forgot her.

The summer months of July and August were very hot in Cairo, well over 90 degrees, and like many families we went to the Mediterranean seashore. For years my family rented a beach cabin in Port Sa'id, 110 miles from Cairo at the gateway to the Suez Canal. In the afternoon my father used to fish from a bridge at the mouth of the Canal. If all the fish he brought home were the same size, we knew he had bought them rather than caught them.

The city of Port Sa'id looked more European than Egyptian, rows of tidy brick houses with white roofs and carefully tended gardens. The wooden cabins that Auntie Zouzou, Auntie Batta and my father rented were right on the beach, set up on stilts so that the water could wash under. The coolest spots were under the houses, and that was where my cousins, our friends and I gathered to play. In the evenings all our relatives gathered in one house to eat, the room lit by kerosene lamps, for there was not yet electricity. I loved the soft light and was very sad at fourteen when electricity came to Port Sa'id.

The very rich usually spent their summers abroad. But I didn't envy them at all. I loved Port Sa'id as a child, spending all day in my bathing suit, swimming in the sea and playing racketball on the sand. At sunset, all the children would gather to play blindman's buff or hide-and-seek while our parents sat together, talking and playing backgammon. Even after dark we stayed on the beach, crowding under the gas lamps which ran the length of the shore, until our dinnertime at 9 P.M.

Alexandria, one hundred miles to the west, was crowded and sophisticated, an international seaside city. Port Sa'id was more of an Egyptian family resort, the same families returning year after year. Often in the evenings we went to the huge outdoor cinema, where we sat on rattan chairs and ate bags of roasted watermelon seeds and *meshabbek,* delicious waffles dipped in honey, found only in Port Sa'id and the port of Domiat. Egypt was producing many fine films at the time, was in fact the second biggest producer of films in the world. I liked films also from America and Europe. I do not know how many times I saw *Gone With the Wind* or watched Esther Williams jump through flower hoops on her water skis. The air was as sweet as the *meshabbek,* and I wanted the summer to go on forever.

On the first Thursday of the month, we followed the same routine as millions of other Egyptians and indeed people all over the Arab world. Gathered around our battery-operated radio in Port Sa'id, in Cairo, wherever we were, we would listen to the live monthly concert of Um Kalthum.

Not before or since has there been a more popular singer in the Arab world. Um Kalthum sang of love and sorrow with such emotion that many people seated in the audience or in their own homes cried. Her voice was magical, her prowess extraordinary. She could hold a single note for a minute and a half. During her concerts she would sing only three songs, the first two lasting nearly two hours, the final song one hour. Over and over she would sing the same refrain, changing the nuance each time the tiniest bit.

Europeans found her songs repetitious, but we did not. To foreigners every dune in the desert looked the same as every other, but we knew that each grain of sand was different. And so was every one of Um Kalthum's Thursday concerts, which drew her devoted followers to Cairo from all over the Arab world, Lebanese businessmen and sheikhs from Kuwait and Saudi Arabia flying in every month to hear her.

So powerful was the aura that we all attached to Um Kalthum that black borders would frame the news in the papers when her voice was silenced by a throat ailment in 1953. No Arab doctor would touch her for fear of doing her legendary voice damage. Finally the U.S. Naval Medical Center in Bethesda, Maryland, volunteered to take the risk of treating her, successfully performing an operation on her throat so that she could sing again. Some would say that this gesture by the Americans was the only thing that held Egyptian–American relations together during the presidency of Gamal Abdel Nasser.

Still later, Um Kalthum and I would become good friends and she would sing at my eldest daughter's engagement party. When she grew too old and ill to perform, I would go to visit and take walks with her. But she got weaker and weaker, eventually becoming bedridden. "Souma," I said to her in 1975 the last time I saw her, calling her by her famous nickname. "I must be away in America for a few weeks. I want you to be strong and healthy when I get back so I will have someone to walk with." "All right, Mrs. Sadat, I promise," she said weakly. By the time I returned, she had died. To honor her memory, Cairo radio chanted verses from the Quran after the evening news, a gesture reserved for the passing of heads of state and the greatest celebrities. And even now, on the radio station Egyptians call the "Um Kalthum Station," there is a program on from five to seven every evening which starts and ends with a song by Um Kalthum.

When I crossed the bridge to go to secondary school in Giza at the age of eleven, my life changed. No longer did I go to school with both girls and boys as I had for primary school. Now I went to an all-girls government school for which my father paid three pounds a month. It was not fair, of course, that only those who could afford these fees received an education. Nonetheless, the education we received was excellent.

Because of the British occupation of Egypt, we had all been taught to read and write English in primary school, as well as to speak it clearly. We had also started to learn Classical Arabic, since the colloquial Arabic we used every day was only a spoken language. In secondary school, in addition to our instruction in mathematics and science, we were given much more instruction in the graceful phrases and expressions of Classical Arabic. Now I would be able to read the Quran, the finest example of Classical Arabic, and to understand also the formal speeches of our statesmen, who often spoke in Classical Arabic.

To enter secondary school, I had to choose between two courses of study. One department would have prepared me to go on to university, stressing geometry, algebra, French, literature and the sciences. The other, more traditional department for girls stressed subjects such as art and music, painting, history, clothes design, sewing and cooking, a preparation really for marriage. Whether out of laziness or because all my friends were making the same choice, I chose the latter.

I have always regretted that decision. I would never allow my daughters to close off their futures that way. But the attitude was different in the forties.

"Which course should I take?" I asked my mother.

She herself was not ambitious. She enjoyed being a good wife and mother. "I'd take sewing and cooking," she said. "You'll need to know that when you're married."

I asked my father.

"You're pretty and you'll probably marry young," he said. "This will prepare you to be a good wife."

There was no thought in anyone's mind, including my own, that I would do anything but marry.

When I was thirteen, tragedy stuck my family. After a long struggle and many weeks in a sanitarium in the desert of Helwan, my cousin 'Awatif, Auntie Batta's eldest daughter, died of tuberculosis. Her body had been weakened not only by two pregnancies very close together but by her insistence on dieting to regain her figure. I had always admired my beautiful cousin and was not only heartbroken but frightened that one so young could be struck down. It was my first experience with death.

A second quickly followed. Within a year, my Uncle Mustafa was dead as well, a victim of typhoid. Once more, I was stunned. Uncle Mustafa was so young, only thirty-nine and so very conscious of cleanliness that he even washed the coins in his pocket every night. My uncle had just begun to learn happiness, having married a relative he had met at the funeral of my cousin. Their marriage, in fact, had been the first which I had arranged.

"You are lonely, Uncle Mustafa," I had told him after the funeral when all the family gathered. "You must marry Nini. She is our cousin and will be perfect for you. You need someone to care for you and bear your children."

Uncle Mustafa had laughed at my impudence. "You naughty girl. Mind your own business," he had scolded me.

But I had not given up. "Uncle Mustafa is lonely. He must marry Nini," I had said to Auntie Zouzou.

She had agreed with me, even though it meant that another woman would move into the house she shared with her brother. "Nini is a relative, so it will be all right," she said. "I will talk to her mother."

Nini's mother, Muntaha, had also agreed, saying such a marriage would honor the family. A year later her daughter, who was four months pregnant, became a widow. I was devastated. And I turned to God.

I felt the need to understand these deaths, to look for the answers in the Quran. I already loved the musical language of the Holy Book, having heard five times daily the call to prayer, and having listened to the cadence of the Quran on the radio. The beautiful language of our Holy Book had inspired me, as it did many Muslims, to try to express myself in poetic verse and to admire poets greatly. Now I sought out my religion for solace.

It was the aunt of my friend Raga', Auntie Ni'mat, who first introduced me to the community of believers, who first taught me to pray. She was very conservative, dressing always in long dresses which covered her arms and legs, wearing a scarf on her head into which she tucked all her hair. This had always intrigued me, because my own family was not so conservative. When Raga' suggested one afternoon we have tea with her aunt, I eagerly accepted. Thus began a long series of afternoon meetings in which I found my identity as a Muslim and a true believer. The experience was to transform me.

Much of Auntie Ni'mat's religious instruction about the Quran I already knew, but had not been old enough to truly embrace or understand. I knew, for example, that the Quran contained the word of God revealed to the Prophet Muhammed by the Angel Gabriel in A.D. 610, and that our Holy Book differed from those of the Christians and Jews because it was the actual word of God rather than man-made record and interpretation of His words. I knew also the five pillars of my religion, the unbreakable ritual and moral laws of Islam: the profession of faith in one God, prayer, alms-giving, fasting and pilgrimage to Mecca for those who could afford the expense. God was compassionate and excused those too poor or weak to make the journey.

I had performed as many of these duties as I could as a child, giving away my pocket money to the blind woman who lived in the tree, fasting with my family during Ramadan. What I was to learn from Auntie Ni'mat was the Muslim ritual of prayer. Prayer is an all-important duty of Islam, a duty so important it is called the "Key of Paradise." No Muslim is ever excused from prayer. If a believer is crippled and unable to make the movements of prayer, he can sit and pray. If a believer is entirely paralyzed and can't speak, he can pray with his eyes. If a believer is traveling or in meetings and is unable to pray during the five separate calls to prayer, he or she can perform all five prayers at once at night. But every believer has to pray. As I learned the carefully prescribed steps of prayer from Auntie Ni'mat, my religion took on a new, internal meaning for me, a sudden emotional relevance.

We did not go to the mosque to pray. It was neither necessary nor our tradition. While the Prophet did not explicitly forbid women to pray publicly in the mosques, he did urge us to pray in the privacy of our homes. When women did attend prayer services in the mosques, they prayed separately, in back of the men. Even though many women wore dresses to the ankles, no one wanted to feel immodest while praying. I preferred to pray by myself or with my family in privacy. My faith in God was personal. And the ritual of prayer was the same wherever it was performed.

First and foremost, we were learning from Auntie Ni'mat, was cleanliness, for God will not accept the prayers of anyone impure and dirty. In the mosques there were large *hanafiyyas*, or faucets from which water runs and where the men perform their ablutions before going in to pray. Most houses, like the one of my friend's aunt, had a small *hanafiyya* of tinned copper in the bathroom for the purification ritual, a religious act in itself called the *wudu'*. If water was not available, the believer in the desert at prayer time could substitute dust or sand.

On Roda, of course, we had ample water. And we were eager pupils. Every afternoon Raga' and I would first go into the bathroom with Auntie Ni'mat, watching closely as she washed her hands three times, rinsed her mouth with water from her right hand, then cleansed her nose, face, arms to the elbows, head, ears, neck, and lastly her feet as high as the ankles. All this took her less than two minutes, while Raga' and I, struggling to get it right, took much longer. Luckily for us, the *wudu'* was not required before each of the five prayers of the day if we had not consciously performed an impure act since our last ablution.

When we had rinsed all the parts of our body three times, Auntie Ni'mat took us into her bedroom, where, barefoot and facing east toward Mecca, we would begin to pray. We always stood several feet behind her. Her age and knowledge made her the imam, the prayer leader, and responsible for timing the movements of the other worshipers, in this case two young schoolgirls in green pullovers. Placing our open hands on each side of our faces and reciting in unison *"Allahu Akbar,"* "God is Great," we would begin the *'asr salah,* the afternoon prayer. Other prayer times would occur just after sunset, during nightfall when it was quite dark, just before daybreak and a little past noon. None of the prayers was to commence at the exact moment of sunrise or sunset, because those were the times pagans had worshiped the sun. After each prayer, the most devout Muslims performed two more optional prayers. But during these afternoons Raga' and I were just beginning to truly follow our faith.

In the name of Allah, most Gracious, most Merciful.
Praise be to Allah, the Cherisher and Sustainer of the Worlds.
Most Gracious, Most Merciful
Master of the Day of Judgment,
You do we worship, and to You alone we pray for help.
Show us the straight path,
The path of those on whom Thou hast bestowed Thy Grace,
Not of those who have incurred your wrath
Nor of those who have gone astray . . .

Holding our left hands within the right in front of us, always we would begin by reciting the Fatiha, the opening passage of the Quran and a passage of tremendous religious significance. I doubt there is a Muslim anywhere in the world who cannot recite the Fatiha by heart in Arabic, even if his native tongue is Indonesian or an African dialect, whether he can read or write. In Egypt, it is the Fatiha which every child learns first, with which we start every prayer, which we recite several times a year over the graves of our loved ones. The first sentence in particular—"In the name of Allah, most Gracious, most Merciful"—is almost always spoken at the beginning of every lecture, speech or sermon given by a Muslim, and written at the top of every piece of paper on which the believer writes. There is even a precise and correct rhythm to be followed in the recital of the Fatiha and all the other verses of the Quran. Raga' and I listened closely to our imam, taking care to shorten and lengthen the specific vowels she did, to pause for breath at the end of certain lines.

"Islam" in Arabic means submission, and "Muslim" one who has submitted. These definitions took on new meaning for me when, after reading a few more passages from the Holy Book together, we followed Auntie Ni'mat in her prostrations. Part of the power of prayer comes from the discipline involved in its execution, a discipline that strengthens your belief. Turning toward Mecca and touching the head to the ground symbolically confirms a believer's commitment to bowing down before Allah. In a similar way, the ablutions which precede prayer symbolize our need to remain clean, pure in the service of God. And the frequency of prayer reminds us never to allow our belief to slip from our minds, for by stopping every three or four hours to recite God's words we ensure that we do not grow away from Him.

How simple Auntie Ni'mat made the prostrations of prayer look. In one long connected motion, she would bow from the hip, straighten, glide to her knees and touch her nose and forehead to the ground while reciting three times during each posture, "God is most Great. I extol the perfection of my Lord, the Most High." Twice she would repeat her prostrations while we struggled to copy her. Returning to the standing position, we would recite together the profession of faith: "There is no God but God, and Muhammad is His messenger."

We would end the ritual by looking first upon the right shoulder and then the left, saying each time to the guardian angels who watch over us, "Peace be upon you and the mercy of God." Others even more devout, Auntie Ni'mat told us, then take their *sebbha*s, strings of ninety-nine beads, and repeat thirty-three times each, "The perfection of God," "Praise be to God" and "God is Great."

During those afternoons with Raga's aunt, I experienced a profound religious birth and an eagerness to learn more. I began to read biographies of the Prophet Muhammad and to commit the Quran to memory, studying it at night and at dawn. Often I would set my alarm for five o'clock in the morning, getting up while my family slept to speak God's words as I watched the sunrise. Always I read the Holy Book aloud, practicing the language of the hardest passages written more than fourteen centuries ago.

Even at thirteen, I heard in the rich melodic Arabic of the Quran something transcendent and, indeed, divine. The Prophet Muhammad was illiterate, as were many of his followers, and for this reason God chose words meant to move the listener as well as to instruct. The beauty of the language used in the Quran is almost inexpressible. The public recitation of its flawlessly constructed rhythms, rhymes and assonances is an art in the Arab world, and those best at it are as famous here as classical musicians are in the West. So stunning is the Arabic of our Holy Book that all who convert to Islam, even those who live outside the Middle East, must learn to read our language aloud.

My religious fervor grew with all the enthusiasm that fuels an adolescent. By the time I was fourteen, I was adding additional short prayers to the five I said every day. Twice a day I read from the Quran. I read the Hadith, the collection of the Prophet's sayings which for Muslims is second only to the Quran in religious importance, and followed its suggestions too. Instead of fasting only during Ramadan, I did so once or twice a week. Although nothing in the Quran required it, I changed the way I dressed, asking my mother to buy me clothes that, like Raga's aunt, covered both my wrists and my ankles. Still unbelievable to me now, I even went to my relatives, my friends, to everyone I knew and asked them to give money to the Muslim Brothers.

The Muslim Brothers were all over our neighborhood in Roda and elsewhere in Cairo, instructing young Muslims about the history of Islam, helping to interpret God's commands as passed down in the Quran, encouraging believers to move along the path of righteousness. As a young girl I thought this fundamentalist group had the highest ideals of religion and morality, their vision of the world not only utopian but obtainable. There were Muslim Brotherhood clinics in the poorest Cairo neighborhoods to give free medical and dental care, Muslim Brotherhood pharmacies which sold medicine at greatly reduced prices, even Muslim Brotherhood insurance for the workers who fell sick and had no way to support their families. And every day I would see the serious young men who worked with the organization at the schoolyards in Roda, offering to teach the young boys about their religion and Islamic history. For the most part, the girls were left to learn about Islam from their families, although some joined the more discreet Muslim Sisters.

I did not mind that my brothers were invited to join the Muslim Brothers' study sessions while I was not. It seemed perfectly normal to me for boys to be treated differently from girls. I was even heartened that such a group was concerned about the young, and I admired greatly the many boys who left the playgrounds for Brotherhood study groups, soccer for the Quran, their childishness for a new, more serious attitude.

The Muslim Brothers were grateful to receive money from anyone, regardless of gender. Once a week I would take the money I had collected, and without telling anyone I would slip off to the home of the man who was second in command in the Brotherhood, Hassan el-Hudaybi. Like the others, Hassan el-Hudaybi was a follower of Hassan el-Banna, the "Supreme Guide" and founder of the Muslim Brotherhood, who in 1928 had created a cadre of young men committed to teaching the principles of Islam. By the time I was fourteen, Hassan el-Banna's original cadre of young men had become an army of young professionals, spread throughout the middle-class neighborhoods of every town and city in Egypt.

Then, as now, membership in the Brotherhood was supposedly secret. But anonymity has never had any meaning in an Egyptian neighborhood. Everyone knows where everyone else lives, what he does, whom he does it with, when it is done. So I knew without asking that Hassan el-Hudaybi's house, less than a block from my own, was the house of one of the Brotherhood's most important members. Knocking on the door, I would simply hand my contribution to the man who met me there. "This is for the Muslim Brothers," I would whisper conspiratorially, enjoying the secrecy I had penetrated. "Thank you, sister," the man would reply. "May I ask where this has come from?" Each time I would shake my head and, turning to go, murmur mysteriously, "From a friend."

While I enjoyed the new fullfillment I had found in religion, I was also discovering a new passion: politics. By the age of twelve I had gotten caught up in the wave of nationalism that was sweeping Egypt. By 1945, World War II was over. The British had won. Why, then, didn't they leave Egypt to be ruled by Egyptians and go home?

It was obvious that the British did not care at all about the Egyptian people. They had built airports and roads from Cairo to Port Sa'id and Suez for their military use which all Egyptians used, but in all the years they had been "protecting" us they had done little for the vast majority of citizens. In the Egyptian countryside, where half the children died before the age of five, where more people were blind than anywhere else in the entire world, where 70 percent of the adults had parasites from drinking Nile water, the British had not set up a single hospital. Nor had they drilled a single well so that the fellaheen could have clean water to drink. Millions of villagers in Egypt could not read, but the British had not built a single school to teach them. Millions could not afford to rent a home, but the British had built no inexpensive housing. I couldn't understand it, and I embraced the rising surge of patriotism felt by all other Egyptians. As a young girl, I became obsessed with the liberation of Egypt from foreign colonialists.

Sentiment, too, was mounting against King Farouk. He did whatever the British asked him to as long as they let him stay on the throne. Instead of helping the needy as our Holy Book demands, he helped only himself, indulging all his childish wishes and fancies. He had green telephones installed in all the bedrooms of his palaces and made a law saying that no one else could use that color telephone. He bought himself two yachts, thirteen airplanes and over two hundred cars, almost half of them Rolls Royces and Cadillacs. He drove the cars extremely recklessly, moving at top speed down even the narrowest roads, once shooting out the tires of a car which tried to pass him. To make sure the police did not stop him for such activities, he painted more than half his cars bright red and made it illegal for anyone else to have a car of the same color.

His government was extraordinarily corrupt, and it was said that many in it sold titles and government positions in exchange for land. Those close to the King, even his barbers and his gardeners, always grew rich, but the farmers whose crops supported Egypt's economy only grew poorer and suffered more. "We are like the needle," the fellaheen began to say. "We clothe others, but we ourselves stay naked."

I wanted to be proud of our King, but instead I was ashamed. Farouk wasn't even Egyptian, but Albanian, the great-great-great-grandson of Muhammad Ali, who had ruled Egypt in the 1840s. Once when we were let out of school to watch the King's motorcade pass by, I could not even bring myself to salute the royal car like all my other classmates. "Egypt belongs to the Egyptians," I kept telling my friends at school, who looked at me as if I were crazy. These were not the usual thoughts of a young teenager. But my yearnings grew and grew. I dreamed of the day when both the British and Farouk would be out of Egypt.

My obsession with politics was puzzling to my family. My

father was not political at all. But I could not stop talking about the dream of liberating Egypt. "Where do you get all these ideas?" my father would say to me, shaking his head in amazement. He barely read the newspapers, while I couldn't stop. Especially after the outbreak of the Palestine war.

During each of the two World Wars Britain had promised Palestine independence in return for Arab support against the Germans. But in May of 1948 the British had gone back on all their promises, withdrawing abruptly from the area and allowing the United Nations to create the new state of Israel. What an outrage. How could Britain, the "protectors" of Palestine, let Israel be created on Arab land? I naively wondered at the time why they didn't put Israel into Australia.

Egypt had gone to war as soon as the last British troops left Palestine, joining Syria and Jordan in the battle against the new state on Arab soil. In Cairo we saw few signs of war, but my heart went out to our troops fighting to protect our country's dignity and that of the Palestinians. It filled me with pride to see the special bands of volunteers armed and trained by the Muslim Brothers as they marched down the streets of Cairo. These fedayeen, whose name literally meant those who give their lives for a cause, included university students and even some *gawwala,* or Eagle Scouts, who still wore their khaki scout uniforms as they went off to war. Even after Egypt and the other Arab states were defeated by Israel two months after the war's beginning, the Muslim Brothers refused to give up, continuing to send volunteers to fight in the Sinai. The banners they held up in their parades expressed my own feelings exactly: "Palestine for the Palestinians! Enough of British Betrayal!"

Ironically, it was my British mother who caused my devotion to Egypt to flower. Over and over again at tea or at dinner, my mother had told us the stories of the brave British pilots and infantrymen who had sacrificed so much for their country during the Second World War. Her special hero, whom she admired above all others, was England's Prime Minister, Winston Churchill. She was just as proud of her civilization, even down to pieces of china she had brought from home. "See, Jean," she would say, turning over a plate or a little cream pitcher, "It says 'Spode. Made in Great Britain.' "

I loved my mother very much and tried to emulate her ways.

If she loved her country with such fierce devotion, then surely I should feel the same way about my own country. That the "enemy" in Egypt were the British did not seem to be a contradiction. The point was loyalty, sacrifice and duty to one's homeland.

While my love for Egypt was fueled by my mother's English patriotism, it was my Auntie Zouzou and her friends who instilled in me a pride in women. As a young girl I, as well as many of my friends, had read the many stories of Egyptian heroines—queens and poetesses, saints and warriors. Time and again I had read the famous story of el-Khansa, a poetess in the time of Muhammad who had won the highest prizes at the prestigious poetry fair held annually near Mecca. Poetesses were very important in Islam, acting as historians, social critics, and eulogizers of those fallen in battle. When el-Khansa lost her brother in combat, it was said she became fully possessed by the spirits who commune only with the best poets. Her grief unlocked verses that epitomized her people's suffering in their constant fight for survival, verses that inspired me greatly and led me to write poetry myself.

The story of Khadija, the Prophet's first wife, also gave me a special feeling, almost of spiritual communion. A rich widow of the Quraish tribe and a business woman engaged in the caravan trade, Khadija had been the first to accept the new religion of Islam. When, in great confusion and fear, Muhammad had revealed to Khadija that the Archangel Gabriel had appeared to him in a cave in Mount Hira and proclaimed him the Messenger of God, she had immediately comforted and supported her husband. "Rejoice, O son of my uncle," she had cried, "and be of good cheer. Verily by Him in whose hand is the soul of Khadija, you will be the Prophet of this People. God will not bring you to shame for He knows your sincerity and your truthfulness." Her courage and the strength of her love kept Muhammad faithful to her all her life. Not until after her death did he take a second wife.

The story of 'Aisha Bint Abi Bakr, a girl of only nine when she was married to the Prophet, was also a favorite of mine. A brave and wise young woman who grew up to be the love of Muhammad's life, 'Aisha brought us much of the Hadith so important to Muslims' understanding of Islam. She also fought for what she believed in, riding her own camel into battle only a few years before the Prophet's death. How devoted Muhammad must have been to her. When he died, his head was on 'Aisha's breast.

There was no end of stories about Muslim heroines, many of whom were saints like Sayyida Zainab, the mother of the handicapped, or Rabi'a el-Adawiyya, the orphaned slave girl who through self-discipline, purity and total devotion to God, rose to the level of sainthood. Though there was no order of priesthood in Islam and no priestly caste, there were many saints, both men and women. All Egyptians flocked to the tombs and mosques of the women saints to ask for *baraka,* blessing, to seek God's mercy and forgiveness, or to ask for miracles, *karamat.* At Friday prayers, the crowds were often so large at the mosques of the women saints that to find a place the worshippers had to arrive several hours early.

I had read also the stories of Western heroines like Madame Curie, who gave up so much in her search for radium and Florence Nightingale, who sacrificed her own comfort and health to nurse the sick. Another of my favorites was the story of Helen Keller, who, in spite of being blind and deaf, fought to be somebody. But most exciting of all to me were Auntie Zouzou's stories about women in modern Egypt.

At tea at Auntie Zouzou's in the afternoons, I would listen in fascination and awe to the talk about Huda Sha'arawi, one of the first women in our country to stand up against the British and for women's rights. Without Huda Sha'arawi, many Egyptian women would never have even gotten an education. It was she who in 1910 opened the first general-education school for girls, scandalizing Cairo. In 1920 she and her friend Siza Nabarawi founded the first women's association, as well as the first feminist magazine, *L'Égyptienne,* which Auntie Zouzou read regularly. Upon Huda Sha'arawi's return to Alexandria from an international women's conference in Rome in 1923, she became the first Egyptian woman to publicly remove her veil, denouncing it as a symbol of male domination and a foreign tradition imported into Egypt by the Turks.

My admiration became boundless for Huda Sha'arawi, who had sacrificed so much for the advancement of Egyptian women, including her marriage. Her husband, who was her first cousin and thirty years her senior, had divorced her when she refused to wear the veil. But she had pressed forward and in 1924 had won at least one of her demands for reform: establishing sixteen as the minimum age for girls to marry instead of the common twelve or thirteen, the age at which Huda had been married. The other reforms she attempted in the twenties —making higher education available to girls, doing away with polygamy and arranged marriages, abolishing prostitution and female circumcision—failed. She was a fighter for women, which elevated her in my eyes. But what made her a major influence in my young life was her stand against the British.

"Tell me again the story of Huda Sha'arawi demonstrating against the British," I would beg Auntie Zouzou. In the national uprising following World War I and the first failed promises of Great Britain to quit Egypt, Huda Sha'arawi had led 350 women to the office of the British High Commissioner to petition for Egypt's liberty. The Commissioner did not respond. A month later Huda Sha'arawi had joined a funeral procession in Cairo for the men and women killed by the British in the ongoing demonstrations. Once more the British opened fire on the crowd, killing even more Egyptians. Suddenly Huda Sha'arawi had stepped forward and faced the captain of the cavalry troops. "Here I am, standing in front of you," Auntie Zouzou now recounted the legendary words of Huda Sha'arawi, which she had spoken in perfect English. "Why don't you shoot me as you shot our other Egyptian women? We want freedom for our country. We will not accept your domination or the disgrace of such domination." Astonished by her bravery, the British officer immediately ordered his troops to hold their fire. This story always held me spellbound. Could I ever be so brave myself?

"Jean, Auntie Zouzou has invited you to spend Ramadan in Suez with her," my mother said to me shortly before my fifteenth birthday. "Would you like to go?"

Of course. I loved to leave Cairo for the holidays, and I looked forward to seeing my cousin 'Aida, whose husband, Hassan Izzat, fit my definition of a hero. During World War II, Hassan had been imprisoned by the British for working with the Germans. Hassan had been one of many Egyptian army officers who believed the Arab proverb "The enemy of our enemy is our friend." A German victory in Egypt, he and others felt, would have led to the final ouster of Britain from Egypt and left us to our own rule.

It was a hot, sunny day when I left for Suez in the summer of 1948. My heart was light as Auntie Zouzou and I drove the eighty miles or so east of Cairo to the Red Sea. The swimming would be wonderful in the clear waters there, the beaches beautiful, backed by the lavender hue of the Ataka Mountains. Hassan, cashiered out of the Air Force by the British and now an engineer, was a wonderful storyteller, and I looked forward to his tales of defying our occupiers. I was a romantic schoolgirl whose imagination knew no bounds. I was just fifteen. And in Suez I was about to meet my destiny.

Chapter 3

el-tha'ir wal taliba

The Revolutionary and the School Girl

i did not recognize him when I first saw him. Perhaps it was because of the hour, two o'clock in the morning, when I was in my aunt's kitchen in Suez helping to prepare *suhur*, the predawn meal, during Ramadan. Perhaps it was because of the improbability of it all. How could this man, this national hero, be just sitting in the hall of my cousin's home? It was unbelievable.

"We have a guest in the house," Hassan Izzat had said as he came into the kitchen, having just driven from Cairo. "He has endured much, so we want to offer him the best we have."

"Who is it?" I asked, my curiosity excited by the thought of another person like my cousin-in-law who had suffered for

Egypt. But when Hassan answered me, I felt as if I had been struck a blow. As I stared at Hassan in disbelief, the mango I had been holding slipped from my hands and splattered on the floor.

"Anwar el-Sadat."

No. It could not be true. Hassan must be teasing me, I thought, picking up the mango. For the three weeks I had been in Suez we had talked of little but Anwar el-Sadat and the ordeal he and fellow defendants were going through. For eight months they had been on trial for the assassination over two years before of the traitor Amin Osman, the Minister of Finance. The trial was finally drawing to a close now, and every day the newspapers featured photographs of the alleged ringleader, Captain Anwar el-Sadat, along with stories about his escapades. I had read every word.

Whether or not Sadat had been involved in Osman's assassination did not matter to me, for certainly Osman's death had been justified. Osman had been a well-known advocate of ties between our government and the British. He had signed his own death warrant when, shortly before he was killed, he made the notorious and highly unpopular statement that Egypt's relationship with Britain was like the bonds of a Catholic marriage, implying it could never be broken. For a Cabinet minister in our own government, an Egyptian, to say this was taken by many as an act of treason. And in January of 1946 Amin Osman had been shot to death. It was Anwar, I later learned, who had taken the men who did it out into the desert and taught them to shoot.

My admiration for Sadat and the other brave men on trial had grown with each newspaper story I read. Every day I would wait impatiently for my cousin to return from the center of town with the newspapers. The deprivation of the Ramadan fast seemed like nothing to me compared with the hardship of waiting for my cousin's arrival. I was totally caught up in the drama of the trial—and the heroism of the accused.

"Abeh Hassan, tell me more about Anwar el-Sadat," I would ask my cousin's husband during the long nights after we had broken the fast—using the Turkish title of respect, "Abeh," for an older brother or cousin. "Please, Abeh," I would beg him. And Hassan would tell me another story about Anwar, having known him intimately while a pilot in the armed forces and later in prison.

I thrilled to the story of how Anwar had first been sent to prison after the British security police searched his house and found a German transmitter that he was trying to fix so that he could send a treaty to Rommel in the desert east of Alexandria. Anwar wanted to offer Rommel Egyptian military support in return for Egyptian independence. For this the British had sent him to prison for two years, from 1942 to 1944.

"Tell me about his time of hiding from the British," I would press Hassan. And my cousin-in-law would weave more stories. Twice during his imprisonment Sadat had escaped, Hassan told me, and he had ended up living as a fugitive from October of '44 to September of '45. He had suffered greatly while avoiding reimprisonment by the British. Growing a beard to disguise himself, he had renamed himself Hajj Muhammad and gone to work for Hassan Izzat as a porter, loading and unloading his truck. "He even delivered fruit and vegetables to the British army camp at Tal el-Kabir in the Canal Zone," Hassan said, laughing. "He always outsmarted them."

From there, Hassan told me, Anwar had found menial work in Mazghuna, near Cairo, where he transported stone rubble from ships anchored in the Nile to the site of a new road being built between Cairo and Aswan in Upper Egypt. He could afford only one meal a day of hot lentil soup and slept in a garage. Digging a new canal was his next work in the town of Abu Kebir in the province of Sharqiyya, and when that was finished he went on to transport marble from a quarry in the desert town of Sannur to a site near the Pyramids in Giza. Like the slaves who built the Pyramids in 2500 B.C., Anwar had to carry the heavy marble slabs on his back. And what was the marble being used for? Hassan laughed again. "To build a rest house for King Farouk," he said.

It was not until the war ended in 1945 and martial law was lifted that Anwar was free to resume his own identity and go home. The British, of course, would not allow him back in the Army. But he had other opportunities. He could have started farming or taken a job in Cairo. But Egypt was still shackled to the British, and Anwar felt that his mission was unfulfilled. Within a month he had founded a secret organization, this time with the intent to rid the country of Egyptian leaders collaborating with the British and, in so doing, to persuade others to withdraw their support. Four months after that he had been arrested once again and charged with the assassination of

Osman. The next two and a half years he spent back in prison, waiting for the trial I was now reading about daily. A guilty verdict would result in the death sentence or hard labor for life.

I had thought of nothing else during my vacation in Suez. This man personified all I admired and wished I could be. He was a hero. His ideals were the highest. He had retained his dignity. He had sacrificed much for Egypt, enduring the punishment of the British while losing neither his courage nor his conviction. One day in the newspaper there was a picture of him standing in the courtroom in the cage built to restrain the accused. "Condemn me to death if you like," he was reported to have shouted, "but stop the public prosecutor from praising British imperalism in the venerable presence of this Egyptian court of law." The verdict was scheduled for early August.

As the day approached I had not been able to sleep and could barely enjoy the delicious fruits and sweets with which we broke the difficult summertime fast. The fate of this man had become my new obsession. While other girls my age thrilled to movie stars or romantic singers, my dreams were filled totally with Anwar el-Sadat. So were my prayers for his safety. "My God, if the court acquits him and his life is spared, I vow to fast another month in thanksgiving," I said the morning of the verdict. For a girl of fifteen who dearly loved to eat, this was no small vow.

I could not wait for my cousin to bring me the newspaper, but, as a young girl, I was not allowed to travel from the house alone. "Come, Saneyya," I called to my aunt's maid. "There is an emergency in Suez that I must attend to." I'm sure she doubted me, for what emergency could a healthy teenage girl have? Nonetheless, she dutifully followed me out of the house, though in my hurry I soon left her behind.

I ran the whole three miles through the summer heat to Suez. The road was covered with sand, and my feet raised puffs of dust behind me. As I rushed along I got many curious stares from children straddling loads of clover and straw on their donkeys, and from women balancing water jugs on their heads and infants on their shoulders. Panting for breath and with an unbearable thirst made even greater because it could not be quenched during the fast, I snatched a newspaper from the first kiosk I saw.

"Sadat Acquitted," the headline read.

In all my years, I do not know when else I have felt such joy and relief. Perhaps I might thirty years later when Anwar would return unharmed from his trip to Jerusalem in 1977. And perhaps I did after the first withdrawal of the Israelis from Sinai in 1979, when I would fast for three months in gratitude. But at this moment in Suez, with the unchecked emotions of an adolescent, I felt as if I were spinning into Paradise. *"Fa Allah khayru hafiz wa huwwa arham el-rahimin,"* I recited from the Quran, tears streaming down my cheeks. God is the best protector and the most merciful. Sadat was saved.

I bought a box of chocolates to celebrate the breaking of the fast on this very special day and treated myself and Saneyya, who had finally caught up with me, to a taxi ride home. I had no idea how special this day was going to become.

Anwar el-Sadat. I continued to stare at Hassan in the kitchen that very night like one struck dumb. "Will I meet him?" I finally managed to get out.

"Of course, you silly girl," Hassan replied, enjoying the shock he had caused me. "He will be staying with us for a while until he decides what he will do."

Absently I drew my hand across my face, leaving a smear of mango juice behind. I looked down at my dress, a simple one still dusty from my hurried trip into Suez. My hands were sticky from the fruit, my hair not neatly brushed. "I must prepare myself," I said to Hassan.

Quickly I darted out of the kitchen to go to my bedroom, not seeing until it was too late the quiet figure sitting in the hall. Paralysis set in again as I stood there, unable to move, utterly tongue-tied. Why was he sitting in the corridor? Why was he not in the sitting room?

Slowly he turned his head toward me. I knew I should drop my eyes, not look at this man—or any man, for that matter—in a bold manner, but at the moment I had no control. It was dark in the hall, but his features were so familiar to me from all the photographs I had seen that it seemed as if the lights were blazing. His eyes resting on mine looked solemn and sad, and I could not look away. His face, even darker in hue than it had appeared in his photographs, seemed burdened with the world. Standing there in the corridor, I felt the weariness he must be feeling.

We remained locked in this moment until somehow I remembered my manners. Forgetting the stickiness of my hand, I held it out to him in welcome. Calmly he accepted it. Not a word passed between us. As I stood there, a memory came to my mind of a hazelnut I had cracked the week before. The kernel had been split in two. On one half the corrugations had seemed to spell out "Anwar" in graceful Arabic characters, while on the other I had clearly seen the word "God." I had taken this to be a good omen for the outcome of his trial. Now I thought it might have been an omen for me.

During our predawn meal, I could not take my eyes off him. He must have been very hungry after the inferior food in prison, but he ate very little. As usual the family joked and told stories, but Anwar did not say a word. Nor, and this was very unusual, did I. Inside I was burning with questions which would have been too forward to ask. Why was he here with us? Why was he not with his wife and children, whom I had read about in the papers? And why was he so silent?

He did not speak for two days. The next morning, after I had spent a sleepless night, still not believing that he was in the same house as I, Hassan offered to drive my aunt to a dentist appointment in Suez. She and I sat in the back seat, Anwar and Hassan in the front. But still there was not a word from him.

"Abeh Hassan has told me of your remarkable courage and heroic patriotism," I finally worked up my courage to say to him.

He nodded at me, murmured his thanks and once more retreated into silence.

I know now that he was thinking, contemplating in silence what actions and decisions he was going to take in the future. Often during our marriage he would meditate in this way, sitting silently for hours in the chair on the terrace while staring at the Nile and puffing on his pipe in total solitude. He would have listened to the advice of his ministers. He would have read all the paperwork, the statistics, the forecasts. Whatever decision he would reach would be his alone. And that was how he would always reach it—alone. Now, in the back seat of the car en route to Suez, I thought his silence made him seem all the more mysterious.

"Daddy, please may I stay longer with Auntie Zouzou?" I telephoned my father in Cairo the next day. "It will be very hot at home and here we can go swimming." I held my breath for his answer. I dared not tell him the real reason I wanted to stay, for surely he would have ordered me to come home. Luckily he gave me his permission to extend my stay without asking me any questions.

I could not have lied to my father, as I loved and respected him very much. But I could not have told him the real reason. He would have been very suspicious—and rightly so—of my feelings toward Anwar. Though I had just turned fifteen, it was not uncommon for Egyptian girls of the middle class to marry at seventeen or so. Already in my family there was talk of whom I would marry. Hassan Izzat's brother Ali had made clear his intention, coming to see my family and me often in Cairo. But I was not really accepting of the idea. Ali was a nice young man, with a high-paying job, even an automobile. But his personality was very dull and he was not witty at all. I also suspected that he was not very brave.

Ali had been in Alexandria during World War II, he told me, when air raid sirens had signaled an imminent attack by Axis planes. There were many such raids during the war, Alexandria being just sixty-five miles from the front in the desert. But Ali had panicked. When the air raid siren sounded, Ali had fallen to the ground in fear. "I was too frightened to move," he told me. "I thought I was going to die." Though his behavior had been perfectly human, my interest in him as a husband had diminished. I wanted a man who would not be frightened of air raids or by the prospect of dying. I had little admiration for a man who would fall flat on the ground.

My cousin, Auntie Batta's son, was also a likely prospect. Ahmed Abu Zaid was very respectable and wealthy, an officer in the military police. Ironically, he had been one of the officers assigned to guard Anwar and the other defendants in the trial in Cairo. It was his responsibility to transport the defendants between Cairo Central Prison and the court, and to keep order among them in the courtroom where they were held in a cage. I did not hold this against Ahmed, for he was only doing his job. But though Auntie Batta strongly wanted a marriage between us, I did not. I loved Ahmed as a cousin, not as a husband.

The son of one of our neighbors, too, had asked to marry me. But I didn't accept that possibility either. He was not at all the man of my dreams, though there were advantages to such a marriage. He was rich, good-looking, only five years older than I, and I knew him quite well. Unlike Western countries, where boys and girls are allowed to court and get to know each other before marriage, in Egypt during my childhood it was not so. From puberty, boys and girls were taught to avoid temptation and were not allowed to be alone in each other's presence.

It never occurred to me or to my family that I might not marry at all. We were middle-class and held property. What my family wanted for me, and what all Egyptians wished for their daughters, was that I marry happily and well. The better off my future husband, the higher my standard of living. The greater his stature, the greater mine. In all ways, his identity would become my identity.

I was finding out from Hassan that Anwar's family was as poor as he was. His father, Muhammad, was a clerk in the military hospital that was in Qubbah, and his mother, Sitt el-Barrein, was the daughter of a Sudanese fellah. Life had always been quite a struggle for Anwar, even when he was a child.

Anwar was born on December 25, 1918, in a farming village in the Nile Delta, the third son of his father's second wife. His village of Mit Abul-Kum had no electricity, no plumbing. His grandmother, Um Muhammad, acted as the village healer, treating sickness with ancient concoctions of herbs, solving the emotional problems of her community with charms and amulets. Like many in the rural areas, Anwar's family had little money to give their children. At the *kuttab,* the Quranic teaching school where Anwar and the other village boys learned the 114 chapters of the Quran by heart, his only meal consisted of bread crusts and bits of dried cheese stuffed into the pocket of his galabiyya.

When he was not in school Anwar would take the cows and the water buffalo to drink from the village canal, drive the oxen pulling the thresher through the fields of wheat, and help to harvest the dates and the cotton. At night, he loved to tell me later, he would lie on the top of the high family *furn,* a primitive oven enclosed in a bench of dried mud, eat the onion he had left to roast in it all day, and listen to his mother and grandmother tell bedtime stories of modern Egyptian heroes standing up to the British. So much did he love this warm moment of the day that later, when he would build our own home in Mit Abul-Kum, Anwar would insist on having a traditional mud *furn* alongside our more modern gas oven.

When Anwar was seven, he had moved from his beloved village of Mit Abul-Kum to Cairo. There, along with his grandmother, his brothers Taalat and Esmat and his sister, Nefisa, he lived with his father and mother in a four-room flat. The flat grew even more crowded when his father took another wife from the village. Amina would bear him nine more children, and all of them too would live in the four rooms.

Anwar's father's salary barely kept bread in the mouths of the thirteen children, and Anwar spent his entire daily allowance on one glass of milky tea. On his way back and forth to school every day he passed one of King Fuad's royal palaces, the Qubbah Palace, whose orchards burst with apricots in the spring. But Anwar dared not pick a single one. Even touching something that belonged to the King could mean death.

Anwar might have been doomed to a life of poverty and obscurity had not the Anglo–Egyptian Treaty of 1936 permitted the Egyptian Army to expand and, most important, to open its previously elitist officers corps for the first time to the lower classes. Since the 1882 revolt against the Khedive Tawfiq in which academy cadets had participated, only rich young Egyptians who owned land and supported the interests of the ruling class had been allowed into the Army as officers. Restricting the control of the Army to the elite had guaranteed the protection of the throne. But such discrimination could not last.

In the rising surge of nationalism following World War I, King Fuad tried to appease the growing unrest among the lower classes by opening the doors of the Army to them as officers. This one simple act would prove to be his son Farouk's undoing. Anwar was one of the first of the lower classes to be graduated from the Royal Military Academy in 1938, with the rank of second lieutenant. Among the other graduates of the academy were Gamal Abdel Nasser, who would lead the coup that toppled King Farouk fourteen years later, and the other young officers who would make up the Revolutionary Command Council.

Anwar's future in the King's Army could have been secure, his social position greatly elevated by his rank. But he had chosen instead to sacrifice everything for the liberation of Egypt. After his first arrest, he had been dismissed from the Army. With his long record of subversiveness against the British, Hassan explained to me, there was little chance he would ever be allowed back into the Army again. If he chose to remain politically active, the chances were equally great that he would once more be imprisoned.

It was what Hassan chose to tell me last, however, which explained Anwar's silence in Suez. Anwar had come to stay with us instead of returning to his own family, Hassan explained, because he was divorcing his wife. She and their young daughters were living with his father in Cairo. Anwar had no home to go to, and, after almost three years in prison, no money at all. Most of what he might make in the future would go to support his children. Not only was that the law, it was also his duty. He was being wracked now by his decisions for his future.

From a practical point of view, what Hassan had told me about Anwar el-Sadat should have quelled my increasingly romantic feelings. But what fifteen-year-old girl is practical? Instead I looked at his skin, much darker than mine and in the opinion of many Egyptians less appealing, and found him very handsome. I looked at his one rumpled white jacket and one pair of trousers, and found him flawlessly dressed. I looked at the age on his face, fifteen years more than mine, and saw the ideals of youth. I listened to his silence and heard a strong personality I could admire. He was the heroic image of my dreams. I could not imagine what he thought of me.

"I have brought you a fig," I said to him, having picked one off a low branch in the garden.

For the first time he looked at me and smiled. "Is it true that you have recently had a birthday?" he asked.

"Yes," I replied, holding my breath in the hope that he would join us on our trip that day to the beach in Isma'iliyya.

"I cannot afford to buy you a gift," he said apologetically. But I did not care. "Will you come with us to the beach?" I asked him. He hesitated and I was frightened that he would refuse, choosing to spend the day instead in silence in our garden. "I will come," he said.

The day was magic from the beginning. In the car I sang all the way to Isma'iliyya, a long drive along the desert on one side and the Red Sea on the other to the end of the Suez Canal. There is something about car rides that always makes me want to sing, a habit that later my drivers would know well. Always they would turn on the radio, looking for the songs of my favorite singer Um Kalthum so that I could sing along with her. But on this day it was not my singing that was extraordinary. It was at long last the voice of Anwar.

"I cannot buy you anything for your birthday," he suddenly said to me in the car. "But I will sing a song for you." I could not believe the change in him as he sang me a song about love by Farid el-Atrash in a singing voice that was quite beautiful. Instead of brooding, his face became alive. Instead of his habit of looking far away into the distance and seeing nothing, he turned in the front seat and looked directly at me. My happiness grew even greater and continued all the way through our lunch by the Red Sea.

All the questions that I had bottled up out of respect for his solitude came pouring out. And with increasing animation he answered them. "How did you pass the time in prison?" I asked him. And he told me about his ordeal, which at first, in the Aliens' Jail in 1942, was not too bad. There, he told me, he had a bed, blankets, a chair, a small table and even cigarettes, although the warden had to light them for him as no matches were allowed in the cells. He was even allowed to read newspapers and books, using much of his time to improve his English from books in that language. During two fifteen-minute breaks a day, he was allowed to walk within the prison walls.

Twice he had been transferred to other prisons, first spending almost a year in a political detention center in a sumptuous palace in Upper Egypt, where he learned German by reading a German-language edition of a novel by Edgar Wallace. The next year he spent at the Zaytun Detention Center near Cairo, where he and his fellow prisoners bred rabbits to pass the time. Another detainee, a count from the Balkans, turned out to be a fine cook of rabbits, and they all ate well until the rabbits contracted a disease and died. But Anwar did not have the patience to stay idly in jail. Germany was heading toward defeat in the war. The British remained entrenched in Egypt. He had to get out. And he did, not once but twice.

"How did you manage your escape?" I asked him as we walked together on the beach after lunch in Isma'iliyya.

He laughed at the memory. "The first time six of us, including Hassan Izzat, made a hole in the roof, climbed through it using a stepladder and let ourselves down into the street. No one even knew we were gone until the following morning."

"Why did you return?" I asked him as I took off my shoes and splashed along at the edge of the water.

He laughed again. "I just wanted to humiliate the government, and I did," he said. "We walked right into Abdin Palace and signed the Royal Ceremonies Book, which many do either to thank the King for any 'royal kindness' or to take their leave. Then we announced to the secretary that we had escaped temporarily from Zaytun to deliver the message to the King not to give in to the British."

My eyes must have been as round with amazement at his daring as the secretary's at Abdin Palace had been.

"What did you do next?" I asked.

"We took a taxi to Zaytun and reported back in," he said.

Nine months later he was still in Zaytun, though by October of '44 the Allies were assured of victory and many political prisoners had been released. Only Anwar and his group remained in prison on the orders of the British. By now, he told me, he was thoroughly fed up and decided to escape for good.

"I went on a hunger strike, which forced them, under the regulations, to put me into the hospital," he said, removing his own shoes and rolling up his trousers as we walked along the beach. "While the hospital was swarming with people at lunchtime, I slipped away from my guard and rushed to find Hassan, who was waiting for me in front of the hospital with his car engine running. I spent the next year as a fugitive," he said.

We had been walking and talking now for an hour, the minutes slipping by. I knew we should return to where my cousin and Hassan Izzat were sitting, but I was so fascinated by Anwar's stories that I allowed this rash behavior and didn't even feel shamed. There was a growing sympathy between us, an understanding that I never felt with anyone else before or since. When we finally returned to my cousin after still another hour, Anwar questioned her over and over about my age, not believing I was just fifteen. So special was this day that we would talk about it often during the coming years, even on the day before he was murdered.

Just as I had bottled up all my questions, so had Anwar kept all his feelings to himself. He was as relieved to talk as I was eager to listen, though he kept looking at me in some bewilderment, seeing that the recipient of his thoughts was a young schoolgirl. Yet little was left unsaid during this first afternoon we shared on the beach in Isma'iliyya and in the remaining afternoons of the summer when we would walk and talk in the fields of Suez. My respect and admiration for him never diminished, while my initial adolescent crush soon softened into love.

He, on the other hand, was becoming increasingly disturbed not only by the great difference in our ages, but by his dedication to politics and his obligations to his first family, which would keep him almost penniless. In his mind at this time, a second marriage was out of the question. During his years in prison he hadn't even been able to support his family from his first. His father had done what he could, but it hadn't been enough.

"How, then, did your family survive?" I asked him.

"Only through the charity of the Muslim Brothers," he replied. "Every month they sent ten pounds to my wife and children, and for that I will always be thankful."

I smiled. "Maybe I contributed, too," I suggested, telling him of how I had raised money for the Brotherhood when I was younger.

Anwar was anguished about his first wife, Ekbal Madi, and their daughters. As was the custom in the villages, Anwar had been young when he married, only twenty-two and a second lieutenant. His wife was a distant relative and from the same village. Such marriages within families were very common and still are in rural areas, solidifying family positions and amassing land. And for Anwar then, a village boy, it had been a suitable match. Their marriage had been arranged in Mit Abul-Kum, where Ekbal's father was the 'umda, the headman of the village. She was seven years older than Anwar, and a good and decent woman. But she was also a country woman with no formal education. She had never even been to Cairo. "I wanted so much to be able to share my life and my dreams with my wife," Anwar told me as we walked and talked on the beach in Isma'iliyya. "But she could not understand, which, of course, was not her fault."

It was during his second imprisonment in 1946, for the assassination of Amin Osman, that Anwar realized the significance

of love—or lack of love—in his life. Unlike his first imprisonment, when the conditions had been at least bearable, his sentence this time, in Cairo Central Prison, had been almost
unbearable. For thirty months he had lived in solitary confine-
ment in a tiny cell. He had no bed, no table, no chair, not even
a lamp, though that didn't really matter as he was not allowed
to read, write or listen to the radio. In the winter, he told me,
cold water would ooze from the cell walls. In the summer,
swarms of cockroaches would cover every surface, including
his sleeping pad—a mat made out of rotting palm fronds covered by a filthy blanket.

"I was grateful at least for the hardiness of my boyhood in
the village," Anwar told me on one of our walks. "It helped
me to endure the suffering." And the suffering was intense,
especially painful for Muslims who must be clean before they
are able to pray. There was one bucket in each cell for water,
and another to be used as a toilet. Naturally there was a scabies
epidemic among the three thousand inmates from the unsani-
tary conditions. Once a day a *ful,* or fava bean, sandwich was
thrown through the small square cut in the door of each cell.
Anwar could rarely eat it. The stress and the deprivation were
ruining his digestion, it turned out, forever. For the rest of his
life Anwar would have to start each day with a glass of Eno's
Salts and even then could eat only very carefully, and very
little. Toward the end, all he would take was a little soup.

Cell 54 became his whole world. And he became his only
company. Alone with his thoughts, he wrestled with the emp-
tiness of his marriage. "How could I punish my wife with
divorce when she has done nothing but wait for me all these
years?" he asked himself time and again. How I admired him
as he described his pain about his duty toward his wife. Few
Egyptian men felt so strongly about their obligations to their
wives or considered their wives' feelings at all. There was a
possibility that she could remarry, of course. But with three
children, there was very little probability.

For a year and a half he suffered over the dilemma of his
marriage, lying down on his mat at night with his temples
throbbing, waking up in the same condition in the morning.
"Among lawful things, the one that God hates most is divorce," cautions the Quran. But Anwar could not see any other
way and finally sent word to his wife that she should stop

coming to see him in prison. Upon his release he told her personally that they could not go on living together. His need to love, he was discovering in Cell 54, could be better spent in his love toward Egypt, toward all living beings, and toward God.

At fifteen, or at any age for that matter, I did not need to be told about the power of love. It is an emotion that comes easily to women, that can overwhelm at times with its joy and also with its pain. All my life I would be ruled by the love I felt for my husband, for my children and for my country, completely and without reservation. Yet, for all of Anwar's preoccupation with love, starting with his desolation in Cell 54, never once in all the years that we were married would the word "love" ever pass personally from Anwar to me. I would tease him endlessly, trying to get him to tell me he loved me, seeking the reassurance every woman wants. But though I knew he loved me, he could not or would not say so. "Don't be so silly, Jehan," he would scold me lightly. "You know how I feel in my attitude toward you, in my respect for you. Everything I have is for you." Stubbornly, I would persist. "Well, I want to hear it from you," I would tease, "otherwise I will be jealous of every woman who looks at you." But he never relented. Perhaps he was too shy.

In Suez, we could not get enough of talking with each other. My aunt and my cousin realized what was happening between us long before I did really, putting them in a very awkward situation. It was unseemly for a young girl to be spending so much time alone in the company of a man.

As the oldest male relative present, Hassan should not have been allowing me to walk alone with Anwar at all. His position was further compromised by the fact that he knew his brother wanted to marry me. Whose side should he be on? Naturally he should have been on the side of his relative rather than this outsider. But Anwar was not just any outsider. He was a national hero.

I didn't think about the risk. All I wanted was to be with Anwar, listening to him talk about his past, his struggles, even the books he had read in prison. I could contribute little to our conversations, having led a very protected and uneventful life. But I couldn't get enough of listening to his loud, deep voice, whose powerful tone I had already gotten used to. Anwar had two voices. One was silent, the other very loud. "Why is Anwar so angry?" people would say to me later after listening to one of his speeches. I would laugh. "He is not angry," I would explain. "This is just the voice in which he speaks."

Only when he spoke in Suez about the books he had read could I participate, and at that very little. In his last six months in Cell 54, he and his fellow prisoners had been allowed to rent pieces of furniture—a mattress stuffed with rice husks, a table, a chair—and, most important, to read. He read all of Jack London, especially enjoying *The Call of the Wild,* in which he identified with the wolf who could not be tamed. He was moved by the Biblical works of Lloyd Douglas, enjoying *The Big Fisherman* and *The Robe.* But it was an article he read by an American psychologist in *Reader's Digest* which had changed his life.

"I developed many complexes from being arrested always in the early hours of the morning and in the bitter cold," he told me. "I became afraid to go to sleep and often woke up at three or four in the morning, shivering and certain that once more I was going to be taken away. I had never known fear before, and in Cell 54 I even began to question whether the suffering I was enduring for Egypt was worth it. Would it make a difference? Or was I being destroyed as a man?"

The answer to his shaken sense of identity came to him in *Reader's Digest.* It was God who sent crises of all sorts to mere mortals, the psychologist had written, to teach them not only to endure, but to battle the consequences. This was not evil of God in any sense, but an act of friendliness to show His creatures how to play the roles assigned to them. With faith and the love of our merciful, just and caring God, all doors could be opened, all adversity conquered. From that moment, Anwar told me, he had achieved peace of mind and a clear sense of his identity. Never again would he be shaken by turbulent events.

"What shall I do?" I asked my cousin as we sat on the terrace of the Beau Rivage Hotel. She, Hassan, Anwar and I had come to Alexandria to celebrate the three-day holiday of 'Aid el-Saghir at the end of Ramadan. "I am falling in love with this man."

"Be careful," she advised me. "Don't walk alone with him in the mornings." But I cherished the walks Anwar and I were taking in the mornings along the beach, though I had been very frightened one morning when we had run into friends of my parents from Cairo. I had nodded to them as we passed, not wanting to pretend I was hiding, but also not wanting to bring attention to myself. Inside I was terrified that they would tell my parents in Cairo. But they had not told.

The risk was becoming too great, however. "I will sit with the two of you so that you can be together," my cousin promised, having received the permission of her husband, Hassan. And she did, over lunch at the Beau Rivage, dinner at the San Stephano, along the seaside Corniche, where the sun turned Anwar's skin even darker and mine, he claimed, more red than that of a crayfish. We were doing the unspeakable in Egypt at that time. We were having a romance, a courtship.

But we couldn't help ourselves. Our emotions were out of control, smashing us, really. We had to be together, stay together, no matter what the cost.

"You are too young," he said to me. "When I am an old man you will just be beginning."

"Think of all the years we'll have in between," I told him. "I love you no matter what the difference is in our ages."

"I have been married before and have my children to support. That is not fair to you," he said.

I shook my head at him. "That is up to me to accept or not."

Was he testing me with all the reasons I should forget him? I did not know, deciding instead he was being more realistic than romantic.

"I have no plans for the future, no employment at all," he said. "You are not used to living in such a reduced way."

But I was fifteen and was convinced I could live on love. "We will be as one," I told him. "That is all that counts."

We had to tell my parents, to receive their consent to marry. But how? It would fall to Hassan Izzat, my relative and Anwar's representative, to present to my parents Anwar's request to marry me. The prospects were not good.

"Let us lie to your father," Hassan Izzat suggested to us at a strategy session. "I will tell him Anwar is a rich man who owns estates and orchards from which he has a large income. They will believe me, for though there have been many stories about Anwar in the newspapers, they have been political stories, not personal ones."

But Anwar refused. "That is unthinkable," he said. "I will not consent to deception."

For once I was the more realistic one. I knew that my father would not accept a penniless man for the husband of his daughter. A little lie now could gain us enough time for my father to come to know Anwar, to respect and love him as I did, and to accept the difficult conditions of our engagement. But it was Anwar, not my father, who first had to be convinced. "You are not deceiving me, and I, after all, am the one who is to be your wife," I said gently to Anwar. "I will tell my father the whole truth before we get married, as I am not in the habit of lying to him. But as it is he will not even agree to the principle of our wish to be married."

Anwar remained silent, which we took to be his painful and unhappy consent.

Hassan's first meeting with my parents upon our return to Cairo was predictably stormy, in spite of his fiction about Anwar's independent income. I was too young, my mother insisted. Anwar belonged to a much more modest family than ours. No one in our family had ever married a divorced man. And, besides, Anwar's complexion was very dark, an irrefutable fact which she knew from having seen his picture in the newspapers so many times.

Hassan had failed. Now it was my turn to plead for my happiness, for never could I have married Anwar or anyone else without my parents' permission. Like all Egyptian children, I was bound by my respect for them as well as by my religion to do my parents' bidding. Obedience to one's parents is mentioned in the Quran as next in importance to obedience to God. It would never have occurred to me to defy my parents' wishes in any matter, especially something as important as marriage. Their approval was imperative.

But my mother remained adamant. "The fifteen-year age difference between you is too much," she said, sounding just like Anwar. "You will regret this later on." She could not think of enough bad things about him to discourage me. "He was married and has children," she went on. "This will disturb your life."

"Why, Mummy?" I asked her.

"Because you will have to look after them and you will be jealous," she said. "He will spend all his money on them and it will spoil your life."

"I love him," I protested. But it was of no use.

"Do you think of love only?" she said, her voice rising. "Your love will quickly disappear when there are so many other things to consider."

"My love covers everything," I insisted. But she had the stubbornness of Winston Churchill.

"Will you at least meet him?" I begged.

"No," she said.

My father was more sympathetic, but no less firm. As a student in Assiut, he too had been arrested for demonstrating against the British. His parents had not known where he was for three days, and when they found him his brief imprisonment had left a devastating impression. Never again would he become involved with politics. Nor did he want me to be.

"Anwar el-Sadat has already been in prison and internment camps," he said as I stood downcast before him. "What guarantee do I have that he will not return in the future if he remains in politics?"

This possibility I could not deny, though to me it was a plus. It was Anwar's patriotism that had drawn me to him in the first place. I actively wanted to be the wife of a patriot, to stand by his side in defense of the ideals we shared. But this was precisely what my father feared.

I could not eat, could not sleep. Now that I was home I could not even see Anwar, who had taken a room in a downtown boardinghouse, and I talked to him only on the phone. My father was becoming concerned about me, as I had always been the first one in the family to joke and sing but now I had become pale and silent.

Once again Hassan came to the house to talk to my father, to argue Anwar's case. I could see that my father was softening, having been convinced of my true feelings and understanding my difficulties in the situation. He too, I realized, had married for love and defied his parents.

"I will consent if he can keep my daughter in a good standard," my father said cautiously. "I don't want her to suffer by marrying someone who has just a small salary and no other income. She is not used to this."

"On the contrary," Hassan insisted. "This man is wealthy." And he went on to describe once again the feddans, the acres of fields and orchards that Anwar supposedly owned.

I felt torn as I sat listening beside them. Why was I cheating my father, who was the nearest one to my heart? Shouldn't I tell him the truth now? My other voice spoke to me: Let the truth wait, Jehan—only that way can you marry Anwar. The struggle waged in me until my cousin left and I burst into tears.

"My father, not a word Hassan has told you is true," I confessed, tears streaming down my face. "Anwar has nothing, but we knew you would not give your consent unless we pretended he did."

My father was not surprised, knowing that Hassan was the sort of man whose word was false 80 percent of the time. But this realization only made me feel worse.

"I love him, Daddy. I love him," I wept. "The money means nothing to me. I don't want any servants. I will cook. I will clean. I will do everything. Even what salary he makes will be too much for me. I pray for your consent."

"If that is what you truly want, Jean, then I will give it," he finally said.

I fell to my knees and kissed his hand in gratitude. I couldn't believe that he had given his consent. But there was still my mother to win over.

"Don't tell Mummy that Anwar has no money," I pleaded. "That, on top of everything else, will keep me always from Anwar."

He nodded in agreement. "You are right, Jehan," he said, stroking my head. "This must be our secret. Otherwise she will say to me, 'Why? Why are you accepting this man?' "

"Will you help me to convince her?" I asked him.

He smiled. "I will try, Jehan," he said. "But she is a very stubborn British woman."

For the next few weeks I tried everything I could to change her mind. But my father's reversal had had little effect.

"Let us be engaged, Mummy, and if after a few months I still love him as I do now, then it will be all right. If not, you'll be right and you can break it off," I promised her.

But she refused. Day and night I pestered her, finally one day falling to the ground in front of her, kissing her hands, her feet, her knees.

"Mummy, please, I beg you," I cried, clinging to her. "At least meet him. If you don't find him proper, then all right, that's up to you." I could sense her relenting a bit and pressed on. "You know I am not a silly young girl going around with romantic ideas in her head," though of course I was. "I truly love this man and cannot live without him."

"All right, all right, I'll meet him," she said reluctantly, trying to disentangle herself from the arms I had wrapped around her legs. A meeting was set for the next week.

Now I was truly terrified. Here was my mother, an English-woman whose love for her country knew no bounds. And here was Anwar, one of the most vocal and nationalistic Egyptians against Britain. Here was my mother who revered the heroism of the British military during World War II, who thought Winston Churchill one of the greatest men of all times. And here was Anwar who had worked against the British in that same war and resented Winston Churchill above all others.

It had been Churchill who, at the request of our Parliament in 1941, had ordered the Egyptian Army to be withdrawn from Marsa Matruh in the western desert, then had punished them by ordering the humiliating confiscation of their weapons. Anwar, then a signals officer in the artillery in Marsa Matruh, had rebelled against this edict and had refused to surrender his arms. Churchill had come into Anwar's life again in a more direct way in 1942, when the British Prime Minister made a secret trip to el-Alamein to boost the morale of the Eighth Army, recently overrun by Rommel. Churchill's decision at the time to change the leadership by appointing Montgomery commander in chief had changed the tide of the war. But during that same trip, Churchill had also changed the tide of Anwar's life. Meeting with the German spies Anwar had been accused of assisting, Churchill promised to spare their lives if they made a full confession. That confession had sent Anwar to jail for the next two years.

What would happen at the meeting between Anwar and my parents? I was petrified. On the day Anwar, my mother, my father and I were to take our tea together, I said extra prayers that it wouldn't be our last. I prayed all day long as the time for Anwar's arrival approached. I was sure my father would love him, the more time they had to sit together. But my mother? I was equally sure that she and Anwar would quarrel, that she would refuse him. I could already hear her voice saying to me, "No, Jean. This marriage shall not be."

Would Anwar bend his principles just once and tell my

mother what she wanted to hear rather than what he believed? It had been noble indeed of him to stand up to the British domination, to denounce the British publicly in court. But this was my mother—and the rest of my life. What would he do? What would she do?

I took my seat at the tea in between my mother and Anwar. I dared not look at either of them, concentrating on the pattern of the rug, which still from that day I can see in my mind. Instead of a polite conversation, from the beginning this meeting was going more like an exam. I said not a word, listening instead to the questions she was hurling at him.

"*Bni'ra 'aanak kteer fil garayyid, ya sayyid el-Sadat,*" she was saying. "We read a good deal about you in the papers, Mr. Sadat. Are you still against the British occupation?" My heart stopped, not for the first time.

"Yes, I am against this occupation," he replied. "As an Egyptian, I do not want any other country to dictate our ways, just as you would not want that for Britain." Fine, I thought. She could understand that.

"Would you like to see all the British people leave Egypt?" my mother pressed him. Again my heart stopped.

But Anwar was splendid. "Of course not," he said. "I have nothing against British people. We are all human beings, after all, with the same dreams and hopes. It is the government to which I am opposed, the government which is occupying my land."

I started sneaking looks at each of them as she questioned and he answered, trying to read their expressions. But there were none. I looked anxiously to my father, but there was no expression on his face either. He did not say a word, knowing that this crucial exam was between my mother and Anwar and not him.

Then came the question I had dreaded above all others. "What do you think of Winston Churchill?" my mother asked Anwar.

Well, this is the end, I thought. I couldn't decide whether I was about to faint or, from the pounding in my chest, to have a heart attack. I tried to catch Anwar's eye, to beg him to at least be gentle. But he was looking directly and clearly at my mother.

"Winston Churchill is a thief," Anwar said firmly. "Egypt has had sovereignty since 1923, yet still he robs our country of its pride and its independence. His are the worst kind of politics, for he seeks his ends for his country through the humiliation of my own. He may be a great leader for the British, but for us he is the hated enemy. With all due respect to you, madam, I feel nothing but contempt for your Mr. Winston Churchill."

My mother stared silently at him over her cup of English tea. I thought I was going to die as Anwar's words still hung in the air.

"You must come see us again, Mr. Sadat," my father finally said into the void. "This has been a very interesting meeting." And he showed him to the door.

Paralyzed, I remained sitting by my mother. Whatever she said next would determine our fate. How would it go?

"I do not agree with anything your Mr. Sadat said about Winston Churchill and British policy," my mother finally said. My heart sank. "But I respect him for speaking in such an honest and straightforward way to me," she continued. "He was not trying to please me. And that is admirable."

My heart leaped with joy. "Then we can become engaged?" I asked my mother.

"I am not sure yet," she said. "I still think you are too young to be engaged. I will see after sitting with him again and discussing it with your father."

For the next few weeks my spirits alternately soared and fell. Frequently Auntie Batta called on my mother, frustrated at the thought of losing the marriage between me and her son and fueling my mother's objections to Anwar. I was pretty. I was young. His future was insecure. Why should my mother marry me off so soon to such an inferior prospect when her son Ahmed was such a suitable match? *"Nar el-qarib walla gannit el-gharib,"* Auntie Batta warned my mother. "The hell of a relative is better than the heaven of an outsider. It is always better to marry someone within the family."

My mother was persuaded. "Why not wait a few years, Jean?" she suggested. "If your love is true, it will wait with you." A few years? That was a lifetime.

Our neighbor's son, who had also asked for my hand, was of no help, either. "Anwar el-Sadat has no future," he said to my father. "How can he provide for Jehan from political prison?"

My father began to express doubts. I was desperate.

"Let us all meet once more with Anwar," I begged my mother, seeing my future with him slipping away again in the face of all these objections. The reservations everyone was voicing were undeniably true. But if my parents, especially my mother, could only know his personality, perhaps their minds would be changed. "Talk about books," I whispered to Anwar over the phone. "She loves to read."

"Charles Dickens is one of my favorite authors," Anwar said to my mother at our next tea.

She was stunned. "You have read Dickens?" she said, addressing him for the first time in English.

"Yes," Anwar replied. And in English they started discussing *Great Expectations* and *Oliver Twist,* which Anwar especially liked because the story involved young orphans and their heroic sacrifices. Orphans had always been a sympathetic subject to Muslims, who consider a child orphaned if either parent has died. The Prophet Muhammad himself had been orphaned at the age of six, and our Holy Book enjoins us to treat all orphans with fairness and kindness.

I listened to their conversation with mounting hope and interest, for Dickens was one of my favorite authors as well. I had read *Oliver Twist* in secondary school and had taken an exam on *A Tale of Two Cities*. And at least my mother and Anwar were not talking about politics. I could see from the expressions on their faces that they were enjoying themselves, finding in each other's conversation subjects of great interest that they had few opportunities to share with others. I watched my mother's face come alive as she talked about one of her beloved English authors in her native language with an educated Egyptian whose accent may have been rough, but whose vocabulary was extensive and precise.

"All right, Jean. All right," she said to me when Anwar left. "I can understand your feelings now about this man. He is intelligent. He has character. He will take good care of you." Then she added a consideration an Egyptian mother would never have thought of: "And you will never be bored."

I hugged her until my arms ached. Our engagement party was set for the following week. I was excited, and a little nervous. I had not yet met Anwar's family. I knew they would be different from mine. And they certainly were.

My father, Safwat Raouf, and my British mother, Gladys Cotrell, in Cairo.

Auntie Zouzou, my Egyptian "mother."

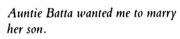

My grandfather, a pioneer surgeon, objected to their marriage.

Auntie Batta wanted me to marry her son.

Me and my cousin 'Awatif's orphaned girls in Port Sa'id.

Anwar, standing at right, with his classmates in Cairo.

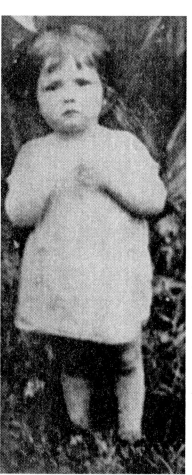

At age two in our garden on Roda Island.

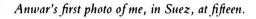

Anwar's first photo of me, in Suez, at fifteen.

My sister Dalia (left), Anwar's sister Sakina, me, Hassan Izzat, Anwar and my mother in Suez after our engagement.

May 29, 1949, the happiest day of my life.

Our first house, at Anwar's post in Rafah.

After our beloved first child, Loubna, was born, in 1954, we took her with us everywhere; on holiday in Port Sa'id; to my sister Dalia's wedding.

Gamal and Noha followed soon
thereafter, shown here in our garden on
the Pyramids Road. When little Jehan,
or Nana, as we called her, was born in
1961, our family was complete.

Anwar was happiest relaxing in his boyhood village of Mit Abul-Kum. Nearby in Talla, I started the Women's Cooperative to teach rural women to sew and give them financial security.

The price of war. During our humiliation in 1967, this veteran (top) was too traumatized to eat. During our victory in '73, I toured the Bar Lev line with General Fuad Aziz Ghali, a Coptic hero, and stole a few moments with Anwar at military headquarters at el-Tahira Palace.

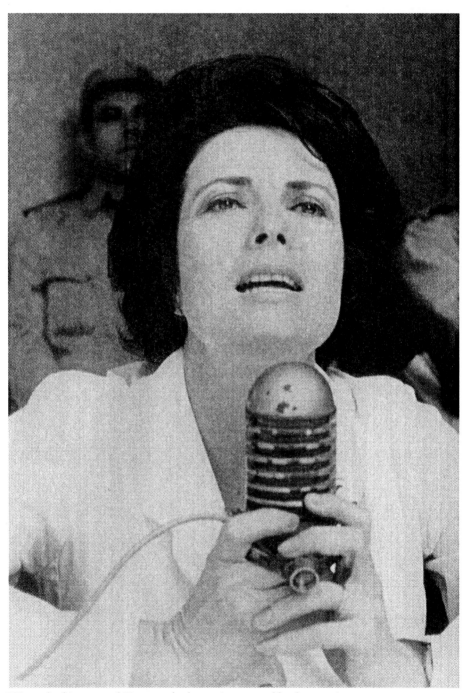

"You who have served Egypt, who have given your blood to regain our dignity, you are our true heroes."

Talaat came. Nefisa came. Sakina, Effat, Zein and Zeinab came. Anwar's father, Muhammad, came with Sitt el-Barrein, Anwar's mother, and his other wife, Amina. Anwar's brother Esmat came with his first of two wives, Zainab. One after another Anwar's relatives arrived at my parents' house to celebrate our engagement. I was shocked by the number of Anwar's family, but it was impossible to be afraid of them. They were relaxed and friendly, having the openness and sense of humor I would later see in other Egyptian families from the countryside. "How did our lucky brother get someone as white as you?" Anwar's brothers and sisters joked with me in a very sweet way. Anwar's father told me warmly how proud he was that I was going to be part of his family. Anwar's mother was so happy she could not speak, but from time to time she ran up to hug and kiss me. So much affection made me feel welcome among them immediately. I just hoped I could remember everybody's name.

Later, when Anwar and I visited his family's house, I would find out how difficult that really was. Anwar's whole family— nieces, nephews, grandchildren, brothers and sisters—all ate dinner together every night. This is more like a tribe than a family, I would think to myself as I looked about me at the three generations gathered around the table. It amazed me, too, to see how many courses Anwar's family prepared every night. Like my mother, I had always placed little importance on what I ate, preferring to save my money to buy a dress or a picture or something to make a corner of a room look beautiful. But Anwar's parents were of a different generation, paying the utmost attention to food and generously serving course after course. "You don't eat at all, Jehan," Sitt el-Barrein would tease me when I apologized and declared that I was full. But actually it was Anwar who ate least of all, having only a little soup and meat each evening. He was much more serious than the rest of his family, too, often leaving them joking and laughing around the table while he went to read a book.

Anwar was different from everyone in his family—and mine. He had a mission. And on our engagement day I glimpsed the tensions and dangers it would bring to our marriage. Defiantly Anwar had dressed in his military uniform, knowing full well that to do so after he had been cashiered from the Army by the British was against the law. The neighbor's son, the one who had wanted to marry me and who was himself an army officer, had seen Anwar come in wearing a uniform and in an act of jealousy had gone to the police to report it. The daughter of the doorman had come upstairs to warn me, but luckily the police had not come and taken Anwar away.

That first moment of danger, however, made up my father's mind about our future. "Anwar," he said, taking him aside, "I love you like a son and have great respect for you, but I cannot give you permission to marry my daughter unless you promise me you will never again involve yourself in politics. This is a perilous life and one I cannot allow for my daughter. So you must choose. It is up to you."

For Anwar, the dilemma posed by my father's request could not have been more difficult. If he gave his promise to my father, it would mean giving up all he had worked and sacrificed for. On the other hand, such a high-risk life would not allow him to guarantee security either for me or for his first family, about whom he felt strongly.

"I promise," he had said reluctantly to my father. Just as reluctantly, he had accepted Hassan Izzat's offer to join him as a partner in his construction business.

I was ecstatic. I looked forward to the future with all my heart. On May 29, 1949, I would become Jehan el-Sadat. I did not know that the eight months of my engagement would be one of the most violent and turbulent periods in Egypt's history.

The mood in Egypt was one of great frustration and anger. Our defeat in the Palestine War had humiliated us and strained our already weak economy. Prices were soaring on food, on clothing, on housing, while massive unemployment was driving per-capita income down. Everyone except the ruling elite was feeling the pinch: employees of the government, the university graduates who could not find work, middle-class members of the military. The rationing that we had all lived with during the war spread now to include such basic commodities as sugar, flour and the kerosene fuel which many urban Egyptian families depended on for cooking and bathing. We were issued identity cards listing the number of people in the family and coupon books to buy rationed goods. But there were few goods to buy anyway. Even *dammour*, the ordinary cotton cloth used by the masses to make their galabiyyas, was very scarce.

Yet the government showed little concern. Most of the members of Parliament were wealthy and repeatedly voted against raising the taxes of the rich. It did not seem at all inequitable to them that 65 percent of Egypt's wealth was held by only 5 percent of our population. They *were* the five percent. And it certainly did not strike them as unfair that a tiny elite of only 2 percent owned more than half of all our country's arable land. Why should it? Most of the high government officials were wealthy landowners themselves, getting richer and richer while the fellaheen who worked for them sank deeper into poverty. Increasingly the poor and unemployed held demonstrations to protest all these injustices. But the government's answer was to arrest the protesters, often treating them very harshly. Reports of this in the press, which was enjoying a relative degree of freedom during this time, advanced the new awareness of class differences and added to the existing tensions.

There was tension everywhere. Efforts to create more agricultural land out of the desert by building new Nile dams and canals could not keep pace with the population growth: from close to 16 million in 1930 to 22 million by 1948. Overcrowding in Cairo was becoming impossible, with as many as ten thousand people packed into a city block. Cairo's buses and trams were breaking down under the strain. Crime, previously rare in Egypt, began to rise. The thousands of fellaheen who had moved to the cities to work during the Second World War now were unemployed. Yet, in spite of an order by King Farouk forbidding the fellaheen to leave their villages, thousands more were arriving in Cairo every day.

As the frustration grew, the Muslim Brotherhood became more and more powerful. By the end of 1948, more than two hundred thousand had joined the organization in Egypt, following the teachings of the Supreme Guide Hassan el-Banna. The fedayeen continued to fight on in the Sinai for the fate of their Muslim sisters and brothers. And they did not stop there. While many Egyptians in the cities grumbled about the corruption in the government and the humiliating occupation by the British, the Muslim Brothers took their religious war to the streets.

There was violence directed at the government, the British, even the foreigners in Egypt with whom we had always lived peacefully. While our troops had fought unsuccessfully in Palestine, foreign and Jewish-owned businesses in Cairo—the fine store David Ades where I had shopped with my mother and sister for china and glassware, the department stores Cicurel, Benzion and Gatinigno's—had all been damaged by bombs. Any non-Egyptian establishment had become a target: the MGM movie theater, the downtown offices of French and British businesses. Though many Egyptian Jews had fled from Egypt to Europe during the German advance toward Alexandria during World War II, still there remained a large colony in Cairo. During the summer of '48, when I was in Suez with Anwar, a bomb set off in the Harat el-Yahud, the Jewish quarter, had killed over twenty inhabitants and injured many more.

Now Egyptians sympathetic to the government began to provide dramatic targets as well. In December of '48, three months after Anwar and I were engaged to be married, the Cairo police chief was assassinated by students who dropped a grenade onto the roof of his car. Suspecting the Muslim Brotherhood, Prime Minister Nukrashi ordered the religious organization dissolved and its property confiscated.

What the police found was terrifying—vast amounts of guns, automatic weapons and ammunition. Groups of the Brothers had banded together to form the Jihaz el-Sirri, a secret paramilitary arm of the Brotherhood one of whose aims, the police said, was to overthrow the government. Most revealing of the Brothers' growing strength was the discovery of their secret paramilitary training centers throughout Egypt, which had been attracting ever-growing numbers of volunteers.

Anwar was deeply disturbed by these revelations, as was I. The sight of all the confiscated weapons pictured in our newspapers and magazines had a chilling effect. Though Anwar greatly admired the Brothers' leader Hassan el-Banna, having met him many times, he did not believe that the formation of the Jihaz el-Sirri was the answer to Egypt's problems. Nor did he think the government would solve anything by outlawing the Brotherhood. "Someone has to do something to end this madness," he often told me during the increasing turbulence. "Violence will only breed more violence. Any action to correct

the corruption and bitterness in Egypt must come in an organized way, from the Army."

Like many of my generation, I too had ambivalent feelings
toward the Brotherhood. I admired the Brothers' tenacity, their
principles and their commitment to our religion. And, like
them, I wanted Farouk and the British out. But I did not want
the Brothers and their repressive ways in. The Brothers' political assassinations and bombing of innocent people made all of
us in Egypt deeply uncomfortable. We had been experiencing
a brief period of political freedom of expression. Our cultural
community was thriving too. La Scala was performing in the
Cairo Opera House, and the Comédie Française was drawing
large audiences in our theaters. Many Egyptians felt that the
Brothers were too rigid in their views, too quick to condemn
anything that was not purely from Islam. If the Brothers gained
power, our government might move not toward the democracy and freedom that many in Egypt hoped for, but toward a
totalitarian regime.

Still, I was apprehensive when the government dissolved the
Brotherhood. I knew in my heart that the problems tearing
apart Egypt were not being met by the government, that the
Muslim Brothers would not give up their fight. What I feared
actually happened: the Brothers just went underground and the
violence continued.

On December 28, three weeks after the official dissolution of
the Brotherhood, Prime Minister Nukrashi was assassinated en
route to his office by a Muslim Brother disguised as a police-
man. Two months after that murder, Farouk's secret police
ambushed and shot the founder of the Muslim Brethren, Hassan el-Banna himself. It was rumored that Farouk's forces left
him to bleed to death in a Cairo street. I was shocked. Everyone
was shocked. Hassan el-Banna had become one of the most
influential men in Egypt, famous all over the country for his
deep spirituality, his sharp intelligence and his ability to mes-
merize an audience for hours with his speeches. Now he had
become the victim of the series of assassinations his own followers had begun.

Prime Minister Nukrashi was dead. Hassan el-Banna was
dead. But nothing had been solved in the escalating violence
between the religious extremists in Egypt and the government.
One act of revenge would be followed by another. New, even

more militant organizations would splinter off from the Brotherhood. Thirty-three years later, such clashes between religious extremists and the government would culminate in the death of my husband.

I woke at dawn the morning of my wedding, relishing what would be the only serenity of the day. "Glory be to Him who made His creatures male and female: the plants of the earth, mankind themselves, and the living things they know nothing of," I read from Sura "Ya Sin" in the Quran, watching the sun turn the mist on the Nile pink. I could not remember feeling so happy. How lucky I was to be marrying a man whom I already knew I loved when so few of my friends would have that same possibility. Even so, my classmates had been amazed when I told them my news—and showed them Anwar's picture. "Is he rich?" they asked. I shook my head. "Is he from a well-known family?" Again I shook my head. "Then why are you marrying him?" they had said, this time shaking their own heads in puzzlement. "He is so old and ugly!"

I held up my hand to admire again the two gold rings Anwar had given me for our engagement, one in the shape of a butterfly, both bought with the help of my father. In Egypt the bridegroom traditionally gives his fiancée an engagement ring and another piece of jewelry as well, a brooch, earrings, something. But Anwar had not been able to afford anything.

"What will we do?" I had asked my father, knowing that Anwar would be too ashamed to admit he could not afford this tradition and knowing too that my mother and my aunts would be looking to make sure I was being well treated.

"Let him come with me and together we'll buy you a ring," my father had suggested.

Anwar had been reluctant. "Can we not wait until I can buy you something myself?" he said. He was then working for Dar el-Hilal, the publishing house which had published his diaries written in prison. Still, he had little money left from his salary after sending most of it to his first family. It was essential, however, for me to be able to display the proof of his love: my mother had not yet found out how poor Anwar really was.

"Please, Anwar, go with my father and choose something very inexpensive," I begged him. "You can pay him back later."

And together they had gone to the jeweler Bayokki and picked out both my rings.

In Egypt, the bride brings a dowry to the marriage, some furniture, a few housewares, linens for the bed. But the Quran instructs the groom to bring a marriage gift to the bride as well. "Give women their dowry as a free gift," reads "Women," the Fourth Sura of the Quran. The amount of the dowry is negotiated by a representative of the bride, usually her father, and the groom, and it is written into the marriage contract before the wedding. Two thirds of the sum is paid at once, the remaining third to be held in reserve for the wife in case of divorce. Though the amount of the dowry varies according to the status of the bride and the groom, the minimum the poorest man can pay is twenty-five piasters. The maximum can go as high as the worth of the groom, sometimes thousands of pounds.

But Anwar could not afford any of our traditional rites of marriage. For me, he contracted for a bargain £E150, and even that he never paid. "You got me for free," I would protest in mock fury throughout our marriage. "What a foolish girl I was."

My father never said a word about the money to my mother, not a word. Instead he made the arrangements for my marriage with generous enthusiasm, even accepting a good offer to sell his family's land so that there would be ample money for the wedding preparations and celebration. My father came with my mother and me to the dressmaker to pick out the materials for the trousseau I had designed using the skills I'd learned at school: linen sheets and tablecloths, hand-embroidered nightgowns of silk and crêpe de chine, dresses and coats. He came with us also to the silver market, where we picked out two kinds of flat silver: plated for everyday use, sterling for guests. We picked out plates, both ordinary and good china for entertaining, and everyday glasses plus a full set of crystal.

Together we searched the neighborhood in Roda for a suitable apartment. In the villages, a young man usually brings his bride to live in the house of his father. In Cairo and the other bigger cities, young couples usually live on their own—but not far from their parents. I was so happy when we found an apartment in a new building just a few minutes from my parents' home. It was lovely, with two bedrooms, salon, dining room, kitchen and three balconies. From one we could look down on both Niles that run beside our island. There was always something happening on the Nile—a parade of motorboats moving up and down the river, white-sailed feluccas making their way back and forth with the wind and the currents, big boats steaming to Upper Egypt with their cargoes of stoves and furniture and returning laden with sugarcane and huge ceramic jars of molasses.

From the balcony on the other side of the flat we could see the desert and the three Pyramids of Cheops, Chefron and Menkaru. Often at dawn we would watch the sun turn the Pyramids red, and at dusk watch the sun set behind them. Between Roda and the desert then there was nothing but green gardens and fields. The line where the green stopped and the desert began was as sharply defined as if cut by a knife. Both held their wonders, the green fields bearing life, the desert and the Pyramids whispering their mysteries.

Many Egyptians hated the desert, fearing its desolation. But I loved it for its sense of vastness and the endurance it demanded. Sometimes I could see camels coming from the Sudan being driven across the Sahara to Cairo, and always there were people riding horses. Anwar would spend much time on the balconies, not only to relish the view but because his years in prison made him feel restless, even claustrophobic, indoors. Even in the whitest heat of the summer, Anwar would remain outdoors.

I had been right about my father's feelings toward Anwar. During the six months of our engagement, when it was not proper for Anwar and me to be alone, Anwar had spent many evenings at our home, my family acting as chaperones. As my father and Anwar began to know each other, often playing backgammon after dinner, they grew to love and respect each other greatly. When Anwar later tried to pay my father back for the rings he had bought, for the furniture, even for my trousseau, my father refused to take a penny. "I am not selling my daughter," he told Anwar. "I am gaining a son."

Anwar would never forget my father's generosity. When later my father retired and Anwar was the Speaker of the Parliament, he would insist that my parents move from their apartment just across the street from us on the Pyramids Road into an extra bedroom in our home.

"He feels that he will be a burden," I told Anwar after talking to my father.

But Anwar was adamant. "Then go to his house and remove his furniture and bring it here," he instructed me. "I owe him many favors from the first years of our marriage which it will be an honor to repay. He will have nothing to fill his days now and I do not want him ever to be lonely. I want him to open his eyes in the morning to find his grandchildren on his bed, to take his breakfast, lunch and supper with all of us."

The tears streamed down my father's face when I arrived with the movers, for he wanted very much to be close to us and his grandchildren but felt constrained because of Anwar's position. One year later my father would pass away, but my mother continued to live with us for the next fourteen years, moving with us into our villa in Giza after Anwar became president. I would nurse her myself during her final illness until her death just before my first trip to Israel. During the last six months of her life she would not utter a word of Arabic, but would speak only in English.

"Jean," my mother now called up to me on my wedding day, "it is time to begin." I was hardly the reluctant bride and welcomed the arrival of my nanny, Shamia, who had come to the house to perform the first ceremony, the *halawa*. In Egypt and throughout the entire Middle East, women for centuries have removed the hair from their arms and legs in this process much like waxing in the West. Carefully Shamia mixed together the juice of lemons with sugar over a low fire, spread on the sweet paste until it hardened, then peeled it off. How clean and sweet-smelling I felt as I dressed and waited for Anwar to come and take me to the dressmaker.

"You look too young," the dressmaker said, looking at me critically in the long beautiful dress and veil I had designed for the wedding. "Why don't we put a little makeup on you?" I had never worn makeup before, and sat thrilled as she painted my face with lipstick and rouge.

Nervously I went on with Anwar to the photographer who was to take our wedding photo. I was not nervous about the photo, but about Anwar, who once again was proudly, but illegally, wearing his military uniform. Only the joking of the photographer kept my mind off the fact that Anwar could be arrested at any moment.

"You are a lucky man," the photographer said to Anwar as we posed for our official wedding photograph. "You are marrying one of the most beautiful brides I have ever seen." I'm sure he said that to every groom, but I, of course, loved it.

"Oh, you lucky man," I teased Anwar as he stood solemnly beside me. "Did you hear him say that I am one of the most beautiful brides he has ever seen?"

Anwar was silent, doing his best to ignore my teasing, just as he would years later when we stood in endless official reception lines. "Mother, tell me a joke," he would sometimes say to me to break the tedium as one person after another would come by to shake our hands. Other times I would make him furious with the quips I whispered to him under my breath. "Just keep quiet," he would mutter at me. "It appears to be possible for everyone but you."

But I could not remain quiet on my wedding day, the most important day, save for the birth of a child, in the life of every Egyptian girl. Already the guests, just the very near members of the family, were gathering at our house in Roda for the marriage ceremony before going on to the reception in the garden of Auntie Zouzou's new house near the Pyramids. Happily I took my seat with my family, making sure my veil was hanging straight, my white dress unrumpled, my bouquet of roses, jasmine and iris safely in my hands. It would not be the bride in this case who would sit face to face with her bridegroom in front of the sheikh who performs the Muslim marriage ceremony. Because of my young age my father would act as my deputy and join hands with Anwar.

At least I was in the same room with them. At many Egyptian weddings where the bride is under twenty-one, the youngest age at which a woman is entitled to sign a legal contract, the bride sits in a separate room with her female attendants while the men in her family seal her marriage contract. She does not even know the moment of her marriage until someone, usually a servant serving cold drinks to the men in the marriage room, bursts into the shrill, quavering cries of joy of the *zaghreet.* Upon hearing it, the bride and the women lend their own tongues to the *zaghreet,* their ululating cries of celebration confirming the passage of the young girl to young wife.

At my wedding, the loudest *zaghreet* would trill from my own throat. I could hardly contain myself when the sheikh first asked my father if I had accepted Anwar as my husband. Every woman in Islam has the right to refuse an unwelcome union, even if it has been arranged. Only in the movies, it seems, does a woman speak up at her own wedding to renounce her groom. But still, the question creates a tiny moment of tension. My father looked at me with a twinkle in his eye when the sheikh asked if I had agreed to the marriage.

"Yes," I nodded with such energy that I nearly dislodged my veil.

"She consents," my father assured the sheikh.

My father and Anwar sat opposite each other on chairs and clasped each other's right hand while pressing their thumbs together. Draping a white handkerchief over their joined hands as if they were the couple marrying, the sheikh then began the brief ceremony.

"I marry to thee my daughter, such a one Jehan, the virgin, for a dowry of one hundred fifty pounds" my father recited to Anwar in the traditional words of the ceremony. "I accept from thee her betrothal to myself and take her under my care, and bind myself to afford her my protection. Ye who are present bear witness of this," Anwar responded three times.

The sheikh then read from the Quran, blessing our marriage. And as the sound of the *zaghreet* finally spilled out into the street, we became husband and wife.

What a party followed at my aunt's house! When we arrived, three dancing horses were gracefully pirouetting around her garden to the sound of a single flute. Flowers were braided into their manes and tails, which were washed whiter than the sand. When all of the guests had arrived, Anwar and I joined the *zaffa,* the traditional marriage procession, led by our entertainers for the evening: singers; belly dancers; musicians playing the 'oud, flutes and drums; the comedian who would regale our guests with jokes and fables.

Once more the air was pierced by the sound of the *zaghreet* as everyone, friends, neighbors, even passersby joined in celebrating this traditional march toward a new life. For luck, we were pelted with coins thrown by our friends and family. And ours was just an average wedding! Often weddings now are held not at home but at Cairo's big hotels, the *zaffa* winding through the lobbies while all the guests throw coins and the *zaghreet* almost deafens. For those of means, weddings can cost $10,000, $20,000 or even more. But for those with little money, the festivities and the joys are the same.

All night until the dawn our marriage celebration went on, Anwar and I sitting on two wedding thrones bedecked with flowers. We ate the buffet, huge platters of meat, salads and desserts, and drank the special celebratory *sharbat,* a sweet red sherbet flavored with strawberry. All night the belly dancers danced, the musicians played, the singers sang of love, and the comedian told naughty jokes.

"We will keep you here until morning," he warned me with a wink.

"All right. You can," I called back, laughing, for I knew I would not be going home with Anwar that night. Our apartment was in a new building and was not yet finished. On our wedding night, Anwar would be returning to his single room in a boardinghouse and I would go back to my family home.

But soon it was no longer night at all. "God bless you," the guests said as they began to file out, shaking our hands and wishing us a successful marriage.

"May God bless you in return. You have honored us," I responded to each one.

Finally Anwar and I were alone. "Come," he said to me. And, taking me by the hand, he led me to the car and drove the short way to the Pyramids.

The silence in the desert was infinite after the noise of the party. Together we walked across the sand to the base of the Great Pyramid of Cheops, looking up, up, up almost five hundred feet to its pointed top. For almost five thousand years the Great Pyramid had stood there, built of stones so perfectly chiseled that it was said not even a razor blade could be passed between them. Many times I had seen the Pyramids and the Sphinx, which stood just a few hundred yards away. But standing there quietly by my new husband, watching the sun first touch its rays on the cool desert, I saw everything through different eyes.

Could we ever be as wise as the Sphinx, which gazed out across Egypt with the tolerance of eternity? The face of this great monument had been used for target practice by the soldiers of Napoleon—could we survive attack with the same dignity? Could our love endure as the Great Pyramid had endured? Never have I felt so full of hope, for my husband, for my country, for all the riches and wonders of Egypt that had gone before, for all the promise that lay ahead.

The sun was high in the sky when finally Anwar took me to my family home and then went on alone to his boardinghouse.

Often I have reflected on that dawn in the desert. Surely it was God's will to draw us there, to reimplant in both of us our destiny and the destiny of our country. From the beginning of our marriage, our love for each other was intertwined with our love for Egypt. From that moment in the desert, Egypt would be a part of every hardship that befell us, every challenge that seemed insurmountable, every sacrifice we made. We would give our love to each other and to our country freely. We were powerless not to.

God had set this path for us. Everything that would happen, good or bad, would come from Him. *Masir.* Destiny. We did not know what God had willed for us, only that it was preordained. From that first dawn at the Pyramids, my husband and I began the journey that had already been carefully charted. Often our routes would be very different. But always our destination would be the same: Love. Dignity. Honor. Peace.

Chapter 4

tahrir misr

The Liberating of Egypt

My wife was in such a bad temper today that she refused to prepare my lunch. Can you believe this? No lunch? If it happens again, I will divorce her."

"It is terrible at my house, everyone fighting all the time. My wife has arranged for our son to marry her niece, but he wants to marry a neighbor girl. All day my wife and son are yelling at each other. I hardly go home at all, for there is no peace there."

"I do not know what to do. I have seen a beautiful young girl at the home of my cousin and dream of marrying her. But already I am paying money to my first wife, and my second wife is again with child. If I divorce her now and then she bears a son, I will have to give up my new wife."

Day after day during our honeymoon in Zagazig, where Anwar was also working, I sat on the balcony outside our hotel room and listened to the conversation of the men below in the outdoor café. Like most Egyptian men, they spoke loudly and passionately as they drank their thick Turkish coffee or sweet mint tea, smoked their water pipes, and gossiped over the back-gammon boards. I was used to the volume of their sound, but not to the way they were speaking about their wives. I had never heard my parents quarrel, never heard my father's voice raised against my mother. They did not even discuss politics, which most Egyptians do constantly and with great intensity. Yet these men in the café were gathering every day to complain publicly about the private affairs of their households.

What an education I was getting in Zagazig, the small Delta city midway between Cairo and Alexandria where Hassan Izzat had sent Anwar to oversee the construction of drinking-water lines to fifty-two villages. With Anwar working sixteen-hour days, there was little for me to do during the month I spent there. For the first time I knew loneliness, the loneliness of a sixteen-year-old Egyptian girl without any of her family around her. Every two or three days I would talk to my sister and my parents on the telephone, but the connection to Cairo was very bad and only made me feel farther away. It was not possible for me to make friends in Zagazig. The girls my age were all in school, and married women were busy taking care of their homes and children. Besides, I was too shy to make friends with people I had not grown up with.

The hotel and our balcony became my entire world. It was unseemly of me to leave the hotel by myself, and save for the market there was no place for me to go anyway. It was not proper for me to visit the cinema by myself, and only men frequented the cafés. From early morning to dusk, when Anwar would return and take me for a walk or a ride in a horse-drawn carriage to a restaurant for our evening meal, I was alone. In the mornings I read. During the afternoons, the men in the café below became my theater while I, upstairs on my balcony, was their unseen and attentive audience.

"Today lunch was late and badly prepared. It is enough. I have divorced her."

"The young girl I met at my cousin's house has accepted me. I have decided not to divorce my wife yet, in case she has a son. I will tell her tonight that my new wife will be moving in with us."

"Jehan, these men are not as sophisticated or educated as those you know in the city," Anwar would tell me in the evenings after I described the dramas of the day. "They talk in a rough way, but many are very decent. Listen to hear the voices of those who are good to their wives and children." I took his advice and listened very carefully. But I heard only one, a man who declined to play backgammon for money one afternoon because he needed it for his family.

Inside I burned with indignation at the cavalier ways these men were treating their wives. It seemed very wrong to me that divorce seemed to be as simple for them as taking a drink of water. Too often these men talked about their marriages as if they were holiday resorts. "Does this place please me?" they seemed to be asking themselves. "If so, I will stay for a while. But as soon as I feel bored, I will try another place." My heart went out to their wives, whose security depended upon the whim of their husbands. How unfair it was. In the back of my mind I would always remember these overheard conversations in Zagazig.

"I am miserable, Jehan," Anwar said to me when we returned to Cairo. "I know now that I cannot be a businessman and work only for money. Such a pursuit denies all that I have based my life on. I am sorry."

Anwar may have thought he was upsetting me, but instead I was thrilled. I hated Anwar's work schedule which kept him away from home so many long hours. I was used to the schedule my family and many others in Egypt lived by, the work day finishing at 2 P.M. Since our return from Zagazig, Anwar's schedule had gotten even worse. Hassan was sending my husband to supervise another water project, this one two and a half hours away in the province of Minia in Upper Egypt. "Leave Jehan in Cairo," Hassan first said. Then he changed his mind. "Take Jehan with you," he said.

I resented the way Hassan was treating us like puppets, as if he alone could pull the strings that controlled our lives. We both saw now why he had been so helpful in making our marriage possible. With Anwar as his partner, his business profits were way up. Yet even with his new prosperity, he had refused to pay Anwar what he owed him, probably to blackmail him into going to Upper Egypt. How clever Hassan had been. He knew I would be totally compromised in my loyalty. I loved his wife, my cousin 'Aida, like a sister. To fight Hassan would mean cutting off our long-standing friendship, for a wife must stand by her husband. Because of these family ties, we were powerless to extract the money Hassan owed Anwar.

"I will not say anything against him," Anwar told me. " 'Aida is your cousin, but when you go visit her now, you must go alone." And, forfeiting his payment, Anwar quit just one month after our marriage.

From the moment of our marriage Anwar had simply handed me his salary, and I had taken care of all the finances. He had no head for figures, and didn't even carry a wallet when we went out. When we went to the movies or had a cold drink in a café, I would slip him the money just before it was time to pay. But not long after Anwar left his job I realized there would be no more movies, and no cold drinks, until Anwar could find another means of support.

We were destitute. For the next seven months I squeezed every piaster I could out of the budget I had set up to pay the £E12 rent on our apartment in Roda, the £E2 for the electrical and water bills, plus the payment of £E10 to Anwar's first family. There was no money for us to eat in restaurants, or even to buy fruit. For the first time in my life, I was hungry. To entertain ourselves, Anwar and I would go for long walks every night along the Nile. As a special treat we would share a round loaf of bread studded with sesame seeds and dusted with oregano which cost only one piaster.

While my friends were at school, I washed the sheets, swept the floors, washed and ironed my husband's suits and shirts by hand. There was much housework to do. The wind constantly brought in sand and dust from the desert, and as soon as I had swept the floor a new layer of dust would settle. What little shopping I could afford to do was a problem in itself. The elevator had not been completed in our building, and every time I came in with bundles I had to climb nine flights of stairs to our apartment.

I wanted to go back to school with my friends, but at that time married women were not allowed to attend school. Instead, I tried to study at home, but it was hard, worrying as much as I did about our finances. Anwar did not want me to take any money from my family, and I didn't.

"Are you well, my daughter?" my father would ask me every day, always coming to call on me after his work. "Do you need anything?"

"I have everything I need," I would reply, eying hungrily the presents of fruit, vegetables and meat he knew instinctively to bring me. We both knew that his worst fears for me were coming true, but never did we mention them aloud, out of respect for Anwar. If my marriage involved sacrifice and suffering, then so be it.

"You eat now. I will have breakfast later," I told Anwar every morning, setting in front of him his dish of fava beans and eggs. Sometimes I would make myself a glass of tea, and sit with him until he went off to the army headquarters, where he was trying to get reinstated, or to the offices of the newspaper where he was also applying for a job. Although I told him that I had no appetite so early in the morning and preferred to eat later on, I ate nothing at all until his return at dusk. We could not afford it.

I told no one, not my friends or my family, how desperate our situation was. Other women, I knew, shared their most intimate problems even with their hairdressers. But never would I do that. Our problems were ours and ours alone to bear and to solve. I pretended to everyone that all was well. And, indeed, much was.

"Does your husband open your mail?" my school friends asked me one afternoon when they came to call.

"No, never," I replied.

"Does he demand to know where you have been all day?" they asked.

I laughed, "No. All this I tell him anyway."

They looked at each other in concern. "Has he struck you yet when you displeased him?"

I was shocked. "Absolutely not," I said firmly.

The expression on their faces grew even more concerned. "Then how can you be sure he cares for you?" they wondered.

By January, however, we were out of money completely. The rent was due the next day. So were the bills we had run up at the grocer. We were both very anxious and unsettled. Though Anwar had applied for permission to rejoin the Army, he was very doubtful that he would be accepted. His military record as an Egyptian patriot was superlative, but his record in the eyes of the British was that of a subversive. What would we do? The question lay silent between us as we went out for our customary evening walk across the Abbas Bridge spanning the Nile between Giza and Roda.

At the open-air café at the foot of the bridge, a fortuneteller approached us. I dug into my pocket for one of my last piasters. If the Gypsy had good news to tell us, then Anwar's somber mood might lift. If he had bad news to tell us, what did it matter? Things could not really get worse.

Taking my hand in his, the fortuneteller studied it carefully, then looked me straight in the eye and said, "You are going to be First Lady of Egypt."

"First Lady of Egypt?" We did not have such a title. "What do you mean?" I asked the Gypsy, not being one to put great store in magic in the first place. Though many Egyptian women, including my sister and my aunts, believed in magic and often went to hear their fortunes read in coffee grounds or whispered from seashells, I was more practical. If these fortunetellers knew so much, why were they not leading the world? No one could know or predict the future except God.

"You are going to be Queen of Egypt," the fortuneteller now told me.

I roared with laughter. Queen of Egypt? All I wanted was the rent money. But the fortuneteller was not through.

"You will have four children," he said, "but only one son. And you will travel the whole world over."

I was hardly listening. The fortune had already worked magic enough for me. For the first time in days, Anwar was smiling.

"You have read the hand of my wife," he told the fortuneteller gently, declining to have his own palm read. "You have given us both our destiny."

The next morning the phone rang. It was Anwar's old friend Yussef Rashad, now the King's royal physician. Our good fortune seemed unbelievable. Yussef had arranged for Anwar to be readmitted into the Army.

Was it magic? Or the will of God? Like a precut puzzle, the tiniest pieces of our lives were leading both of us toward the completion of the picture. Never could Anwar have been readmitted to the Army had it not been for a simple act of charity he had performed for Yussef Rashad in the desert eight years before. Anwar had met the young doctor while stationed at an army encampment between Alexandria and the border of Libya. Rashad had been worried about his small son, who had pneumonia, and wanted to stay in touch with his home by phone. Anwar, who was the communications officer and had all the telephones in his tent, exchanged lodgings with the doctor so that Rashad could have use of the phones during the nights. Rashad had never forgotten that act of kindness.

Another piece of the puzzle had followed soon. After the war, King Farouk had been speeding along the desert road from Ras el-Tin in one of his many sports cars and had smashed into a British truck. The King had been rushed to the nearest hospital, where Yussef Rashad happened to be on duty. Impressed by the medical attention he received from Yussef, King Farouk appointed him to his personal staff and embraced him as a confidant. Another piece had fallen into place. Rashad was now in a position of influence with the throne. And he had a debt of gratitude to pay to Anwar.

"Go see el-Farik Muhammad Haidar Pasha," Rashad told Anwar on January 10, 1950. "He is expecting you."

Anwar went to see the Commander in Chief of the Armed Forces. "This boy is to be reinstated in the Army from today," Haidar Pasha barked to his secretary. And on January 15, 1950, Anwar was once again a captain in the Army.

Anwar's salary at first was low, just £E34 a month, and we would continue to suffer. But at least Anwar and I had our own life together without the interference of outsiders like Hassan. And there were other advantages as well. The Egyptian Army provided its officers with a car, a driver, even an aide. The biggest employer in Egypt, the Army also paid higher salaries to graduates of the military academy than other graduates could hope to make.

Not only was Egypt's army the largest of any in the Arab countries, but it was the most respected by far. To be accepted as an officer in the military had always been the dream of many Egyptian youths, for such a position afforded a status in our country that they could not achieve any other way. So honored were our military officers that their very presence in uniform brought special attention from people in the street, in cafés, in shops. Everyone respected our officers.

Anwar could not believe his good luck. To be an officer was in his blood. His picture of himself was as a defender of Egypt, dressed in his country's uniform, pursuing his dreams for Egypt's independence. No other career could have satisfied him. I too was ecstatic. Now our future was secure.

"*Mabruk*. Congratulations," phoned one of his old friends, a classmate from the military academy, Abdel Hakim Amer.

Gamal Abdel Nasser phoned, too. "*Mabruk, Anwar.*"

Our good fortune rose again when Anwar, after brief tours of duty in Isma'iliyya and Qantara along the Suez Canal, was posted to al-'Arish and Rafah in the Sinai. The Sinai was considered a hardship post, and Anwar's pay was doubled. What a relief. We would have no rent bills, no electricity charges, not even food bills, for all these were paid by the Army. We could even begin to save a little money. To celebrate our new solvency, we bought a Vauxhall car, borrowing half the price.

When Anwar went to the Sinai I moved in with my parents, for even as a married woman it was not proper for me to stay alone in our apartment. I was intent on completing my secondary schooling, and since I was not allowed to return to school, I had private tutors at home. I worked hard to make up the time I had lost. I had completed three of the four years of school when I married. The final examinations, however, would cover not only the last year of studies, but all four years. To my curriculum of home management I also added geometry, science and algebra so that I would qualify for university. All day I bent over my books. At night I was lonely for Anwar, reading and rereading his letters of encouragement for my studies. One month before my exams began, I joined Anwar in Rafah for the first time in the small house he had found for us.

It was lovely, set out by itself in the desert. Anwar was not sociable and had asked for permission to live outside the military compound where the rest of the officers were staying. At seventeen, I was still shy, and welcomed the privacy. Anwar and I kept our own company, taking long walks in the desert in the evenings, bringing a picnic with us to the beach on Fridays, talking always about history and politics. Often Anwar went into the desert to pray, feeling closer to God in the midst of such natural serenity.

We grew ever closer to each other, our separate strengths becoming the strengths of the other. Anwar tended to brood, to lose himself in contemplation. I was more lighthearted and open. Often I could tease him out of a black mood. Other times I could not. I knew by watching his face. The clouds of his despair could lift and blow away in a second when I teased him, turning his dark face into one filled with light and laughter.

But sometimes I could not penetrate his darkness no matter how hard I tried. "Jehan, I must think," he would say to me gently. And immediately I would withdraw, respecting his solitude.

One week a month, and for the winter, which was very cold in the desert, I returned to my parents' house in Cairo. After the austere life we were leading in the northern Sinai, Cairo seemed filled with luxuries. When Anwar was on leave we would go constantly to the many outdoor cinemas downtown, seeing one movie from three to six in the afternoon, then going right into another from six to nine. There were no restaurants in our military outpost, so I couldn't get enough of eating out during my times at home. I had failed miserably as a cook myself in Rafah, producing one inedible meal after another until Anwar brought in a cook so that we wouldn't starve. Luckily Anwar did not care that much about food, so he was never angry at my poor attempts in the kitchen.

When I was in the Sinai with Anwar, I was shocked by what I saw. The war had left its mark on everything and everyone. Wherever I went I saw Palestinians who had been forced from their homeland by the creation of Israel and the fighting that had ensued in 1948. Dressed in black, mothers with their children squatted silently alongside the roads, in the towns, around the marketplaces in Rafah, el-'Arish and Gaza. More than one million Arabs had suddenly become homeless, depending on the United Nations Relief Fund for subsistence. Their vacant stares and the suffering that was etched into their faces as they waited with their straw baskets for the food delivery broke my heart.

What a study in contrasts Gaza was at that time. On the Mediterranean 160 miles east of the Suez Canal, it had always been a beautiful summer resort for those landlocked by the heat of the desert to the south. Wealthy families from the Arab countries had come each year to cool off in the deep blue waters, to eat the fresh fish which were plentiful and enjoy the ripe vegetables, fruits and green almonds which grew easily so close to the sea. No more. Every week Anwar and I would drive in an army jeep to the market in Gaza, and though the road to Gaza was still beautiful, it had become a scene of despair.

Refugee camps lined the roads, the tents so close they seemed like a canvas city. I worried about the women's cooking fires. If one tent caught fire, they would all go up. A makeshift school had been set up outdoors, but most of the children wandered restlessly up and down the tent rows with nothing to do. Everywhere there were groups of men squatting together, passing the time playing *siga,* a game played with pebbles in a pattern etched in the sand. Through this scene the black-robed women walked, carrying firewood and water jugs on their heads.

"Is your family faring well?" I asked our cook, a Palestinian woman from one of the refugee camps.

She dropped her eyes. "It is not like before," she said quietly.

"Tell me," I urged her, admiring her high forehead and the wide-set eyes that distinguished so many Palestinians.

"From the camp we can see the tops of the lemon and orange trees on our old farm," she said slowly, as if reluctant to remember. "On our land it was always green and warm, but here in the desert it is very cold. At night in our tent now we all sleep very close to each other for warmth."

I shuddered, thinking of the rain that beat so hard on the aluminum roof of our house some nights that I could barely sleep, of the winter nights in the desert so cold I could not stand them. I thought, too, of the scorpions that lived in the desert. One had stung my sister when she came to visit Anwar and me, and after we had taken her to the military hospital for treatment we had slept for days with the legs of our beds set in buckets of water. The Palestinians had no beds at all, few blankets, and no hospitals to treat them if they fell sick.

"Tell me about your husband," I pressed. "What work does he do?"

The woman's eyes dropped even lower. "At home he was a farmer. Here in the desert there is nothing for him. All day he plays *siga* in the sand with the other men."

"So only you are working?" I said in astonishment.

"Yes," she whispered.

That night I sent her home with extra blankets from our house and a dozen eggs I had bought from the Bedouin women who came in every day from the desert to sell their produce at the military camps.

How silly my studies in needlework and cooking suddenly seemed. I could not look away from the suffering of these people whose religion I shared, whose language I shared, whose history I shared. I looked at the women exhausted by their struggles for their families and saw myself. I looked at the children so thin and listless and saw the children I knew I would have. I looked at these people from a region they could no longer call home and knew that, for all its problems, I could never live without Egypt. All around me, it seemed, I could see the fabric of my world unraveling.

The Palestinian refugees had not been the only victims of the war. Egyptians too had suffered. While Anwar had spent the Palestine War in frustration in Cell 54, the frustration had been even greater for his fellow officers on the front. The weapons provided by the government had been defective, supply lines nonexistent, military strategy vague. "What was happening at Falluja was only what was happening in Egypt," Anwar's colleague Gamal Abdel Nasser would write later about the beleaguered town he had defended. "She too had been besieged by difficulties, as well as ravaged by an enemy. She too had been cheated and pushed into a fight for which she was not prepared. Greed, intrigue and passion had used her as a plaything, too, and had placed her under fire, without arms."

Resentment toward Farouk was growing rapidly among the military, among the fellaheen, among everybody. The King seemed not to care at all that we had lost a war, spending more time at parties in his palaces, villas and royal rest houses than he did in the Parliament. And it was obvious that Egypt's problems were not causing him to lose his appetite. Our King was growing grotesquely fat, and all of us heard stories of his gluttony. For breakfast he ate thirty eggs. At dinner he had six or seven plates of meat and vegetables. Each day he drank thirty bottles of lemonade or juice. He grew so heavy that he walked with difficulty, and special chairs had to be built for him to sit on in his palaces.

These excesses and lack of self-discipline shamed all of us in Egypt, but the behavior of the King in public we found even more embarrassing. He flew barbers from Europe to cut his hair, and had a manicurist for each hand when he went to the beach. The Quran says that Muslims must not gamble, and yet our Muslim King went to casinos constantly. In Monte Carlo, Farouk played games of chance with thousand-dollar chips, losing up to $50,000 in a single evening. In Alexandria, at the casinos catering to foreigners, the King spent less but played more frequently. In wintertime, when Farouk stayed in Cairo, the royal cars were seen parked every night in front of night-clubs by the Pyramids, where the King caroused openly with dancing girls.

In this time of growing nationalism, Farouk was also being condemned as a foreigner. It was well known and much discussed that he preferred speaking in French or English to speaking in Arabic. He socialized with foreigners at the Gezira Sporting Club, and his best friend was an Italian handyman. Since he was not of Egyptian descent, Farouk tried hard to prove himself descended from the Prophet Muhammad, but he could not. When he divorced the popular Queen Farida because she had not given birth to a son, resentment against him rose higher still. The proud legacy of his ancestor Muhammad Ali, the first ruler of Egypt to institute a state system of education and send educational missions abroad, the first to revolutionize our agriculture and begin national industries, the first to build a very strong army, was now working against him. The royal line had grown weak, Egyptians were saying. By the time it had come down to Farouk it was no longer good.

There were forces agitating for change on the radical right and, less effectively, on the radical left. The King was fighting the Wafd, our nationalist political party led by Mustafa el-Nahhas Pasha, for control. The Wafd was fighting him, while handing out patronage jobs. And anti-British sentiment was rising steadily. Fearing Egyptians' growing animosity, the British command by 1950 had moved its headquarters from Cairo to Suez. The British barracks which had filled so large an area of the downtown were gone. Often so were the soldiers' uniforms. In an effort to ensure their safety, British troops in Cairo were advised to wear civilian instead of military clothing.

I could not believe that Anwar was not somehow involved in the increasing unrest. And I was right. While I was studying for my exams in Cairo and commuting back and forth to Rafah early in 1951, Anwar had been secretly reinstated by Gamal Abdel Nasser into the Free Officers' Organization, joining a group of officers who were plotting the overthrow of the government. Anwar told me nothing about it, remembering the pledge he had made to my father not to return to politics.

In November of 1951, friction between the British and the government came to a head. Responding to mounting nationalist pressure, Prime Minister el-Nahhas canceled the Anglo–Egyptian Treaty of 1936, the treaty which had allowed Anwar and his fellow revolutionaries to become army officers in the first place. To many, the cancellation of the treaty meant that the British no longer had the right to have their military camps in Egypt. Nearly 100,000 Egyptians employed by the British command refused to go to work. Egyptian railroad engineers stopped driving trains with British soldiers or supplies aboard. Egyptian customs officials found they had no time to clear the goods the British ordered from abroad. Even merchants and tradesmen canceled their British accounts. On the streets of Cairo I began to see Egyptians jostling British soldiers who crossed their path.

Attacks against the British garrisons flared in the Canal Zone, in Suez, Isma'iliyya and Port Sa'id. The Egyptian Army could not officially participate, but Anwar and some other officers supplied arms and training to fedayeen, who in turn harassed the British. After three months of fighting, the British cut off all communication between the Suez and the rest of the country and effectively cordoned off the entire Canal Zone.

But then the British went too far. In January of '52 they retaliated to the attacks of the fedayeen by attempting to occupy Isma'iliyya. British troops armed with machine guns ordered the Egyptian police there to surrender their arms and leave the city. Though they were armed with only a few, primitive rifles, the Egyptians were ordered by the government to stand their ground. The British showed them no mercy, massacring fifty of them and wounding many others. The next morning, January 26, Cairo went up in flames.

What a horrible, horrible sight it was. From my bedroom in my parents' house in Roda I heard one explosion, then another, then another. I rushed with my parents to our roof to see clouds of black smoke and flames shooting up all over the city. Even the Nile seemed on fire with the reflection. It was terrifying watching our city burn—and not knowing why. I rushed back and forth on the roof as still there were more explosions and more flames until it looked as if the whole country, not just Cairo, must be on fire. What was happening? Were we under attack from a foreign country, perhaps again from Israel? Or was this the beginning of a coup?

From the radio we learned that what had started as a student demonstration against the government and the King was escalating into a full-scale riot. We watched from our roof all day while the explosions and the fires continued unchecked into the late afternoon. Why didn't the government contain the chaos? The police couldn't, for they were on strike that day to protest the murder of their colleagues in Isma'iliyya, enraged that the government had delivered them totally unprotected to their British enemies. But the government seemed to be doing nothing. Later, we would find out that Farouk had been too busy honoring his newborn son and heir, Fuad, at a sit-down luncheon for six hundred to concern himself with reports of a riot.

On what would become known as Black Saturday, mobs of Egyptians swept through downtown Cairo, looting stores and burning buildings. Any business associated with the foreign presence was set aflame. The Rivoli and Metro cinemas where Anwar and I had often gone, the Jewish-owned department stores where I had shopped for my trousseau, Ford's automobile showroom, Barclay's bank: all these were burned.

Liquor stores and the great downtown bars and restaurants —the Cecil, the St. James, the Hermitage and the Turf Club— were all firebombed as well, the flames changing color and growing even higher when the liquor bottles sitting on the shelves of these establishments exploded. The few foreigners unlucky enough to be caught in the Turf Club were killed. Some people claimed to have seen youths on motorbikes speeding through town to light one bonfire after another. Others swore they saw men driving jeeps full of torches and barrels of gasoline.

Last to burn was the world-famous Shepheard's Hotel, which had once been the palace of a Turkish bey. Anwar and I had never been there, for it was too fancy and expensive for us. But the hotel's terrace had been a favorite haunt of British officers, and its Louis XIV ballroom the site of many costume balls where foreign tourists dressed up as Egyptians. Some said that on Black Saturday, when the firemen came to save Shepheard's from the flames, the mob slashed their hoses with knives.

By nightfall, more than forty people had been killed and hundreds injured. The crowds had come within a thousand yards of 'Abdin Palace. At last the government ordered a curfew, sending out troops to stop the burning and destruction in the streets. Anwar called from Rafah to make sure we were all right. "I beg you, Jehan, be careful," he said. "Do not go out until the streets are completely calm. No one knows yet what the riots mean."

By the next morning we knew the riots had not been a prelude to a coup, because there had been no attempt to take over the government. The burning of Cairo, however, had been too organized to be spontaneous. Who had incited the crowd? No one ever knew for sure. Some suspected the Communists, the term we use in Egypt to include Marxists, Russian sympathizers and members of anti-Western groups. Others suspected the Muslim Brothers. Some even suspected the King himself. But as the last dark clouds of smoke lingered over Cairo, there was an eerie certainty that the end of Farouk's time was near. No longer did Egyptians ask one another whether the government would be overthrown. The only question now was when.

The day of the Great Cairo Fire seared itself in Egypt's memory and changed the course of history. The dissatisfaction with the government had burst into the open and shaken the throne. Not suspecting that Anwar was a member of the antiroyalist conspiracy, Yussef Rashad confided to him that the riots had so frightened Farouk that the King was preparing to flee the country. The Free Officers then moved up their target date for the revolution originally set for 1955 to November of '53, just one year away.

Yussef Rashad was one of the most important people in Anwar's life at the time, though I didn't know it. Farouk had recently named Yussef head of his Royal Intelligence Service, creating a direct pipeline to the palace for Anwar. Determined not to let the Free Officers' plot fail, Anwar was using Yussef to send false information to the King. He had to. After the Cairo fire, rumors of impending revolution were everywhere. Some said the Muslim Brothers would lead the coup. Others claimed that the Army would take over. Farouk was trying to investigate all of these rumors, which put Anwar and his fellow officers in jeopardy. Knowing he and his colleagues could be arrested for conspiracy at any time, Anwar in May and June of '52 began to travel to Alexandria, where Yussef was summering with the King. The King had nothing to worry about from the army officers, Anwar kept telling Yussef. The rumors were without truth.

I was in Alexandria with Anwar in early July when one of his meetings with Yussef took place. We'd had a lovely day on the beach, so I was quite content to stay in the car when Anwar told me he had to have a word with Yussef at the Automobile Club, one of the most elegant social clubs in Alexandria. When Yussef heard I was outside in the car, he insisted that Anwar and I join him for dinner. I was delighted. After our day in the fresh air, I was ravenous, and had been dreaming of a meal of the huge grilled shrimp much like lobster tails that come from the Mediterranean.

I never even got to taste them. Shortly after we sat down, another party arrived at the table next to us. Immediately I felt the strength of someone's eyes on me. Looking up, I gazed directly into the face of King Farouk.

I was panic-stricken. Farouk's reputation was known from one end of Egypt to the other. Whenever he saw a woman he wanted, he simply sent for her—and had her. Recently all Egypt had been talking about a man who had been killed after the King had taken his wife. It was not clear whether the King had shot the husband or whether the husband had shot himself. At this moment in the Automobile Club, the details did not matter. Here I was face to face with the immoral King. I knew I was not bad-looking. And I was eighteen, Farouk's favorite age.

"Dr. Rashad, His Majesty asks that you join him," one of Farouk's aides said to Yussef, coming over to our table.

I froze. He must be asking who I am, I thought. I wanted to look at Anwar, to plead with him to leave, but I did not dare raise my eyes. Every time I tried, the King's gaze was on me. "I must go to the bathroom," I managed to whisper to Anwar as I left the table. When I came back I sat in Yussef's chair so that my back, not my face, would be towards Farouk.

"The King wanted to know whom I was sitting with," Yussef said nonchalantly, rejoining us. "I told him you are my friends."

I thought I was going to faint, staring down at the shrimp for which I no longer had any appetite.

"Dr. Rashad, the King requires to speak to you." Again Rashad was summoned to the King's table. And then again.

With each summons, Anwar was getting more and more agitated. I thought he was concerned for me, but I realized later he was worried that the King was going to identify him with the rumored plots among the army officers. Anwar knew there had been reports not only about the Free Officers, but about him in particular. The last thing he wanted at this moment was to capture the attention of the King. The last thing I wanted at any time was to capture the attention of the King. For our separate reasons we were both close to panic.

"Hurry and eat, Jehan," he snapped at me. "We must be going."

But I couldn't eat. I couldn't even move, my heart was beating so fast. The King is going to send for me tomorrow, I thought to myself. What am I going to do? Of course I will not go. But then he will kill me or kill Anwar. My imagination ran wild, for although I was a married woman, I was still a child. I will make myself ugly, I decided. I will burn a cork and blacken my face. No, that's ridiculous, I chided myself. Instead I will barricade the door and not answer the bell no matter who comes.

Immediately after dinner Anwar and I left to drive back to Cairo. Anwar said very little, preoccupied with his fears. I didn't talk much, either, preoccupied with my own. I didn't share them with him, not wishing to upset him when he seemed quite upset enough already. At home in our apartment I stayed awake all night waiting for the dreaded day. I will kill myself, I decided, absolutely certain that someone from the palace was going to come to our front door. In the morning, when Anwar went off to report to Abdel Nasser, I bolted the door. I will use the peephole to see who is calling, I told myself. Only if it is my sister will I open it. But no one came.

That night Anwar returned to Rafah, and with relief I went to my parents' house.

Farouk certainly had enough on his mind already. Once again his government was heading for collapse. In the six months since Black Saturday, he had dismissed one Cabinet and two more had resigned. Now, on July 20, the King's Cabinet resigned again only three weeks after its formation. It was rumored that the Cabinet Farouk formed to replace it would include his brother-in-law "Colonel" Isma'il Shirin, who wore the uniform of an officer but had never even graduated from the military academy. The Army felt insulted by the idea of Shirin's appointment. Never would they accept it.

"Jehan, I'm coming home on leave," Anwar phoned me two days later from Rafah, on July 22. On leave? He had just been on leave. "My mother is ill," he explained. His mother ill? I had just visited Sitt el-Barrein that day in her home and found her in good health. What was this mystery?

I went to meet him at the train station. "Let us go for a drive along the Pyramids Road," he suggested as soon as he arrived.

"Jehan, do you remember the promise I made to your father not to involve myself in politics?" Anwar asked me as we drove through the desert.

"Of course," I said, looking curiously at my husband, who was smoking cigarette after cigarette.

"Well, I'm not actually working in politics, but sometimes I sit and talk to my friends about politics and then I feel guilty," he said, then added quickly, "You understand I am not working in politics, just sharing my ideas with my friends."

I was not surprised at all. In fact, I was relieved. "If you were not sharing your political ideas with your friends, then you wouldn't be the Sadat I married," I answered, though I felt sure Anwar was not telling me the whole truth. "You were a devoted patriot. How could you just stop?"

"But I made a promise to your father which I am not exactly keeping," Anwar said, his eyes fixed on the road.

I reached to touch his arm. "Anwar, my father asked you to make that promise because of me, and you gave it to him because of me. Both sides of that promise were about me. But no one asked me how I felt."

"How, then, do you feel?" Anwar asked quietly.

I did not hesitate in my reply, knowing the importance of my answer. A promise made between relatives, which Anwar and my father now were, was not easily broken. "Most wives would not want their husbands to live in danger, to jeopardize their own security by risking their husbands going to prison," I said. "But you are not an ordinary husband. Nor do I want you to be. The Anwar who made that promise to my father was not the Anwar whom I married, not the Anwar who is here now talking to me. What my father did was his duty toward his daughter. But now I am your wife. Do not even think of that promise."

Immediately Anwar relaxed. "Let us go to the cinema with your parents tonight," he suggested. It was amazing how just a few words seemed to have released such a great burden from him. But still I did not know why he was in Cairo.

"Jehan, would you like an ice cream?"

"Jehan, would you like some chocolates?"

"Come, Jehan. Have another ice cream."

"Oh, Anwar. I have had enough. I am going to blow up."

"No. No. I want you to have whatever you want without even thinking about it."

He showed me more affection than usual during the film, always keeping his arm around me. I could not imagine what was making him so loving, though of course I did not discourage him. Even when the lights on the projector went out twice during the film, causing quite a delay, he did not get angry or impatient. What I didn't know was that Anwar was in fact saying goodbye to me.

In Rafah he had gotten a message from Nasser under his code name, Abu Menkar, saying that the Revolution would take place sometime between the twenty-second of July and the fifteenth of August and that he should come immediately to Cairo. Once more the time for the coup had been moved up, this time because of the rumor that the King's new Cabinet would include not only Isma'il Shirin but also Hussein Sirry Amer, a man who personally knew seven of the Free Officers and was threatening to reveal their plans to the King. "We will have to eat Amer for lunch before he eats us for dinner," Nasser had said to Anwar, using a common Arabic expression.

Suddenly the Free Officers were racing a very dangerous time clock. If they were exposed, the Revolution would fail before it began and its supporters put to death. If they went ahead with the Revolution and the coup failed, then again they would be facing certain death. While I was happily accepting Anwar's presents of chocolates and ice cream, he was well aware that this could be the last time we would ever be together. Knowing the very real dangers that lay ahead, Anwar wanted me to have a special last evening with him to fill my memories.

"Where is your husband?" the porter said to me when we got back to my parents' house around midnight.

"He is parking the car in the garage," I said.

The porter handed me a note. "A man has been here twice looking for him and finally left him this card."

On our way up the steps to collect our things to go to our own apartment, I gave the message to Anwar. Immediately the blood drained from his face.

"I must leave at once," he said, rushing past me into the house.

I ran after him into our bedroom, where he was pulling off his summer shirt and trousers and hurrying into his military uniform.

"Where are you going so late at night?" I asked him.

"One of my friends is very ill and I must go to him."

"In your military uniform?"

He paused for a moment. "If I have to take him to the hospital or get medicine for him at this late hour, my uniform will make everything easier," he blurted out. Giving me a kiss on the cheek, he started to rush down the stairs.

"Anwar, if you go to prison I will not visit you," I called out.

He froze halfway down the stairs. "What did you say, Jehan?" he said with intensity, looking up at me with his dark eyes blazing.

I laughed, not knowing what I had said. But there was something about him that cut my laughter short. I understood him very well. There were times for me to laugh and joke with him, and there were times for me to say nothing at all. This was one of those times. I could feel it from his eyes as they bored into me on the stairs, hear it in his measured and deep voice.

"God bless you, Anwar," I said quietly to him. And he was gone.

I waited all night for Anwar to return, or at least to call. But there was no word from him.

"Absence has its own excuse," my father kept telling me as he too waited up for word from Anwar.

It was 6:45 in the morning when the phone finally rang. My relief at hearing Anwar's voice turned quickly into anger at him for so upsetting me. "Where are you? Where did you spend the night?" I sputtered at him.

Turn on the radio, Jehan, and you will know everything," he said. Again, there was that something in his voice which was bigger than my suspicions, even my anxiety.

"Are you all right?" I asked him.

"Perfectly," he replied.

"Then God be with you and grant you success in whatever you are doing," I said.

Immediately I turned on the radio, but heard only the normal broadcasting of the Quran being read by a sheikh. What was going on? Then suddenly, at 7:30 A.M., I—and all Egypt—heard Anwar's voice reading a declaration from the Free Officers:

"Egypt has gone through a difficult period in its recent history, which was plagued by bribery, graft and corruption. The corrupt elements were responsible for our defeat in the Palestine War. That is why we have carried out a purge. The Army is now in the hands of men in whose ability, integrity and patriotism you can have complete confidence."

He said nothing about a coup nor a word about King Farouk. At the beginning of the Revolution, there was no mention of deposing the King. There was no mention of changes in the country. When I went down the street to visit my childhood friend Ola, I had no idea that I would not hear Anwar's voice again for three days.

Roda was quiet the morning of July 23, with no signs of anything different. But the news from Ola's cousin, who had planned to join us, was alarming. She could not come, she phoned, because the streets downtown were filled with army tanks and soldiers, and all the roads had been blocked. Tanks? Soldiers in the streets? I had never seen that and became increasingly frightened. Where was Anwar? Had the King arrested him? Or had the military deposed the King?

I hurried back to my parents' home, to find my father home early from his office. He and his colleagues in the government had no more idea of what was going on than anyone else, he told me, just that there had been reforms in the Army.

"Then Farouk is still in power?" I asked him anxiously.

"I don't know, Jehan. Probably, but who knows?" he replied.

My father was no different from many other Egyptians. Few were prepared emotionally for revolution. For more than fourteen hundred years we had been ruled by foreigners, whether they called themselves kings or caliphs or khedives or sultans or emperors. Egypt had been invaded by the Hyksos, the Persians, the Greeks and the Romans, invaded in the seventh century by the Arabs whose legacy was our religion of Islam, invaded again from the twelfth to the sixteenth centuries by the armies of the Fatimids, the Ayyubids and the Ottomans. Napoleon had mounted his expedition to Egypt in 1798. Since 1882, we had been occupied by the British. It was little wonder that the concept of revolution and even of self-rule was very new and frightening to us. At the beginning, it was very difficult for Egyptians to realize we were having a revolution at all.

It was just as difficult for the eleven revolutionary leaders, I found out later. After they had quickly secured the airports, the radio station, the major roads and bridges and the center of Cairo with infantry units and tanks, it would take the revolutionaries three more days to form a government and to decide how best to handle the King in Alexandria. Some wanted to kill him. Others wanted to exile him immediately. Others wanted to keep him in Egypt but force him to appoint yet another new Cabinet. Still others, including Anwar, wanted a negotiated and bloodless settlement with the King which would lead to his voluntary abdication. "Once blood started to flow, it might never have stopped," Anwar would tell me later.

But, for those three days, we were told very little. In Roda we saw none of the tanks, weapons and soldiers that we had heard were stationed downtown. Everywhere I went people were clustered around the radios in shops, in cafés or at home, waiting for more news. People spent hours talking to one another on the telephone, trying to find out the latest rumors. The streets, always bustling with cars, were oddly empty. Still, the very air seemed charged with tension in the summer heat. No one knew anything, including me. As each day passed I grew more and more hopeful that the Army had rid the country of Farouk. But I also grew more and more afraid that I would never see my husband again. The King's forces or the British could capture my husband and kill him at any time.

It was a fear that I would have many times in my life— Anwar is in danger . . . he will be killed . . . he will never come home. But even during the Revolution I did not show my true feelings. My fears were my burden and mine alone. At eighteen, I was learning to keep everything inside me. I did not want the people around me to feel my suffering, nor did I want to disturb them. "All I know is that Anwar phoned me the morning he went on the radio and told me to listen," I told the people who asked me repeatedly for information. "I know no more than you do."

Rumors were flying, many of them turning out to be true. In order to keep King Farouk from fleeing from one palace to another, troops loyal to the Revolution had surrounded the Ras el-Tin Palace in Alexandria at seven in the morning of July 25, the third day of the Revolution. Shots had been exchanged between the Royal Guard and the revolutionary forces, but the King had ordered his men to cease fire and to close the palace gates. Frightened that he might be killed by his own guard, Farouk had called on the American ambassador for protection. Knowing how unpopular the King had become and anxious not to antagonize the revolutionary forces, the ambassador had sent him only his private secretary.

I did not know that Anwar, along with Gamal Salem and Muhammad Naguib, two other revolutionaries, was also in Alexandria by the morning of July 26. They had gone to deliver an ultimatum to the King: If Farouk did not leave the country by six that night, the Free Officers would not be responsible for the consequences. Farouk took only five minutes to accept. So frightened was he for his life that when he went to sign the abdication papers, transferring his throne to his infant son Crown Prince Ahmed Fuad, his hands shook so that he misspelled his name and had to sign twice. To many, the misspelling took on a nationalistic meaning: Farouk could not even spell his own name in Arabic, proof positive that he was a foreigner through and through.

Gamal Salem and Muhammad Naguib then went to ready the royal yacht, the *Mahroussa,* for the King's departure into exile, while Anwar ordered the Air Force and the Coast Guard to salute the King as he left Egypt's territorial waters. This was a sign of respect, but it was also a form of insurance, as some among the Coast Guard had threated to fire on the royal yacht. Anwar and the revolutionists wanted no blood shed whatsoever, and the plan worked. Promptly at 6 P.M. the *Mahroussa* set sail, taking King Farouk, his new Queen, Nariman, and their little baby Prince into exile. While Anwar and Gamal Salem oversaw the departure from the deck of an Egyptian battleship, a twenty-one-gun salute thundered over the harbor. The Revolution had been completed.

In Cairo, we had no inkling that all of this was going on in

Alexandria. And when the announcement of Farouk's departure came on the radio, I missed it altogether. It was broadcast while I was en route to the dentist.

"Mrs. Sadat, come right in," the dentist, himself an army officer, called to me when I arrived at his clinic on the evening of July 26.

I looked around at all the other people waiting ahead of me. "Do I not have to wait my turn?" I said to the dentist with some puzzlement.

"Have you not heard, Mrs. Sadat?" the dentist said. "The Army has expelled the King. It's all over. Your husband is now one of the leaders of Egypt."

I was stunned. All the rumors, the few radio announcements, came to a head. There really had been a revolution. I didn't know whether to laugh or cry. The King was out. That was wonderful. But what would the British do? Would they, with all their troops in Egypt, just stand back and watch? What would happen to Anwar now? I couldn't spend this moment at the dentist.

Running out into the street, I saw that the atmosphere had changed completely. Where the streets had been empty, now they were filled with people dancing and cheering. Where the cafés had been quiet, with everyone huddled around the radios, now they were noisy and full. "All drinks are free today," one café owner was shouting.

At home I joined my family around the radio. My excitement grew along with my fear not only for Anwar but for the anger of my father. "Please do not be angry with Anwar for breaking his promise to you," I pleaded with him. But my father was too preoccupied with the news to even think about it. All I could think about was my husband. Where was he?

I couldn't hold back my tears when Anwar suddenly arrived home the next day, exhausted but exhilarated. "Quickly, I want a hot bath, hot food and a change of uniform," he said.

I rushed to do his bidding, peppering him with questions. "Where have you been? What's going on?" I asked him over and over.

"Later, Jehan. Later," he told me. And over dinner he told my whole family the meaning of what had happened.

"Egypt is now going to be a country for all people, not just the rich minority," Anwar said over our evening meal before leaving for a meeting with Nasser. "Never again will kings use forced-labor gangs to build canals and palaces, or waste our country's money on things that benefit only themselves. Land will be given to those who for years have farmed the land of others. And the British will at last be forced to let us govern ourselves."

I could not take my eyes off of Anwar, nor hear enough of his words. His dream for Egypt had come true. My dream for Egypt had come true. Even my mother was happy, for all the people close to her heart were Egyptian.

As we sat at the table I began to absorb the fact that for the first time since the Persians invaded Egypt in 522 B.C., Egypt would be governed by Egyptians. My husband, Anwar el-Sadat, would be one of them. As his wife, it would be my duty to stand at his side no matter what course our country took. I wondered at the prophecy of the fortuneteller, and wished that I were better prepared for the responsibilities that lay ahead for me. My birthday was just two days away. I would be nineteen.

Chapter 5

fatret abdel nasser

The Time of Nasser

W ill all private land be nationalized?"

"Is the country on its way to becoming Communist?"

"Is it true that the foreigners are being forced to leave the country?"

Wherever we went after the Revolution, Anwar was questioned intently by our friends—engineers, doctors, lawyers, university professors, small landowners—as to what the new laws emanating from the Revolutionary Command Council meant. Nobody knew what was going to happen, and there was great confusion.

Night after night we were invited to dinner by friends anxious to learn what the Revolution would mean to them. And night after night Anwar would be late, very late, arriving. "Go on without me. I will meet you at the dinner," he would say to me early in the morning before going to the meetings of the newly formed Revolutionary Command Council. At nine o'clock he wouldn't have arrived at our host's house. Ten o'clock would go by, as would eleven often or even midnight. Inside I would be getting more and more nervous, not knowing what had happened to him, but as the wife of one of the Revolutionists I couldn't show my anxiety. "Anwar will be coming soon," I would reassure the guests calmly. I dared not even show my relief when eventually he would arrive.

"Will the government nationalize the factories?" the questions would start. "Is it true that everyone is going to get a free education?"

All the questions were appropriate, for Egypt was going through a period of drastic social change. Over the course of the next twenty years there would be more changes in the structure of Egyptian life than there had been in fourteen centuries. And the changes had started right away. Two months after the Revolution took place the Agrarian Reform Law was passed and the huge feudal estates throughout Egypt were divided up and given to the fellaheen. Now no single owner could own more than two hundred feddans, or acres, a maximum which nine years later would be further reduced to one hundred feddans. Before the Revolution, eight million fellaheen had owned no land at all. Now the requisitioned land, for which the landowners received bonds, was divided among the fellaheen in five-feddan lots. The 600,000 feddans owned by the royal family, one tenth of all the arable land in Egypt, was requisitioned with no compensation at all.

My father and his relatives had sold their land four years before the Revolution, so they were not affected. Besides, they had owned a legal amount of land in the first stage of reform. But the holdings of the large landowners were greatly restricted, much to the satisfaction of the fellaheen. In thirty years of parliamentary government, not one measure had been passed for their benefit. Many of the farmers had earned only £E5 a month while the landowners they worked for had grown rich, taking more than 80 percent of the harvest for themselves. This sweeping new land reform was closest to the hearts of the fellaheen, and to the hearts of the army officers on the Revolutionary Command Council. Many of the Revolutionists themselves had come from farming villages and had seen firsthand the inequities of land ownership in our agriculture-based economy. The members of the Revolutionary Command Council were determined to get rid of the "old order" who had controlled Egypt so unfairly for so long.

One family I knew of who owned thousands and thousands of feddans in the Nile Delta used to hire guards to bring to the bank the money they had made after the cotton harvest. The fellaheen who had cultivated the soil, sown the seed, irrigated the crop, picked the worms off by hand and gathered in the cotton would watch while trucks piled high with sacks of money went by. Why couldn't the landowners have distributed at least some of the money to the fellaheen who had worked the land for them? It was too much, really, in a country where the majority were poor.

Another rich family in Upper Egypt who also owned thousands of feddans was known for the large parties they gave. Instead of giving the leftover food to the peasants and the servants who had served the guests, the family ordered a big hole to be dug and the food buried. If the fellaheen ever tasted this kind of food, the family reasoned, they would want it for themselves and feel bitterness toward the family. It was better to throw the fancy food away and leave the poor to their customary meals of bread, a piece of white cheese and some green leaves from the field. Such an attitude was very, very cruel and deserved to be ended.

Countless other reforms quickly followed. Government cooperatives were set up in rural areas for loans to farmers, minimum wages guaranteed, work hours reduced for both farmers and factory workers and land rents fixed. Government-financed medical clinics were opened in the villages. More schools were built in one year than had been built in the previous twenty, with education becoming compulsory for all children, boys and girls, even in the rural areas. The universities, once just the province of the privileged, were opened to every Egyptian, and a government job was guaranteed for every college graduate. In the new egalitarian spirit, the old Turkish titles of Pasha, Bey and Effendi were abolished, bringing an outburst of joy from a society that had been so hierarchical. The significance of self-rule and the almost instant dismantling of the *ancien régime* were the obvious promise of things to come.

The anticipation grew when Farouk's four palaces were searched, the extent of his personal wealth achieved at the expense of poor Egyptians proving to be more than we had ever suspected. Though Farouk had taken hundreds of suitcases with him when he set sail from Alexandria, he had left behind so many valuable items in the four hundred rooms at Qubbah Palace that foreign experts from Sotheby's, London's famous auction house, flew in to evaluate them before auctioning them off. Farouk's collection of gold coins and medals alone added up to over eighty thousand pieces. His collection of ornate paperweights, many encrusted with precious stones, was the largest in the world. There were artifacts of gold in room after room, including a gold holder for his Coca-Cola bottles and a piece by Fabergé, the famous Russian jeweler.

In the west wing, where Farouk had his living quarters, the sunken bathtubs were made of green alabaster. Hung in his huge wardrobes were more than one hundred suits and neckties. Rumors flew about his moral character. On a board in the King's private quarters, it was said, hung the keys to fifty Cairo apartments, each labeled with the name of a different young woman. And everywhere there were objects of erotica, on the playing cards in his gaming room with its roulette and chemin-de-fer gaming tables, in the poses of his marble statues, in oil paintings, watches, even music boxes.

It was sad, really, for Egyptians to have to recognize the depravity and greed of our King. But the money raised from the auction would finally go to the poor who deserved it. When the confiscated property of the royal family was finally totaled up it reached £E 70 million, a sum which the government soon used to establish health centers, hospitals and schools in the villages.

The new Revolutionary government also moved quickly to expel our occupiers, opening negotiations with the British to set a timetable for their departure. This was what Anwar had been fighting for all his life, and these days should have been the happiest for him. But instead Anwar was becoming increasingly distressed over the political infighting in the Revolutionary Command Council, especially the hostility of the Council's chairman, Muhammad Naguib.

Because the officers who had led the Revolution were quite young, to reassure the public—and themselves—they had appointed the older Naguib as their chairman and, shortly thereafter, as the first president of the new Republic of Egypt. But, for some reason, Naguib and Anwar had started out on the wrong foot. Naguib's relations with Gamal Abdel Nasser and other members of the Council were beginning to sour generally, but his relations with Anwar were particularly bad, marked by jealously and suspicion. He went so far as spreading rumors about my husband, claiming that Anwar wanted the presidency of Egypt for himself. Anwar had been disgusted at first, then increasingly depressed as the Revolutionary Command Council, instead of concentrating on setting new economic policies, redefining Egypt's international relations or directing social reforms at home, was spending much time fighting among themselves. This was not what Anwar had spent almost all of his life fighting and sacrificing for.

I was almost drawn into the conflict between Anwar and Naguib myself. On one of the most important feast days of this difficult year, while Anwar was away on pilgrimage with Abdel Nasser, I heard the scream of sirens fill the street in front of our apartment building. From the balcony, I looked down on a caravan of motorcycles, police cars and military vehicles approaching from Cairo. In the center of this procession rode President Naguib in a long open car. I and all the others who had come to their windows and balconies watched the President's entourage pull up to the door of our building and stop, motors still roaring and sirens blaring.

What was Naguib doing here? It was traditional after the morning prayer on feast days to visit close friends and relatives to wish them *'aid sa'id,* a happy holiday. But Naguib knew quite well that Anwar was away in Mecca. I decided the President had come to visit Sadat's wife anyway, making a big show of his importance and hoping to downplay his campaign against my husband.

The neighbors may have been impressed with the attention of the President, but I was not. I had no intention of welcoming into my home someone who had made Anwar's life so difficult. "Run down and tell the President there is no one at home," I told our maid. "Tell him you do not expect me back for many hours." I was relieved when I saw Naguib's entourage wheel around and head back across the Nile.

Anwar's depression deepened. He wanted to put the day's quarrels and burdens behind him, to leave his work far away from our home, but there were many times when he just could not.

"Jehan, this shirt is missing a button," he would shout at me. Immediately I would run to get a needle and thread.

"Jehan, I could not sleep at all last night, the sheets were so rumpled. Can you not see that they are ironed better?"

"Jehan, this room has not been cleaned for at least two days," he said one day.

"That cannot be true, Anwar. The rooms are cleaned every day."

But he was determined to find something wrong. "I left a handkerchief in the corner two days ago and still it is there," he insisted.

"You must have dropped it there at lunchtime."

When he saw I was nearly in tears, he backed down. "You are right, Jehan. I am sorry."

I was not too upset by these outbursts, for I knew that his discontent was not coming from me but from the infighting among the Revolutionists. I was more distressed by his depression. Often during the early months of the Revolution, I would find him sitting alone on one of our balconies, not reading or writing or doing anything but just thinking. His look of sadness during those times made me feel just as sad. Often I would sit quietly by him for an hour or so, in case he wanted to share his burden. "What's wrong, Anwar?" I would finally say. Sometimes he would answer me. And sometimes he wouldn't.

I rarely felt that his silences came from anger or disappointment in me. We quarreled, of course, like any husband and wife. But seldom. And, even then, we had discovered from the beginning of our marriage that neither of us was the insulting kind. Because of that, we met on many things. We respected each other very much. And I understood him totally, even in his moments of greatest distress.

"Jehan, we are leaving the country," he announced to me one night.

Leave Egypt? For once I was speechless.

"I cannot endure these rumors Naguib is sending around about me any longer. The Council is divided and all we are doing is fighting one another. I am sickened and have written my letter of resignation."

I stared at him, my mind whirling with the concept of leaving my country, my home, my parents.

"Will you come with me?" he said.

"Of course," I managed to get out. "Wherever you go I'll be with you."

"Good," Anwar said. "Let us start with Lebanon. It is a beautiful country, it is Arab and I'll be able to find work in Beirut."

He must have known that I would go with him, for immediately he produced our two tickets, newly issued passports and exit visas. But luckily his friends on the Revolutionary Command Council, Abdel Hakim Amer and Gamal Abdel Nasser, persuaded him to withdraw his resignation and we remained in Cairo.

With his background in publishing, Anwar did not immediately join the new government full time, but started a newspaper, *el-Gumhuriyya,* or *The Republic,* to present the views of the new regime. He seemed never to be home, leaving early in the morning and arriving back only to sleep. And though I respected what he was doing for our country, I had too much time alone to be satisfied. I couldn't even chide him the way other Egyptian wives did, asking their husbands why they were so late coming home. I knew where Anwar was—and why.

Married women were allowed to attend school now, and I myself enrolled so that I could finish my final year of study. But it didn't work. Anwar was so busy, sometimes coming home just to change his clothes or to quickly eat something. I never knew what his schedule would be, nor did he. But, as his wife, it was my duty to be at home whenever he appeared there. Like every Egyptian husband, he expected this, and I never questioned it. "I'm sorry," I said to my teachers after I had had to break appointment after appointment. "I will have to drop out of my studies for now." If they were disappointed, they did not show it, for they too understood clearly what my responsibilities were as a wife.

I became very conscious of my appearance, wanting to look dignified at all times. I was careful never to wear short-sleeved dresses or a dress without a high neck. Egyptians are very conservative, and in no way did I want my husband to be criticized for any sign of disrespect from me. I also dressed very simply and practically, wanting there to be as little gap as possible between me and the many poor people in our country. It was this gap between the arrogant rich and the millions of poor that had been one of the reasons for the Revolution in the first place. Now all Egyptians were as one, including the leaders.

In spite of the egalitarian message of the Revolution, to my great discomfort the people in our neighborhood persisted in treating me like a celebrity. Never would they allow me to stand in line at the movie theater or to wait my turn at the medical clinics. Instead I would be ushered to the head of the queue. "Will you still be buying meat from me?" our butcher asked anxiously. To my amazement, the pharmacist, the vegetable seller, even the stationer from whom I bought paper and pens, were just as concerned. "Of course," I reassured each of them. "Our position may have changed, but we are still the same people." Signs began to appear in shop windows: "Mrs. Sadat shops here."

At one store where I bought clothes for Anwar, the change was dramatic. Just before the Revolution I had been in there when a minister from the old regime had come in with his entire entourage, smoking a cigar. Immediately the woman waiting on me had rushed away to serve him, and I had left the store, knowing that nobody would pay any attention to me for a long time. When I returned after the Revolution and my husband had become speaker of the Parliament, the same people in the shop rushed to serve me, neglecting everyone else. My God, there is no difference even now, I thought to myself. But to the salesperson I said, "Please, wait on those who came in before me. I will wait my turn."

Inevitably, Anwar and I lost our privacy. Wherever we drove in our car, people recognized us and cheered us in a very warm way. If we went to a movie or ate in a restaurant, we would be constantly interrupted by people coming up to Anwar and shaking his hand. "God bless you, Mr. Sadat," they would say over and over. Sometimes I would yearn for time alone with my husband, but rarely did I feel the attention drawn by Anwar an imposition. I was happy as his wife to be welcomed by the people. At the same time that we were giving to our country, we were also taking the good feelings people showed toward us. "Isn't it a burden?" my friends would ask me. "Not at all," I would reply. And my feelings never changed.

"Are we still going to call you Jehan?" my friends from school asked me.

"Of course," I told them. "What is different between us?"

"You have become very important now," they told me.

But I felt no different toward them. "I may seem important to others, but I am just the same with you," I assured them. And we laughed together, remembering our days in school.

"Do you remember the time I kicked you in the playground when the teacher wasn't watching?" one friend asked me.

"Oh yes," I told her, hugging her. "Now I'll take my revenge. You'll see."

Many of my new responsibilities, however, caught me by surprise. No sooner had Farouk left the country than I found myself approached by hundreds of women who thought I might do them favors.

"Please help me, Mrs. Sadat," said one woman waiting for me outside my apartment. "My husband has lost his job. Will you tell his employer to give it back?"

"Madam! Madam!" a woman shopping near me whispered another day. "My son did not get into medical school at Cairo University. Will you please contact the dean for me and tell him they must let him in?"

Each day as I returned home I found four or five women with petitions in their hands, waiting for me to give them an audience. On Fridays, our religious holiday, even more clustered around my door.

My mail too was suddenly filled with petitions from people who wanted my influence in everything, from finding them an apartment to speaking to a job supervisor about a missed promotion. Hundred of letters poured in as if I were queen and could grant royal favors. I could not erase from my mind the words of the fortuneteller in Roda, nor my own childhood premonition that one day I would have the opportunity to help others. Now, overnight, I had been put into just that position. It was quite frightening. At nineteen, I still thought of myself more as a schoolgirl.

I answered every letter I received and set aside every afternoon to greet the petitioners lined up outside my door. In listening to their problems, I learned a patience that went beyond my nature. Often they would repeat and repeat what they wanted—a child admitted into a school, a husband to be released from prison—but I never said, "That's enough. You've told the same story over and over." I felt that I had been given a mission to help the people, to try my best to better their lives.

This opportunity had come from God. It was up to me to use it. From the time of these first petitioners to the time Anwar would pass away, I wouldn't rest, working night and day to fulfill what I saw as my God-given obligations.

I refused no one and did everything I could to fulfill their wishes. I called the owners of buildings to help secure apartments. I called the heads of businesses to try to find jobs. I did as much as I could to help solve the problems I was hearing. This was the way the system worked in Egypt then and had for centuries, the less fortunate having to beg for favors from the powerful beys and pashas. Anwar himself owed his military career to such a patronage tradition, his father having solicited the help of Major General Ibrahim Khayri Pasha for his son to be accepted into the Royal Military Academy. The Revolution had done away with the traditional Turkish titles awarded to the powerful, but the powerless still depended on others to open doors they felt they couldn't open for themselves. It was a humiliating system really and kept the poorer classes dependent on the whims of others who would arbitrarily decide to help—or not to.

This did little to foster self-sufficiency among the people and was counterproductive to the goals of the Revolution. But it was engrained in Egyptian society. It was Anwar who would try to put an end to such a demeaning and servile tradition when he became president, introducing institutions and laws which treated everyone fairly and with one standard. Even our own son, Gamal, would be admitted not to the medical school at Cairo University, but to the faculty of engineering because he did not have the necessary scores for enrollment. During Nasser's time, however, the petitioners came and came, and I did what I could.

I got over my shyness. I had to in my dealings with so many people. And I became increasingly moved and disturbed really by the letters I was reading from women. I had never even met these women, yet they were pouring out their hearts to me on paper. "My children and I are very hungry, for my husband has left us. He promised to pay alimony, but he has disappeared," wrote one woman. Another wrote: "My husband has brought another wife to live with us and I don't know what to do." These were all letters from broken lives and very private. Still, the women clung to the hope that I could do something.

"If you fear a breach between a man and his wife, appoint an arbiter from his people and another from hers," the Quran instructs us. "If they wish to be reconciled, Allah will bring them together again." Now I was being considered such an "arbiter."

"I have received a letter from your wife, who wants you to return to your marriage," I telephoned one man, a doctor. "I am sorry if you think I am interfering in your private life, for I am not. I am calling you as a sister to see if I can do something to help you and your wife reconcile. Will you come see me? It is up to you."

He came, standing nervously in my living room. "If you would like me to return to my wife I will, Mrs. Sadat," he said. "But if you knew what I had suffered from her, you would understand." And he told me how his wife had become so jealous that she followed him everywhere, even into his clinic while he treated his patients.

I agreed that no man could put up with such jealousy. "I was hoping I could help, but I see I can't," I said.

"But you can," he insisted. "I send her alimony every month, but she denies that she has received it. Could someone from your home deliver the money to her so you will know she has gotten it?"

"Of course," I said. And every month I had his alimony delivered to her.

But the jealousy of his wife and the suspicions of so many other women I was hearing from disturbed me deeply. They were living their lives in terror of losing their husbands and, in the process, were often driving their husbands away. Their dependencies on their husbands for money, for shelter, even for their own identities were making them more prisoners of marriage than marriage partners. To live fully and freely, the women had to learn to stand on their own.

I called for the doctor's wife to come visit me. "Your marriage is finished," I said to her. "You have to face your life now and rebuild it. Why don't you get a job?"

"A job?" she cried.

"Yes," I said. "I will help you to find one." And I did, changing her life completely. Now she is remarried, still working, and very happy.

Other problems were simpler. Some couples I did reconcile

by letting them talk through me to each other. Other women were creating their own problems. "You have to treat your husband better or you will lose him," I advised one woman after listening to her unjustified complaints. "Make your own money instead of always nagging at him to give you more."

At night I told Anwar the stories I had heard during the day and what I had done about them.

"Why do you get so involved?" he said. "The private lives of these people are none of your business."

"Then why are they coming to me as if I could work miracles?" I said. "Would you just send them away?" And I continued to help wherever I could.

The new leaders of Egypt were not satisfying everyone, of course. And only six months after the Revolution a plot by several party leaders and certain army officers to overthrow the new regime was revealed. Immediately the Revolutionary Command Council disbanded all the old political parties, arresting the politicians and court-martialing the army officers. A year later, on January 12, 1954, the Muslim Brotherhood too tried to wrest power from the government. Using their old tactics, the Brothers incited students at Cairo University to antigovernment demonstrations and riots during a memorial meeting for those who had lost their lives fighting the British in the Canal Zone.

The Revolutionary Command Council responded swiftly, arresting the Brothers' leaders and disbanding their organization. But once again the fundamentalist sect just went underground. In March, members of the outlawed Brotherhood defiantly marched on the newly named Republican Palace at Abdin, waving bloody cloths and chanting slogans against the Revolution. Nothing, it seemed, could satisfy them. It was not enough for the Muslim Brothers that the new government had begun to lessen foreign involvement in Egypt, or that the unpious King had been deposed. They wanted total power and would stop at nothing to get it.

It was such a turbulent time. Rarely in the early years of the Revolution was Anwar home, often meeting late into the night with the other Revolutionists. Once again, I was spending much of my time alone. But this time I hardly noticed, for I had a project of my own. I was pregnant.

Just after the Revolution I had had a miscarriage. I thought it was because I had foolishly walked for hours after hearing my good news to order maternity clothes and materials for the baby. Now in the summer of '54 I refused to take any chances at all and put myself to bed. "Get out of bed and walk. Your muscles need exercise," the doctor kept telling me, but I refused. At age twenty, I didn't know I was being ridiculous. I was convinced that if I stood up, the baby would drop out. I didn't even dare think of myself as a mother for fear of losing the baby, but lay still in bed reading books, learning to knit and crochet and do *petit point*. My mother, father and sister came sometimes to sit with me. And I was content, turning out enough embroidered bureau scarves, lampshades and antimacassars to furnish several homes!

In spite of my precautions, I went into labor early, only in my seventh month. On September 7, 1954, Anwar sat beside me all night long in the hospital while the doctors looked increasingly worried.

"What is the matter?" I kept asking. "Is the baby going to be all right?"

Through my pain, Anwar's face began to blur together with the faces of my mother, my father, my sister, my brothers. "Shhhh. Relax," these faces kept saying to me. I did not hear the doctors telling Anwar that the baby was in the wrong position, the feet down instead of the head, that its heartbeat was weak, that it had only a 50 percent chance to live. And Anwar said nothing about it to me.

"We have a lovely girl, Jehan," he told me as soon I came out from under my anesthetic. "I couldn't believe my eyes when I saw her. She is beautiful, with fair skin and blue eyes."

I wanted nothing more than to hold my baby girl. I moved Loubna's tiny fingers, wiggled her tiny toes. But my happiness soon turned to tears. One of Loubna's feet moved when I tickled it; the other didn't.

"There is something wrong," I cried to the doctor.

During the difficult delivery, he told me, the nerves in Loubna's right foot had almost been severed. Her foot was numb, though he assured me it was only temporary. That afternoon he put a leather brace on her foot to keep it flexed so that it could develop properly.

I do not consider myself a superstitious person at all, but I immediately put a blue bead in Loubna's bassinet to ward off "the mischief of the envier, when he envies" described in the Daybreak Surah of the Quran. In Egypt we believe that the color blue keeps the evil eye of the envier away.

On the seventh day after our daughter was born, we held Loubna's *sebu'a*, or birth celebration. There is not a child born in Egypt, rich or poor, who does not have a *sebu'a*, for the gift of a child is the greatest gift of all.

As is our custom, I lay in bed during the *sebu'a*, while my female relatives, friends and neighbors crowded into the room to see Loubna in her bassinette. As a precaution, I had pinned some blue beads to my bedjacket. Not only could a young woman after having given birth be thought to be beautiful, but she could also be envied for her baby. To protect myself, as did many other young mothers, I wore the blue beads so that my milk would not dry up in the night.

Beside my bed was Loubna's *qollah*, an earthen water jug which my relatives had decorated the night before with the traditional ribbons, pieces of lace, even tiny earrings to signify the birth of a girl. Now my aunts, cousins and other women friends each took sips of water from the *qollah* either as good luck for Loubna or as a symbol of fertility, I never could remember which. And the *sebu'a* began.

Carefully Aunt Zouzou laid Loubna in a *ghorbal*, a woven leather sieve from our kitchen, to allow any evil spirits or envy from the evil eye to seep from her body during the ceremony. My cousin 'Aida began to strike a brass mortar and pestle together like a drum. "*Halaatak. Bergalatak,*" the women crowded into my room began to sing: "Obey your mother. Obey your father." They all lit candles. And with Aunt Zouzou carrying Loubna in the *ghorbal*, just as she had carried me at my own *sebu'a*, the traditional procession set off around our flat.

My sister Dalia led the way, banging away with the mortar and pestle, the women following her each holding a candle. Happily I lay in my bed, listening to the joyful sounds of the *zaghreet* and the singing fill the air. In each room the women threw seeds of grain as symbols of the baby's prosperity and grains of salt in warning. "The salt be in the eye of the person who doth not bless the Prophet," they chanted. "The foul salt be in the eye of the envier." And in every room they charged

Loubna to obey her parents and respect her elders, the traditional message to every newborn. Even now it is said that disobedient sons and daughters were probably not placed in the sieve on the seventh day.

In my bed I felt completely content as I listened to the sounds of the *zaghreet* following Loubna around our flat. I sipped the glass of *mughat* by my bed, our traditional very rich drink for new mothers made of *helba,* or fenugreek, sugar and cream, then topped with almonds and pistachio nuts. Not only did it taste delicious, but it was very healthy for the milk of young mothers as well. In the sitting room was another large bowl of *mughat* and platters of chocolates waiting for our guests and anyone else who might drop by to visit Loubna. Except for my worry about Loubna's foot, my happiness was complete.

For the next three months, I took Loubna to the doctor every single day for electric-shock therapy on her foot. At home I massaged it and moved it as the doctor had instructed me, to develop her muscles. Not once did I leave Loubna's side, not even on Fridays. "Let us just stay home with the baby instead of going for a drive," I would suggest to Anwar. And he stayed home with us, understanding my obsession with my baby.

So as not to disturb Anwar's sleep, I moved into the bedroom with Loubna, watching over her twenty-four hours a day. The only time I left the house without her I was miserable. I had neglected my appearance since her birth, so, leaving Loubna with my mother and sister, I had gone to the hair salon. But, as I sat under the dryer, tears streamed down my face. Was Loubna all right? Was she hungry? Was she crying? I rushed back to our flat still with tears in my eyes. "She is fine," my mother soothed me. "She is fine." And suddenly, she was fine.

Her toe! Her toe moved! I saw it, disbelieved it, saw it move again. I rushed her to the doctor. "She is moving her toe!" I cried.

He tested her, saw the toe move for himself. "She will be all right now," he said.

I lost all composure, hugging the doctor. My baby was going to grow up healthy and strong. This should have been the happiest day of my life. But in a pattern that was to dominate the rest of my life, political events were casting their shadows over my personal happiness. Loubna would be fine now. But what about my husband? Only a month after Loubna's birth, the fear that was to dominate the rest of my life with Anwar had begun.

"There has been an assassination attempt against Gamal Abdel Nasser in Alexandria," the news bulletin had come over the radio on October 26. "Eight shots have been fired, but Nasser appears to be unharmed."

I was at home with Loubna when I heard the terrifying news. An attempt to kill Abdel Nasser? Why? This should have been a time for celebration, not violence. Just the week before, the Anglo–Egyptian Evacuation Agreement had been signed, finally ending our seventy-five years of occupation by the British. Nasser, who had led the Egyptian delegation in the negotiations with the British, had gone to celebrate the signing at a rally in el-Manshiah Square in Alexandria. There a young plumber from Cairo had suddenly pulled out a pistol and started firing. Nasser had almost been killed. The plumber was thought to have ties to the Muslim Brothers. And the repercussions began.

Thousands were called in for questioning, and hundreds arrested, as police investigations revealed an elaborate Brotherhood plot to overthrow the government. In Cairo, it seemed that conspiracy was all around us. Two of my most devout second cousins fled the country, fearing imprisonment as members of the Brotherhood. So did Abdel Mun'em Raouf, a colleague and friend of Anwar's who was reported to be the leader of a pro-Brotherhood faction in the Army. Even Naguib himself was revealed to have ties with the Brotherhood. He was dismissed as president of the country and placed under house arrest.

In November of 1954, a "People's Court" was set up to try all the traitors to the new regime. Anwar, who had become the Minister of State only a few days before the birth of our daughter, was now appointed by Nasser to be one of the three judges on the People's Court. All in all, the People's Court and the military courts would try over one thousand people accused of high treason, sentencing six members of the Muslim Brotherhood to death. And the phone calls began.

"Is this the home of Sadat?"

"Yes. Who is calling, please?"

"Is he there?"

"No. He is not here right now."

"Who is this speaking?"

"I am his wife."

"Then take notice. We are going to kill your husband."

"Who are you!"

"That is not important. Just know that we are going to kill Sadat for what he has done to the Muslim Brothers." And the phone line would go dead.

Sometimes the threats would come in the mail. Other times from reports from government intelligence. Sitting with my little baby in our apartment, I began to dread the sound of the phone. Every time it rang, my heart would start beating, beating, beating with terror. "Just hang up," Anwar advised me. "Or don't answer the phone at all." But usually I couldn't prevent myself. I always listened very carefully in case there was some way I could protect him.

I tried hard to conceal my fears from Anwar. He had to do his duty in the court without worrying about me. But some nights when I would answer these calls my tears would come flooding. How could the Muslim Brothers think of killing my husband, the Revolutionist who had been closest to them before the Revolution? Would I become a widow at twenty-one? Would our baby Loubna grow up without a father?

"Don't worry," Anwar would try to reassure me. "The ones who actually kill never call to say they are going to kill. They are threatening me over the phone just to trouble you, to make you worry."

I would cling to his words, trying to believe them. But then the next phone call would come.

Bodyguards were assigned to protect us, one stationed in the hallway just outside the door to our apartment, others on the street in front of the building. In one way I welcomed their presence, but in another the very fact that they were necessary reminded me constantly of the danger Anwar was in. I was convinced he was going to be killed. What could I do to save him? I thought of little else. I myself did not feel threatened. Later, after Anwar became president of Egypt and I traveled throughout the country working on my own projects, I too would occasionally be threatened. In the beginning, however, it was Anwar whose life was greatly at risk.

Shots. I hear shots. I jump out of bed and run out on the balcony, peering down nine stories to search for his body in the street. I know it has finally happened. My husband has been shot. But I can see nothing. Quickly I dress, ready to rush down the stairs to search for his body, to get him immediately to the hospital. But I stop myself. What will the bodyguards think, the soldiers stationed around the building? Will they think Mrs. Sadat is afraid? Or will they think she is a madwoman, dashing into the street at 2 A.M.? Better not go, I tell myself. I have to be very respectable and calm. My other voice speaks: Just go quietly downstairs and inquire calmly what the trouble is. No, Jehan, don't listen to this voice. Be a good wife and stay in a dignified manner at home. Both voices rage in my head as I rush back and forth between the front door to go to Anwar and the balcony to listen for more shots.

Fifteen minutes later the key turns in the front door and suddenly Anwar is there with his big smile. "What is wrong with you, Jehan?" he says as I throw myself into his arms, sobbing.

"I thought they had killed you," I say, telling him about the shots I had heard.

He laughs, that lovely deep laugh of his. "Listen to me very carefully, Jehan," he says, tipping my face up to his to make sure I am listening. "When it is time for the end of my life, neither you nor I nor anyone else will be able to prevent it. Remember the words of the Quran: 'Wherever you may be, death shall overtake you, even though you be in fortified castles.' When my time comes, it will come whether you are there to rush me to the hospital, or not. It will make no difference. So quiet yourself and be calm. Nothing you can do will add one day to my life, not even one moment."

I knew he was right of course. *Masir*. There is nothing that anyone on earth can do to change what God has willed for us. For the rest of my life I would remember the words Anwar spoke to me that night, that nothing I could ever do would add one moment to his life. And it was true. I could do nothing for him the day he died. It happened exactly the way he said it would.

Still, the possibility would always nag at me throughout our life together that it could be my destiny to save Anwar, to prevent or at least to delay the taking of his life. I could never really accept deep in my heart my passive helplessness in protecting him. A man, questioning our Prophet about the idea of fate, asked him if he should tie his camel up when he went in to pray or simply trust God to guard it for him. "Tie up your camel," said the Prophet, "and trust in God." I could not tie up Anwar, of course. But perhaps there was something I could do to help him. Always I was in conflict. Would I recognize the moment to fulfill my destiny and save him? Or was his protection really out of my hands altogether?

I began to develop the severe headaches that would plague me until he passed away and in fact still continue to this day. From the time of these first threats from the Muslim Brothers, the symptoms have been the same. The pain starts in the back of my neck, then climbs gradually up and through my head until I feel that my head is being crushed. My stomach can hold nothing down. My vision becomes blurred and any light touching my eyes feels like the blade of a hot knife. Nothing any doctor here in Egypt or during our travels abroad has prescribed has done any good, no tablets, no injections, nothing.

"You are suffering from tension headaches," the doctors always tell me after examining me and finding nothing clinically wrong. This, of course, I know. What they cannot comprehend is the stress I have always lived under.

"How do you deal with your pain?" one doctor in Paris asked me. "Do you ever scream or cry out?"

"No, never," I told him.

"Then what do you do?" he persisted.

"The maximum is to excuse myself wherever I am, lock myself in the bathroom and let my tears come," I told him. "Then I wash my face so no one will notice." And that has been the pattern of my life, hiding my pain inside while making everyone around me believe I feel secure and satisfied. This seeming serenity was my duty toward my country, and especially toward my husband. My headaches were the price of our love.

"Teach me to drive, Anwar," I said to my husband one Friday, the one day he always spent with me. Most young wives I knew wanted to learn to drive so that they could go to shops in different neighborhoods or take their children out of

Cairo into the countryside. But my motive was different. If we were driving alone and a fanatic attacked my husband, what was I going to do? Just sit there helplessly while he bled to death? No. If I knew how to drive, at least I could shove him into the other seat and drive him to the hospital. I learned how to drive.

"Teach me to shoot, Anwar."

He looked at me quizically, but asked me no questions. "All right," he said.

The next Friday he took me to the desert at the Pyramids, handed me a small pistol, showed me how it worked and how to aim it, then set up a tin can in the sand. "I don't agree with you wanting a gun," he said to me.

"I know," I told him. "But it will make me feel more secure when I am with you."

"I understand," he said. "I just hope you won't do something wrong with it."

I laughed at him. "Do you expect me to rob a bank?"

"Just hit the can," he said.

Again and again I shot at it, but it was no use. I was as nearsighted then as I am now. The pistol kicked each time in my hand, sending the bullet way over the can. And I couldn't stop jumping at the loud sound of the explosion. "I'm sorry, Anwar," I said to my husband. "I'll just have to scream and shout for bodyguards to come save you. That will be easier than learning to shoot."

He looked very relieved.

Anwar and Nasser were spending much time together, Anwar taking his dinner at Nasser's home or he in ours. Occasionally both Anwar and I went to Nasser's home to visit with him and his wife, Tahia. Their relationship seemed very formal and old-fashioned to me. Tahia never addressed her husband by his name, but always as *el-ra'is,* "the President," even in front of us. So did his five children. Very shy and modest, Tahia rarely spoke during the meals we shared, even looked uncomfortable sitting with the men. Never did she join in the talk of politics, the constant subject at the table.

Anwar loved and respected Abdel Nasser very much, as did I. But sometimes Nasser could be very difficult. He was very suspicious, a common trait in those from Upper Egypt, where many are hot-tempered and jealous. I felt sorry sometimes for Nasser, knowing how tormented he was about the loyalty of those around him. But I understood him.

His naturally suspicious nature had been enflamed by the success of the Revolution itself. The ten-year secrecy surrounding the Free Officers' Organization had been so successful in a country where there are many secrets known to everybody, that Nasser increasingly felt the possibility of the same sort of conspiracy against himself. His suspicions were further fed by his inner circle, who tried to prove their own loyalty by adding imaginary plots every week to the real ones coming from the fundamentalists and other political factions.

Nasser trusted Anwar more than most, knowing he was less interested in power for himself than he was in the success of the Revolution. But he was almost paranoid about the loyalty and the intentions of others. Knowing this, his entourage continued to amass power for themselves, getting rid of all their adversaries by denouncing them as enemies of the Revolution. Arrest after arrest was made for suspected subversiveness. No one felt he or she could say anything openly and frankly without fear of being arrested or at least questioned. There was a popular story during this time of one man saying to another, "Oof, this weather is so hot," to which his companion quickly replied, "Didn't we agree not to discuss politics?"

The uneasiness that ran through Egypt was very upsetting to Anwar. "It's in his blood," I told my husband. "Nasser can't help it."

Most seemed to agree, for Nasser remained very popular with the people. Unlike the more formal politicians in the days of King Farouk, Nasser spoke to the people not in Classical Arabic but in everyday colloquial language. The people saw Nasser, the son of a postman, as one of their own, a man like them who ate *ful* for breakfast, who prayed every Friday in the mosque and who canceled his plans every first Thursday of the month to listen to Um Kalthum's concert on Radio Cairo. Nasser was an Egyptian, through and through.

He instilled a new pride and dignity among Egyptians. Though many remained very poor, at last we were masters of our own house, the air made fresh by the new egalitarian spirit. Upper-class Egyptians no longer spoke to one another in French, but in Arabic. Egypt was run no longer from the British Embassy, but from the offices of the Egyptian ministries. After thousands of years of foreign rule, we were rediscovering our heritage.

Under Nasser, Egypt began to cut her European ties and to reach out to Arab and other Muslim countries. In 1955 Nasser named Anwar secretary general of the newly formed Islamic Congress. Over the next few years Anwar would spend much time visiting King Hussein in Jordan, President Chamoun in Beirut and King Muhammad V in Morroco. He would also travel to Malaysia, Indonesia, Pakistan and nearly all the Muslim countries, becoming close to the ruling families of the Gulf States and the royal family in Saudi Arabia.

The road ahead was not to be easy for Nasser, however. There was danger to Egypt from within and without. In January of 1955, Nasser was pressured by Prime Minister Anthony Eden of Great Britain to join with Turkey, Iraq and Pakistan in the Baghdad Pact, a bilateral defense treaty controlled by Britain. Nasser naturally refused, having just successfully negotiated the end of the British military presence in Egypt. In swift retaliation, Israel, backed by Britain and the United States, then launched a series of bloody attacks on our Egyptian army camps in the demilitarized zone in the Sinai, attacking Gaza, Kuntilla and Sabha. These attacks on the last day of February 1955 were to change the course of the Revolution, of Nasser and of the whole Middle East.

Weapons. Suddenly weapons were foremost on the minds of Nasser, Anwar and the other Revolutionists. Until that moment, the revolutionary government had not considered the possibility of war with Israel. All Nasser had talked about, both in public and in private, had been the reform of Egyptian society, the need for the government to spend its money on eradicating the three traditional enemies of Egypt: poverty, illiteracy and disease. Now all he talked about was buying arms. Our Army was still equipped with the outdated and broken weapons bought by Farouk, the weapons which had failed Egypt so miserably in the Palestine War.

Nasser first turned to the United States and Great Britain for weapons, only to have unacceptable conditions laid down by U.S. Secretary of State John Foster Dulles and British Prime Minister Eden. At first Eden was reluctant to sell arms to the Egyptians until the new government had reached an agreement on the status of the Suez Canal, the Western Bloc's lucrative passageway to India and the East. Then Eden upped his demands. Unless Egypt signed a new Anglo–Egyptian defense pact, he declared, Britian would not sell us any arms at all. Naturally, Nasser refused.

The proposal from Dulles was even more patronizing: U.S. arms could go to Egypt only if they were controlled by American military advisers. Nasser turned down Dulles' offer as well, refusing to sacrifice Egypt's newly won independence to become a military puppet of the United States.

Both Western leaders were angry at Nasser for not accepting their conditions. But Nasser was determined not to be controlled by them. Egypt had had a long tradition of neutrality, endorsed time and again by the Wafd government under both King Farouk and President Naguib. In April of 1955, Nasser made Egypt's neutrality official. After attending the first Asian-African Conference of Nonaligned Nations in Bandung, Indonesia, Nasser announced that Egypt would join the group of unaligned Third World countries. That finished for good all arms talks between Egypt and the United States and Britain, forcing Nasser to turn toward the East for his military needs. In September of '55, Nasser signed an arms agreement with Czechoslovakia and the Soviet Union.

By 1956, the Revolution in Egypt was entering its second phase. A new Constitution was put into effect which gave Egypt a new system of government with an elected President. When the first presidential plebiscite was held in June, nobody was surprised by Nasser's overwhelming victory. I voted for him myself with great excitement, not only because I thought him a great leader, but because for the first time women had been given the right to vote. The future seemed bright. Egyptians danced in the streets shortly after the elections when the last British soldier left Egyptian soil and Nasser himself raised our flag over the former British military base in the Canal Zone.

We were totally unprepared for the shock which followed just one month later. To punish Egypt for its impudence and its arms deals with the Eastern Bloc, Britain and the United States canceled their commitment to help finance one of Egypt's most urgent needs: the High Dam at Aswan in Upper Egypt. Nasser was shocked to his core when the Western countries broke their word. Long the dream of Egypt, the High Dam was essential to our future.

Egypt could no longer afford to depend on an economy based only on agriculture. The High Dam would have generated the thousands of kilowatts needed to start the essential process of industrialization. The High Dam would have helped to feed our exploding population as well, making it possible to irrigate one million feddans of land now lying barren in the desert and allowing the fellaheen to grow three crops a year instead of just one. In addition, the dam would have provided much-needed electricity to the millions of villagers who for centuries had lived and worked by oil lamps. This was no idle project. The High Dam had lain at the heart of the Revolutionists' dreams for Egypt. And the United States and Britain had killed it.

Once more Nasser turned to the East, and quickly the Soviet Union offered funding for the High Dam. The essential project was saved. But nobody knew how deeply betrayed by the West Nasser felt until he delivered a speech in Alexandria on July 26, 1956, to commemorate the fourth anniversary of Farouk's departure from Egyptian soil. He had asked Anwar to join him in Alexandria, but at the last minute Anwar couldn't go, feeling ill from an attack of gastroenteritis.

"I'm sorry you won't be with me," Nasser told Anwar. Then he made what seemed to Anwar to be a rather strange request. "Please listen to my speech on the radio," Nasser said.

While Anwar listened to Nasser's speech in Cairo, I listened to it in Port Sa'id, where I was staying with my family. Millions of other Egyptians listened to it from their villages all the way from Aswan in Upper Egypt to Alexandria. And no one could believe their ears. What we were hearing now was beyond our wildest dreams.

"We shall never repeat the past, but we shall eliminate the past," Nasser was saying. "We shall eliminate the past by regaining our rights to the Suez Canal . . . this canal belongs to Egypt." In Port Sa'id, my parents and I stared at each other in amazement. What was Nasser saying? "While I talk to you at this moment," he continued, "some of your Egyptian brothers are proceeding to administer the Canal Company. Right now, at this very moment, they are taking over the Canal Company —the Egyptian Canal Company, not the 'Foreign Canal' company! From now on we are going to build our future with dignity!"

All over Egypt, demonstrations erupted. In the streets of Port Sa'id, men linked arms and danced while women clapped with joy and gave tongue in the *zaghreet*. Others in the city celebrated by dynamiting the bronze statue of Ferdinand de Lesseps, the French builder of the Canal. I tried not to get too excited myself, because I was two months pregnant with my second child. But Nasser's words and his daring action had transformed us all.

With utmost courage, he had stood up to the powers which had dominated Egypt for so long and given Egypt back its pride. With one sentence, Nasser had nationalized the West's most valuable property—the Suez Canal—and become an almost mythical hero to all Egyptians. From that moment, Nasser had proclaimed, the $35 million a year revenue from the Canal would no longer go to the Anglo–French company which controlled it, but to its rightful owner Egypt. The money would now be ours to build the High Dam if we so chose. And the sacrifice of the 120,000 Egyptians who had died digging the Canal would be honored.

I ran to the telephone and placed a call to Anwar in Cairo. "Anwar," I shouted excitedly, "are you listening to the radio? Did you hear Nasser say that the Suez Canal once more is ours?" I couldn't hear his reply, the noise of cheering from the people gathering in our house was so great. "What is it? What did you say, Anwar?" I said over the phone to Cairo, straining to hear Anwar's reply.

His words cast a chill on my excitement. "I share in the happiness, but I am worried about the repercussions," I finally heard him say. "The West cannot afford to lose the Canal. And we are not yet ready to go to war."

Can there be a sound more frightening than the wail of an air raid siren? Save for the sound of gunfire, I have not heard any sound more terrifying. And on October 29, 1956, I first heard the sound that was to make me shudder for the rest of my life.

Nasser had stood firm even after the governments of Britain, France and the United States had frozen all Egyptian assets in their countries to punish him for nationalizing the Suez Canal. Now, unbelievably, Israel invaded the Sinai, while at the same time British and French planes started bombing Cairo. What was to become known to us as the Tri-Partite Aggression, and to the West as the Suez War, had begun.

We were all stunned. How could it be possible that two of the strongest countries in the world had joined forces with Israel to attack one poor country—Egypt? Even Nasser, when told of the attack, could not believe it until he stood on the roof of his house and saw that the planes buzzing Cairo had French and British insignias on their wings. But still he would not be intimidated. On the day of the first attack, the British and the French had issued an ultimatum giving Nasser twelve hours to withdraw our forces ten miles west from the Canal, tantamount to our relinquishing not only the Canal, but the whole Sinai Peninsula. Nasser had rejected the ultimatum, refusing to give in to the bullying tactics of the super-powers.

And the planes came.

"Hush, Loubna, do not be frightened," I soothed our little daughter, who clung to me in terror while the sirens wailed. We had been instructed to go down to air raid shelters during the raids, but I was six months pregnant by then, and climbing up and down the nine flights of stairs carrying Loubna was exhausting. Instead, we stayed in our apartment, where, outside, the night sky was as bright as daylight, lit by the flares dropped from the planes so that the British and French bombers could see where to drop their loads. Inside the flat, however, was total darkness because of the blackout which the government had ordered all over Egypt.

"Turn on the light," Loubna kept pleading, burying her head in my neck. Her fear escalated as the sounds of the bombs exploding sent tremors through our apartment. "I'm scared. Make the noise stop," Loubna wailed night after night. But of course I could not.

"See how pretty the sky is," I tried one night, carrying her out of the darkness in the apartment onto our balcony. All over Cairo, we could see enemy planes dropping their flares, illuminating the city with an eerie brightness. The too-bright light washed out all natural color and made the buildings look somewhat like X rays. I hid my own fear to try to divert Loubna's. "Doesn't the sky look like the fireworks you've seen on the July Twenty-third celebration?" But even at two, Loubna knew better.

For seven days the propaganda broadcast on Israeli radio warned us that one night Israeli planes were going to bomb the factories, another night the radio station, another the offices of the three newspapers. This psychological warfare was very frightening to all of us. To set an example for the workers at *el-Gumhuriyya*, Anwar defiantly started sleeping at his office at the newspaper. I stayed at home by Loubna's bed, singing to her and telling her stories in the dark until she fell into an exhausted sleep. But every morning when I woke up, Loubna was in my bed, her arms wrapped around my neck. It was terrible to see the suffering of our daughter, terrible, too, to imagine the suffering of the baby now inside me.

Only once did Loubna and I go down to the shelter, ordered to by the air raid marshals who pounded on our door. I went willingly, for this nighttime raid was particularly worrisome. The Israelis had declared their target to be the bridges of Cairo, and our building stood right next to the Abbas Bridge.

As the sirens began their wail, everyone in the building crowded onto the first-floor landing. Loubna and I were pushed against the owner of the building, who was screaming and screaming.

"Why are you screaming?" I shouted at her, trying to make myself heard over the sirens and her own loud shrieks. "You are making everyone else very anxious."

"Can't you hear the sirens, Mrs. Sadat?" she shouted back, her eyes rolling in terror.

"Of course I hear them. It is horrible," I told her. "But your screaming will not make the sirens stop. It would be nice if it did, but it cannot."

She looked at me, shocked. I shifted Loubna onto my other hip. The child was trembling, her eyes squeezed shut and her ears blocked by her hands.

"If we are going to die, let us at least die in a dignified way," I said to the landlady. "There is nothing we can do, so we might as well be calm."

"I don't understand you, Mrs. Sadat," the lady said to me. But she stopped screaming. And the raid passed.

We never went to the shelter again. "You will go with Loubna to stay with your sister in the country," Anwar said the next morning.

I shook my head. "I will send Loubna, but I want to stay

with you," I told him. "Here at least, we are in danger together."

But Anwar was adamant. "You must go with Loubna," he ordered me. "I do not want to be torn with worry about you. Until the aggression ends, I will have to stay at the newspaper day and night."

And so I went with my parents and Loubna to my brother-in-law's family ranch in Buheira province, two hours from Cairo.

I sat by the radio day and night listening to the news of the war. I still couldn't believe what was happening to us. All the news was bad. Our new aircraft recently delivered by the Soviets had been destroyed before our pilots had had time to learn how to fly them. The lovely city of Port Sa'id was being bombed to the ground, as were the canal cities of Suez and Isma'iliyya where I had summered as a child and first met Anwar. We were defenseless, but still the aggressors came. Nasser had withdrawn most of our troops from the Sinai Peninsula in order to better defend the Egyptian mainland against the expected invasion. In two days the Israelis had swept across the Sinai, and they were now at the Suez Canal.

With utmost bravery, the fedayeen in the Canal Zone once more were fighting alone against the foreign invaders. Women, claiming they were bringing in food to their relatives, smuggled weapons in baskets into the blockaded city of Port Sa'id which the men then used to attack the British and French troops. Foreign barracks in the city were set ablaze by homemade bombs. Teenage girls lured the foreign soldiers into alleys so that their brothers and cousins could cut their throats. There was no way that these ordinary citizens could singlehandedly stop the foreign invaders, but the unfair aggression was spawning a new wave of nationalism and a surge of heroism. One of my childhood friends from Port Sa'id was killed trying to blow up a trainload of British soldiers.

Three days after the bombing raids began, the United Nations called for a cease-fire, which Egypt immediately accepted, but which Britain and France vetoed. Five days later, on June 8, there was a call for a second cease fire, which all countries involved accepted. But fighting continued in the Canal Zone. Not much physical damage had been inflicted on Cairo, the original raids centering on and around Cairo airport, but much psychological harm had been done to the people. Including me.

I was going through mental agony in Buheira. What was happening in Cairo? Would my husband and all the other Revolutionists be killed? I could not show my fears, of course, as everyone in the countryside was looking to me as the wife of one of the Revolutionists. All day I joked and laughed with the family of Mahmoud Abu Wafia, my brother-in-law, while following the news. But inside I was frightened. Nasser's speeches on the radio were sharply criticizing our attackers while praising the bravery of Egyptians. Nasser seemed so confident, so sure, and I clung to every word, as did all Egyptians. But at night I sometimes lost heart. Will you ever see your father again? I thought as I looked at Loubna, who was still too traumatized by the bombings to sleep alone. Or will you be an orphan girl?

On November 12, two weeks after the first planes had strafed Cairo, the pains began. "No," I cried out. "It is too soon." But the pains continued. "Oh, please, no," I cried again. "I am only six months and two weeks pregnant. The baby will die. Please, no." But the strain of the war and the air raids had been too much. And the pains escalated.

"We must call Anwar," my sister said to me in the morning.

I shook my head. "I do not want to add a further burden on him," I said. "I will go through this like any peasant woman or any other woman."

In the afternoon, my sister called in a local doctor.

"Have you ever delivered a baby?" I asked him.

"Yes," he said a little nervously, for he also admitted he was not a specialist at all but a general practitioner.

My anxiety grew close to hysteria as night fell. Surely without special care my baby born so prematurely would die. But we could not go to a hospital. There were no private hospitals in the area, the government hospitals were filled with the wounded, and even the hospitals had to observe the blackouts at night.

I had to hang on. I had to. But could I? By dinnertime I was almost out of my head with pain and worry. Please let the labor stop, I prayed to God. Please let me keep my baby longer. But the pains simply came more intensely and quickly. My brother-in-law called from Cairo to see how we all were. "Jehan is in premature labor," my sister said to him. She looked at me. "Can he tell Anwar?" she asked. I nodded. I was too exhausted to resist alone any longer.

I hardly saw the doctor arrive at 3 A.M. on November 13 through the haze of my pain. I did not find out until later that Anwar had immediately sent a car for Dr. Muhammad Magdi Ibrahim, the doctor who had delivered the son of Farouk. Dr. Magdi had collected the oxygen, anesthesia and surgical instruments that would have been available in a hospital and had rushed to Buheira with an obstetrical nurse. The journey, which normally took two hours, took them four. There was a curfew on all civilian travel, and over and over they had to stop at military checkpoints and explain their mission. There were many army vehicles on the road, and because of the blackout they had to drive without lights. But I knew none of this.

As soon as I saw Dr. Magdi's familiar face, I let go. "Now I can have my baby," I told him just before he placed the anesthesia mask over my face. And all the worry I had kept hidden in the last two weeks erupted.

"God will save our country!" I cried out time and again to the startled doctor. "God will save Gamal Abdel Nasser!" Under the anesthesia my anxious patriotism reached new heights. "Why are the British destroying our country?" I shouted. "Long live Egypt! Long live our President!"

When I regained consciousness I had a little boy, a very little boy weighing just over one kilo, only three pounds.

My patriotic labor had not gone unnoticed. "It was my first political delivery," the doctor would laughingly tell everyone later.

My son was small, much too small. The November night was cold, and quickly he and I were wrapped in blankets and rushed to Dr. Magdi's hospital in Cairo one hundred miles away. The nurse held an oxygen mask over the baby's tiny face, but he kept making unnatural noises, like a chicken more than a baby, and I knew that something was wrong with his lungs. Again and again we were stopped at roadblocks. "Who are you and where are you going?" we were asked. I was too weak to say anything. Only after the military police shined a flashlight in my face were we allowed to continue.

I was still groggy from the anesthetic. In the car I was convinced we were playing out the scene from *Gone With the Wind* where Scarlet delivers Melanie's baby in the middle of the Civil War without any of the proper instruments or supplies. I refused a wheelchair when we finally arrived at the hospital, but after two steps I hemorrhaged and had to be wheeled inside. The baby was rushed into an oxygen tent because his lungs were not developed enough for him to breathe by himself.

My head kept whirling in my hospital room as I floated on the edge of consciousness. At one point Anwar's father came in and, without saying a word to me, began to prostrate himself in prayer over and over again on the floor. "Thank God my son has a son," he kept repeating. Anwar's mother, Sitt el-Barrein, clad all in black, arrived too. My eyes blurred as she whirled around the room, dancing in an hysterical way, pausing only to kiss me. Through my haze I saw my father sitting in the room, my brothers and my sister sitting in the room, Sitt el-Barrein jumping and jumping, my father-in-law standing and bowing, standing and bowing, all the time thanking God. This must be what it feels like to be drunk, I thought before closing my eyes to all of them.

"Do not even bother to look at the baby," Anwar said to me the next morning when he arrived at the hospital. "He looks like a monkey. Our daughter is much prettier."

I did not know then that Anwar had spoken to the doctor, that he had been told that this time our baby's chances for life were not even 50 percent. All I knew was that my heart went out to Anwar at that moment, for I knew exactly what he was really telling me: *I am trying to prepare you for our son's death. Do not care for this boy and do not worry about me, whatever happens. I am very pleased with you and Loubna.* But I refused to believe him.

We had planned to name a boy Safwat after my father. But because of the aggression against Egypt and the courage of Nasser, we decided to name him Gamal in honor of the President of the regime. Little Gamal had to live. He had to. "You are a fighter, just like your namesake," I whispered to the tiny creature.

At first Gamal could not swallow, could not even suck. I tried saturating a cotton swab with milk and putting it into his tiny mouth, but he was too weak to draw any sustenance from it.

"Get me an eyedropper," I said to the nurse.

That seemed to work. But the stress from the war and Gamal's birth was drying up my milk. The nurses went to all the other new mothers in the hospital and collected milk from them so that I could feed my baby. "It is too bad our children will never be able to marry," the mother of a baby girl joked with me later, referring to the Quranic injunction against marriage between those who have suckled at the same breast. "They are certainly brother and sister."

For the next month, while Gamal stayed in his incubator in the hospital, I would squeeze milk into his mouth every hour around the clock. At night I sat in the nursery while he slept.

"You are exhausted, Jehan," Anwar said to me. "Let the nurses take care of him just for a little while."

But I refused. I was willing my baby to live.

What joy there should have been for the birth of Anwar's first son after our girl and his three daughters from his first marriage. But I couldn't feel the happiness I should have felt. Anwar came to the hospital as often as he could, but it was not often. He took me for drives to try to get me out of my depression, but it wouldn't lift. Everything upset me. Loubna could not stay with me in the hospital, and my sister had taken her away to her home. Anwar could not sit with me like a normal husband. My country was occupied. My little son was fighting for his life. I felt torn between them all, even my mother.

She was my mother, but she was also British. It was the British who were bombing my country, yet still I loved her. My feelings were in terrible conflict. "Mummy, why did your country invade my country. Why? We have done nothing against them," I asked her over and over in the hospital.

"Jehan, it's not me, darling. It's not me," she would soothe me.

"I know that, Mummy. But why are the British fighting us?" I'd press her. "It was our right to nationalize our own Canal."

"Shhh, Jehan," she'd say, stroking my hair. "The British were wrong. They were wrong."

Slowly, Gamal took strength, beginning to close his mouth around the eyedropper and to suck. By the time he was strong enough to leave the hospital, I could have qualified as a nurse for the premature. Always after that, whenever I visited other countries, I would study the latest equipment in treating the babies born too early and make sure we brought back that equipment to Egypt.

"Gamal's birth was like a lovely dream in the midst of a

nightmare," Anwar would tell me later. But even the happiest moments in our life, it seemed, always had something attached to them which wouldn't let us feel total happiness. Because of the war, Gamal had no birth celebration, no *sebu'a*. Everyone was too worried. There was no time and no possibility for parties or any pleasure at all.

Nasser, through Shukri el-Kuwatli, the President of Syria, had appealed to the Soviet Union to use its influence in helping Egypt against the British and French occupation, but Khrushchev and Bulganin had refused. Nasser had then appealed to the Americans. And unlike the Russian leaders, President Eisenhower had responded. He was furious at the deceit of the British and the French, who had told him nothing of their plans to attack Egypt. Now the American President was putting much pressure on Britain, France and Israel to withdraw. This Britain and France finally did, one month after their initial attacks on Egypt. Israel followed three months later, in March of '57, using a scorched-earth policy, destroying all our roads, railways and military installations on the way back to their own state. The United Nations then ordered a peacekeeping force into the Sinai; it would remain there until 1967.

The war had taken a terrible toll. Anti-Jewish sentiment which had started after the Palestine War in '48 now reached fever pitch across Egypt. Thousands and thousands of Egyptian Jews with whom we had always lived peacefully either were expelled or fled.

In human terms, their departure was a great loss for our country. The Jews had played a great part in the culture of Egypt and had been totally accepted in our society. The *Who's Who* of Egypt in the fifties had been at least one-quarter Jews, including many who were among our most famous and popular actors, writers, lawyers, bankers and industrialists. During World War II, when the Nazis had come within sixty-five miles of Alexandria, Muslim and Christian families in that city had hidden Jewish families in the basements and attics of their houses. In Cairo, Jews had lived peacefully for generations. Muslims had often gone to the homes of the most religious Jews on Saturday, the Jewish Sabbath, to turn on their lights for them and perform other small chores which Jewish law prohibited on the day of rest. But the creation of Israel and the Suez War had destroyed this harmony. Egyptian Jews were leaving in droves, making a last expression of commitment to their country by emigrating not to Israel, but to Europe, the United States and South America. Only their names—Cicurel, David Ades, Ben Zion, Shallon and Gabriel—remained behind them, on the stores which in my childhood had been the most prestigious in Cairo.

Westerners who had lived in Egypt for years were also being looked upon with suspicion and hatred. For two weeks my own mother hid inside her house in Cairo, afraid to set foot outside. In retaliation for the Suez War, Nasser began to "Eyptianize" the large banks and insurance companies held by the British and the French, taking control of more than fifteen thousand of them by the end of 1956. Fearing that their businesses would be next, even Greeks, Turks and Armenians who had lived in Egypt all their lives were now leaving, going "home" to countries they had never even seen before or moving on to new destinations in Europe, America or Australia. Wherever I later traveled in the world, I would always find people with European names who spoke Egyptian Arabic and who were hungry for news of Cairo.

Nasser would complete the nationalization process in 1961, when he would pass laws socializing all industry, banks, trade and insurance companies, and expropriating the land owned by foreigners. And while his policies would move him further and further from Britain and the United States, they would open a new era of cooperation between Egypt and the Eastern Bloc. Advisers from Czechoslovakia would bring with them not only new arms, but also new manufacturing and building equipment. East Germany would agree to build a new bridge spanning the Nile between Roda and Giza, while the Russians would work with our scientists to set up our first nuclear laboratory. In Cairo, Eastern European singers, dancers and circuses would be featured in our theaters, and books from Rumania, Bulgaria and Hungary would appear in bookstores. Stores downtown would begin to carry Russian goods. Even our cinemas would play some Russian films, catering to the growing number of Eastern Europeans who had come to live among us.

When I returned to our home in Roda with Gamal in December 1956, our family had grown too large to stay in our apartment and we had to move. I loved the apartment with its views of the Nile. But it wasn't fair to the children, I thought, to bring them up without a garden to play in. I had also had a terrible fright one day when I had caught Loubna trying to climb out our ninth-story window to get to the outdoors.

"I have seen a house for rent on the Pyramids Road," Anwar said to me one morning shortly after I brought Gamal home. "Come and take a look at it."

I cried when I first saw it. Even though many of the houses on the Pyramids Road, built by Khedive Ismail to transport the foreign guests from Cairo to the Pyramids during the opening ceremonies of the Suez Canal, were lovely, this one wasn't. It was huge and gloomy. Paint was peeling off the walls, and there were large holes in the plaster where the former owner had ripped out the light fixtures when he left. The garden, though very big, had been totally neglected.

"I can't stay in this house," I cried to Anwar as we stood in the dilapidated front hall.

But he was fascinated by it. "Don't look at it the way it looks now," he urged. "See it instead all repainted."

He was right, of course, and I grew to love the house, which we would live in for the next fifteen years. I furnished it with secondhand furniture and antiques I found at auctions or at the Attarine, an old area in Alexandria. When we first moved in, the masses of foreigners leaving Egypt after the war were selling many of their household items and it was possible to buy French antique furniture, crystal chandeliers, Gallet vases and many other lovely pieces for only one tenth of their original prices. I also bought replicas of Egyptian antiquities to give our home the flavor of Egypt. What I couldn't use right away I stored in our big basement for the dowries of my children.

I love nature. I love green. I love flowers. And slowly we fixed up the garden, planting many shrubs and trees. From the balcony off my second-floor bedroom I could pick the grapes from the grapevine which grew from the terrace below and dates from the palm. Soon my mother and father moved to an apartment across the street while my sister Dalia, her husband, Mahmoud, and their four children moved into the house next to ours. We opened the gates between our gardens so that the children could always be watched by a member of the family.

In December of 1958, Nasser formed a union with Syria,

changing the name of Egypt to the United Arab Republic. I know this date very well because in 1958 I had my second daughter—and a big fight with Anwar over her name. Anwar had been in the air flying home from Syria when the baby was born. "*Mabruk*. You have a daughter. Congratulations," he was told on the plane. When he arrived at the hospital directly from the plane he told me he wanted to call our new daughter Zenoubiyya.

"Zenoubiyya?" I said to Anwar in disbelief.

"Yes," he said. "Zenoubiyya was the name of an ancient Queen of Palmyra who herself forged a unity between Egypt and Syria. Our daughter was born while I was coming home from working out the same sort of unity between our two countries, so the name is fitting."

"We are not going to call her Zenoubiyya," I said to him firmly.

"Yes, we are," he said just as firmly, and left to report to Nasser on his trip.

I was furious, and when Mrs. Nasser came to see me in the hospital right after Anwar had left I told her about my husband's choice of a name. "I can just see this poor little girl in school and all the children laughing when the teacher calls her name," I said to Tahia. "Anwar said she could be called by a nickname, Zizette, but I know the teacher won't. It will be horrible for her."

When Tahia went back to her home, Anwar was still there with her husband and she told them both how unhappy I was.

"Anwar, why are you insisting on such an awkward name?" Abdel Nasser chided Anwar. "Who carried this baby for nine months? Who went through all the pain and difficulties of birth?"

"Of course Jehan," Anwar had to reply.

"Well, then, leave Jehan to name the baby what she wants," Nasser said.

I named our baby Noha, which, the newspapers dutifully reported, meant unity. But it didn't. Noha means intelligent, and that is exactly what she was—and still is. There would be no argument over the name of our last child, born in 1961. She would be formally called Jehan after me, but she would be known by her nickname, Nana.

I did not have a nanny for my children, though most of the other government wives did. I gave my whole life to them when they were young, reading to them, feeding them, playing with them, bathing them all together in the bathtub, braiding their hair, making sure they had their vitamins and drank milk for their bones, carrot juice for their skin and eyes. When they were playing in the garden, I either watched them from the balcony or went down into the garden with them. When sometimes I took a nap in the afternoons, I brought them into my bedroom with me and locked the door so that none of them could wander away and get hurt.

I felt about my children as if they were plants. If you give a plant enough water and attention, later it will give you fruit. When they were babies I spoiled them. But when they were five or so I tried to instill in them very clearly my principles and values, and a sense of respect. They knew never to cross their legs when they sat in front of their elders, for example, for to do so was disrespectful. They addressed their father as *hadritak,* or "sir," just as they called me *hadritik,* or "ma'am." When either of us came into a room, the children always stood and offered us their chairs. If they were impolite I scolded them, and if they talked back to me I did not hesitate to smack them with a soft slipper. " 'Show your parents no sign of impatience, nor rebuke them,' " I would recite to them from the Quran.

Often we prayed together in our living room as a family, Anwar acting as the imam. Although Gamal was only five or six when he began to pray, he would stand behind his father, and my daughters and I would stand at the rear. This seemed quite natural and right to all of us. At home or in the mosques, women traditionally prayed behind the men. On Fridays, when Anwar took Gamal to the mosque to pray, I would pray at home with my daughters. Acting as the imam, it was I who would then lead them in the ritual.

Both Anwar and I wanted the children to gain the peace and understanding we ourselves had gained from our religion. Very early I taught the children to know the Holy Book, to pray and to fast. They were too young to fast for the whole month of Ramadan, so at first I encouraged them to fast for just one day so that they would not hate it. "If you complete the first day, I'll put twenty pounds in the bank for you," I encouraged them, tempting the children, for whom pennies were the norm. At age ten, my oldest daughter succeeded. But Gamal at age eight broke down completely. "Mummy," he cried, "I don't want money. I don't want toys. I just want a sandwich." By eleven or twelve, they had all worked up to fasting throughout the whole month.

I taught them also our beliefs as Muslims about death, that the spirit lives on even when its physical shell does not. Twice a year on our religious feasts, and on the birthdays of relatives who had passed away, we went as a family to the City of the Dead, the huge cemetery that stretches to the east of Cairo. On the days of the feasts, the road to the cemetery would be jammed with traffic—cars and donkey carts bearing loads of flowers and food. Like many other families, we gave away gifts of food and money to the needy who gathered there, and read verses from the Quran to bring light into even the darkest graves and comfort the souls of those no longer on earth.

Sadly, just one year after we had moved into the house on the Pyramids Road, it was my father's grave that we would all be visiting. While we were breaking the Ramadan fast at the home of my husband's secretary, Fawzi Abdel Hafez, one night, our cook and loyal friend Osman had called us to say my father was not feeling well. Immediately we rushed home, but I knew as soon as we walked in and saw Osman crying in the living room that something was terribly wrong. My father had seemed suddenly very weak, Osman told us. Osman had called immediately for the doctor and then, on impulse, had begged my father to say the Shihada, the Muslim testimony of faith. My father, trusting the advice of the man who had worked for our family since before I was born, had obeyed.

"There is no God but God, and Muhammad is His messenger," he had whispered. Moments later, he had died of a heart attack.

After my father's funeral and burial the next day, Anwar, my two brothers and my sister's husband, Mahmoud Abu Wafia, received condolences from the men in a tent we rented in front of a downtown mosque. My mother, my sister and I received condolences from the women at home. *"El-ba'iyya fiy hayatik,"* the wives of my father's friends murmured to each of us. "May the remainder of his years be added to yours." Because it was Ramadan, we could not offer those who paid respect the traditional cups of black coffee or cigarettes, but still they came, for my father had been much loved. His death affected me deeply, sending me into a deep depression. To console myself, I brought fresh flowers to his tomb every day for weeks and read many books about the soul and its flight into heaven.

When they were old enough not to be frightened by the cemetery, I took my children often to visit my father's grave near those of Auntie Zouzou, Auntie Batta and my Uncle Mustafa. To learn about life, I told them, we must first learn about death. "We came from dust and we return to dust," I would tell them as we stood in front of the tombs. "It does no good to be greedy or anxious for material things. We are all buried with nothing."

My children thought me very strict, and perhaps I was. When they returned home from school I always sat with them while they did their homework. "What words do you have for spelling?" I would ask them. Then I would make them spell the words for me. If they had a reading assignment, again I would act as the teacher, making them read it aloud. Rarely did I leave them alone. At night I sat on a couch in the hallway outside their rooms to make sure they went straight to sleep. "Watch out. Here comes the lion," they would joke when I came into their rooms.

I also made sure they did not associate with children whose families I did not know. "Jehan, why won't you let them go to this birthday party?" Anwar would say to me, being much softer with them than I was. "You are too severe with them." "But you don't know the family," I would say to Anwar.

Anwar would shake his head at me. "Still, Jehan, they should be allowed to mingle with their friends," he'd say.

It would be my turn to shake my head. "Please, Anwar, they are my children. Leave me to do my duty."

Sometimes he would overrule me and let the children do as they wanted, which made me furious. But we never quarreled in front of them. And usually we agreed.

Often Anwar told the children bedtime stories, which they liked much better than mine. Their father's stories, the children told me, were always different, while they accused me of repeating mine over and over. Often after dinner I would find

Anwar musing on the balcony, creating the story of the evening, which would always have a moral. On Friday afternoons he would play soccer with the children in the garden or games like hide-and-seek. For hours, it seemed, they would all run and laugh together.

"Anwar, you are much younger than I," I would sigh. And, indeed, I felt he was. "Why don't you have wrinkles?" I'd ask, looking at his face with envy. "You are fifteen years older, but I'm the one with the wrinkles."

"That is because of all the powder you put on your skin," he'd reply.

But I knew it wasn't. His soul was always youthful and decent, and it showed.

In 1959, two of Anwar's daughters from his first marriage, Rawia, then thirteen, and Camelia, eleven, came to live with us. Their older sister, Rokaya, was married and living with her husband. They were charming girls and I was delighted that finally they had joined us. For years I had been pestering Anwar to invite them to live with us, but he had resisted. When we had first been married, he hadn't even wanted me to meet them. "You are too young," he had told me. "There will be time."

It was not until Anwar had taken me with him to see Rawia, who was in the hospital with appendicitis, that I had met one of his first children—and Ekbal, his first wife. No one had introduced us in the hospital room, but I knew instinctively as soon as I saw her who she was. To my children's delight, Rawia and Camelia would live with us for two years on Pyramids Road. My children loved their "new" sisters and looked up to them as older and wiser. They would miss Rawia and Camelia very much when they married from our house in October of 1961.

No children are perfect, of course. Nor were my own. Sometimes they were very naughty indeed. Once I caught them smoking cigarette butts they had picked up out of the ashtrays, though they tried to hide them. "Let me smell your breath," I said to them. And I smacked them. I had to smack Loubna once, too, when I asked her to bring me something and I heard her sigh in complaint. " 'Show your parents no sign of impatience,' " I reminded her, something she already knew well. But I felt a bit sorry for Loubna. As the oldest, she had to set the example for the others.

Sometimes they ganged up on me. In Alexandria one day when Gamal was thirteen or so, I saw that he needed a haircut. "Go to the barber," I told him. The next day he hadn't gone. Nor the day after. A week later I sat him down in the chair and cut his hair myself, not very smoothly. "Perhaps now you will go to the barber to get your hair shaped better," I told him. He cried the whole time I was cutting his hair. He was outraged. And so, it turned out, was his youngest sister, Nana.

In the garden at the time we had a pet monkey, Bani, whom they knew I loved dearly, feeding him fruit and sometimes ginger ale from the bottle. "Come on, Gamal," Nana said to her brother. "Let's go cut the monkey's hair and see how Mummy feels then." I couldn't believe it when I saw the monkey. His looks were completely spoiled, much worse than Gamal's. I knew immediately it must be Nana, for she was a little devil. But I also knew she had done it to make her brother feel better. And I didn't punish either of them.

As much as I loved the house on Pyramids Road, it was quite isolated and far from the children's schools. Though many foreigners had left Egypt, the foreign schools remained open and continued to offer a better education than the new government schools. In light traffic the trip to Loubna's German school and Gamal's British school took twenty minutes, but it took more than an hour during rush hour. The trip was eased when I put all the children together in the Port Sa'id School, a private school in Zamalek, but by then there were also the afternoon music lessons which they attended in the Conservatoire.

I grew weary, too, of the mosquitoes which plagued us night and day, for the Pyramids Road was close to a branch of the Nile. The children always had spots from mosquito bites as if they had the measles, and we all had to have nets around our beds. At night I felt I was climbing into a prison made of gauze. As the children grew older, I began to look for a house nearer their schools. Most appealing was a former merchant's house in Giza that had been leased by one of Nasser's daughters. But Anwar never seemed to be home to look at it with me.

In 1960, Nasser asked Anwar to run for speaker of the National Assembly. He did and was elected. Overnight our lives changed again as Anwar began to work even harder and to travel more. The children and I rarely saw him. He was either traveling or in meetings with Nasser in Cairo or in Alexandria, where the President took all the leaders of his government to spend the summer.

I loved our house in Ma'amoura just outside Alexandria that the government allocated for us. It was isolated and private, overlooking the beach. In front of the house was our own island with a cabin on it for bathing. Because the beach was private, my daughters and I could swim and enjoy the sea. My children loved snorkeling and collecting seashells. And the garden was lovely, with a tennis court. The children were very happy there and so was I. The atmosphere was very relaxed in Alexandria, and often the Nassers, who lived next door, would come to visit us. While Anwar and the President played backgammon, Tahia and I would go for long walks around the garden.

I was startled at how much bigger Alexandria was than Port Sa'id, and how long the beach was, almost fifteen miles. Everywhere in Alexandria we were surrounded by history. It was almost too much to comprehend that this ancient seaport was first built as a city by Alexander the Great in 332 B.C., after he had conquered Egypt. For centuries Alexandria had remained the capital of the Ptolemies, housing one of the Seven Wonders of the World, the 220-foot lighthouse Tower of Pharos. The Ptolemy Queen Cleopatra had chosen Marsa Matruh, west of Alexandria, as the site for the beautiful palaces in which she lived with Julius Caesar. Legend has it that Cleopatra caused two tunnels to be drilled through the rock in a nearby lagoon to let fresh seawater in and out for her favorite swimming spot, still called Cleopatra's Bath. I took the children to swim there, and to see the ruins of the Roman amphitheater in Alexandria, where Cleopatra is said to have met with her lover Antony just before the Roman conquest in 30 B.C.

In Roman times, Alexandria had the two most celebrated royal libraries in the world and the oldest university in history. The Rosetta Stone which was the key to deciphering our ancient hieroglyphics was discovered by one of Napoleon's soldiers in 1799 just thirty-five miles east of Alexandria. When I was ten, the pivotal battle of el-Alamein in World War I had been fought sixty-five miles west of Alexandria. Bedouin tribes still roamed the desert, though leftover land mines planted by the Germans and the British had blown up many of their flocks of sheep and goats and had made them more cautious. I used to drive out to visit the Bedouin women in the desert, admiring their brightly embroidered dresses and their heavy silver bracelets and anklets covered with bells.

Although most of the Greeks, Italians and Jews had left Alexandria after the '56 war, the city still had a Mediterranean rather than an Oriental atmosphere. All along the fifteen-mile Corniche running by the sea, outdoor restaurants served grilled fish and pigeons, and vendors sold ice creams from the seaside kiosks. There were sports clubs for tennis and squash, and dining clubs right by the water. Anwar and I made many friends at the Automobile Club, the same club where before we had had our encounter with King Farouk. We could spend very little time with our friends, though, for there were many government functions we had to attend.

In Alexandria, as in Cairo, there was much official entertaining of visiting foreign delegations from Europe and the Arab world. Often the wives of our government leaders would be asked to entertain the wives of whoever was visiting. I went endlessly to lunches and meetings with the other wives, only to chat about fashion and our children. Having spent so much of my married life alone reading books on history, on politics, on the lives of women I admired, I found these functions a frustrating waste of time. Though I still hadn't been able to resume my formal schooling, the education I'd been giving myself was very satisfying. These meetings weren't. Besides, the meals were so lavish and we were spending so much time eating them I was getting fat.

"Let us try to make use of our meetings instead of wasting the time," I proposed at one of these luncheons to a group of startled government wives. "Let us have just one course to eat and then invite someone to speak to us about a different subject. We could invite Salah Abdul Sabour to speak to us about poetry, or invite the wives of the Arab ambassadors to tell us about Kuwait or Saudi Arabia. What do we know of the full picture of these countries, their economies, the political situations, the status of women?" The women looked amazed. "The next lunch will be at my house and we will have a speaker," I said.

My idea worked. And over the next year we all became more knowledgeable. At one meeting Amina el-Sa'id, the first woman publisher in Egypt and one of our first women journalists, told us how she had gotten her start working as an assistant to our most famous feminist, Huda Sha'arawi. Amina had had to publish her first articles under a man's name because no paper would agree to run the byline of a woman. At another meeting, Somayya, the wife of the Palestinian ambassador to the Arab League, showed us a film about the Israeli-occupied lands of Palestine and told us of the hardships suffered by the Palestinian refugees who now had no passports, no home and nowhere to go. After that meeting we voted to donate the money we saved on our formerly extravagent luncheons to the Palestinians, and to solicit other contributions as well.

For the first time our conversations and our interests ranged beyond the affairs of our homes and families. If our husbands were involved in domestic and world affairs, was it not our duty to be informed ourselves? Anwar was surprised when when I told him about these lunch meetings, believing that the women would have preferred to talk more about their families than social and political issues. Maybe some of them would have. But I did not want to sit silently in ignorance beside my husband while we entertained foreign diplomats. I wanted to participate. And there was so much to learn. Whenever I was invited to someone else's house I would always ask, "Whom are we going to hear?" If the hostess wanted me to help her organize it, I did. And the meetings turned out to be not only such an education for all of us but invaluable preparation for me.

For the first time I had to stand up in front of a group and speak: "Dear friends, we are going to make good use of our time today. We are going to hear our guest, Dr. So-and-so, speak to us about the status of women before and after Islam." At first I was very nervous. Like most Egyptian women, I had had no training in public speaking except for reciting my lessons in school. Indeed, my generation of women had been encouraged to remain silent, especially if there were men present. Luckily no men attended these first meetings, so I had only my own nerves to overcome and not tradition as well.

But I felt increasingly constrained. These meetings had stirred something in me I didn't know was there. The women who spoke to us were very bright and well educated. The women listening responded eagerly, taking notes and asking questions. Why shouldn't women share information and speak out like this all the time? We had minds, too, our own opinions and thoughts. Why didn't our customs allow us to express them?

"Jehan, the Indian philosopher Narayan is coming to our house for dinner tonight," Anwar told me one morning.

"I will be delighted to receive him," I replied.

When we sat down, the conversation quickly turned to Israel. Narayan wanted Egypt to reconcile its differences with Israel and couldn't understand why our two countries were enemies. "All the land on earth belongs to God, not to man," he said. "So there is no need for country to wage war against country for something that doesn't belong to either of them in the first place."

I stiffened in my chair, thinking what Israel had cost us already. Anwar shot me a nervous look, but I was going to be silent no longer. "The Israelis have tried to take land in the Sinai that does not belong to them," I said. "If they tried to take your land in India, would you say then that all the land belonged to God? Would you?" The man was silent. "We don't hate the Israelis," I went on. "But that is our land and we want it."

Still the man was silent, and out of the corner of my eye I could see Anwar looking a little nervous at my forwardness, but proud now as well. I hadn't been rude. But I had challenged this man. And he had had no answer.

"You will bring me trouble, Jehan," Anwar said to me later. "Of course you were right to say what you did. Still, it is hard for others to get used to your ways."

"I am sorry, Anwar," I told him. "But I am not content with either remaining silent or talking about the weather when there is much on my mind."

Soon it was Anwar who had much on his mind. In the spring of 1960 Anwar was working almost around the clock. Egypt's union with Syria was not going well. Tensions were high among the old members of the Revolutionary Command Council. Gossip was resurfacing about Anwar's political ambitions, causing the naturally suspicious Nasser to briefly turn against his old friend. Anwar was relieved to leave Egypt in May of 1960 to chair a conference in Conakry, West Africa, but the weather there was very hot and humid, the sort of weather which did not agree with him.

He did not look very well when we sat down to lunch on May 15, a few days after he had returned to Cairo. Though on the surface Anwar was always able to give the impression of being calm and even distanced from the petty squabbles of opportunistic politicians, inside him his disappointment and anger raged. On this day he was also worried about the health of Nasser, who had recently contracted diabetes. The strain of leading Egypt through the Revolution was beginning to exact its price.

Anwar had been up the whole night before, writing a speech. After resting for just two hours he had gone to his office, then returned home for lunch. He looked unnaturally pale as we sat down. "I think I will lie down," he said after lunch.

"That is a good idea," I told him, hiding my anxiety at his appearance. "I will keep the children very quiet."

But instead of being able to sleep Anwar began to vomit, with increasing intensity. The pain started, first in his chest, then spreading down his left arm.

I called the doctor, who arrived immediately with an electro-cardiogram machine. "He must stay in bed for three weeks without moving at all," the doctor cautioned me, looking closely at the printout of Anwar's heart rhythms. "He is not to be disturbed by anyone, or receive any phone calls. He is not even to get out of bed to use the bathroom."

"What is it, Doctor? What has happened?" I asked, my own heart pounding.

The doctor lowered his voice so that Anwar would not hear him. "He has had a heart attack," he told me.

A heart attack? Anwar was just a young man, only forty-two. A heart attack? "Is he going to die?" I asked the doctor.

He looked at me sympathetically. "Not if you take very good care of him," he said.

"Does he know he's had a heart attack?" I asked.

He shook his head. "That will just add to his worries," he said.

For the next three weeks I guarded Anwar, at times severely. The doctor had a bed from the hospital sent over so that I could crank him up and down, and I never left his side. I read to him, kept him calm with stories about the children, took away his cigarettes because the doctor had said he could no longer smoke. I let nobody come into his room, nobody, even his sister, who got extremely annoyed.

"If you really care for your brother, don't ask to see him," I told her. "If you get in, then so will your brothers and their children as well. I don't want him to make the effort to talk or to answer any questions."

I began to have nightmares. In my dreams I could see Anwar but he couldn't see me. I would call out to him, try to touch him, but he neither heard me or felt me. My children came into my dreams. What was going to happen to these little, little children? It was horrifying to think of myself as a widow, for I loved Anwar very much. During the days when I sat by his side my fears would return. Often I went into the bathroom to cry. Then I would wash my face and come back out smiling at him.

He was being a difficult patient, insisting on getting up to use the bathroom instead of the bedpan. "I can't stop him," I said to the doctor.

"Then we must tell him he's had a heart attack," the doctor said. After Anwar realized what had happened to him, he stayed in bed as he had been told.

His heart attack at such a young age changed his life, and started him on a pattern which he would follow to the end. He never smoked cigarettes again, but switched to a pipe even though the doctor in Bad Nauheim, Germany, where we went for two more weeks of convalescence, told him to smoke if the desire to smoke made him tense. Anwar was also told to take walks for his health and his nerves. After three weeks in bed at home, he started walking in our garden, first for five minutes, then ten. In Germany we spent every morning in the sanitarium and walked in the town every afternoon. And for the rest of his life Anwar would walk at least one hour almost every day, sometimes by himself, sometimes with me, sometimes with Gamal or his friend Osman Ahmad Osman, our daughter Jehan's father-in-law. When he couldn't walk he would use an exercycle.

He learned relaxing exercises. In the afternoons he would lie on our bedroom floor with a scarf over his eyes for half an hour. The children loved that, of course, and would jump on him as if he were a train or a horse. Quickly I would try to shoo them away, but Anwar always stopped me. He loved it. Yet he continued to work too hard. In 1969 he would have a second but much milder heart attack while Nasser was in Russia taking treatment for his diabetes and Anwar was acting president. Again he was struck at noontime, not vomiting this time but with the same pain. The spasm was a warning, the doctor told him, that he was putting too much stress on his heart and that he'd have to take better care of himself. And he did.

From then on, even when he became president of Egypt, he cut way back on the amount of time he worked. He learned and believed that a man who works eighteen hours a day will be no more effective than the man who works hard for eight hours and then takes his rest. Clarity of mind and the purity of thought needed to make the best decisions are best achieved before 6 P.M., he decided. Unless there was a national emergency, Anwar refused to work at night. He would sit and read reports, and answer phone calls from his ministers if they were important. But most nights he would watch cowboy movies in our basement, where we had set up a projector and some old comfortable couches and chairs. He was very careful about his rest. While I would get up at 5 A.M., Anwar would sleep sometimes until 8.

It took two heart attacks for Anwar to finally learn how to take care of himself. And I was greatly relieved. More and more he began to spend as much time as he could in Mit Abul-Kum, the village of his childhood. It was only there, in the simplicity of village life where everyone shared in the work, the laughter and the sorrows, that Anwar could truly relax. His roots were there. His heart was there. And so, increasingly, was I.

Chapter 6

el-hayah fil qura

Life in the Villages

U m Gamal, is your son well?"

"Um Gamal, I feel so sorry for you. You must have more children."

It did not matter to the women in Anwar's village of Mit Abul-Kum that I had three beautiful daughters as well as a son. No. I was known in the village only as Um Gamal, the Mother of Gamal. No matter how much I protested, in the village my daughters—or anyone's daughters—did not count. "You have only one child," the women would chide me even after my youngest daughter, Jehan, was born in 1961.

"I have four," I'd reply.

"But you have only one son. You must try to have another so he won't be all alone."

"He is not alone. He has three sisters and three half sisters as well," I would answer.

But the women would exchange side glances and shake their heads. "You should have more children," they would pronounce gravely. "Otherwise you might lose your husband."

I loved going to Anwar's village with him in the Nile Delta. The two-hour drive from Cairo was beautiful, the road lined with sycamore and eucalyptus trees and passing through miles and miles of cotton fields which were bright green in winter and filled with pale-yellow flowers in summer. As soon as we arrived in Mit Abul-Kum, my husband was transformed. Shedding his city business suit and putting on the long white galabiyya worn by all the men in the village, Anwar would go for long walks with me and the children, laughing while they rolled in the clover like puppies. Often Anwar would sing in his very loud voice the mournful songs of peasants toiling in the fields and I would wait for the neighbors to complain, but they never did. At home he taught the children to bake bread just the way he had loved to as a child, breaking an egg over the dough just before it went into the oven. They practiced and practiced to get it just right.

Anwar had been very nervous when he first brought me to his village. "You cannot go out during the day at all. You must stay inside until evening," he had told me. Not go out?

"Why?" I asked him.

"Because the people in my village will not understand you," he said.

"Anwar, what is it?" I pressed him.

He looked uneasy. "You are a woman used to the ways of the city," he explained. "The people in my village are very conservative. They will not respect you if they see you in your city clothes showing your arms and legs with your head uncovered. Such dress for women is not in our tradition."

Why, then, could I be seen in the evenings?

"That is the time set aside for visiting when the landowners and those with government jobs go out in the villages," Anwar explained. "The people are used to different ways then and accept it."

The next day I went to Tanta where I bought material for a long dress like those of the fellaheen, and a colorful scarf which I fixed to my head, as they did, with a band of flowers. And the next time we went to the village, I went out.

At first Mit Abul-Kum seemed as foreign to me as if we had gone not only to a different country but into a different century. The streets were unpaved, enveloping all who passed in their own little clouds of dust. The houses were made of baked mud and had very few windows; openings in the palm-thatched roofs let smoke out. On most roofs were piled stacks of fuel cakes made from animal dung and straw, drying in the sun. Deeply superstitious, many in the village painted their doors blue to ward off the jinns, the evil spirits described in the Quran. For more insurance against the evil eye and the curses of the envious, villagers also dipped their hands into blue paint and placed their palmprints on the outside walls to evoke the protective symbol of Fatima, the Prophet's daughter. Horse-shoes and ceramic hands bearing blue beads were also hung over the doors to the houses, fixed to the harnesses of their farm animals, even hung over the peasants' beds.

The lucky few in the village who had made their pilgrimage to Mecca had painted the story of their sacred journey on the outside walls of their houses as well. If they had crossed the Red Sea to Saudi Arabia by boat, there was a painting of a ship crossing the water. If they had flown, there was a painting of an airplane. Some had gone part of the way by bus or car. All this was depicted colorfully on the house walls, along with a rendition of the Kaaba, the black boxlike structure in the Great Mosque in Mecca which is the most sacred shrine in Islam.

The mud houses were very secure, as there was little rain, but they were very primitive. Before the power plant at the Aswan Dam was completed in 1968, there was no electricity in Mit Abul-Kum, no indoor plumbing or running water. The villagers rose by the sun and went to bed by the moon. Most of the houses were divided into two rooms, one used by the family to cook, sleep and pray in, the other to shelter their water buffaloes, donkeys, cows or even a camel, along with a few geese, ducks and chickens. In between the rooms there was usually an open area where the women hung their *hasiras*, or bamboo mats. Salted yogurt was placed in them to drip until the yogurt turned into cheese.

In the center of the village there was a high tower for the pigeons to roost in, always noisy with the flapping of wings. The beautiful white birds were a food staple to the fellaheen as well as a product to sell on market day. The only building taller than the pigeon tower was the village mosque, built shortly after the Revolution. Anwar had contributed some of its con-struction costs himself, donating his first paycheck from *el-Gumhuriyya* so that the small mud mosque of Mit Abul-Kum could be replaced by one built with red bricks and a high minaret.

The sight of the village women depressed me at first. Older women over forty dressed always in black from head to toe and the women of all ages worked harder than the men. At dawn the women rose to the voice of the muezzin calling the faithful to the morning prayer, and then prepared the morning meal of white cheese and very sweet black tea for their families. Then there were the dirt floors of their houses to sweep out, the animals to feed, the dough to make for fresh bread, water which the women pumped by hand from the village well and carried back in jugs on their heads. Just in time they then hurried to carry lunch to their husbands in the fields, where, after the meal, they joined the men for the remainder of the day, weeding, hoeing and harvesting the crops of cotton, corn, clover and wheat.

The scene in Mit Abul-Kum was always the same, the dawn sky lighting the procession of the men in their galabiyyas toward the fields, followed by the children taking the water buffaloes and the cows out to graze and drink. Flocks of white egrets would fly behind them, settling in the early-morning fields to catch the worms which had come to the surface during the night. The egrets to me made the fields look like green carpets covered with white polka dots. By midmorning the egrets had moved, settling now on the animals, where they enthusiastically picked off the bugs from their backs.

At dusk the procession would be reversed, but it was now of a different shape. The flat horizon would silhouette not only the animals and the men in their robes, but the shapeless profiles of their long-robed wives walking behind, often carrying large loads of produce on their backs. The egrets would follow them home to roost in the trees, turning the branches totally white.

Though this view was always beautiful, I shivered when first I saw it. The women seemed like nothing but beasts of burden —or even less, because the men cared more for their cows than they did for their wives. The cow was the man's livelihood, bringing him milk and cheese and butter to eat and to sell. If his wife died he would be sad, of course. But if his cow died, he would be heartbroken, having lost his life savings and his economic future. It was cheaper, after all, for a man to add another wife than it was for him to buy a new cow.

The women were constantly kept in their place by the men. "Kill your cat on your wedding night," the men would say to each other after they married, stressing their need to be the dominant one in a marriage. The birth of a daughter was joyous, as all Egyptians love children, but it did not come close to the birth of a son. *"Illi taht el-tarha malhash farha"* was a common village expression: "What is under a veil brings no joy." The men hardly referred to their wives by name, always calling out to them "Ya sitt," or "Hey, woman!" A woman could not interrupt her husband while he was talking with his friends, and had to walk behind him rather than beside him as they went to market. How miserable the women must be, I thought. I was wrong.

Why are you looking so pleased, Amina?" one woman asked another at the waterwheel where all gathered to chat and gossip at noon before the women took the midday meal to their husbands in the fields.

"I sold three chickens and fourteen eggs yesterday at the market," Amina replied. "Now I can buy enough sugar and tea for the rest of the winter."

Another woman was also smiling. "Our cow is giving so much milk that I was able to sell ten kilos of cheese. My daughter's wedding will be the most splendid in the village."

Every day I joined the women at the waterwheel to listen to their conversation. And every day, while the yoked donkey or water buffalo drew the water by walking around and around the well, wearing a blindfold so that it wouldn't get dizzy and stop, my perception of these women changed. By modern standards they were disadvantaged, the great majority being illiterate. But compared to many middle-class women in Egypt in the fifties and even the sixties, the women of the village had far more freedom and independence.

What choices did middle-class women have except for those living in Cairo or Alexandria? In the smaller cities women had little education, certainly not enough to get a good job. Their husbands from the same class clung to the old traditions, expecting their wives to stay at home and care only for them and their children. These middle-class women lived in social isolation, sharing nothing of their husbands' lives and having no lives of their own outside the home.

In the rural areas the women worked side by side with the

men, sharing in all aspects of their daily lives. Together they irrigated the fields, weeded and harvested the crops, sowed the new seeds. When the time came for a cow to bear a calf, the wife gladly assisted her husband in the delivery, for the birth of a calf was a blessing on any home. Not only would the family have milk to drink, but they would also prosper by having extra milk and cheese to sell. Individually, the women had their own businesses as well. They raised their own chickens and geese, collected the eggs, made their own cheese and sold what they could spare on market day. These were small freedoms, but it is many small things which make a whole. And in a way I envied them. They were certainly participating more in outside activities than I was when my children were small.

I loved the direct way the women talked. They were very bright and full of life, like my friend Hanem whose son was a nurse in the new village clinic. Hanem could neither read nor write, but because she, like many of the other women, listened to her portable radio all day, she was better informed than many of her contemporaries in the cities. Often I felt as though I were listening to a current-affairs professor when I visited with Hanem, she was so knowledgeable about events happening outside Egypt.

Though the men would certainly not admit it, it was the women in the village who made many of the decisions for the family, deciding when to build an extra room on their houses or to buy new animals to raise and sell. "The man is a river and the woman is a dike," went one popular expression in the villages. In Mit Abul-Kum the women had even organized a *gam'iyya*, a financial cooperative. Every month each woman would pay a small amount of money into a single fund, and each month a different woman would take the whole pot. In that way it was possible even for a very poor woman to get enough money to pay her son's brideprice or to buy a new sofa, straw rugs for her home, or a new dress which she would rush to show us all at the water wheel.

The women helped each other in many ways. The oldest women in the village looked after the young children while their mothers worked in the fields. When one woman fell sick or had a baby, the other women served food to her family and cleaned her house. If a husband died—or a child—the women took turns bringing food to the poor widow, knowing she probably had little money and was not in the mood to cook anyway.

I had not been in the village long when Um Muhammad lost her son in a military accident. When I went to pay condolences, I had no difficulty locating her house. I simply followed sounds of grief. When I entered Um Muhammad's house, I found at least sixty women all dressed in black surrounding the poor mother, crying as if their own sons had died.

"I remember him as a little boy. I can see him now dressed in his military uniform coming to the village in a Jeep just like a prince," one woman was crying out as I came through the door. Immediately all the women burst into wails, some beating their breasts and tearing at their clothes.

When the crying died down a little, another woman spoke. "I remember sitting at his wedding just five years ago," she cried out. "Never had he looked so beautiful dressed in his white galabiyya and a silk shawl. He looked like an angel." And again the women burst into shrieks of pain.

The atmosphere of loss was palpable. I began to cry myself, to feel the pain of the mother, and to share it. "We are never going to see Muhammad again," another woman sobbed, her arms around Um Muhammad. "Such a wonderful son. I remember when he brought you his first paycheck. 'Mother, this first salary is for you,' he said. 'You have suffered and sacrificed for me. You have been strict with me because you wanted to see me as an officer. Now it is my honor to thank you.'"

For three days the women came to lament with Um Muhammad, from the first rays of dawn until the evening, when they had to go tend to their own families. The village women did not leave their grieving sister for one minute. One third of them would bring lunch for everyone one day, another third the next, and so on. But they did not bring very good food, nor when they poured coffee and tea for those paying condolences did they offer sugar to sweeten it. This was not a time for pleasure. Only the food and drink offered to Um Muhammad, who would not eat, was sweetened.

"Try just this one bite of pigeon and take one swallow of this lemonade," the women urged Um Muhammad.

"Let me die," she cried out again and again. "Can there ever be happiness living without my son, never being able to see him again?" Immediately all the women would wail again.

The lamenting reached new peaks when Um Muhammad's grandchildren, who had been sent to another house during the day, returned at night. "See how small they are," the lament now ran. "It is too early for them to be orphans."

By the end of the three days, everyone, including Um Muhammad, was exhausted. By calling up every measure of grief at the young man's death, the women had helped to cleanse Um Muhammad's pain and to leave behind no hard grief. Nor did they desert her after the three days. Her close friends and neighbors stayed with her after that. And every Thursday afternoon until the fortieth-day ceremony, all the women returned to lament, though more quietly, with Um Muhammad while her grief began to fade. In Cairo we treated death much more privately and kept our sorrow to ourselves. But in the village everyone shared in everything.

Everyone had clearly defined roles, including the children, who worked all day beside their parents during the harvest of the corn, cotton and fruits. "O you who planted the oranges, who planted and who suffered," the harvest song would rise in the morning air. "Now at long last comes the time of the harvest." Before the Revolution, even children as young as five or six had spent long, hot hours in the fields, while supervisors hired by the rich landowners had moved among them with long sticks looking to smack any who were lazy or were telling jokes. All day the children had weeded the cotton crop, looking especially for the eggs of the black, ugly cotton worms, which they removed from the plants and stuffed into their galabiyyas. I was terrified of these worms, though I do not know why, and to this day cannot bear to be near a worm of any kind. I can feel whether a piece of fruit has a worm in it before I even cut into it! If I am suspicious, I won't even touch it. I would rather face a lion than a tiny worm.

Now the village children went to school. But they continued to have daily tasks as well, helping in the fields and taking the water buffaloes and cows to graze and to cool off in the Nile.

"Mummy, we took our cow to swim with those of the other children," my children would say with great excitement, eager to share in the communal responsibilities which Anwar especially wanted them to learn.

"If all Egypt could be like one village," he would say, "then together we could accomplish anything."

Every year our whole family traveled to the village for the spring school holidays, for at least two weeks of the summer before going on to Alexandria, and again for Anwar's birthday on December 25. "The children must learn their roots," Anwar would insist when the children were teenagers and preferred the more sophisticated life in Alexandria. "The village is the heart of Egypt."

For Anwar, Mit Abul-Kum represented everything that was good and enduring in life, except for the relentless poverty. And this he would try to correct by donating all the money he would make from his books to Mit Abul-Kum, as well as the money from the Nobel Peace Prize he would share with Menachem Begin of Israel after the signing of the Camp David Peace Accords in 1978. Because of this strong link between my husband and his village, my children and I still return to Mit Abul-Kum every year to honor his birthday.

When first we came to Mit Abul-Kum, Anwar and I stayed at his father's house, a small mud building much like all the others in the village. Later Anwar would buy a few feddans of land and build a small brick house which we would add on to, bit by bit. At first, though, we lived very simply, without even the butane-gas water heater we used in Cairo. For a hot bath we heated large pots of water on the primus stove, then poured it into the tub. For light we used kerosene lamps. For warmth in the winter we sat around our copper brazier, which was filled with glowing coals. To fuel the mud oven we gathered sticks and dried cornstalks. Later we would put in a hot-water heater and even a washing machine. But Anwar would insist on keeping the mud oven from his childhood for baking.

In our garden we planted fruit trees of every kind, orange, tangerine, peach, prune, mango and guava, and grew our own grapes as well. The soil was so fertile that to start a date palm we had only to put a shoot into the ground. We grew our own vegetables too, cucumbers, lettuce, marrows and tomatoes, which we flavored from our herb garden of coriander, basil and parsley. We also kept a few animals of our own, a donkey for the children to ride and a cow for milk. When we weren't there, Sharaby, a man from the village, looked after the house and gardens. Twenty-five years later, he still does.

I loved the simple food and cooking of the village. Immediately when we arrived from Cairo I would send the children to gather fuel so that we could bake milk and rice, making a delicious village pudding. I also learned to make the white cheese from the milk of our cow, and to make butter by beating together salt and cream with a wooden spoon. I never did manage to milk the cow myself. I believe there has to be a certain relationship between a cow and a person to allow the milk to flow, and that I never achieved. But I did learn to make *mish,* a salty, very pungent cheese almost like roquefort which the peasants ripen for months in a water jug with hot green peppers and the skin of a lareng, a fruit somewhere between a tangerine and an orange. For sweets we ate *naddagha* made from black molasses, and for sharpness pickled turnips and carrots which the villagers marinated in vinegar, lemon juice and herbs.

Anwar could not believe how quickly I took to the ways of the village and how quickly the women accepted me. But in almost any village, the people are completely welcoming. Any stranger walking down the dirt paths that interlace Mit Abul-Kum would hear "Welcome!" shouted out from inside the houses, followed by an invitation to share a cup of tea. No matter how poor, the villagers extend an invitation to share whatever they have with a stranger, and feel deeply disappointed if they are turned down. Not only does the Quran exhort us to be hospitable to strangers, but, as in all Arab countries, the desert tradition of feeding and even sheltering travelers can make the difference between life and death. In Iraq, for example, tribal rest houses are set aside to provide food and shelter to any traveler for three days with no questions asked. On a lesser scale, Mit Abul-Kum was no different.

"Where have you been?" Anwar asked me one evening when I came home at eight o'clock.

"I have been taking my dinner with one of the women in her house," I told him.

Anwar looked a little concerned. "What did you eat?" he asked.

"A delicious meal of marrows stuffed with rice which she had stored inside a wooden chest. Two other women dropped by and she invited them to join us, too."

"And you feel well?" he asked me.

"Very well," I replied.

His face lit up with pleasure. "Then I never have to worry about you again," he said. "You have enough immunity now to protect you from anything."

Anwar was right to be concerned about sickness, however. In his childhood, life expectancy in the villages was only thirty-three years. I supervised my children carefully, looking especially at their playmates' eyes to see if they were running or had any discharge at all, symptoms of ophthalmia. For centuries eye disease had been one of Egypt's greatest health problems, and some in the village were blind. Before the clinic came to Mit Abul-Kum, the villagers protected their babies' eyes by lining the lids with kohl, the black powder that Egyptian women had been using for eye makeup since before the days of Cleopatra. Though kohl might have helped, there was still much eye disease all over Egypt from all the dust and the flies which carried the infection from one person to the next.

There was malaria in the village, too, transmitted by the mosquitoes breeding in the swampy areas. Later I would have medical students from the university fill in the wet places where the mosquitoes bred. Two or three times we also had outbreaks of cholera, though it was certainly not as prevalent as in India. Most of the time cholera was brought back by those who had made their pilgrimage to Mecca and had mixed there with the Indians and other Asians. The government was very conscious of the danger from cholera and would immediately quarantine the area in which it was found and send some vaccine. Still, we were vulnerable to polio, to measles, to any contagious diseases and infections that breed in hot and not always sanitary conditions.

The greatest sickness in Mit Abul-Kum and in all the farming villages, however, was bilharzia, a parasite carried by snails living in the stagnant waters of the irrigation ditches and canals off the Nile. Before the Revolution brought clinics to the village, 70 percent of the villagers suffered from bilharzia, for there was no one in the village who did not come into daily contact with the water. The women washed their families' clothes and dishes in it. The children stood in the water to wash down the family animals and to cool themselves off in the scorching Egyptian sun. The men waded in it, clearing the ditches for better irrigation.

There was no way to avoid the parasites from the bilharzia-infected snails, which lived by the thousands just on the edge of the water. Like the tiniest of worms, visible only through a microscope, the parasites entered the bloodstream through the skin of the peasants and their children and settled in their livers and spleens, eventually causing cancer. The first symptoms, which the peasants often ignored, were aching joints, a low fever and a feeling of exhaustion. Often it was not until they found blood in their urine that they realized they were infected. By then there was little they could do about it.

Now bilharzia can be diagnosed and is easily treated by an injection which kills the worm. And the cure has come just in time. It is ironic that the Aswan High Dam, in addition to providing great benefits to the farmer, has also increased the incidence of bilharzia by not allowing the Nile to flood and naturally cleanse itself. So the peasants keep infecting and rein-fecting themselves with the invisible worm as they continue to work in the water.

Although the Revolution brought many new health clinics to the rural areas, many among the fellaheen believed more in the healing power of religion than they did in science. Many villages had a sheikh or sheikha, a man or woman who acted as the local healer, exorcist, sorcerer, and manipulator of fortune. In Mit Abul-Kum, these duties were performed by Sheikh Has-san, one of the few in the village who could read or write, and the only one believed to be effective in devising the *hegab*, tiny bits of paper on which were written specific verses of the Quran selected for whatever was troubling the villagers. Perhaps a jealous wife wished her husband to lose interest in his second wife, or a woman with many daughters wished to be blessed with a son. Whatever the quest, the sheikh would prescribe a *hegab* for a small fee of ten piasters, then specify where it should best be placed to be effective—in the undergarments, in a pouch around the neck, maybe even sewn into a corner of a bedsheet.

The sheikh would also prescribe certain rites to supplement the power of the Holy Book: for infertility, perhaps the sacri-fice of a black duck; for fever, a diet limited to the white meat of chicken or a green leaf consumed at the exact moment of sunset. I did not believe at all in the magic powers of these healers, but Anwar had believed in them when he was young. As a child he had developed a white spot on his arm which was very obvious because of his dark skin. His father worked in the military hospitals and so could take Anwar to the best doctors, but none of the many medicines they prescribed did anything. Finally his father took him to the woman in the village who made tatoos. She put needles around the white spot and told Anwar's father the spot would turn green and soon disappear. It did.

Though I did not believe in magic, I did believe in the natural herbs many Egyptians used and still use to heal, especially in the villages. When my children were sick I took them to the new clinic and followed the directions of the doctor. But I also used the natural remedies. When they suffered from stomachaches, I gave them tea made from cumin or camomile. Constipation was relieved by aloe and bitter apple leaves. When they had coughs, I gave them boiled guava leaves, and when they seemed rundown a brew of boiled hibiscus leaves which strengthened the blood. These natural cures have been carried down from generation to generation and in many cases are still more effective than chemicals and synthetics. Even now when I get sunburned I remember Auntie Zouzou saying to my mother many years ago after a day on the beach, "No, no. Don't use Nivea. Put on yogurt." And Auntie Zouzou had been right. Immediately the yogurt had drawn the heat from my shoulders, and the burn had quickly healed.

There were some things in the village, however, I could never accept or get used to. I would not let my children near the water in Mit Abul-Kum for fear of bilharzia, nor could I ever bring myself to look closely into the canals, even though I knew that the parasitic worms were invisible. Even the thought of a worm made me feel faint. One of the favorite hobbies of Egyptian children was to buy a silkworm and keep it in a box with leaves and a stick. If they were lucky, the children would then watch the worm spin a cocoon and see it emerge months later as a butterfly. But my children were forbidden even to bring a silkworm into the house and had to watch it and feed it instead at the house of a friend. I was even nervous of the scarab, the large beetle which the ancient Egyptians considered sacred and reproduced so often in their temples. To me they were just large bugs, and I discouraged my children from playing a favorite village game of making a small water wheel out of cornstalks and tying a scarab to it. In its frenzy to get away, the scarab would fly in furious circles, rotating the pretend water wheel just as the blindfolded donkeys and buffaloes did the real ones.

Trickery was also a part of village life, I was learning from the women at the waterwheel, especially in achieving a good marriage for a daughter. One woman had duped a boy's family into a marriage contract with her daughter, who was quite ugly, by showing them her younger and prettier sister; after the deal was struck, the other sister was substituted. Another got around the minimum age of sixteen for marriage by sending an older daughter to the doctor to get a certificate for her age, then substituting her fourteen-year-old daughter at the actual ceremony. Still, village girls rarely entered marriage reluctantly. Instead of the Western custom of leaving a baby tooth under a pillow to be rewarded with a wish by the Tooth Fairy, little girls in the villages had only one wish. Throwing their teeth into the air, they would chant, "*Khudi sinnit el-gamusa widdini sinnit el-'arusa!* Take the teeth of the buffalo and give me the teeth of the bride!"

Marriage. Marriage. Marriage. Around the waterwheel it seemed to be the core of every village woman's life. For the mothers of sons, marriage meant a rest and lifelong security, because their daughters-in-law not only came to live in their homes but took over all the cooking and cleaning as well. For the mothers of daughters, marriage not only meant the end of their financial support but the successful fruition of all the dreams they had held for their girls. There were no other alternatives for women in the village, and a daughter who remained single was considered an embarrassment to the whole family. Marriage was better, no matter what the cost.

"See what my husband did to me yesterday," one woman moaned as we sat around the water wheel one evening. Ostensibly she was looking for sympathy for her swollen cheek, but actually she was proud that her husband cared enough about her to beat her. A game of one-upmanship followed, the women talking more openly than women in the cities ever did about their intimacies with their husbands. Perhaps such bragging was healthy, and understandable really in a society where a woman's greatest fear was that her husband might divorce her. But always my face would burn with embarrassment. I would never share such intimacies with anyone, not even my mother, to whom I was very close. But then, marriages in the village were very public affairs and wedding days the most joyous of all celebrations.

I went to hundreds of weddings in Mit Abul-Kum. Hundreds. And the rituals were always the same. With all the other village women, I would crowd into the home of the bride's family to pay my respects to the bride-to-be on the morning of her wedding day. Every bride always looked her best, for the night before her friends had gathered to bathe her, to lay out her clothes and jewelry in preparation, and to stain the palms of her hands and the soles of her feet with henna. Henna has been used as a cosmetic in Egypt since the time of the ancient Egyptians, its color considered not only beautiful but a sign of purity. In other parts of the Arab world, women stained their hands and feet with the rich orange-red dye each week, while I, like many others, have always used it for the health of my hair.

Though only women visited the bride before her wedding, everyone from the richest landowner to the poorest beggar gathered just before sunset to celebrate the bride's move to her new home. "A woman makes two outings in her life," runs an old village proverb. "One from the house of her father to the house of her husband, and the other from her husband's house to her grave." The excitement grew as the wedding parade made its way through the narrow streets of Mit Abul-Kum.

First, beating on drums, clapping and singing special songs to celebrate the marriage, came all the young girls in the village, including my daughters. Next, the bride's trousseau—her shining new copper pots, a brightly painted wooden chest, all her bedroom furniture, a new mattress, a bed, a new wardrobe, a sofa—was put into an open car or donkey-drawn carts and shown off to the crowd. All of us shouted our congratulations as the carts rolled through the streets, and shouted even louder as the bride's family ceremoniously carried the great trays of ducks, geese, vegetables, rice, beans, bread and sweets which would make up the wedding feast. But the loudest shouts of all came when the bride and groom themselves paraded through the streets.

Seated in an open car covered with flowers or in a cart drawn by a flower-bedecked donkey, the bride and some of her women relatives headed the procession. Often the men fired ceremonial shots into the air as the bride's party passed, while the women and I made the *zaghreet* and threw pinches of salt into the air to ward off the evil eye. The bridegroom, coming from the house of his best friend, followed behind the bride. He too had been bathed by his friends and had henna put on his hands. They had dressed him in a turban and galabiyya of the finest cotton and given him a sword to carry in his hand. Now, carrying candles and torches, his friends made a ring around him and walked with him until he reached his bride waiting for him at his family's house. While the sheikh made the marriage contract between the bride's father and the groom, the bride and her friends performed one last ritual.

The bride sat in a chair surrounded by her friends, a Quran in her lap as a good omen that God would take care of her. To ensure her future prosperity, the bride put her feet into a large copper pot of water, warmed if the marriage was taking place in the winter or cooled during the summer, while her friends draped green leaves on her head and dropped more leaves into the water. So that her new life would start sweetly, they also brought sugar to put into her mouth. When the contract was signed, the villagers celebrated all night until dawn the passage of the young girl and boy to lives of responsibility of wife and husband.

The birth of a child prompted no less an outpouring of joy. Proud new parents often announced their news by outlining their houses with lights or stringing lights on their trees or shrubs. During the *sebu'a* on the seventh day, everyone in the village brought a present to the family, a duck, a goose, sometimes even a sheep, loaves of bread or *fetir meshaltet,* a very rich loaf baked with cream and eaten with honey. Some brought presents of money, which was then considered a debt. When the donor had a baby, that same amount had to be returned.

But because the gift of a child was the greatest gift we could receive, the parents were often frightened of envy. The most welcome birth presents, which Anwar and I usually gave, were ones to ward off the evil eye, perhaps a replica of the hand of Fatima, the Prophet's daughter, or a gold locket or bracelet engraved with inscriptions from the sura "Ya Sin." For added protection, new parents in the village braided a blue bead into the front of the baby's hair so that anyone admiring the baby would first see the color blue. When our granddaughter Jehan was born during Anwar's trip to Jerusalem, the former Prime Minister of Israel, Golda Meir, would send birth presents of a golden hand of Fatima and earrings of blue beads.

A few new parents in the villages went to even greater lengths to downplay their good fortune. Some expectant parents made no preparations at all for the birth, not even preparing a carry-cot or making the baby's clothes until their child was safely born. Even after the birth some new parents continued to refuse to buy anything at all for their new baby, believing that envy of them would be higher if the infant looked well clothed and prosperous. Instead these parents tried to disguise their good luck by begging others to clothe their poor and forlorn offspring.

This superstition was more understandable when the infant mortality rate in Egypt was 50 percent. But even after the Revolution when medical services were available to everyone, some of the superstitions and rituals remained intact. So that no one would envy their good fortune, a few anxious mothers continued to dress their young babies in rags and even to neglect their health until the children were three or four years old. Because boys were more valued than girls and therefore more susceptible to the evil eye, some parents even dressed their sons in girl's clothing for the first year.

To this day in the villages, never do you say to a new mother, "What a beautiful baby." No. That would be inviting disaster. "Isn't he or she ugly" or "What a horrible little creature" are the reactions the mother wants to hear. Even the child's name is sometimes chosen to protect him. One of the men who worked for my parents was named Shahhat, which means beggar. "Why did your parents give you such a humiliating name?" I asked him as a child. "Because every baby my mother had died," Shahhat told me. "They decided before I was born to call me 'beggar' so no one would envy me and I would live. It must have worked."

These superstitions and rituals were not limited to just weddings and births in the villages. There were rituals for almost everything, from freshening a cow whose milk had dried up to ensuring the birth of a son. Women who couldn't conceive a child at all often ate a handful of Nile mud to bring fertility.

Women whose babies had been stillborn sometimes buried the afterbirth under the threshold of the house or in a wall, believing that this would help their next babies to be born alive.

One of my favorite rituals occurred once a week. After the Friday noon prayers, the lovely smell of *bukhur* often spread through the houses of the village, the scent of incense. To purge any envy from their homes, many fellaheen celebrated our holy day by heating lumps of resin on their *furns* or on glowing coals in clay pots. The fresh and pungent smell of the smoke was beautiful, much like the scent from frankincense and myrrh, treasured all over the world in ancient times. Now the *bukhur* was from the mistika tree but no less aromatic. I often joined in this age-old ceremony myself, carrying our own smoking clay pot of *bukhur* from room to room to bless our home. In other village houses, the fellaheen added another ritual, ceremoniously crossing through the smoke of the *bukhur* seven times to ensure a wish.

The villagers also worried continuously about outsmarting the jinns, believing that the devilish spirits could ruin their lives. Fingernail parings and sheared hair had to be buried because the villagers feared that the jinns could use them to cause mischief, even to possess their bodies. The most superstitious were careful to take off their clothes properly at night, for the jinns could step into anybody's clothing left inside out. Even the long modest dresses of the women and the galabiyyas of the men which shielded the ground where they walked were thought to discourage the jinns who could enchant people by watching where they walked and stepping in their footsteps.

Some of these superstitions frustrated me, for they prevented women especially from participating in a more modern life. I will never forget the chance encounter I had with a young woman one morning on the road from Mit Abul-Kum to Alexandria. My car had two flat tires, and the driver had left me to work on my papers in the car while he went in search of a new tire. Seeing the stranded car, the landowner who owned the fields on both sides of the road had come to see if he could help.

"Will you wait in my home with my wife?" he inquired politely when he recognized me.

"No, thank you. It is a lovely day," I told him. "I will just wait here."

But his good intentions would not be diverted. "Then I shall send you someone to keep you company," he told me.

She was thin, very thin. As she approached me from the fields, tucking her sparse hair into her head scarf, I was struck by her pallor and her fragility. When she reached my side and we started to chat, I could see from the sunken hollows under her cheekbones and the white spots on her skin that she was seriously ill.

Though she was obviously sick, she was certainly not shy. In the direct way of most women in the countryside, she quickly asked me my name, whether I was married and whether I had any children. I told her I was called Jehan, but when she heard about my son she addressed me only as Um Gamal.

"You are blessed by God, Um Gamal, to have a son," she said to me sadly. "I have none, and my husband has just brought a second wife who is young and healthy into his home." That alone might have explained why she was so thin, since it was not uncommon for wives to worry themselves sick over the fear of another wife coming into the house, or the more dreaded fear of divorce. But this young woman looked near death.

"What medicine are you taking for your health?" I asked her gently. "What is the doctor giving you?"

"Doctor?" she said to me, shaking her head. "There is nothing a doctor can do for me, Um Gamal. It is an evil spirit which has possessed me, that has ruined my health and taken away my chances to have a son." And she told me about her "possession" four years before when two big black birds which had flown before her one morning had suddenly turned to look at her. "At the instant their eyes met mine I felt the jinn leap up from the grass and fix itself inside me," she said. "I knew immediately what had happened and went that night to the sorcerer. But none of the *hegab* he has written for me since have ever worked and now I have no more money to give him. Soon I will be too weak to work and my husband will divorce me."

I looked at her sadly, sympathizing with her story but believing that her suffering was unnecessary. I had seen symptoms like hers before and suspected she was suffering from severe anemia, a condition that could be reversed.

"Please," I urged her, "please come with me now to see a doctor."

But she refused, insisting that her problem was not physical but came from the spirits. I could see the driver returning and knew I was running out of time. If I could not convince this young woman to get medical help now, the next time I would pass by on this road she might be dead.

"If you will not come with me to see a doctor, then come and try my sorcerer instead," I said to her quickly. "He is famous in all Cairo and makes his *hegab* very, very small. He rolls them into tiny colored balls and these you do not wear around your neck or sew into your clothes. Instead you swallow them and they remain inside you where the jinn is. Few spirits are strong enough to resist the *hegab* at such close quarters, and almost all are driven off."

She seemed more interested in this proposal, and I elaborated, hoping to win her over. "This sorcerer is rich and dresses only in white," I told her. "The rooms he practices in are huge, but still you find that people must line up to see him. He has taught others a little of his magic, and they too are dressed in white and move about the room to help him."

She looked at me as spellbound as if I too were magic. "I will come to your sorcerer," she said.

The next week I picked her up on my way home to Cairo and took her to my doctor, whispering to him the problem. She started swallowing the *hegab* he prescribed, and every week for the next months when I again would pick her up to take her to Cairo her color looked better and the white spots were less apparent. The last time I drove her home she told me the sorcerer had pronounced her health in good order. I never saw her again, although I always looked for her as I drove by the field she worked in. In my mind, I picture her spending her time at home, looking after her son.

I was frustrated, too, by the poverty so many in the villages were living in, and the helplessness so many women felt. My ears rang with all the pleas for help I was getting from women wherever I went in Mit Abul-Kum and in the neighboring villages as well.

"Madam, have you any money to spare? My husband has been sick for three months and still cannot leave his bed to work."

"Madam, God keep you, just ten pounds. Three daughters I have, but not a single son. And now my husband has left me for another."

"Madam, what can I do? My husband has gambled away all of his money and he beats me. I want to take my children and run away from him, but last week he sold my sewing machine and now I have no way to support my family. Can you help me?"

"What is your name?" I asked the woman whose husband had sold her sewing machine.

"Nawwal," she replied, her eyes downcast.

I gave her ten pounds, as I did to almost all the women who asked, but I could not keep giving forever. My husband was speaker of the Parliament, not a rich king. And the women's pleas for money were so counterproductive. What good would the gift of ten pounds or even twenty pounds do? It would last maybe two weeks in the rural areas, and then they would have to beg for more.

There had to be some way these women could get together and make enough money to support their families without having to depend totally on their sometimes tyrannical husbands. I thought of the cooperative effort about which I had learned so much while sitting around the water wheel in Mit Abul-Kum. If women in the village could cooperate when one was sick or pregnant or marrying off a child, why, then, could not all women group together to help one another make money and support themselves? Egypt had won her independence from foreign occupiers, but Egyptian women in the villages had not yet won theirs. Was it not time for them to begin their own Revolution? But how?

Over and over, the women's pleas for money played themselves in my mind. I felt haunted and had difficulty sleeping. Since Anwar had been elected speaker of the Parliament, as his wife I had some degree of influence or at least access to powerful people. But what could I do to help? Nawwal's story about the loss of her sewing machine because of her husband's gambling disturbed me greatly. Here she had owned something with which she could have made money, only to lose it. A sewing machine. A sewing machine!

"I'm here to see the Governor, please."

"Yes, Mrs. Sadat, how nice to see you. How can I help you?"

"I want a building."

"A building?"

"Yes, I want to start a project training women to work. And I also want some sewing machines."

"Sewing machines?"

"Yes. I am going to start a sewing cooperative so that the women in your governorate can support themselves."

The Governor of Munufiyya province, in which Mit Abul-Kum was located, looked at me dumbfounded. "The Delta is crowded, madam, as you well know. And all the mansions once owned by the big landowners have long been taken over as government offices."

I was expecting that. "There must be a building somewhere," I insisted. "We do not need a palace, only something with four walls to keep out the flies and dust."

The Governor thought for a minute. "There is an old empty police station in the town of Talla," he finally said. "The walls are cracked and it will not be long before the building falls down. But it might be usable."

"I'll take it," I told him. "And the sewing machines?"

"Perhaps there are some left in the government storerooms," he said, beginning to enjoy this. "I remember there was a project which never was completed . . ."

The Governor was right. The police station in Talla, a town slightly larger than Mit Abul-Kum, certainly was no palace. But it existed. Now I had to see if any women would actually work for money, having been trained for centuries to ask for it instead. There was only one way to find out.

"Women who want to work! Come to the abandoned police station tomorrow night." Borrowing a loudspeaker and a microphone from the Governor and putting the speaker on top of my car, I asked the driver to take me around the narrow, dusty streets of Talla. "Come if you are single, married, widowed or divorced," I shouted through the public-address system. "Come if you have a skill or if you want to be trained in one. But do not come if you are lazy. Come only if you are ready to work hard and fast to earn money for your families. Come to the police station tomorrow night during the hour of visiting."

All day long my heart was pounding. I had asked Anwar what he thought of my idea, and he had been neither encouraging nor discouraging, not really believing I would go through with it. Now the meeting at the police station was about to begin, and I was not sure of my plan myself. How many would come? Would anyone come at all? I arrived early in Talla. To my great relief, there was already a crowd of people waiting for the meeting to start. Men were sitting on one side of the room, curious to see how women could possibly make money, and curious to see the woman who had been shouting from her car in the streets. The women were sitting on the other side, eager but puzzled. And the questions began.

"How can we afford sewing machines?"

"The government will buy all the materials first," I answered. "Then from our profits we shall pay them back."

"Who will look after the children while we are working?"

"We will," I said. "We will set up a nursery in the building for your children and for other children in the village as well. And we won't work too long hours, so there will still be time to prepare the meals for our families."

"Whom can we sell the clothes to? Nobody in the village will be able to afford them."

"We will take them to Cairo and sell them there," I said.

A buzz ran around the room. Cairo? Few had ever even been there.

"The clothes must be as well made as are the clothes in the city," I warned them. "If they are, I know there are shops that will buy them from us."

"What if the clothes we make are not good enough to sell?"

"Then we will make jam or pickles, anything so we can make money," I said. "We will start at this same time next week. Come if you want to start a new life. Come if you want to earn self-respect and the respect of your husbands. Surprise those who do not think their wives can make money of their own."

Nawwal was first in line at the police station the next week, along with twenty-five other women who knew how to cut and sew. At first we made simple aprons while the more expert sewers hand-embroidered scarves and cloths. When all the women were well trained, we moved on to men's work clothes, bush shirts and trousers, as well as children's clothes and embroidered nightgowns for women. Every day I drove two hours from Cairo to supervise and encourage the women, then two hours back so that I could be with my family.

"This seam is not straight," I would chide one woman. "Look how uneven this hem is," I would criticize another.

Soon the clothes were nearly perfect. "What is wrong, Madame Jehan?" the women asked with concern. "You are so quiet. Do you no longer love us?"

One day soon afterward, a friend of mine in Cairo with a factory of her own told me about her contracts with the Army and large factory owners to make uniforms and work clothes. "Why don't you see whether you can make local contracts in Munufiyya for clothes from the Talla cooperative?" she asked me. "I will lend you my cutter, who is very experienced. He can do all the measuring and cutting. The women at Talla can do the sewing."

I was very grateful to her and excited about the idea. At some point the Talla cooperative had to make enough money to become self-supporting. Why not now? The next time I was in Talla, I called on the owner of a local cloth manufacturing company. "We can make excellent work clothes for your employees cheaply and quickly," I told him. "Why send your orders out of Munufiyya when the women at Talla can provide what you need locally?"

The owner called in his factory supervisor. "Do we need work suits?" he asked him.

"Yes," the supervisor said.

We got the order.

I was thrilled. True to her word, my friend in Cairo loaned us her cutter, who went to the cloth factory and measured all the workers, then went back to Talla to cut the material. In no time the women sewed all the uniforms, close to five thousand shirts and pants. Bursting with pride, I delivered the work suits to the factory owner.

"The women in Talla are excellent workers," I gushed to the owner, sitting with him in his office. "You will be very pleased, even amazed, at the quality of their work."

A knock came at the door. "Would you like to see the work clothes?" the factory supervisor asked. And with that, nine men walked into the office. If they were short, their shirtsleeves hung below their hands. It they were tall, the trousers stopped at the knees and looked like shorts.

I felt my face growing red and willed the earth to swallow me up. "This is our fault," I managed to say to the owner. "I will take all of the uniforms back to the women. Give us just two weeks and you will have the proper sizes."

I was furious at the cutter. "You have destroyed all that we have worked for," I said to him, wanting to kill him. "You said you were an expert, that you would work with the women and make sure there were no mistakes. If we were not ready to deliver these uniforms, then why didn't you tell me?"

He seemed remarkably calm. "Do not worry, madam," he assured me. "Give me ten days. You will see. We know our work."

I went back to Cairo in great distress. What was the point of my working so hard with the women at Talla if this was the result? I had taken much time away from my family. I would do better just to stay at home and tend to my children. I was so upset I couldn't sleep, tossing and turning with conflict and self-doubt. Why had I thought I could benefit the women? I had done nothing but bring embarrassment and humiliation on them. The cutter had seemed so confident. How could I ever trust him—or myself—again?

Ten days later, I returned to the factory in Munufiyya. "Are the clothes ready?" I asked the cutter.

"Yes, madam," he assured me. "You will see."

When I sat once again with the owner, I felt none of the confidence and exhilaration I had had at our prior meeting. My heart sank further still when I heard the knock on the door.

"Would you like to see the clothes?" the supervisor asked.

I nodded, not knowing whether I could bear to be so humiliated again. And the line of workers entered, one after another, dressed this time in beautifully made, well-fitting new uniforms. I couldn't believe my eyes. Was I at a fashion show? The clothes were 100 percent perfect!

"Excellent," the factory owner said.

"How did you do it?" I asked the cutter afterward. "These new clothes are perfection!"

"They are not new," he told me. "I did nothing."

I was totally confused. "But they must be new," I insisted. "The last time nothing fit at all."

"The last time I forgot to bribe the supervisor," the cutter explained. "He dressed the workers like that on purpose, putting the smallest clothes on the tallest men, the biggest sizes on the smallest."

I felt my breath fall away. What was he saying? It had never occurred to me to bribe the supervisor.

For weeks afterward I struggled with the principles of it. How naive and innocent I had been, just an idealistic housewife. I had done my best for the women at Talla, but that hadn't been enough. If I was to continue, I would have to face the reality of the ways of doing business. Not everyone, I was sure, was as corrupt as the supervisor. But how would I ever know? At least I should be prepared. Sure enough, it happened again when I ordered hundreds of yards of lace to be cut for the women to sew on the hemlines of nightgowns. All the lace came up short until I went to the woman who measured the lace, bearing gifts of perfume and the best coffee from Yemen. Suddenly all the lace was the right length. How simple. If this was the way we had to do business, then so be it. The women at Talla needed the money and the dignity of their new profession.

I was as thrilled as they were. At last the women had an opportunity to support themselves and to help their families. Finally I had something concrete to offer them so they wouldn't feel so dependent and vulnerable. Around the waterwheel in Mit Abul-Kum, the conversation changed.

"I don't know what will become of us," Fatima cried one morning. "My husband has left me. How am I to feed our six children?"

"Be patient. He will come back," the other women tried to calm her.

But Fatima was inconsolable. "He said the children were always rude, pushing and shoving each other. But he was the one who wanted so many children."

"I feel sympathy for you," I told Fatima. "But this is your fate. Instead of crying, why don't you do something to occupy yourself? Come and work at Talla."

Fatima only cried harder. "But I can't sew," she said.

"Then we will train you," I said.

Instead of waiting around the next day for her husband to return, she came with me to Talla. Soon she was busy and supporting her children on her own, for her husband never did return.

The work of the women continued to improve while at the same time they were learning more and more designs. A year after the uniform incident, the women were ready to display their full line of goods. Packing up three hundred boxes of clothes and handicrafts, twenty-five women and I set out in minibuses for Cairo and a display that other volunteers had helped to arrange in the lobby of the Sheraton Hotel. The Talla women, many of whom had never seen Cairo, could not believe their eyes when the tall buildings came into view. "Will they fall?" one asked me anxiously. With every car horn blast the women jumped in fright, then clung to one another on the crowded, bustling pavement in front of the hotel. Never had they seen so many people in such a hurry, people they did not even know. But what happened inside the hotel rendered them speechless.

Besides our display, an *haute couture* fashion show was taking place. While the women from Talla, covered in black from head to toe, looked on in disbelief, fashion models swept in and out of the dressing rooms wearing practically nothing at all. When one model went out to display a silk nightgown, several of the women covered their eyes. "There is a man," I heard one of them scream. And sure enough, there was the designer in the dressing room with his models while they stripped down to their underwear before putting on the next outfit. This was not strange to the models, but it was unheard of to the women from the village. It was all I could do to get them to set out the clothes we had brought to sell from Talla, they were so spellbound by all they were seeing so suddenly in Cairo.

They were just as spellbound by their success. When the buses returned to Talla that night, every single item we had brought had been sold. Half the profits would go to the women, the other half to improve the cooperative.

How I loved the spirit of the village women. No longer was I lonely when Anwar was away, for wherever I went the women now knew me by name and would rush to hug and kiss me. Emotions run very close to the surface in the villages, and the fellaheen express affection and sorrow easily and openly. They are almost telepathic to anything happening in the villages. Because of this sensitivity, they knew something was very wrong one day in 1965 when I drove very fast through our village without returning their cries of welcome.

"Mummy, Gamal has put his eye out," my daughter Loubna had sobbed when I returned at lunchtime from Talla. "Pappi has taken him to the hospital."

Gamal? Gamal! I thought I was going to faint. All I could

think of was my son walking around with a patch on his eye like Moshe Dayan.

"He was running after the duck to save him from being eaten by the dogs, and he fell on the spikes of the iron fence," Loubna went on. "There was blood everywhere on him and Pappi took him away to the hospital."

I had to go to my son. But which hospital was he in? We had no phone, but the Governor of Munufiyya did. I would go there first to save time. En route I sped by the women working in the cooperative, only to meet Anwar's car in the road returning home.

"Gamal! Gamal!" I cried, seeing the bandage on his eye through the window.

"He is all right," Anwar quickly assured me. "He cut his face under his eye, and it was so swollen and there was so much blood it seemed as if he had put out his eye. The doctors have stitched up his wound and he will be fine."

"Thank God," I said, taking our nine-year-old son home to recover from the anesthesia in bed.

"*Salma, ya salaama, Gamal rigi' bil salaama.*" What was this sound of singing? "Safely, oh safe one, Gamal has come home safely . . . " I looked out the window to see two cattle trucks stopping in front of our home, filled in the back with the women from my project and other women from the village as well. Singing and dancing, they crowded into Gamal's room, clapping in rhythm to our traditional song of celebration for a soldier returned from war.

How had they known he'd been hurt? How had they known he was all right? As if there were an invisible telephone linking all in the village together, the women had immediately known what had gone wrong, and what had gone right. Tears rolled down my cheeks from relief over Gamal and love for these women. For half an hour they danced and celebrated in Gamal's bedroom, then left as quickly as they had arrived. Only a small scar would remain under Gamal's eye, a scar his father had in the exact same place from a fall he had taken at the same age. But the warmth and support the women left behind was very large. There was nothing I would not do to try to help them.

After the cooperative's first sellout success in Cairo, I worked even harder. More and more women came to join what became known as the Society for Social Development. From twenty-five sewing machines we would grow to one hundred and twenty-five. The Ministry of Social Affairs would build us a new building just before the police station fell down, and we would add a carpentry workshop for men. Our production would rise from sixty work suits a day to four thousand as we opened two other workshop cooperatives in Munufiyya as well as one each in Beni Suef and Alexandria.

Still Nawwal is working in Talla. When last I saw her, she, like the other women, had been quick to study the new fashions in Cairo and now was wearing a dress with the sleeves tapered tight to the elbow, then opening out like a flower. She was also wearing new gold bracelets on both her wrists and was full of enthusiasm. "My husband no longer gambles or beats me," she told me happily. "Now he has respect for me."

I was very satisfied with my first project.

"What do you think?" I asked Anwar the day a branch of the Talla workshop opened in Mit Abul-Kum.

"Excellent. Never would I have believed it was possible," he told me. "But be careful, for not everyone is happy to see women out of the home and working. They still have to do their duties as wives. And so do you."

I laughed. "You will always be a village man, Anwar," I teased him. "But you cannot have your Revolution only for the men. Some of it must belong to the women."

He smiled. "Well, then, I shall leave the women of Egypt to you," he said. "I shall put my mind on the other matters facing the country."

"I accept this arrangement," I told him. "You will see how proud you will be."

Neither of us would be proud, however, of a new and sinister turn the Revolution had taken.

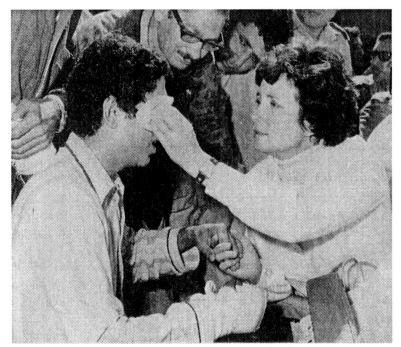

<u>*awga' misr*</u>

The Agony of Egypt

Madam, what is happening in the village of Kamshish is inhuman," a village leader whispered to me one day in the summer of 1966 in Mit Abul-Kum. "Yesterday military-police officers dragged the father of the el-Fiqqi family out of his house and tied a rope around his neck. 'Get down on your hands and knees like a donkey,' they yelled at him. Then they made him crawl around the streets of the village, ordering the fellaheen to spit on him as a symbol of feudalism."

Nervously the leader averted his eyes, knowing he should not be criticizing the government to the wife of the Speaker of the Assembly and one of the Revolutionists. But his heart was breaking from what he had seen. "Mrs. Sadat, we love your husband and we love the Revolution," he said in anguish. "But the people will hate the Revolution if they see things like this. I have never liked this rich family, but to see a man treated even worse than an animal will bring more sympathy to the family than to the Revolution. It's too humiliating."

Fear. Repression. Betrayal. Humiliation. These would be the bitter legacy of the government's terrible, two-year-long campaign to purge the enemies of the Revolution in the mid-sixties. Amid reports that the Muslim Brotherhood was hatching yet another plot against the government, Defense Minister Abdel Hakim Amer in 1965 had been ordered to use his military police to root out and arrest all militant fundamentalists. Not long afterward, President Nasser had moved as well against the other great obstacle to the goals of the Revolution, the last vestiges of the landowning elite. It had long been rumored that several hundred "feudal" families in the rural areas continued to hold and farm great quantities of land illegally. In the spring of 1966 Nasser had decided to strip these feudalists of their property. The highly controversial "Committee for the Liquidation of Feudalism" was formed to document and sequester the property of all who had dared to violate the laws of land reform. As with the campaign against the Muslim Brotherhood, Defense Minister Amer had been placed at the head of this effort to complete the socialist ideals of the government. And a reign of terror had begun.

There was nothing wrong with Nasser's intent, but much wrong with the way Amer's forty-member committee was implementing it. Many of Amer's influential colleagues were running out of control, using their new positions of power to crush anyone they disliked and to stifle all criticism of the government. No one was exempt from the new wave of suspicions and arrests. Anyone suspected of being a member of the Brothers or even knowing one was being seized for questioning and often tortured. The property of former politicians was being appropriated in the name of the state. Members of the Army were taking charge of all public services, and anyone who criticized the lack of housing, the untrustworthy telephones or the overburdened public transport was arrested. So were thousands who were guilty of nothing at all. In one twenty-four-hour period, over eighteen people were arrested as suspected members of the Brotherhood and sent to detention camps.

Often the military police would wait to search a house for suspected traitors until late at night, earning the dreaded name of Zuwwar el-Fagr, or Visitors of the Dawn. No one knew where they were going to strike next. Everyone was insecure, wondering whether the Visitors of the Dawn would burst into their houses while they were sleeping and take away the men of the family. When they did, the families were never told where the men were going or why they were being taken. Often the men themselves didn't know why.

"Jehan, you must get your husband to help us," one of my friends from the nearby village of Kirdassa cried one day, coming to my home on the Pyramids Road with her two sisters-in-law. "The Zuwwar el-Fagr came to our house last night looking for two of the Muslim Brethren who have escaped from prison and are thought to be hiding in the village. Our husbands knew nothing about it, but they took them away with many other men from the village to prison."

I was shocked. Camelia and her husband were our very close friends and came from a highly respected family. I was sure they had never conspired against the government or the Revolution. The army officers had lost their senses. Recently they had arrested an entire busload of people in search of the escaped Muslim Brothers, and then had tried to beat confessions out of the innocent passengers. Now Amer's troops had arbitrarily rounded up another group, including our friends.

"Anwar is on pilgrimage in Saudi Arabia with Abdel Nasser and will not be back for a few days," I told Camelia.

"Then we will wait here in your home until he returns," she said. "We will not rest until our husbands are returned to us."

Anwar was just as shocked when he got home and met with the women. Immediately he called the Minister of Defense. "Hakim, why did you take these two from Kirdassa? They are our friends and are innocent." Amer said he knew nothing about the arrests and quickly called the prison to secure their release. But when the men were returned to our home, I saw first hand the brutal and humiliating tactics of the military police.

The backs of the men were raw from whippings, their flesh knotted and flayed. Every hour, they told us, they had been taken out of their cells and whipped until they began to faint. "Where are the two members of the Brethren?" the soldiers had yelled at them again and again. I was sickened by the pain and humiliation our friends had been forced to suffer. As Muslim men, they were fastidious about their appearance, each having a mustache which was considered very dignified. The devils in the prison had shaved off one eyebrow each from their faces, and one half of their mustaches to degrade them and mark them as traitors. And this was just one incident out of thousands.

Egyptians are a very resilient and proud people. Egyptians can endure almost anything—hunger, poverty, sickness, even death—but they cannot accept the loss of their pride. They care tremendously about their reputations, about their honor and their dignity. The richest man will give up all to protect his family name. The most willful child will not disobey his or her parents. Yet in this atmosphere of repression, the pride of many Egyptians was being broken.

I did not want to believe what I was hearing and seeing, for Abdel Hakim Amer was an old colleague and friend of Anwar's. Our two families had visited frequently together, especially during the summers in Alexandria, and had become very close. My children looked on Amer almost as part of the family, calling him "Uncle" and rushing to find the chocolates and gum he hid in his pockets for them whenever he came to visit. It seemed impossible to me that Amer, one of the original Revolutionists, could now be responsible for what was happening in Egypt.

On the day the village official in Mit Abul-Kum told me the ordeal of el-Fiqqi being treated like a donkey, I was delighted when I returned to Cairo to find the chairman of the Committee for the Liquidation of Feudalism visiting with Anwar in our drawing room. I was trembling with anger, almost crying, as I told both Anwar and Amer the story I had just heard in the village.

"If this man has committed a crime against the Revolution, if he has done something wrong, why don't you put him on trial?" I said to Amer. "Even if the court decides to put him to death, it will be more dignified for him than being so humiliated and degraded."

Amer seemed upset. "Nobody ordered the soldiers to treat the rich like animals," he said. "They must be taking their personal revenge."

"Then why don't you stop it?" I asked him. "People are beginning to hate the Revolution. The sympathy is no longer with your goals, but with the people who are being so abused."

Amer put a stop to the humiliation being inflicted on the el-Fiqqi family, just as he interceded in every case that was brought to his attention. But few people dared to tell him the truth. And the overall abuse continued.

Perhaps out of friendship, Nasser himself was turning a deaf ear to the stories that were circulating around the country about Amer's men. Together Nasser and Amer had fought in the war for Palestine. Together they had organized the Free Officers and guided Egypt to revolution. The two men had even named their sons after each other. Amer was fiercely loyal to our President. But Nasser, knowing that anyone who controlled the Army controlled Egypt, was growing increasingly suspicious of his old friend.

Other members of the Committee for the Liquidation of Feudalism, known as Marakiz el-Quwwa, or the Centers of Power, were growing increasingly more controlling themselves. Systematically they were crushing their opponents in the government and in the courts. Each of them, it was rumored, had a black book in which to write the names of those he envied or disliked. Everyone whose name was entered was arrested or had his property sequestered.

In March of '67 the committee stepped up its tyrannical campaign to impound the property of the bourgeoisie. The tactics of the Zuwar el-Fagr became even more merciless. Often the young officers didn't even know what they were looking for. "Show us what you have," they would demand after pushing their way into the homes of those suspected of being rich. They would even enter the bedrooms where the women were huddled in fear, stripping their hands of their rings, snatching off their bracelets and their earrings, often putting the jewelry right into their own pockets along with whatever money they had found. Some families had their houses impounded, generations of grandmothers, cousins, little children, being literally turned out into the streets. And nobody dared to protest. There was no mention of these atrocities in the newspapers. If a paper had printed these stories, it would have been banned or closed down.

The petitioners who lined up in front of my door now were

more apt to be the formerly rich and powerful than the poor and powerless. Some asked me for help in regaining their property. Others asked me for money or an increase in the small pensions the government had awarded them. Our religion instructs us to help all who ask for it, so I took all their petitions and gave them to Anwar. But there was nothing more I could do. I was torn. I believed completely in the concept of the Committee for the Liquidation of Feudalism, to redistribute the wealth of the few among the many poor. But I felt great sympathy for the suffering of these rich women. I agreed with the ends of the government's socialist goals, but certainly not the means of obtaining them.

It was as if the soldiers, of whom many came from poor families, were taking their revenge against members of the large, respectable families whose names were known all over Egypt. Some were friends of mine, like Nefisa Abdel Ga'far, who came to me in tears.

"Please, Nefisa. You are my sister. Please let me give you some money," I said to her.

She refused. "I cannot accept charity," she said.

"Then think of it as a loan and repay me when you can," I begged her.

But she still refused.

"How are you living?" I asked her.

"By selling bit by bit the family jewelry that I hid from the Zuwwar el-Fagr," she told me.

Other stories I heard later. Gladys Soursuk, a member of a large landowning family, told me of her ordeal when she returned to Egypt to visit after fleeing to France during this terrible period. "The Zuwwar el-Fagr pounded on my door in Zamalek in the middle of the night," she told me. "They pushed past me with their pads and pencils to note down every single piece of furniture, china and silver. 'You cannot touch or sell anything,' they told me. 'It now belongs to the state.' There was no point going to the bank either, they said, for our accounts had been frozen by the government.

" 'You have three days to get out of your house,' the soldiers told me. I didn't know what to do. My husband was in Europe on business and I had no money and nowhere to go. 'Go to the courts,' they said. The next day I went to the court and they promised me a pension, but it was not enough for us to live on. When I returned to my home they had sealed all the cabinets with red wax so they would know if I tried to open them. 'You can take nothing with you,' they said. I phoned my husband in France. 'Don't come back. You will be arrested,' I told him. 'For what?' he asked. 'For being rich,' I told him."

Gladys and I both had tears in our eyes when she finished her story, for she was a dear friend of mine. She lives now in Paris, where she and her husband had to start from zero to build a new life.

Another friend of mine, I'timad el-Tarabulsi, whose family owned hundreds of feddans in Sharqiyya province, was at least allowed to stay in her house in Dokki when her family land was taken, though she was treated like a prisoner by the Zuwwar el-Fagr. Several times a week, this very courageous woman told me, the officers returned to her home to make sure she had not touched any of her belongings. Like many of the well-to-do, I'timad had taken courses in painting and sewing just to fill the time. Now, suddenly, the courses did not seem like idle pastimes and helped her through this hard period. "The pension the court gave me was not enough even to buy food for breakfast or medicine for my mother," she said. "My sister and I borrowed money from the bank, bought a sewing machine and several weaving machines, and started to weave silk material and make clothes for a living. 'I can't believe that you are kneeling on the ground and doing this job after being such a rich woman,' one of my customers said to me. 'It's an honor to depend on myself instead of just sitting and crying about being poor,' I told her. And then she tried to bargain the price of the dress down. When she left I locked the door behind her and cried."

Even members of my own family were affected. "Jehan, will you keep this for me in a safe place?" my sister's father-in-law, Abu Wafia, asked me, handing me a small package. He had been very kind to me during the '56 war, for it was at his ranch that I had given birth prematurely to Gamal. I was willing to do anything for him after what he had done for me.

"Of course," I said to him. "What is in it?"

"Just some jewelry belonging to my wife," he told me.

"How much?" I asked so that I could be sure none was missing when he took it back.

"You don't need to know," he said. "I trust this house and I need your help."

I put the package into my bedroom closet without telling Anwar and locked the door. But I was so worried about it that for a short time I didn't dare leave the house. I knew that if something was taken from the bag Abu Wafia would never tell me about it, and that would be an awful feeling for me to bear. I got so worried that one morning I locked myself in the bedroom and paced up and down in front of the closet. This is ridiculous, I finally said to myself. But six long months would pass before I could return the bag to him.

I felt terrible. Mistreating the well-to-do and driving them out of the country had not been the point of the Revolution. The army officers were supposed to take an inventory of people's valuables, but not to touch or take them. And the brutality of the dreaded Zuwwar el-Fagr toward those they suspected to be against the regime went against everything I believed in. Never, no matter what a person had done or is suspected of doing, does he deserve to be tortured. No. If he has murdered another, then he deserves to be executed himself. I agree with such a form of capital punishment. But not with torture. It was rumored that many devout Muslims, fearing arrest, had hidden their Qurans. There were even stories of wives being brought into the prisons and threatened with being beaten in front of their husbands to make the men confess. The stories were sickening, the repercussions demoralizing.

The middle class was turning against the regime. They hated Amer. They hated Nasser. They hated all of the Revolutionists, even my husband. The fellaheen too were losing respect for the campaign to rid the country of feudalism. My defense of the Revolution began to sound hollow even to me. "To change from capitalism to socialism, someone has to be a victim," I repeated over and over to my friends and other groups of people. "You cannot please each person with each law. But the majority will benefit."

In this one brief period, several hundred "feudalists" were arrested and sixty thousand feddans of land seized by the military police. Many properties were taken so arbitrarily that some would soon be returned to their owners, first by the courts, and then later by my husband when he reinstituted the rule of law in Egypt. What a shameful time for our country. It would take a new provocation from Israel to end the diabolical actions of the Committee for the Liquidation of Feudalism and turn the government's attention from fighting the suspected enemy within to confronting our true enemy on our eastern border.

War. By May of 1967, a military confrontation with Israel seemed imminent. For six months tensions had been escalating. In November, Israel had staged a full-scale attack thirty miles inside Jordan on the village of el-Samu, destroying 125 homes, the village clinic, the school and the mosque. Claiming that the village was a base for the Palestine Liberation Organization, the Israelis had killed seventeen people, wounded fifty-four and used tanks and armored cars to route the population of five thousand from their homes.

It was now the duty of all Arabs, Syrian President Nur el-Din Attasi charged publicly in February, "to move from defensive positions to offensive positions and enter the battle to liberate the usurped land. Everyone must face the test and enter the battle to the end."

On April 7, Israeli and Syrian planes clashed near Damascus, the Israeli Air Force shooting down six MiGs. Israel might "have to teach Syria a sharper lesson than that of April seventh," Israeli Prime Minister Levi Eshkol announced on Radio Israel on May 12. "It is quite clear that Syria is the focal point of terrorists, and we shall choose the time, place and means to counter the aggressor."

Because Egypt had a common defense pact with Syria, our government took this threat very seriously. In April while on a trip to Moscow, Anwar had been told by Premier Alexei Kosygin that Israel had massed troops on the Syrian border and planned to attack in mid-May. On May 15 Abdel Nasser ordered Defense Minister Amer to send Egyptian soldiers across the Sinai to the Israeli border.

Our Arab brothers, especially President Attasi of Syria and King Hussein of Jordan, were not satisfied with Nasser's commitment of troops, thinking he was merely saber-rattling. What Nasser needed to do, Radio Jordan announced, was to stop hiding behind the United Nations peacekeeping force in the Sinai. Sharm el-Sheikh, the Egyptian city in the Sinai which commanded the Straits of Tiran at the mouth of the Gulf of Aqaba, Israel's only outlet to the Red Sea, was still being policed by the UN troops which guaranteed open passage to the Israelis. It was time, the Arab leaders urged Nasser, for him to do something about it.

Meanwhile, the Israeli propaganda machine was working to convince the world that Israel, a tiny country of two million, was being threatened by a hundred million hostile Arabs. The Israelis were clever, really, convincing the world that Israel was an innocent victim when it was they who had massed their troops on the Syrian border. Every day another story of the Israeli propaganda campaign ran in our newspapers, on the radio and on TV. The Israelis were making much out of Ahmad el-Shukeiri's statement after the formation of the PLO in 1964 that the Arabs would not rest until Israel was driven into the sea.

This one little sentence of Shukeiri's would cost us millions and millions of dollars' worth of Western support. Again and again the Israelis would use it over the years to prove to the West that the Arabs were planning another Holocaust. It was infuriating to us in Egypt to see support and sympathy grow for Israel based on such false propaganda. How could we drive Israel into the sea? Israel with her American backers was more powerful than all the Arab armies put together.

In the spring of 1967, the Israelis were also aiming their shameless propaganda directly at the Arabs. Most of us, they claimed, were poor, ignorant and dirty. "If you put all the Arabs into a *ghorbal* and shook it, almost all of them would fall through," claimed Israeli Foreign Minister Golda Meir, implying that we had quantity because of our great numbers but no quality whatsoever. Later she would say that Arab women were especially frivolous and superficial, buying makeup and dresses rather than spending money on education and self-improvement. It was true, of course, that some Arabs were living in a backward way compared with the Israelis. But I resented deeply Mrs. Meir's generalizations and the Israelis' implication that Arabs, many of whom could barely afford to feed their families, were actively choosing a more primitive way of life instead of the more modern, privileged one available in Israel.

By mid-May, every day was bringing us closer to war. On May 14 and 15, Syria, Egypt and Israel declared a state of emergency, and troops in all three countries were called up. On

May 18, responding to the pressure from the other Arab leaders, Nasser petitioned the United Nations to remove its peacekeeping forces from Egyptian soil. In an effort to keep the peacekeeping forces in the region, UN Secretary General U Thant called upon Israel to accept the UN troops, pointing out that the original United Nations plan drawn up after the 1956 war had been to place the troops on both sides of the Egyptian–Israeli frontier. But just as Israel had refused to accept the UN troops after the Suez War, she now refused again. U Thant was forced to remove the peacekeeping forces from our region altogether.

Overnight, Nasser became an even greater hero in the Arab world. Once more foreign soldiers had been forced from Egyptian soil. Without firing a shot, Nasser had reversed Egypt's humiliation in the '56 war. Still, all of us in Egypt knew that the departure of the United Nations meant that another war was coming, for only the presence of the peacekeeping forces had been keeping the Israelis and the Arabs apart. The time grew closer when, on May 21, Nasser ordered Egyptian troops into the all-important Sharm el-Sheikh, regaining control of the Straits of Tiran for the first time in eleven years. Nasser did not close the straits, hoping that just the threat would be enough to bring Israel to the negotiating table. But the Israelis refused to talk, and the risk of war escalated.

"Are our armed forces ready for conflict?" Nasser asked Field Marshal Abdel Hakim Amer at a Supreme Executive Committee meeting that same day.

"Let it be on my head," the Defense Minister replied. "Everything is ready to go."

Israel made no move toward negotiation. And on May 22, Nasser closed the Straits of Tiran.

Israel's prestige was on the line. She had to do something to show the world she would not let the Arabs push her around. "Israel cannot accept or remain indifferent to what has taken place," an article in *el-Ahram* ran on May 26. "Let Israel begin. Let our second blow, then, be ready! Let it be a knockout."

Two days later, Nasser declared to the foreign press that he did not want war but he would fight for the honor of the Arabs if Israel attacked. There was, after all, no one else to take the Arab side. The United States, Nasser said, was "biased toward and taking the side of Israel one hundred percent." The other

Western powers were talking only about the rights of Israel and siding with Israel. "Where are the rights of the Arabs?" he asked the reporters from *The New York Times,* the London *Times, Le Monde* and other Western papers. "There is not one man who is talking about the rights of the Arabs or the rights of the Palestinian people in their own country and homeland."

Pride swelled in Egypt and throughout the Middle East as we all listened to Nasser, the first leader to stand up for the Arabs against the superpowers in the West and Europe. In Cairo we willingly braced ourselves for the Israeli retaliation sure to come. In cafés and in our homes, we clustered around our radios, waiting to hear the first news of an attack. Our confidence was high, our mission clear. "We are going back by force of arms. We are going back like morning after the dark night," sang Um Kalthum in a song written expressly about the impending war. "Army of Arabism, may God be with you. . . . The tragedy of Palestine pushes you toward the borders. All are with you in the flaming battle."

To raise money for the war effort, Um Kalthum gave concerts all over the Arab world, donating the proceeds to the Egyptian government. Other Egyptians contributed in any way they could, giving money and supplies to the organizations that were raising funds for the Army. Like many women, I gave my wedding and engagement rings. My three daughters, then thirteen, eight and six, donated their gold bracelets.

Anwar was gone from dawn to midnight, meeting with the other leaders of our government. At home I anguished alone about the safety of our four children and the future of our country. "Is Israel going to attack us?" I asked Anwar whenever I caught a glimpse of him.

"Anything can happen now, Jehan," he would say as he changed into a clean uniform and rushed off again.

But I was sure we were on the brink of war. And rather than just sitting around and worrying, I decided to put my energy toward preparing for it. I did not know that that decision would forever change my life.

I called the women who had come regularly to our lunch meetings, the heads of women's organizations, the wives of the Arab ambassadors, any women I knew in public service. "Let us go together to the Qasr el-'Aini State Hospital and give our blood to the blood bank," I said to each of them. "That way when the wounded arrive there will be blood on hand." I alerted the newspapers as well. If there were news photos of women coming forward to give blood, perhaps other people would follow. And they did.

I went to the headquarters of the Red Crescent, our equivalent of the Red Cross. "I wish to join your organization and help you prepare in any way I can for war if it comes," I said to the startled officers. I had not joined the Red Crescent during the last war, having been pregnant then with Gamal. But now I was ready and eager.

"What would you like us to do, Mrs. Sadat?" they asked, startling me in turn, for they were older and far more experienced than I.

"Let's be practical," I suggested. "Instead of waiting for the war to begin and then wasting time finding cotton for bandages and material for hospital gowns, let's begin now so that everything will be ready."

I was filled with a sense of urgency. "Call your friends, your relatives, your neighbors," I told the women who came to the first meeting at the Red Crescent. "Tell them the heroes of Egypt are going to need their help."

One woman called another, who called another, who called another, and soon there was an army of women working as volunteers in the Red Crescent. From the material in the basement of the Red Crescent, we cut and sewed underwear and hospital gowns for the wounded, and when that material was finished we went out and bought more. We put together bedside parcels containing a bar of soap, a washcloth, a towel, a razor, a bottle of eau de cologne, one pair of pajamas, a galabiyya, and a Quran for the Muslim soldiers or a Bible for the Copts. Every day we distributed these parcels to the different hospitals so that they would be ready.

"What shortages do you have?" I asked the hospitals' administrators. "What do you need that we can provide?"

Some replied that they needed more sheets, others equipment such as food blenders to mince food for wounded who wouldn't be able to eat anything whole. We brought in what we could spare of our own things, then asked for contributions to buy more. I was slightly surprised at myself for not asking Anwar's permission or even advice before embarking on such a project. But there hadn't been time. And I felt increasingly filled with confidence and purpose as I watched the enthusiasm grow among the women volunteers, many of whom had done very little outside their homes before.

It was also heartening to see how readily the hospitals were accepting our help, for this was the first time they had been approached by so many middle-class, married Egyptian women eager to get involved. A new respect for women was born, and I was very proud. If war had to come, the women of Egypt, in the true spirit of the Revolution, would be ready to stand by their countrymen and participate.

Meanwhile, diplomats around the world were trying to resolve the crisis in the Middle East by peaceful means, though more pressure was being put on Egypt than on the aggressor, Israel. The Soviet Union warned Nasser that he was risking military conflict by escalating events. The Americans were urging him to avoid any military confrontation while the State Department tried to mediate a reconciliation between Israel, Egypt and the Arab countries. Mediation was, of course, what Nasser had wanted all along, and naturally he was relieved when a State Department official assured him on June 3 that Israel was pursuing diplomatic means to resolve the situation. In a press conference on that same day in Jerusalem, Israeli Defense Minister Moshe Dayan sent out a false message of hope. When asked about the time being consumed by diplomacy, Dayan replied, "[It is] too late to react regarding our chances in the military field . . . and too early to draw conclusions as to the diplomatic way of handling the matter."

Dayan was lying. Two days later, on June 5, 1967, just after I had seen the children off to school in the morning, the sky exploded. Jet fighters ripped through the sky above Cairo, stunning everyone caught in the morning rush hour. On the Pyramids Road the roar was deafening, and our house began to shudder from one tremendous impact after another. All over the house the glass rattled in the windows, strained to the point of shattering. Our Air Force must be repulsing the Israeli invaders, I thought. I rushed to Anwar, who had been reading the morning paper in bed.

"Anwar, this is it, isn't it?" I said to him. "We have gone to war!"

He smiled at me, calmly putting on his uniform. "It appears

so," he said, adding with great confidence, "This time we will teach the Israelis a lesson they will never forget."

The children. I had to get to their schools to bring them home. "Don't worry. They will be safe there," Anwar said. But I wanted my children to be home where my mother and my sister could look after them while I went to the Red Crescent. I knew I would not be able to concentrate on the work that lay ahead of me if I did not know my children were with my family. I had to hurry. "Have you seen the driver?" I asked the maid as I hurried toward the car. He was on an errand, I was told, so I took the car myself.

The road to Zamalek was horrible, blocked by trucks and buses, pedestrians and bicycles. Everyone was trying to get home or into a shelter. So many other parents had rushed to pick up their children that I could not even get near the school. The sound of air raid sirens had joined the terrible thudding of the explosions, and black clouds of smoke rose over the desert. I didn't know whether I would even live to get to my children. Everyone along the way was rushing this way and that, looking fearfully up at the sky. In spite of the chaos, we were all proud to think that our Air Force was fighting the Israeli warplanes over Cairo.

I switched on the car radio, turning it very high so that I could hear it over the noise outside. "The brave Egyptian Air Force has shot down one hundred and fifteen of the Israeli enemy aircraft!" the announcer was shouting on the Voice of the Arabs program broadcast from Cairo, reading excitedly from government bulletins. I was thrilled, as were the people jammed around the transistor radios in cafés and kiosks all over Cairo. Many did not even go to air raid shelters in spite of the sirens, dancing instead in the streets. None of us knew then that this radio announcer, Ahmad Sa'id, would become famous for these jubilant war reports, all issued by the government.

Dropping the children at my sister's house, I went straight to the hospital. "Good morning, my friends, my sisters," I said proudly to the three hundred volunteers pouring into the Red Crescent. "The war has come and we are ready."

I divided them into teams headed by a chairwoman and assigned each group to a different military hospital to await the arrival of the wounded. In the afternoon I went with each team to its appointed hospital, introducing the volunteers to the hospitals' directors. We could still hear the roar of the jets and the antiaircraft guns, but little seemed to be damaged in Cairo. I was exhausted when I arrived home, but elated. Our teams were in place. And the news of the war over the radio continued to be excellent.

"Where is your father?" I asked the children, wanting to share immediately the triumph of the day.

"He is upstairs on his balcony," Loubna said.

I ran up the stairs. "Anwar," I called out as I rushed onto the balcony, "I have such good news. The women are ready at all the hospitals to receive our wounded. Everything is in place."

He did not answer me or even look at me.

"Anwar," I continued with excitement, "not a single moment will be wasted. The wounded soldiers will be cared for as never before."

Still he sat and stared.

"What is it, Anwar?" I said, worried that perhaps his heart was bothering him again. "Are you feeling ill?"

"No. It is something much worse than that," he said, finally turning to look at me. I had never seen his face so filled with torment. "We have lost the war," he said.

Lost the war? The war had just begun, and all the news reports were signaling a victory. "You must be wrong, Anwar," I told him in disbelief. "Just outside, in the road in front of our house, whole companies of people are dancing and cheering. Truckloads of people have even come in from the country to celebrate."

His eyes never left mine. "Jehan, I have just come back from speaking with Amer and Nasser," he said slowly, as if he too did not want to believe. "Every one of our planes is lost. Israeli infantry have already captured el-Arish. Our soldiers are on the run. This is a disaster for Egypt."

I could not believe what I was hearing. Evidently, between the time I had left my home to pick up my children from school and the time I safely delivered them home, the war had been lost. In just two hours, Israeli fighter planes had completed a devastating attack on Egyptian territory. Defense Minister Amer had been in a plane himself during this critical time, touring our air bases, and orders had been issued not to fire any antiaircraft missiles while his plane was in the air. By the time Amer's plane had landed, the Israelis had bombed every airfield from Cairo to Alexandria. Our Air Force had been destroyed while still on the ground. Our airport runways had been damaged so severely that no plane would be able to take off for weeks.

At the same time, Israeli land forces had swept rapidly across the border into the Sinai. Many of our military units were still fighting in Yemen, and the ground troops stationed in the Sinai had not even had a chance to fight back. Yet even now, as I stood paralyzed by Anwar's words, I could hear the crowds chanting victory slogans: "*Hanharib! Hanharib! Kull el-nass hatharib!* We'll fight! We'll fight! Everyone will fight!"

I felt the strength drain from my body. "Why, Anwar?" I finally managed to say. "What went wrong?"

Still he sat stunned. "Amer's war plan was not good," he said. "The Israelis took him by surprise, destroying everything. Now we have no air cover for our soldiers in the Sinai. They will be slaughtered."

"But the radio . . ." I protested weakly.

"It is all propaganda," Anwar said. "Nasser does not wish to demoralize the people by telling them the truth. Nor can you."

I stood and stared at my husband on the balcony, trying to comprehend what he had told me.

Slowly he turned his face away from mine to gaze back out over the garden. "It is finished," he said, more to himself than to me.

As I left him to arrange dinner for the children, I realized that the explosions I had heard in the morning were not from our planes firing on the Israelis, but from the Israelis bombing the Cairo West airfield.

For four days Israeli planes swept over Cairo. Some days they dropped bombs. More often they didn't. Day after day they flew low and very fast over the city, the terrifying explosions of their sonic booms shaking the apartment buildings and shattering glass. Some people boarded up their windows. Those who couldn't afford the wood used tape to keep the glass from exploding. Brick walls were hastily built a few feet in front of every doorway to shelter those coming in and out. At night people huddled inside their flats with their lights off, not knowing what to expect.

Using their old tactics, the Israelis launched a propaganda campaign to increase our terror. Rumors planted by their spies ran wild through Cairo: "Tomorrow they are going to bomb Heliopolis." "Friday is the day for Ma'adi." Cairenes took their children and fled from one suburb to another in advance of these threatened attacks that rarely took place. The Israelis knew that if they bombed Cairo we would eventually retaliate against Tel Aviv. But their rumors and their terrorizing low flights over Cairo made us feel as if we were being continually bombed. "We want you to know how easily our planes can reach you," they were implying. At home, my youngest daughter, Jehan, began to scream and tremble whenever she heard the faintest sound of a plane. I had to send her and my older children to Mit Abul-Kum with their cousins, my mother and my sister. Their nerves would be calmer there, and so would mine not having to worry about them while I worked in the hospitals.

Eighty Israeli aircraft destroyed! Sixty Israeli aircraft destroyed! "Isn't it wonderful?" the women volunteers said to me every morning at the hospitals. I smiled and nodded, though inside my heart was like stone. For the next two days I walked through the rows of the first wounded to arrive, listening to the lies of victory on the radio I carried in the pocket of my uniform. Still the government claimed we were winning.

When the truth began to come out in the foreign newscasts, the Voice of America and the BBC, Egypt went into shock. Disillusionment and depression replaced the euphoria of the people. "We will never trust the government again," parents of the wounded began to tell me in the hospitals. One of the first of the wounded to arrive told me his brigade had come to the Sinai only twelve hours before the attack. "Israeli planes strafed us at dawn with no warning," he said. "We had no weapons ready yet, no radios. Our soldiers were cut down where they stood." Other soldiers were just as demoralized by the bad military planning. "We didn't even get a chance to fire a shot," one soldier who had lost an arm said to me in tears. "We were prepared to give our lives in the fight, but there was no fight. We were shot down as we were retreating."

On June 8, three days after the first attack, the air raid sirens sounded again while a friend and I were on our way home from the hospital. Quickly we went to the bomb shelter in the basement of her building, where we were to spend the entire night. It was the worst night of my life. We sat in total darkness, while overhead we could hear the scream of the flares dropped by the Israeli planes, and underneath us the ground shuddered. Will I die here alone, I wondered, far from my children at Mit Abul-Kum and my husband, who was with Nasser?

I was not afraid of the dark, remembering my mother's nightly lessons in our garden. But others were. In the blackness some were crying and some were screaming, while others were trying to soothe their babies. The whole atmosphere was desperate. It was as if we were watching a film of war, but this time it was happening to us. And still the government-controlled news on the radio in my pocket claimed we were winning the war.

It was too much. Finally Nasser could not keep the truth from the people any longer. By the next afternoon, Ahmad Sa'id was announcing on Cairo Radio that the fighting had stopped and that Nasser would address the people that evening. At seven o'clock on June 9, his face ill with strain, Nasser announced on television and radio that Egypt had suffered a *nakba*, a setback. The responsibility and the shame were his, he said, his eyes filling with tears, his voice thick and shaking. I myself cried as I watched his speech on the television set at the hospital. I could not bear to see our President this way, this bold, strong man now so broken. He had always been so proud, so dignified. But what he said next was the most shattering of all.

"I have decided to give up completely and finally every official post and every political role," he said, "to return to the ranks of the public to do my duty with them like every other citizen."

I was shattered. Abdel Nasser resign? He could not, he must not. He was our leader, and more than ever now we needed him. We had been defeated, yes. But we needed him to lead us out of defeat towards retribution. We couldn't do it without him. He was everything to Egypt. I felt close to panic. And so did everyone else.

"*Nasser!*" "*Only Nasser!*" The chant began to rise from the street even before our President had finished speaking. "*Nasser!*" "*Nasser!*"

From the windows of the hospital I could see hundreds, thousands, some dressed in their nightclothes, pouring out of the buildings, running toward the Radio and Television Building in downtown Cairo as if they could stop the President from resigning by stopping the broadcast.

"*Nasser!*" "*Nasser!*"

I rushed to the phone to call my husband at his office. "Anwar, don't let him resign," I pleaded. "We need him to continue. It is up to him to take us out of this defeat and prepare for our retaliation. Pleace convince the members of Parliament not to accept his resignation!"

"Be calm, Jehan," he told me. "The members have already voted not to accept the resignation." But could they prevent Nasser from stepping down anyway?

For the next unbelievable seventeen hours in Cairo, the massive demonstrations continued. Putting aside all accusations of blame for our defeat, the people flooded by the tens of thousands into the streets to cry out their support for Nasser while air raid sirens wailed their own lament. "*Ya Nasser, Nasser, ihna ma'ak. Lan neqbal el-hazima,*" rang through the air. "Nasser, Nasser. We are with you. We will not accept defeat."

Close to half a million people massed around Nasser's home in Manshiet el-Bakri through the night, while I stayed on the telephone with the hospital volunteers. "We must show our support for the President." I urged one after another. "Make signs saying he must not resign. Call all your friends to help us demonstrate together tomorrow."

We set up meeting places, and the next morning I led five hundred women dressed in their white hospital aprons across the Gala'a Bridge and the Tahrir Bridge toward the Parliament Building. "Stay, Nasser. Stay!" I chanted, the women echoing their response. Thousands of people milled around us, pushing, shoving, calling out their own pleas to Nasser: "*Nasser! Nasser! Don't leave us. We need you!*" There were people going in all directions at once. The police were helpless to bring order.

What a saving grace this outpouring of emotion was. For a few short hours anyway, we were able to forget the horrors of our defeat. I found myself laughing aloud as my feelings of depression were replaced by the elation of purpose. "Nasser! Stay, Nasser!" I called out at the top of my voice as we were swept along in the crowd toward the Assembly. A man fainted, and someone, seeing my white uniform, asked me to attend to him. Using the treatment for hysterical shock, I smacked his face. It worked and he regained consciousness.

When we reached Qasr el-'Aini Street in front of the Hilton Hotel, we were met by policemen with water cannons. There were too many people to control, and the crowd was on the verge of rioting. The police had to act, and on came the cannons. The force of the water knocked me right off my feet, and, right beside me, the wig off my friend's head. The tears were rolling down our cheeks, we were laughing so hard while we searched in vain for her wig. I was still drenched when I got home, and sat soaking wet in the kitchen listening for news on the radio. It was not long before I heard what I most hoped for, the news that Nasser had decided to stay on as president. It was Anwar himself who read Nasser's letter thanking the people for their support. Outside, I heard the shouting of the crowds turn into cheers, the chants into songs of celebration.

The exhilaration was short-lived as the reality of what we had lost sank in. Jerusalem, the most sacred city to Muslims next to Mecca and Medina, was now completely under Israeli control. Our land in the Sinai was under Israeli occupation, as were the West Bank in Jordan and the Golan Heights in Syria. In the six days of the war, Israel had occupied more than three times the amount of territory it had controlled before the fighting.

Over fifteen thousand Egyptian soldiers had been killed and many more wounded. One million Palestinians had been placed under Israeli occupation and hundreds of thousands of others forced off their land to become refugees. Yet Israel was still refusing to admit that the Palestinians' country was being destroyed, or even that the Palestinians had a national identity at all. "There is no such thing as the Palestinian people," Golda Meir, now Prime Minister of Israel, declared shortly after the war in remarks quoted widely in our newspapers. How could she so heartlessly dismiss a people who had flourished for thousands of years? The Israelis had gained a homeland by taking away the homeland of others. Just as the Europeans had persecuted the Jews, the Jews were now persecuting the Palestinians.

From one end of Egypt to the other, the people felt nothing but total humiliation. How could it have happened? Three times now we had been defeated by Israel, but this defeat was the worst. It had been impossible to expect victory over the combined forces of Britain, France and Israel in '56. But this time there was no excuse, and the loss went much deeper. It was very hard for any of us to bear.

Everyone started blaming everyone else: the leadership of Abdel Nasser, the bad planning of Defense Minister Amer, the generals who did not lead their troops to victory. Even the soldiers were blamed for their ineptitude, while they in turn blamed the Russian weapons for not being as advanced as those of the Americans on the Israeli side. The whole military was disgraced. "Look, one of the running soldiers. Why didn't you win the war?" people jeered at anyone in uniform in the streets. For a time the soldiers didn't even dare to wear their uniforms in public. Even military vehicles were scarce, the officers feeling safer driving ordinary cars and trucks. We had lost our pride. Everyone was torn.

The war had also left Egypt in desperate financial straits. We had lost two of our major sources of revenue, our oil wells in the Sinai and the income from the Suez Canal, which had been blocked by sunken ships during the fighting. Tourism had also dropped dramatically because of the war. Sympathizing with Egypt because of the Israeli aggression, Saudi Arabia, Kuwait and Libya banded together to offer us £E95 million in aid each year. But over the next three years almost a quarter of our budget would go to buying new weapons instead of the services Egyptians so desperately needed. And the depression of the people deepened.

Our very faith as Muslims came into question. Articles appeared in our papers claiming that the Jews had won because they were pious whereas we had strayed from the Divine way. Attendance at our mosques went up by 600 percent, every place of worship being filled to capacity on Fridays. On Sundays the churches were fuller than they had been in years. More and more men started wearing galabiyyas in the streets, while women took on the *hegab,* the head covering which looks much like a nun's coif. For more than a month, hundreds of Copts saw an apparition of the Virgin Mary floating in the air above a church in one of our most densely populated areas. When the elders of the church interpreted the Virgin's message as "I know, Egyptians, that you can no longer come to see me in Jerusalem, so I have come to see you in Cairo," it made the front page of *el-Ahram,* our most respected and widely read newspaper.

Demonstrations broke out, more from a sense of frustration than from anger. Angry crowds threw incendiary bombs at the United States Information Library, for it was well known that the Americans had armed Israel not only with modern weapons but with devastating intelligence reports. With the help of the Americans, the Israelis had broken all our army codes and used them to order our troops in the Sinai to locations where their troops were waiting in ambush.

Over the next weeks, while the wounded poured into the hospitals, their agony became my own. Anwar too was suffering terribly. As one of the government leaders, Anwar felt responsible for our defeat, though he had not taken part in any of the military decisions. I battled my depression by working harder and longer in the hospitals. Anwar reacted in an opposite way. And it was devastating.

"Did Mr. Sadat go out today?" I asked the cook each evening when I returned from the hospitals. Day after day his answer was no. I was used to Anwar's way of sitting alone and thinking when he had problems on his mind. I knew when I saw him this way that there was little I could do except keep the children quiet to protect his solitude. But this depression following our defeat was deeper and more distressing than ever before. For three weeks he sat motionless in his chair, without talking phone calls, without speaking to anyone.

"Anwar, why don't you go to military headquarters?" I said to him one evening.

"What is the point?" he said.

I tried a different tack another evening. "Anwar, the soldiers in the hospital need to see one of their leaders. Will you come with me and visit them?"

He sat staring out over the garden. For a military man like Anwar, Egypt's humiliating defeat was almost too much to bear. Nasser too closeted himself in his presidential villa, shattered by the tragedy.

Truckload after truckload of the wounded arrived from the Sinai, making the vulnerability of our troops clear. Many of our soldiers were horribly burned from the napalm the Israelis had dropped on them as they ran for their lives through the desert. Many had lost arms and legs, and others were blinded. Among the survivors were hundreds who also had been severely damaged psychologically by the futility of their suffering. There was hardly a family in all Egypt which had not lost a husband, a son, a nephew, a grandson. Several of my cousins and Anwar's cousins were horribly wounded.

I do not know where my energy came from or how I had the courage to face so many dreadfully injured men. Perhaps sustenance came to me and to the other women volunteers from our experience as mothers. Our instincts told us how to soothe, to comfort, even to scold when necessary. "Um el-Shuhada," the patients called me, Mother of the Martyrs. And that is how I felt.

"Mother, I cannot see," one soldier cried to me one day. I looked at the doctor who was accompanying me on my rounds. He shook his head, for this soldier, like many others, was suffering from traumatic, not physiological, blindness. He could see. He just didn't want to. I sat with him for two hours, chatting about the family that was waiting for him to come home, about how brave a soldier he had been. I came back every day to visit him until one day he said, "I see you are wearing white."

Other soliders were just as traumatized, more than one insisting that he was the Prophet, others screaming in terror from the sounds they still heard of bombs and planes. Some stared vacantly, not moving their eyes at all, while the eyes of others darted frantically.

After hearing stories about the Israeli ground forces, I could understand our soldier's mental distress. Lost in the desert, many of our troops had stumbled across Israeli units. After falsely comforting our young soldiers with water and fruit, some Israeli soldiers had opened fire on them. At other times the Israelis had been truly kind, aiding our soldiers in their retreat toward home. No wonder our soldiers were so traumatized. They did not know whom to trust, including the Bedouin tribes who roamed the Sinai. For a price, some of the Bedouins had disguised some of our troops in galabiyyas and hidden them from the Israelis. Others among the Bedouin had taken money from our men and then sold them for a higher price to the Israeli desert units.

I searched for words to defuse the bitterness and feelings of futility shared by so many of our wounded. Many held the government leaders responsible for their suffering, making it doubly difficult for me as the wife of one of them.

"I didn't lose my foot to the Israelis, I lost it to our own bad command," a young officer said to me with scorn.

"Why did you enroll at a military academy instead of becoming a poet or joining the faculty of medicine or law?" I asked him. "To go through war and lose your foot was your fate, not the fault of your leaders. We are not the first country to be defeated. But so that we will not be defeated again, why don't you write on a piece of paper what you have seen that was wrong in our military plans and give it to your commander so that it will not happen again."

I found myself performing duties I never thought I was capable of. As I was talking to the boy who had lost his foot, another officer was wheeled in from the operating room still groggy from the anesthetic, his head so swathed in bandages only his mouth showed. Out of the corner of my eye I saw the man begin to vomit, but because the hospitals were overcrowded and understaffed there was no one to call. Quickly I looked for a receptacle, but there wasn't one. Without thinking, I cupped my hands for the officer to vomit into, then washed my hands in the sink in the room and cleaned around his mouth. When I visited him the next day, he kept kissing my hand. "With your permission I will call the first daughter that I have Jehan," he told me.

"I would be honored," I replied.

Still, nothing I said to Anwar when I got home could break through his depression, until one day in Ma'adi Hospital I happened to visit with Major General Kamal Hassan Ali, who would later become our prime minister. "Mrs. Sadat, I wish to speak with you privately," the wounded General said. When the room was cleared he said, "It is very important that I speak with your husband. There are facts about the war which I must tell him."

That night I gave Anwar the General's message, and for the first time in three weeks he showed some interest. The next day Anwar went to see Major General Hassan Ali and from there went to report to Abdel Nasser. Anwar never told me what Hassan Ali had told him. But I was happy enough that my husband had finally found reason to come back to life.

For five months I was up at dawn and in the hospitals. I worked until late at night, when I would speak with the director of each hospital to see what was needed before going on to the Red Crescent to meet with the chairwoman of each volunteer team. To help meet the hospitals' demands, we established an international network among the wives of the Egyptian ambassadors abroad. When the military hospital in Heliopolis told me they needed special equipment for burn victims so that their limbs could be saved instead of amputated, I called the wife of our ambassador in London and the equipment was sent immediately from England. Many lives were saved in this way.

Other lives were beyond saving. On the shores of the Suez in Sinai, where I traveled with other members of the Red Crescent in July, the suffering was excruciating. Every day more soldiers would stumble in from the desert to the eastern bank of the Canal, victims of the chaotic military withdrawal. In spite of the cease-fire sporadic fighting continued along the Canal, and not until the artillery fire stopped at sunset could small Egyptian fellucas ferry our poor soldiers across the Canal to safety. Often they were escorted by the women volunteers supposedly safe in their white uniforms bearing the badge of the Red Crescent. But continually the women were harassed by the Israeli soldiers on the east bank. "You son of a dog," one of my friends muttered under her breath, thinking she had been shot after an Israeli soldier threw a lemon at her, hitting her hard in the shoulder. She was an excitable person with a stammer, and for the next half hour she couldn't stop saying "Son of a dog . . . son of a dog . . ."

Not only soldiers but civilians too were fleeing the Canal Zone cities of Isma'iliyya, Port Sa'id, Qantara and Suez. The Israelis had first attacked these cities from the air and were now continuing to shell them from the other side of the canal. Thousands of refugees, many of them wounded, now came to our Red Crescent headquarters in Isma'iliyya. We sent many to the very simple housing in the desert which had been set up for workers on a land reclamation project, and when those rooms were full we set up tents in the courtyards of mosques and schools all over the governorates next to the Canal Zone. It was pathetic to see so many innocent families carrying their children on their backs, knowing that their homes, everything that they owned, had been destroyed.

Of all the people in Egypt, it was those from the Canal Zone who suffered most from the war. Anwar would try to compensate them when he reopened the Canal in '75, making Port Sa'id a free-trade zone. In the center of Suez would be left a memorial to the years of fighting the people had endured: an American tank captured from the Israelis.

I wanted to cross the Canal myself to tend to the Egyptian soldiers coming in from the desert, but the military command in Isma'iliyya persuaded me that the danger of my being kidnapped or ridiculed by the Israelis in plain view on the other shore was too great. Instead I waited on the Egyptian side to greet our men, never really getting used to the terrible condition so many of them were in.

Their legs were hideously swollen from walking through the heat of the desert by day and the cold at night. Their feet were cracked and bleeding. Many had been without water for so long that that their tongues were black and so thick they had trouble speaking. "Oh Mother, Mother," they would croak as I bathed their legs and feet and gave them juice to drink.

"Do not try to talk," I urged them. "Save your strength to get well."

The ones suffering only from their cruel exposure in the desert were sent to a recovery camp. The wounded were sent to the hospital.

In the crowded burn wards, the air was thick with the smell of charred flesh, almost like that of rotting meat. Only by concentrating deeply on the soldiers I was trying to comfort could I overcome my revulsion. "You are a hero to Egypt," I told each burn victim, remaining by his side sometimes for hours until he slept. "You are luckier than I am, for you have a wound to show your honor." Sometimes their eyes would be the only part of their bodies without bandages. Often they died right in front of me. "*Ya ayyatuha al-nafs al-mutma'ina. Irja'i ila rabbiki radiyya murdiyya.* O soul at peace! Return unto thy Lord, Content in his good pleasure," I would recite from the Quran over their bodies. Never did their deaths get easier.

Only once did I lose my nerve. One evening, as the other women and I moved routinely through a group of wounded newly arrived from across the Canal, I started soaking the swollen feet and legs of one young soldier in warm water. "God bless you, Mother," he said weakly as I poured him a glass of juice. But as my hand got closer to his mouth, I froze. Between his lips and his nose was a deep and ugly wound, the flesh completely torn away. And crawling in the wound were worms.

I stood paralyzed, the glass in my hand trembling. I willed myself to ignore the worms, to finish raising the glass to his lips. But I could not. I am going to die, I thought, unable to take my eyes off the worms. I felt myself growing faint. How could I tell this boy that he had worms in his body, that I was too frightened of worms to care for him after he had endured so much? Finally I broke out of my paralysis. "Just one moment, my son," I said. And I rushed to a nearby room.

"What is the matter, Mrs. Sadat?" asked one of the volunteers, Akila el-Sama'. "You look very pale and your whole body is shaking. Are you ill?"

When I got my breath back I told her about the boy with the worms in his body and my complex about them.

"Don't worry, I'll take care of it," she reassured me. And she did, cleaning out his wounds with Dettol and warm water, then covering them until the doctor could see him.

"Where is Mrs. Sadat? I was so happy to see her," the soldier asked her.

"She is extremely tired and thought she was going to faint," the brave woman explained. "She didn't want to show you how tired she was, and now she is having a little rest."

"Tell her thank you from me," the soldier said.

The Israelis were using their military-intelligence reports to further intimidate our soldiers who had made it to the Canal. "You will find Mrs. Sadat waiting for you on the other side," the Israeli soldiers told the Egyptian soldiers. Naturally our troops did not believe them, for no government wives had traveled to the front before. And when they saw me, they cried out in fear. "They know everything," more than one soldier said, trembling.

"You are safe now," I would soothe each of them. "There is nothing for you to be frightened of now. You must save your energy to get well."

Peace. Who can see the things that I have seen and not believe in peace? In the summer of 1967 I was learning firsthand that war should never be the answer to any conflict. The price was too dear. And the wounded kept arriving.

Throughout the summer and the fall I shuttled between the wounded in Cairo and the Canal Zone and my children in Mit Abul-Kum. When I was sure that the attacks on Cairo had ceased, I brought the children home. I could spend little time with them, for I was so busy in the hospitals. But I wasn't worried. They were being well cared for by their grandmother and aunt and entertained by their cousins, with whom they were growing up. As a mother I had no guilt at all about the children, who sometimes came to the hospitals to read poetry and books to the soldiers and to write letters for them. But Anwar had been getting increasingly impatient with me. Though intellectually he was for the freedom of women and certainly proud of what I was doing, at heart he was still an Oriental man.

"Jehan, you are neglecting your home, neglecting your husband, neglecting your children," Anwar scolded me morning after morning. "They are still very young and I want you to be home at two P.M. Who else is going to look over their homework? Who is going to find out how they are doing in school? If you want to leave home to go to the hospitals at five in the morning, fine, you can go. But at two I want you home, the way you used to be."

I shook my head in protest. "Nothing is the way it used to be, Anwar," I told him. "Our country has been defeated. We have thousands of wounded and dying in the hospitals. And for the first time women have come forward to help. They need me."

"So do I," he would argue. "I am a man. And I want my wife to be home at two P.M.."

The arguments were always the same. "Anwar," I would persist. "If I have something I can do for a wounded soldier, or if one is finally telling me how he really feels and then I look at my watch and say 'oh—it's two o'clock and my husband wants me home, bye-bye, I can't listen to you anymore,' how would that make you feel?"

But my husband remained resolute. "You heard my message. That's all I can say," he'd wind up.

"All right," I'd say, torn between pleasing Anwar and doing my duty as a citizen. "I'll do my best." The next day I would come home at two, the day after at two-thirty, then three and four until I was back into my full-time schedule.

On the nights I had to stay in the hospitals very late, I tiptoed into the house, carrying my shoes up the stairs in my hand so that Anwar wouldn't hear me. But often he did.

"You know I was not out at a party or a nightclub," I would respond to his frowns when he would look first at his watch and then pointedly at me. "You know exactly where I was."

When I was in Port Sa'id or Isma'iliyya I rarely called him, not wanting to get into another dispute over the phone. And when I was home, I tried to get out of the house with as little fuss as possible because I hate to quarrel in the morning.

"Be home by two," he would warn me.

"I will try, Anwar," I promised.

I understood Anwar, of course. There wasn't a single Egyptian man, or probably any man anywhere, who didn't want his wife to be home waiting for him with a big smile and a hug, with his meal cooked and ready. The house should be in perfect order, the children neat and respectful with their homework done, the atmosphere joyous and happy. Truly most men want their wives to be like computers, to always look well and be in a good mood. And Anwar was no different.

Little by little after the war, when my friends and I would turn our energies to working in the government hospitals and upgrading the care of the patients, his resistance lessened. He had to accept my independence, really. I knew by then that I had found my lifework: caring for the sick and disabled, aiding those who could not help themselves, working for peace, raising the standard of women. My pursuit of these goals would become easier for me after Anwar became President. Then both our schedules would be so full that neither of us had time to worry about who was—and wasn't—at home. But there was no doubt that our life as husband and wife was sometimes difficult during the June War and its aftermath. One shock seemed to be followed immediately by another.

Defense Minister Abdel Hakim Amer, once Nasser's closest friend, now was rumored to be mounting a military insurrection against him. Amer, who had assured Nasser before the '67 war that Egypt was totally prepared for victory, felt betrayed and abandoned by his old friend. In the crisis following our defeat, all the Cabinet Ministers had offered to resign along with Nasser. Only Amer had refused, seeing this as a plot to place the whole burden of responsibility for our defeat squarely on his shoulders. In his increasingly troubled mind, he could see no reason why he should resign while Nasser remained in office. It was as if he and Nasser were twins, the fate of one being intertwined with that of the other. Finally Nasser was forced to dismiss him, and to appoint a new Defense Minister, Lieutenant General Muhammad Fawzi, in his place.

To regain his position, Amer began to solidify his support in the military and to stockpile weapons in his home. The mutual suspicion between Nasser and Amer grew even deeper, intensified on Nasser's part by the broad power base Amer had created for himself as head of the Committee for the Liquidation of Feudalism. Because of Amer's popularity among his army officers, Nasser feared that the Army might rebelliously force him to return Amer to his post, or even overthrow the government. But still Abdel Nasser was reluctant to move against his old friend. The situation grew increasingly dangerous during the summer. When unexpectedly in that tense period I found Amer at home with Anwar after I had returned from the hospitals, I realized how pained and confused the former Defense Minister had become.

"How could Abdel Nasser treat me this way?" he was saying in bewilderment to Anwar on our balcony. "Always I have felt toward him like a brother." I was shocked at how old and shaken Amer looked.

"It's not a matter of whether Nasser loves you or he doesn't," I said gently to him, hoping that perhaps I could reason with this shattered man. "This is a crucial time for Egypt, and not the time to challenge him. I tell you this like a sister: go to your hometown of Estal and relax with your family. When this time passes, then you will be able to reconcile with your old friend. If you continue to pressure Nasser, it will not be to your benefit. I beg you, Hakim, please listen to me."

But Amer had been too preoccupied to listen. "The defeat was not my responsibility alone," he insisted. "We all shared it."

"It doesn't matter whose fault it was or wasn't," I told him. "Whether you like it or not, the people see the outcome of the war as your responsibility. As a leader, you must accept this. If something went wrong in the Red Crescent, it would not satisfy the people to be told that it was the fault of Mrs. X or Mr. Y. No. It would be the fault of Jehan Sadat. And so it is with you."

But I couldn't convince him. Amer just shook his head and didn't answer me at all. Two weeks later he tried to go to the Radio and Television Building to plead his case to the people and was put under house arrest. Three weeks later, on September 14, he swallowed a capsule of cyanide and killed himself.

I wept as I stood alone by Amer's tomb in his village of Estal, reading the Fatiha from the Quran. Because of Amer's threat to the regime, Nasser had asked the Revolutionists not to attend the funeral of their old friend and colleague. But I had been so saddened when I heard the tragic news that I had left Alexandria immediately to go to Amer's home in Upper Egypt to pay my respects to his family. They had already returned to Giza, and I went to call on them there the next day.

I was not welcomed. "He didn't commit suicide," his daughters screamed in a hysterical way when they saw me. "The government killed him!"

But I had come as a friend, not as a representative of the regime. In the garden I met one of Amer's sons, an army officer. "Why, Auntie, why?" he cried out to me. I couldn't tell him, could not explain myself why this man had become so unrealistic and finally an enemy of his best friend. If Amer had felt so desperate, he should have followed military tradition and taken his life at the moment of our defeat on the fifth of June, 1967. Then everyone would have understood that his pride could not have borne Egypt's shame, and his suicide would have been honorable. Now it was pitiful.

In Cairo Abdel Nasser was taking the news very hard. The disloyalty and the death of his friend combined with our defeat in the war were making him ill. His diabetes flared up and he looked terrible. At least once a week during this terrible time Nasser had come to our house on the Pyramids Road to talk to Anwar. And every time it had pained me more to look at him. His body was stooped, as if he was carrying mountains and mountains of grief, and he developed a rash so painful that even the touch of his clothes was agony. How much more would Nasser, would Egypt, have to endure?

Egyptians were still fighting and dying. Though the June War was officially over, skirmishes would continue for the next six years in the Canal Zone, in Upper Egypt and occasionally in Cairo itself. During this dreadful period when we had no declared war—and no peace—the Israelis continued to pound our cities of Suez, Isma'iliyya and Port Sa'id while we fought back against their growing fortifications along the Bar Lev Line. By 1969 the skirmishes had escalated into what was called the War of Attrition, this time the Israelis striking at industrial and civilian targets as well as military ones.

The strain on Nasser was terrible. In September of 1969 he

had a heart attack, though the public was told he had the flu. Feeling his own mortality and facing one political intrigue after another, Nasser turned to his one true friend. On December 20 he asked Anwar to bring his Quran with him when he came to see him off for an Arab summit conference in Morocco. At his home before going to the airport, Nasser swore in Anwar as his Vice President. And the War of Attrition continued.

In the Canal Zone cities, the scene was one of *mahgoura,* no life, no people living there anymore. Not a single building was left standing in Isma'iliyya on the western side of the Canal. Anyone seeing the wreckage wept as I did, looking at the shattered homes with the staircases going up to nowhere, the closets still hung with dresses, the beds of the families burned. What dreams were destroyed there? How many people lost? I could not hold back my tears. The streets were as empty as the houses, for everyone had been evacuated to camps in the desert.

Israeli planes were bombarding industrial targets all over Egypt as well, even along the Upper Nile as far south as Aswan. Though the High Dam was very well fortified, everyone was frightened the Israelis would destroy it, sending a wall of water ten feet high to flood our villages and even Cairo. One day while I was visiting a hospital in Sharqiyya governorate, I watched a fight from the balcony between our planes and those of Israel. "Go inside," the military guards shouted at me. But I stayed outside to watch. I never had the feeling of danger to myself. If I had, I could not have continued as I did. But it was very hard to see the suffering continue. Four thousand Egyptian technicians alone would be killed in this nondeclared war.

In January of 1970, air raid sirens sounded again in Cairo. As everyone scrambled to safety past the brick walls and sandbags still outside the buildings, we heard the first bombs drop. Seventy workers died in a factory on the outskirts of the city. When we heard about the second barrage of bombs, a new wave of fury swept the country. The Israelis had bombed the Bahr el-Baqar primary school in Sharqiyya province, near Bilbais.

Could the Israelis really have meant to attack little children? I couldn't believe they could be so cruel, though many Egyptians did. Through my tears I moved through the hospitals unable to find the words to comfort the little children lying there without legs, without arms. Though such pain and loss were certainly hard for the war veterans, at least they knew that their duty was to defend the country, that their job entailed risk. But not these innocent children. For weeks afterward I would hear their screams of pain and terror. It was hard for me, for all of us working in the hospitals, to control ourselves while we tried to comfort the children of Bahr el-Baqar.

Somebody had to intervene. Somebody had to stop this senseless carnage. In November of '67 the United Nations had adopted Resolution 242, which proposed Israeli withdrawal from the occupied territories in exchange for Arab recognition of Israel's right to exist within safe boundaries. Both Israel and Egypt had accepted the resolution, but Israel had never kept her half of the promise. The resolution didn't say "all the territories," the Israelis had claimed, using this semantic argument to continue their occupation of our land in the Sinai.

Now Israel's greatest ally tried to resolve the dispute. In May of 1970, the Americans under President Nixon came forth with the Rogers Plan, named after Secretary of State William Rogers. This plan called for Israeli withdrawal, a ninety-day cease-fire, and mediation by the United Nations to settle the Palestinian problem. Nasser accepted it. The Israelis rejected it.

How much more would we have to sacrifice before the Israelis negotiated? Already the Palestinians were infuriated with Egypt, and the more radical Arabs were turning against the more conservative ones. The Palestinians felt that Nasser had abandoned their cause, and they swore violence against him and anyone else whom they considered the enemy. The situation deteriorated especially quickly in Jordan, where militant Palestinians mounted an insurrection against the regime. Arab unity was disintegrating.

Two months later, in July of '70, Nasser called an Arab summit conference in Cairo to try to restore peace at least in Jordan. For four exhausting days, Nasser and Anwar attended meetings and sometimes shouting matches around the clock in the Hilton Hotel. Every Arab king and head of state was there. So was Yasir Arafat, chairman of the recently formed Palestinian Liberation Organization, and Libya's new revolutionary leader, Muammar el-Qadaffi.

I had met President Qadaffi shortly before the summit at a dinner given by Abdel Nasser, a meeting which I had briefly feared had cost me Nasser's friendship. It had all begun when

Qadaffi's wife, Fathiyya, addressing Nasser, complained that her husband had given orders to arrest her uncle. To be polite, Nasser had then turned to Qadaffi. "Why did you do this to your wife's relative, Brother Muammar?" he asked pleasantly. "You really must order his release."

All the dinner guests agreed, while Qadaffi's face darkened. "I had the man arrested because he is an enemy of the Revolution," he said firmly. A short silence had followed, which I broke.

"I agree with President Qadaffi," I said to Nasser. "Any revolution has to defend itself, expecially during its early phases, against those who are trying to undermine it."

There was almost a gasp, for few dared disagree with Nasser in public, especially a woman. I avoided looking directly at Anwar, but out of the corner of my eye I could see him wince. And Nasser was clearly irritated.

"Pay no attention to her," he said briskly to Qadaffi. "After all, her mother is British."

I was stung. "Perhaps you have forgotten, Mr. President, the story of Gawad Hosny, one of our most famous patriots, who fought against the British in the Canal Zone," I said to the astonished Nasser. "His mother was also British, but he would not admit it when the English soldiers arrested and tortured him, giving him no water at all. He knew they would be less cruel to him if they knew he was half British, but he told them nothing. This university student lived as an Egyptian hero and he died as an Egyptian hero, torn apart by the pack of dogs the British cruelly set on him. Being half British did not mean that he was any less Egyptian."

Again came a silence which someone had finally broken, shifting the conversation to safer grounds. "You are bringing me trouble, Jehan," Anwar had scolded me on the way home. But I regretted nothing. "Would you allow your heritage to be insulted?" I asked. Anwar laughed. "You are right," he said. "But it's hard for others to get used to your ways." Nasser, though, was not angry with my forwardness. "Your wife is a proper Upper Egyptian," he had laughingly told Anwar sometime after the dinner. "Like all of us, she was intent on taking her revenge immediately."

On the day the summit ended, I woke with a start and sat bolt upright in bed, my heart pounding. I rushed to Anwar's bedroom. "I have had a very bad dream," I told Anwar anxiously.

"What is it, Jehan?" he said, half asleep.

"Something is wrong with Nasser," I told him.

"Nonsense," Anwar said. "I was with him yesterday and there was nothing wrong at all. He is exhausted from the summit meetings, but today the leaders are leaving and he can rest."

"Anwar, please listen to me," I begged him. "There must be something the matter. In my dream I was standing on the balcony of my parents' house in Roda just after sunset when I saw people, many people, coming toward me in the street. I looked closely and I saw President Numeiry of the Sudan crying, crying, crying, with two other people who were crying, too. Then I saw Qadaffi with his whole entourage, all of them crying."

"What were they crying about?" Anwar said, more to calm me than anything else.

"Qadaffi was saying over and over again, 'It's unbelievable. Unbelievable. What has happened to Nasser? What has happened to Nasser?'"

Anwar yawned. "Well, there's nothing the matter with Nasser," he told me. "Don't worry about that dream."

The phone rang. It was Nasser. "Oh, thank God," I wanted to say when I heard his voice, but I controlled myself.

"Jehan, I would like to come take my dinner tonight with Anwar," he told me.

"You will be welcome, Mr. President," I told him, passing the phone on to Anwar. I was extremely happy he was coming, which he did often. He loved the children and they loved him, especially little Jehan. "I will kiss you a very strong kiss," she always told him, and together they would laugh. After he had visited with the children I would take them away, then serve Anwar and Nasser their meal.

"Our President is coming to have dinner with us today," I now went to tell the cook. "Let us just have a few simple things, kebab, salad, some stuffed grape leaves." But why didn't I feel better? Abdel Nasser was well. I would see him for myself in a few hours. What was the matter with me?

Perhaps I am getting a cold, I thought. I took two aspirins and went back to bed, something I almost never did. I had to be feeling stronger by the afternoon so that I could make sure the table was properly set and the flowers arranged the way I liked them. But I only felt worse. After I had eaten lunch my body felt as if it weighed two hundred kilos. I could hardly drag one foot in front of the other, I felt so heavy and tired. Perhaps it was not a cold, but the flu. I left a note for Anwar, who was coming home at 3 P.M., and I went back to bed for the afternoon.

At six the phone rang. "Would you please ask Mr. Sadat to come to the residence of President Nasser," the caller said. I thought it was a bit odd, but Anwar didn't think a thing about it when I told him.

"He has probably changed his mind about coming here," he said. "It's better for him to relax at home after such a hectic day." That made sense, for Nasser had been at the airport all day, personally seeing off every one of the Arab leaders in their separate planes. When Anwar left for the forty-five-minute trip to Nasser's home, he told me he'd call me if the President wanted to come back to our home for dinner.

But the message that came from Anwar an hour and a half later was quite different. Now I too was to go to Nasser's home. This was very unusual. In Cairo, Anwar and I never went together to Nasser's home except for official receptions and dinners. Otherwise Anwar went alone to meet with Nasser while I would go alone at other times to call on Mrs. Nasser. In Alexandria we would all meet together in the summertime for more social visits. Then we would all chat for a while and have some cold juice. Afterward Mrs. Nasser would usually take me for a stroll in her garden while Anwar and Abdel Nasser talked or watched a film together. That was normal in Alexandria. But in Cairo, no.

It was the eyes of the driver looking at me in the rearview mirror of the car which sent the first chill of premonition through me. He was not my normal driver. He was the same driver with the same eyes in the same mirror looking at me in the same way as he had three years before when he had driven me to bury my father. I knew at that instant someone had died at Nasser's home.

"Please switch on the radio," I asked him, wanting to take my mind off my forebodings. Immediately came the voice of Nagat el-Saghira singing her famous song "O My Beloved Egypt" about all those leaving Egypt to study, to work or teach or do anything abroad. On the radio now, she was singing of the exact moment the man is leaving his country. "Please switch off the radio," I asked the driver. He looked at me questioningly, but I turned to stare out the window. "I'm sorry," I told him. "I don't know why, but I don't want to talk."

The nightmare began. When I walked into Nasser's home, I found the Minister of the Interior sitting on the stairs, his head in his hands.

"What is wrong?" I asked. But he didn't answer. I went outside to the garden, to find one of Nasser's aides crying. "Has something happened to our President?" I asked one of the servants. But he was too upset to speak. "Where is Mrs. Nasser?" I pressed him gently.

"She is in her bedroom. The doctor has given her something to calm her," he managed to tell me.

I went up the stairs toward her room. In the hall I met their oldest son, Khalid. "Can I see your mother?" I asked him.

"I don't think so," he said. "They have put her to sleep."

No one told me what had happened, making the daze I had been in all day grow worse. I felt unable to make any decision at all. What should I do? And where was Anwar? Absently I looked down and realized I was wearing a bright-blue dress. Whatever had happened here, my dress was inappropriate. I will go home to change, I thought; then I will be ready to help receive the visitors who might come, to sit with the other women, to do what I can do. In the car I began to feel close to panic. I must sort out what I knew. It couldn't be Mrs. Nasser who had died, because she was under sedation. I had seen Khalid, so nothing had happened to him.

It must be Abdel Nasser. But it couldn't be. How would we survive without Nasser? I felt frightened, as if there were no other leader in the whole country, in the whole world, who could replace him. Egypt had been his ship, and he the sole captain. For eighteen years he had led us. It had never occurred to us that he wouldn't lead us for at least eighteen more.

I couldn't stop my tears. "What's wrong, Mrs. Sadat?" the driver asked.

"I don't know," I told him, which was true. But I couldn't stop my tears.

"What's wrong, Mrs. Sadat?" the driver kept asking me.

"I don't know. I don't know. Nobody told me anything," I said to him. "Please stop asking." And immediately he was quiet.

At home I turned on the television set, but there was no announcement of anything happening to Nasser. Instead there were films of him at the airport from that very afternoon, seeing off the last of the Arab leaders. I looked closely and saw him resting his head on the Amir of Kuwait's shoulder while they embraced. Nasser did look extremely tired and not his usual bold self. I switched back and forth between the two channels. There were no announcements. I turned on the radio. Nothing.

"Why are you crying, Mummy?" my children asked anxiously. "Has something happened to Pappi?"

"It's not your father," I reassured them over and over. "It's not your father." I climbed a stepladder to find my black wool dresses stored in the top of the closet. My summer dresses were all too light in color.

The phone rang. "What's wrong with Abdel Nasser?" asked the wife of a member of Parliament and a close friend.

"I don't know," I said.

But she was crying and so was I. "We are coming over to be with you," she said. "Everyone is saying that Abdel Nasser is dead." How did they know? It is impossible to explain. But the rumor was spreading like a brushfire. Nasser is dead. Nasser is dead. A silent wail seemed to come from the streets, where already people were gathering. Nasser is dead. Nasser is dead.

The apprehension heightened all over Egypt when the television screens went suddenly blank at seven o'clock and verses from the Quran appeared. Everyone's worst fears were confirmed at eight o'clock when Anwar's image came on the screen. I knew—everyone knew—just by looking at Anwar's face. He did not cry, nor even have tears in his eyes. His grief and suffering went beyond that.

" 'O soul at peace! Return unto thy Lord, Content in His good pleasure!' " Anwar recited. His shock was causing him to stop often to swallow or to take a deep breath. "I bring you the saddest news of the bravest of men, the noblest of men" he said slowly. "President Gamal Abdel Nasser has died after a brief illness which modern medicine has failed to cure."

How could Nasser be dead? He was only fifty-two years old.

For me, for almost everyone in Egypt, this seemed too sudden, impossible. But those closest to the President knew that he had been yet another casualty of the war. Nasser's health had been broken by the June War, our terrible defeat stripping him of his strength and self-confidence. "Gamal moved and talked after the war, but you could see death in his pale face and hands," Anwar would tell me later. "He did not die on September 28, 1970. He died the morning of June 5, 1967."

Five million grief-stricken people lined the streets of Cairo on Thursday, October 1, 1970, the day Nasser was buried. Because so many world leaders had wanted to attend Abdel Nasser's funeral, we had broken our tradition of burial on the day of death, waiting instead for three days to begin the ceremony. And what a tribute it was. Nasser's funeral was the largest ever witnessed in the world. As if my dream were occurring all over again, I watched President Numeiri coming down the steps of his plane in tears. Immediately afterward came the grief-stricken Qadaffi surrounded by his entourage. "Unbelievable," Qadaffi was saying. "Unbelievable."

I hardly saw Anwar in the days before the funeral. All day and all night he was in meetings, greeting the leaders as they arrived, arranging for the ceremony, preparing for their security. He didn't even come home, but moved into the Qubbah Palace where Abdel Nasser's body lay in state. On the day of the funeral, Anwar collapsed out of exhaustion and was taken to the Revolutionary Command Council building to rest. He awoke five hours later, terrified that Nasser's body had been carried off by the hysterical mourners along the street.

While Anwar prepared for the funeral, I sat with Mrs. Nasser, her relatives and the other government wives at her home. During the seven days of condolences after her husband was buried, I continued to sit with her while she received the hundreds, the thousands, paying her their respects. What a burden it must have been for her, what a hard position to be in. Her grief at her loss may have been private, but her mourning had to be public. Often she broke down. "Don't think about it," I would murmur to her, putting my arms around her shoulders. "It is God's will." My own sadness did not lift, either.

"*Mabruk,* Mrs. Sadat," one woman whispered to me as she came along the line. "Congratulations."

I glared at her, not believing her lack of tact.

I did not want to be the wife of the President of Egypt. I did not want the burden or the responsibility. And I did not want the loss of privacy, which would be more, much more, than what we had already lost. Anwar too was very depressed in the days following Nasser's death. He had never even considered becoming president of Egypt. He had welcomed what responsibilities he had had serving his country and Nasser whom he loved. But always the ultimate responsibility had rested with the late President.

Now the burden would be Anwar's, though officially he wouldn't be elected president for a month. And the strain would be great. We had been defeated in war, and our land was occupied. Our treasury was so low that it would soon be difficult to pay our soldiers on the front and our civil servants. Suspicion and dissent had filled our jails with more than 23,000 political prisoners, the great majority of them Muslim Brothers. And the only foreign power we had ties with was the Soviet Union, a regime Anwar distrusted completely.

I had the greatest confidence in Anwar. Of all the possible leaders to follow Nasser, I knew Anwar was the most capable, the most courageous. I knew that his true belief in God made my husband very, very strong inside, that God would be with him always. Still I was frightened for him. There had always been an ambitious clique in the government around Nasser, the same power elite who had fueled Nasser's suspicions to get rid of all who opposed them. Now they would be the ministers in Anwar's government.

I knew they were going to be opposed to Anwar, to give him trouble. Because of their opposition, Anwar would have to face all Egypt's problems alone. He would have around him people who were not faithful to him, who would try to hurt him. I knew this immediately. I knew this from the moment Abdel Nasser passed away and my husband became president of Egypt.

el-khiyana wal ghadr

Treachery and Traitors

i am standing in our garden in Giza. All around me there is a threatening orange glow, flickering off the magnolias and the fir tree that stands higher than our house. What is this ominous light? I look up at our home. It is on fire! Inside I can see the flames burning, burning, shooting out of all the windows at once. I try to run toward the house, to save my children, my husband, my mother. But I cannot move. I want to scream, to cry out for help. But my voice makes no sound. Helpless, I stand there, watching the smoke now billowing out over the Nile. But wait. The smoke is not black. It is white! There is still hope. "Please help us, God," I say. "Please help us save Egypt."

Anwar. I had to tell Anwar. I rushed to his bedroom to tell him my dream. "The plot against you will not suceed," I said excitedly. "Your enemies will try to kill you and take over the country, but they will not be able to reach you. This I believe because the smoke from the fire they set in my dream burned white and not black. Egypt will be saved and so will you!"

My husband smiled at me, but said nothing. I did not know whether he believed in my dreams or whether even I did. But the dream about Nasser's end had come true. Was this to be another? It made me feel better to think so. But the danger to Anwar was great, and I was still very frightened.

Anwar was fighting the most stubborn kind of opposition: the power of a ghost. His vision for Egypt was very different from that of Abdel Nasser, to whom many in our country were still fiercely loyal. Unlike Nasser, Anwar wanted to reduce censorship and encourage political debate. Unlike Nasser, Anwar wanted to open Egypt to the lucrative markets of the West. Unlike the Nasserists, Anwar did not want to continue the War of Attrition against the Israelis. But my husband's position as president was very delicate. Some did not think he should be president at all.

Almost every one of the leaders in the government Anwar had inherited from Nasser was against him: Prime Minister Ali Sabri, Minister of the Interior Sha'arawi Gom'a, Minister of Presidential Affairs Sami Sharaf, Minister of Defense Muhammad Fawzi, Minister of Information Muhammad Fayek, as well as the head of General Intelligence, Amin Howeidi. Over the years these men, many of whom had served on the dreaded Committee for the Liquidation of Feudalism, had amassed great power and influence, arresting or blackmailing their opponents, tapping phones and monitoring the opinions of thousands of ordinary Egyptians. Under Nasser this group had grown increasingly influential, forming a power block which was virtually uncontrollable. Under Sadat, they had no intention of giving up any of their power.

From the beginning of my husband's presidency Anwar's actions enraged this power bloc. Rather than forming committees which arbitrarily seized the property and wealth of the middle classes, Anwar only two months after taking office lifted the sequestration decrees which put private property under government custodianship. Rather than bugging telephones and keeping blacklists as Nasser's ministers had always done, Anwar made it illegal to tap a telephone without a court order. So dedicated was Anwar to a citizen's right to privacy that he refused even to read the mounds of transcriptions of telephone calls between Egyptians formerly under suspicion.

Each of these steps toward democracy were condemned by Anwar's Cabinet. Nasser had been very close to the Soviet Union, and so now were his loyalists. In a time when Europe and America were expressing optimism about what they called "the Cairo Spring," my husband's enemies were using their propaganda to criticize his every move. "Sadat and his supporters represent the forces of reaction," they told the members of the Arab Socialist Union. "The reactionaries are regrouping so that they can negate the gains of the workers and the fellaheen." Five of the eight members of the Supreme Executive Committee of the Arab Socialist Union, our country's only political party, were so pro-Soviet that Anwar bitterly nicknamed them "the Politburo." The "Politburo" made no secret of their attitudes, discrediting my husband to all who would listen. Even the newspapers began to echo their criticisms of my husband's policies. So did the foreign diplomats. "Sadat won't last six weeks," United States envoy Eliot Richardson reported to President Nixon after returning from Nasser's funeral. The Soviets agreed.

But what was angering the government members opposed to Anwar was greatly pleasing the people. Egyptians were rejoicing in their new freedoms, especially the lifting of the decree which had made it almost impossible for Egyptians to travel abroad. No longer was it necessary to have government interviews, get government stamps and fill out endless official forms just to get an exit visa. Wealthier Egyptians who had fled Egypt began to trickle home. The isolation that had shrouded Egypt was lifting. And the campaign of the Nasserists to overthrow my husband began.

"The Minister of the Interior was talking harshly against your husband at dinner last night," one of my friends warned me shortly after Anwar's inauguration. Said another, "I heard from Sami Sharaf that your husband is weak and none of the ministers respect him." Those who knew our telephone number called me with one rumor after another. Those who didn't started coming to our door. Loyal Egyptians I'd never even met put themselves in danger by coming furtively to see me at our home at every hour of the day or night to report a new threat, a new slight to Anwar. I met with all who came, instructing the staff to let everyone in regardless of the hour. The danger of a coup was growing, and I wanted to know exactly what was going on behind my husband's back.

The rumors intensified when Anwar announced a new peace initiative to the Parliament four months after he assumed power. If Israel would withdraw her forces from the Sinai, Anwar proposed, Egypt would be willing to reopen the Suez Canal. He also announced his plan to extend the cease-fire proposed by the Rogers Plan from three months to six, and to restore diplomatic relations with the United States.

Most startling of all was his proposal to sign a peace agreement with Israel through the mediation of the United Nations. In the twenty-two years of Israel's existence, no Arab leader had ever taken such initiative. Alarmed by this radical proposal, Anwar's enemies redoubled their efforts to discredit him. Anwar's policies were gaining public support and thus becoming dangerous. His leaning away from the Soviet Union and socialism toward the West and democracy was a trend they had to crush.

Every night I told Anwar about the new rumors and smears I was hearing. By April, six months after his inauguration, Anwar's enemies were boasting about the "rumor centers" they had set up, claiming they could launch an anti-Sadat story in Cairo and have it circulate throughout the country and be back to Cairo in an hour. Telephone conversations I was making from our private phones were reported back to me, proving that our own home—the President's own residence—was bugged. "Why does your husband leave power in the hands of his enemies?" those faithful to Anwar kept asking. "Why does he allow his ministers to persuade the people that he is just some kind of figurehead like the Queen of England, that they are really the ones ruling Egypt?" "He is just waiting for the right time," I would answer. But I myself was losing patience with Anwar.

"Anwar, what are you waiting for? Are you waiting for them to arrest you, to put you in prison, to kill you?" I asked him in exasperation one night in April. "I'm worried about you as your wife, yes, but I'm also worried for Egypt. If the Communists take over the country, they will close it up again. You are leading Egypt toward democracy, toward peace with Israel and improved relations with many other countries, but they will reverse it." I tried to remain calm, to talk quietly, but I couldn't. "You are in a race with your enemies, and the winner will be the one who is quickest to get rid of the other," I said a little loudly. "All of them are against you, and they have the power to move the masses. What are you waiting for, Anwar? Tell me."

After the '73 war, I took the women hospital volunteers to Mecca with me to give thanks and traveled to the Canal Zone to thank our soldiers still stationed there.

At the age of forty-one, I enrolled in Cairo University. Six years later, I sat for my master's degree in Arabic literature, supported not only by (from left) Nana; Gamal's wife, Dina; Loubna and Noha but by thousands of Egyptians watching on television.

My dear friend the late Queen Alia of Jordan (top) visited me in Cairo, as did Safiyya Qadaffi on her first trip alone outside Libya (bottom). In 1974, two hundred women from 30 countries attended the first conference of African and Arab women convened in Cairo.

I made many friends on our trips abroad, including Queen Elizabeth, who invited my whole family to lunch at Buckingham Palace, and Rosalynn Carter, with whom I shared many anxieties during the peace process.

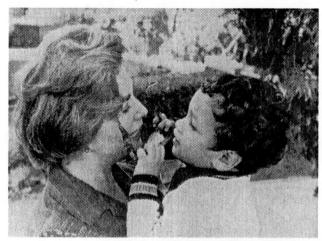

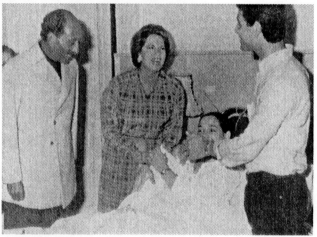

Always my heart was with my family; my grandson Sherif; Gamal and Dina at the birth of their daughter, Yasmin; our family gathered nervously in Isma 'iliyya before Anwar's trip to Jerusalem.

Mrs. Begin, Mrs. Carter and I sat together (above, front row right) at the signing of the Camp David Accords in 1979. But peace with Israel and our welcome of the deposed Shah and Shahbanu of Iran in 1980 angered the fundamentalist minority of Egypt.

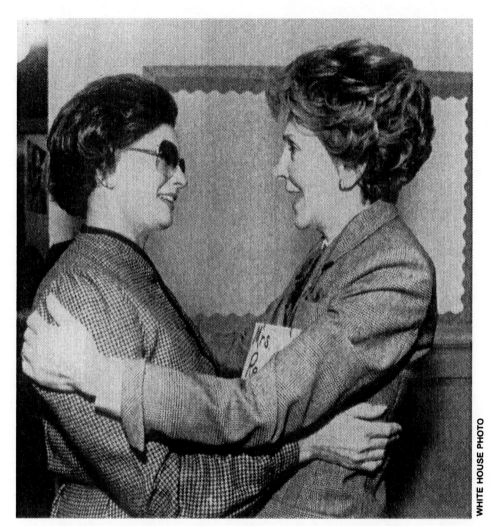

With Mrs. Nancy Reagan, who would become one of my best friends in Washington.

October 6, 1981. Someone took this snapshot of me and Sherif before the review, while in the stands below, Anwar (seated between Vice President Mubarak and the Minister of Defense) awaited his destiny. Three days later, the world mourned the passing of a man of peace.

Anwar smiled. "Well, Jehan, you have forgotten something very important," he said gently. He pointed to the sky. "God is with me," he said.

"Yes, I'm sure God is with you," I replied. "But God does not always help those who do not help themselves. Maybe God is impatient with you, too, saying 'Do something, my son, and I'll be with you.' It's not enough, Anwar, just to say 'God is with me.' "

But Anwar kept smiling. "I am not saying that, Jehan," he said. "Of course I am taking steps, but quietly. I am not as impatient as you. Nor do I care about the empty threats of words. When the time comes, you will see that I am prepared."

"What can I do to help you prepare?" I asked him, wanting really some reassurance that he had a plan.

"Ask the people who are telling you these rumors to write them down, to sign them and give them to me," he said.

I felt greatly relieved, thinking that he was telling me indirectly of his plans to arrest the insurrectionists and to use the signed reports of their lies as evidence against them in court. The next day I asked a woman member of Parliament to write down what she had told me and to sign it.

"The ministers addressing the Arab Socialist Union declared that our leadership was weak, that they had no trust in the leadership and that Egypt's latest policies went against everything that Nasser stood for," she dutifully reported.

"Good," Anwar said when I gave him the report. "I will show this to the Minister of the Interior."

The Minister of the Interior? The leader of the opposition? I was shocked. "Anwar, how could you?" I cried. "You will be putting this good woman who has helped us by giving us information into the mouth of the lion!"

But Anwar was firm. "I know what I'm doing, Jehan," he said. "You will see."

I knew that my husband was a man of principle. But why would he jeopardize the men and women who were trying to help us by sharing this information with the enemy? Later I would understand his strategy. By showing these threatening reports to the ministers who were against him, Anwar was letting his enemies know that he knew their intentions. He was showing them that he was entirely sure of himself. He knew, and they knew, that as President he held the ultimate power and could arrest them anytime he chose. But if he issued such orders, would the Army be loyal to Anwar or to his enemy, the Minister of Defense?

"That was such a nice officer your husband sent to our house yesterday," a neighbor said to me one morning. Officer? What officer? "He came with the Minister of the Interior and asked if he could inspect your house from our upper floor. They said they needed to know how best to defend your house if anyone tried to attack your husband."

I expressed my thanks to her, for she thought she had done us a favor. But I suspected that the truth was very different. They were looking for the best way to attack when they came to arrest Anwar.

Never had I felt so alone. We had no one to turn to, no one even to talk to. I moved into Anwar's bedroom at night, feeling safer next to him and the pistol he always kept on his bedside table. "Lock the door," I told him.

"Why?" he asked. "We never lock the door."

"Well, now we must," I insisted.

He looked at me in his bemused way which infuriated me.

"At least when they come to arrest you in the middle of the night they won't be able to get into the bedroom immediately and you will have time to wake up and get your pistol ready," I blurted out. "You will be able to kill two or three of them before they kill you."

"Oh, Jehan," Anwar said. "Your imagination will kill us all." But he said nothing further when I got up and locked the door.

The Nasserists were almost as opposed to me. From the beginning they had criticized me, even sabotaged me, for the public role I had chosen to take. While I sat with Mrs. Nasser during the period of mourning for her husband, I had wrestled with the options ahead of me. As the wife of Egypt's new President, was I going to follow in Mrs. Nasser's traditional footsteps, staying always at home, being known as a good wife and mother, fulfilling only the bare minimum of my public obligations? Or was I going to continue to serve the people?

I knew that anything I did in public would be controversial, for no leader's wife in our country had ever worked outside the home. In ancient Egypt, of course, women themselves had been greatly respected as leaders, Queen Hatshepsut having launched the military expeditions which increased Egypt's sovereignty over Somalia and Djibouti. As proof of her power, Hatshepsut had ordered the images of herself that were carved on her huge tomb in Luxor to be shown wearing a beard. It was only in more recent times that Egyptian women had been relegated to inferior roles. And most had submitted.

But I could not—I would not—give up the public work I had started. I felt that God had given me the power to help the people and the ability to understand their problems and to work with them. As the wife of the new President, I could be the link between Anwar and the people, sharing their suffering and studying their problems. I knew that some would criticize me for my work, and that Anwar too would be attacked for allowing his wife to appear in public. But those who objected to my role I was determined to ignore. How I made use of this gift from God would be up to me.

The confrontation with those clinging to the old ways had begun immediately. On the night of Anwar's inauguration, a reception was held at Abdin Palace for the foreign ambassadors. This was traditional. But Anwar's message was not. "Tell your leaders Egypt wants peace, but we will not accept our land being occupied," Anwar told the diplomats.

To further show the world that this administration would be different, Anwar made another unprecedented move. When my husband and I entered the reception, he asked me to walk beside him rather than five steps behind him as Mrs. Nasser had always done with her husband. Moreover, when the reception line was formed, Anwar placed me ahead of him so that each guest shook my hand before his. Even I was startled, for it was unheard of for a Muslim leader to show such deference to a woman. But Anwar wanted to show the world—as did I—that Egypt would now be under new and modern leadership. The flashbulbs never stopped recording this unprecedented event. And the backlash began.

"Don't serve the guests yourself," the wife of the Minister of the Interior hissed at me as I handed each foreign diplomat his plate. "You are the wife of the President!" She thought I was being undignified, while on the contrary I felt I was sending out the new message of equality.

"What can I lose by being polite?" I said, smiling at her, as I continued to assist the diplomats. "What I would do in my own home for our guests I want to start here. If our foreign guests see that I am secure, they will in turn respect me." And once again the flashbulbs lit up the room.

The confrontation came to a head the next day. Photographs of the wives of King Farouk had very rarely been in the newspaper. Very rarely, too, had there been photos of Mrs. Nasser. And there would be none of me. The photos in the newspaper the next morning showed the foreign wives of all the ambassadors, their husbands, my husband standing in the receiving line—and my hand. It made me laugh and feel furious at the same time. If Nasser's old guard wanted a fight over the new status of women, they were going to get it. Immediately I phoned Fawzi Abdel Hafez, Anwar's secretary. "Call the Minister of Presidential Affairs and ask him why he removed me from the photograph," I asked him. "Tell him he should be proud to show the wife of the President in the newspaper and never to cut out my photo again without my permission."

"All right, madam," Fawzi answered reluctantly. I should have known when I heard the resistance in his voice that he wouldn't relay such a controversial message.

An hour later I was on my way downstairs to greet a guest when Fawzi called me back. "The Minister of Presidential Affairs is on his way to see you," he told me.

"Did you give him my message?" I asked him.

"No," he said unhappily.

"Swear. Did you tell him?" I pressed.

"I swear, no," he replied.

"Then what you are telling me is far worse," I said.

"Why?" Fawzi asked.

"It proves our phones are bugged," I said. "How else could he have known of my displeasure if you didn't tell him?"

The Minister's explanation for removing me from the photo was as ridiculous as the situation was ominous. "I apologize for not running your photo, madam," Sami Sharaf said to me when he arrived at the house. "I was thinking of our troops who have been suffering in the desert on the front for four years and what they would think when they saw your photograph."

"What is wrong with seeing the wife of the President?" I asked him.

The perspiration was flowing off Sharaf. "The troops would think that while they are suffering for their country, their leaders are having parties in Cairo," he said lamely.

"Parties? What kind of parties?" I responded. "We were doing our duty in greeting the ambassadors. We were not dancing or entertaining our friends. This was our work."

"I did not want to offend our troops," he persisted.

"Well, you have offended me," I told him firmly. "Do you think I should have been hidden away at home behind a veil so that no man would see me?"

"I am sorry, madam," he told me. "I'm sure the magazines will run your picture."

"How can it be right for a magazine and not for a newspaper?" I asked. The poor man could think of no explanation.

Another incident quickly followed. The only woman in the Cabinet, Minister of Social Affairs Dr. Hikmat Abu Zeid, invited me to a reception for the first female Russian astronaut. It was a lovely dinner. But when Dr. Hikmat called me a few days later, what she said chilled me. She had sent me a cable, she told me, asking if I had a message for her to convey to a women's group she was going to address in the Sudan. Cable? I had never received her cable. I soon discovered that the Minister of Presidential Affairs had hidden the cable to prevent me from being publicly identified as an activist or even a participant in the modernization of Egyptian women.

I was furious, and once more sent for Minister Sharaf, who claimed never to have received the cable. Only after I insisted that he find it was it delivered to my office. It was clear that I, like Anwar, was going to have to wage war against my increasingly powerful enemies in the government. Like many other Egyptian men, the Nasserists believed that a good wife stayed modestly at home.

But I did not agree. For too long Egyptian men had gotten away with treating women as possessions, robots whose function was to be invisible and obey. And there was no basis for it. None.

Nothing in our religion supported the total subservience of women. In no place in the Quran is it written that women must remain at home and do no work in public. No. The Quran treats men and women equally, in life and in death. "If any do deeds of righteousness, be they male or female, and have faith, they will enter Paradise," reads the 124th Sura of our Holy Book. The Quran, in fact, extols the leadership of women. "I found a woman ruling over them, and she has been given abundance of all things, and hers is a mighty throne," reads 27:23 of "The Ant."

It was neither our Holy Book nor the teachings of our Prophet Muhammed that had reduced the status of Muslim women. It was the centuries-old tradition of male supremacy throughout the Arab world. Succumbing to male dominance had become a habit for generations of Muslim women. But habits could change.

Where to begin? Assiut. That is where I would go. In the face of the official opposition to my active participation, I knew I would need the support of the people, especially that of the most religious. It was in Assiut in Upper Egypt where the most conservative and even fanatic Muslims and Coptic Christians lived, and where the supposedly Islamic costume of the veil for women and galabiyyas for men was most entrenched. Like the religiously conservative anywhere in the world, the devout in Assiut would be the most resistant to change. If I could win the support of the dozens of sheikhs in Assiut, the fundamentalist students in the university there, and the Copts, then half the battle would be won.

I did not write a formal speech, nor even make any notes. I wanted to plead my case before this most difficult audience from the heart, though I must admit that my heart faltered somewhat as I looked out over the audience almost totally composed of men. "I have come to Assiut because you are the most conservative people in all of Egypt," I said. "I know that you greatly respect women who stay at home to care for their husbands and children as do I. But I want to ask a question of you.

"I have two choices. As the wife of your President, I can stay at home and spend my time relaxing with my husband and children, attending a few official dinners for the wives of visiting dignitaries, and traveling to the airport to say goodbye. That would be a very easy and comfortable life for me. But these are not comfortable times. And I would like to hear your answer to my second choice.

"As I speak to you, our land is occupied. I feel as if my country is my home, and my own garden is occupied. The choice is whether I stay inside my house, unable to go out into my own garden, or whether I try to help my husband to get our garden back. Am I going to share the burdens of Egypt, working with women and children, the disabled and the poor, or am I going to leave it to my husband to do everything all alone? Which is the proper role for a wife?

"I know what I want to do. I want to help my husband, to do whatever I can for our country, to play a role. I will receive no money for it. Instead I will sacrifice my time, my health sometimes from being overtired, my comfort in being well cared for at home. In one way, this role will not be enjoyable. But in another it will, for I believe that God has sent me this mission. And I want to do it." I took a deep breath.

"What is your answer?" I asked. "I want to hear it."

There was a moment of silence. And then the applause started, growing and swelling until my heart was full.

"Thank you so much," I called out to the crowd. "I appreciate your answer very much. I promise you that I will do the best I can for the benefit of our country."

From Assiut I went directly to the front in Suez to seek the support of our military troops, a crucial factor in the role I wanted to play for Egypt. Our early Islamic history, I reminded them, was filled with examples of women famous for their strength and bravery. Nusiba Bint Ka'ab el-Ansariyya, for example, had taken up a sword and fought in the Muslims' many battles against their enemies, in one case striking down a man who was about to kill the Prophet. Um Muslim el-Milhan had fought alongside the Prophet, too, going into battle even when she was pregnant. 'Aisha, the Prophet's favorite wife, had ridden her own camel into battle, and had not been condemned as a bad Muslim. On the contrary, the Prophet had singled 'Aisha out as an example for all to follow, advising men and women believers both, "Take half your religion from her."

Nor were such examples limited to the distant past, I told them, reminding them of the famous Algerian heroine Gamila Bou'hered, who, like so many other Algerian women, had smuggled bombs and weapons in her handbag to fight in Algeria's revolution against France. Gamila Bou'hered had been caught and cruelly tortured by the French, but she never told them the identities of the other fedayeen. "Like the Algerians, we are all one family facing danger," I told the troops. "Our duty as wives and mothers is to be the partners of our fighters, not just to sit at home and let the burden be on them." The response of the soldiers was as heartwarming as had been the support I had found in Assiut. *"Allah ma'aki,"* they chanted, "may God be with you." Filled with confidence, I returned to Cairo.

I knew there would be some resistance to the new role I was trying to create for women. I soon found out how bitter it would be. Soon after I returned from the front, the most conservative students at Cairo University staged a demonstration against me, charging that my appearance before so many soldiers had been improper and shameful. *"Hukm* Dayan *walla hukm* Jehan," they shouted. "Rule by Dayan is better than rule by Jehan!" I could not believe my ears. Would these students really prefer to be ruled by the Israeli Minister of Defense simply because he was a man? I was shocked. But from the beginning I knew I had to learn to take the criticisms if I was to change anything at all. I hoped I would have the courage.

Every day now in Cairo the wives of the men Nasser's regime had imprisoned were coming to my home to petition me for their husbands' release. And I met with every one of them. "Mrs. Sadat is wasting her time on people who don't deserve it," the criticism began, circulated by the Nasserists who had imprisoned these men in the first place. But I paid no attention. "Tell those who repeat this criticism that I am here to meet with anybody in need," I told Fawzi Abdel Hafez, Anwar's secretary. I continued to meet with the prisoners' wives and to pass their petitions on to Anwar. Later, these prisoners and thousands of others would be released by my husband as he brought Egypt closer and closer to democracy.

I also managed somehow to continue visiting with the wives of the government ministers opposed to us, all the time pretending I knew nothing of their husbands' intentions to overthrow Anwar. While we chatted on about our children as if we had nothing else on our minds, I listened for clues in whatever they said, any slips of the tongue that would disclose their husbands' plotting. I felt such conflict as I shared cold drinks and small talk with these women whom I had known as friends for so long. Did they know the sinister plans of their husbands? I drew comfort from one of my favorite sayings which kept echoing in my mind: "Who ever digs a hole for another to fall into, he is the one who will end up falling."

On May 1, the crisis began to come to a head. Because of our relationship with the Soviet Union, this was our Labor

Day, a day of celebration for all of Egypt's workers. Anwar was to make a speech. The Minister of Labor was to make a speech. So were the Governor and the heads of all the labor syndicates. All of Egypt was watching on television, including me. And what we saw was horrifying.

Every time the crowd applauded one of the speakers, the men in the front rows held up large photographs of Abdel Nasser. "Sadat is nothing compared to Abdel Nasser," these demonstrators were implying to the millions of Egyptians watching. "Pay no attention to what he is telling you and listen only to those who remain true to our greatest leader." I couldn't believe it. The first six rows of the audience had been filled with men the ministers had recruited against my husband!

I felt close to panic. The conspiracy was out in the open now. And obviously it was well organized, because the photos of Nasser rose as if by one hand. Now everyone in Egypt knew that Sadat's own Cabinet ministers were against him. Was Anwar doomed? Or were they?

I rushed to Anwar when he got home. "Anwar, what are you going to do?" I cried out to him.

"You will see tomorrow, Jehan," he said calmly. The next day he dismissed Ali Sabri, one of his two Vice-Presidents and the top Soviet advocate in Egypt.

The race was on. Every morning when I woke up behind our locked bedroom door I was amazed Anwar had survived the night. "Take special care of the President," I said every day to his bodyguards. "Be very, very cautious." Still people came to our door both day and night with the latest rumors. The most ominous message came from Muhammad Heikal, the editor of *el-Ahram*.

"Mrs. Sadat, swear not to tell anyone what I am going to say to you," Heikal said to me. "The President is acting so calmly that I do not think he realizes how dangerous the situation is. I have heard plans in many meetings to remove him from office. Your husband must not go near the radio and television center. The Minister of Defense has ordered guards to surround the building in case the President decides to broadcast the plot against him to the people. They have orders to arrest him if he tries."

I rushed to Fawzi Abdel Hafez, who was responsible for Anwar's security. "Do not let my husband go to the television building," I said to him. "I cannot tell you why or how I know, but there is the greatest danger to him there."

"All right, madam," Fawzi said, his face grim.

A few days later, Anwar announced his plan for a May 13 visit to el-Tahrir province, where a pilot experiment in land reclamation was under way. "Please, Anwar, please cancel your trip," I begged him. "I have a feeling that something terrible will happen in el-Tahrir, that you will be ambushed and killed."

Whether he believed my intuition or not, Anwar postponed the trip. "I have much to do here," he told me. "There is no need to go just now."

My head pounded. I felt threats all around me. I had to protect Anwar. But how? He still refused to move against his enemies. In spite of my intuition and all the overt warnings, Anwar continued to feel that he did not have the concrete evidence for a court conviction.

"Please, Anwar, arrest these men before they kill you," I pleaded with him.

But he continued to refuse. "This is a country of laws," he told me. "I will not resort to the old police-state tactics of preventive detention unless I have sufficient evidence for conviction."

The evidence arrived on May 11. "Mrs. Sadat, I must speak with you immediately," said Fawzi, entering the salon where I was sitting with my sister and her husband, a member of Parliament, before dinner.

I excused myself and went out into the hall.

"A police officer loyal to your husband has just brought a tape recording of what he says is a conversation between Farid Abdel Karim and Mahmoud el-Sa'dani which reveals the plot to overthrow the regime and kill the President," Fawzi told me quietly.

"Oh, God bless him," I said. "But we must act perfectly normally. There may be spies even among our household staff. We must wait until my sister and her husband leave after our meal to listen to the tape."

I sat in agony throughout the evening, discussing the political situation with my sister and brother-in-law, but not mentioning the tape. Anwar had joined us late and knew nothing. "Leave. Please go home," I kept silently willing my sister. It was almost midnight before they finally left and I could tell Anwar what had happened. Together we went upstairs to the terrace on the third floor, where Fawzi brought us the tape. The reel was too big to play on our tape recorder.

"We have a larger one in the basement," I told Anwar. "I will go fetch it." I went calmly to the basement in case someone in our household was watching for anything out of the ordinary, and finally returned with the right machine.

I trembled as the harsh words filled the air. This was my husband these devils were planning to kill, the leader of their own party, the President of their own country. I sucked in my breath when I heard Abdel Karim, the head of the Arab Socialist Union in Giza tell journalist and party member Mahmoud el-Sa'dani of Anwar's plan to visit el-Tahrir. "We will get rid of him when he goes to the land reclamation project," Abdel Karim said.

I gasped. My intuition had been right.

The incriminating tape wound on. "What if he goes to Broadcast House to appeal to the people on television? Do we have that covered?"

"Of course," came the response. "Our guards are stationed there to stop him from entering and will arrest him on the spot."

I gasped again. "That is just what Muhammad Heikal told me," I said to Fawzi.

Anwar stopped the tape recorder. "Muhammad Heikal told you that?" he asked me incredulously, his face growing dark with anger. "Did you already know this and not tell me?"

"Yes," I admitted.

"Why, Jehan, why?" Anwar said, his voice rising.

"Because Heikal made me swear not to tell anybody," I confessed. "I told Fawzi only to keep you away from Broadcast House, knowing that if you went there you would not be permitted to enter."

"Who dared say this?" Anwar shouted. "To take over our national communications and to prevent the President from addressing his people is a real plot. Words are one thing. But this action is quite another. I must speak to Heikal myself immediately."

We couldn't call because our telephone was tapped and it was after 1 A.M. But Heikal lived only a few blocks away. Early the next morning I woke our thirteen-year-old daughter. "Run, Noha," I told her. "Tell Heikal your father wants him immediately!" Soon Noha returned with Heikal.

"Muhammad, you told Jehan about the plot at the television station. Why didn't you tell me?" Anwar asked Heikal. Heikal's response was very hesitant, as if he did not want to cast his lot with either side. "I just wanted you to know that you have to be very careful, to be even more cautious," he said.

The tape had given Anwar all the evidence of a coup he needed. But though it was clear now who was against us, who was with us?

The next day, May 12, Anwar arranged to meet with the Army. Anwar was sure of their loyalty, knowing he was far more beloved by the troops than was Defense Minister Muhammad Fawzi, now a leader of the conspirators. Anwar also knew that this meeting would be a critical showdown. Defense Minister Fawzi would be there, and everyone knew that whoever had the loyalty of the Army controlled Egypt.

"I won't allow any 'spheres of influence' to come into being or any kind of power struggle to continue," Anwar said firmly at the meeting, bringing the challenge of his political adversaries to a head. "Anyone who acts against the interests of Egypt will be ground into mincemeat."

I trembled as I watched on television the stony face of Defense Minister Fawzi, who was sitting right beside my husband. The tension was incredible. How would the Army react?

"*Yahya* Sadat! Long live Sadat!" the officers cheered, their support for Anwar overwhelming. No one had realized how tired the officers had become of the Nasserists' police-state tactics and untrustworthy ways.

Now everybody knew that the crisis had reached the boiling point. On the next morning, the thirteenth, Anwar fired the Minister of the Interior, Sha'arawi Gom'a, another leader of the traitors. He also summoned General el-Leithy Nassif, commander of the Presidential Guard, whose sole duty it was to safeguard the President, and whose orders came only from the President and not his Cabinet. The loyalty of the Presidential Guard would be critical as the showdown neared. And though Anwar knew that General Nassif was a man of principle, a man who had faith in God, he also knew that Nassif had served Nasser faithfully and for years had worked closely with all the ministers now involved in the plot. They were not only his colleagues but his close friends.

"Leithy," Anwar now asked him, "if I were to ask you to arrest the Cabinet ministers, could you do it?"

"Yes, Mr. President," General Nassif replied with no hesitation. "It is my duty to do whatever you ask."

"Do you have the forces and the armed equipment ready to arrest each one at his home?" Anwar asked.

"I am prepared," the commander answered. But was he? Anwar and I knew that Nassif must be torn. Though he might be sure the ministers were wrong, still they were all friends of long standing.

"Do not tell anyone of this conversation," Anwar cautioned him.

"Of course not, Mr. President," Nassif said.

The conspirators made their move that night. Anwar and I were watching the ten-o'clock news, the last television programming of the day, when there was a knock on the door. It was Nasser's son-in-law, Ashraf Marawan, who worked in the office of Sami Sharaf, the Minister of Presidential Affairs. We welcomed Ashraf, for he was our personal friend. But what he brought us were the final cards in the planned coup: letters of resignation from the Speaker of the National Assembly, the Minister of Defense, the Minister of Information and the Minister of Presidential Affairs, as well as the resignations of several members of the Central Committee and the Supreme Executive Committee. "The resignations will be announced on television in a few minutes," Ashraf said, somewhat sheepishly.

The moment of truth had finally come. By announcing their joint resignations and thereby creating a constitutional crisis, the Cabinet ministers were sure Anwar would be forced to submit his resignation as president as well. With him out of the way, they would be free to reinstate themselves and take over the country. Their timing was critical—they planned to use the last moments of television broadcasting so that Anwar would not have time to respond immediately to their resignations and explain the situation to the people.

Anwar looked at Ashraf, shaking his head in disbelief.

"We have just been handed a news bulletin," the announcer was saying. "The Minister of Information has resigned. The Minister of Defense has resigned. The Minister . . . "

"Ashraf, why didn't you tell us this earlier so that my husband would have had time to prepare a response?" I asked the young man standing there so uncomfortably.

"The ministers wouldn't let me leave the office," he said.

That might have been true. Ashraf, after all, was just an employee and had to obey his superiors. I didn't know what to believe anymore.

The conspirators had underestimated Anwar. Though the timing of their mass resignation was clever, the rest of their strategy was very stupid. "They have made it much easier for me," Anwar mused as we watched the television. "They have announced all their resignations, but not mine. They have done my work for me." He glowered at the television screen. "As president of Egypt, I accept your resignations. And now you are all under arrest."

He summoned General Nassif, who had prepared for such an emergency. "It is time," Anwar told the commander of the Presidential Guard. "Place all the ministers and the other government conspirators under house arrest immediately and cut off any comunication between them."

"Yes, Mr. President," General Nassif replied. Immediately he dispatched his guards to surround each of their homes.

The plot against us was about to be over. Or was it? Fawzi Abdel Hafez phoned me at midnight. "Mrs. Sadat, there are tanks moving toward your home. Did the President order them to your home for protection?"

I hurried to the bathroom, where Anwar was shaving, preparing himself to leave the house at the crack of dawn. "Did you give orders for tanks to come here?" I asked him.

"I gave no such orders," Anwar said.

I hurried back to the phone, my fear mounting. "No, Fawzi," I said.

Whose tanks were they? Who had given the orders? Had the Defense Minister managed to turn the Army against us? Why else would tanks be coming to our house except to attack and take Anwar prisoner? The children. I had to get them out of the danger rumbling toward us in the dark streets. I rushed to speak to my eldest daughter, Loubna, taking a deep breath before entering her room because I did not want to appear frightened. I had kept as much of the plot against their father from the children as I could, not wanting to alarm them. They were still quite young, Loubna sixteen, Gamal fourteen, Noha thirteen and little Jehan only ten. But of course, like all children, they knew far more than their parents realized.

"Loubna," I said gently, "there is so much commotion here, people coming and going all day and all night. Why don't you take your brother and sisters and go now to your aunt's house, where you will all be much more relaxed."

Loubna looked me straight in the eye. "Do you want to send us away because there is danger here?" she asked.

"Maybe," I admitted.

But Loubna was way ahead of me. "In your mind, the worst that can happen is that our home will be attacked and we'll all be killed," she said. "But to me the worst would be that we were sent away and you and Pappi were killed. We have talked about it and have decided that we do not want to live without you. Even if we are all about to be killed, at least we will all be together."

"You have talked about this with the others?" I said incredulously.

Loubna nodded. "With Gamal," she said.

Gamal. I went to his room and found his bed empty. "Where is Gamal?" I demanded of Loubna.

"He is outside with his shotgun," Loubna said. My mouth fell open. "He has been patrolling the garden for several nights to defend the house, insisting that he can protect Pappi if his enemies come."

I rushed down to our front door, to find Gamal sitting on the steps, the gun he used to hunt birds with his father across his knees.

"Gamal," I said, putting my arms around him, "your father will be very proud of you for your bravery, but you can do nothing to protect your father with this gun. Now come to bed."

But he refused. "I know it is not a powerful gun," he said, "but in the dark perhaps his enemies will not know that. At least I will be able to warn Pappi, to give him time to prepare. If I see a stranger coming through the gate, I will shoot him, which will make a loud noise. Then I'll run to tell Pappi they are coming before they have time to reach him."

My heart broke for this young boy, sitting there so bravely in the dark with his bird gun. Even at fourteen he felt it was his duty to protect his father, to put his own life before that of his father. What a burden we had handed to our children. Though I had tried from the moment my children were born to protect them from the harshness of our destiny, I never really could. God had ordained this sacrifice for them as much as He had ordered it for Anwar and me. And so on the night of May 15, 1971, I left Gamal on the steps of our house with his gun and left the other children in their rooms. It the tanks were coming to harm us, it was better that we all face the consequences together. "Oh God, please help us," I prayed as I went back into the house.

The phone rang. It was General Nassif telling my husband not to worry. "I ordered tanks to your house to protect you in case there was trouble," he told Anwar. "But everything is now secure. The conspirators have all been arrested. It is over."

I ran to bring Gamal inside and to tell Loubna the news. Immediately Anwar went to Broadcast House to tell the people that the coup had failed, that those responsible were under arrest, and that the new freedoms he had promised Egypt were safe.

From such a night of tension came a morning of rejoicing. As Anwar spoke from his heart over radio and television, people began to pour into the streets. "Any force against my country, any threat to the new liberty and freedom I am giving to you all, I will grind into mincemeat," he promised with great emotion. The people went mad with joy, picking up on the phrase that had come to identify my husband during what would be called the Corrective Revolution. *"Ufrum, Sadat, ufrum!"* they chanted in the streets, massing in front of our house. "Grind, Sadat, grind!" Soon we could see hand-painted posters among the crowd, cartoons of the various ministers falling into meat grinders and coming out as mincemeat. "We are behind you, Sadat," the mobs called. "We are with you!"

The new spirit was infectious. In the next few months Anwar ordered all the infamous detention centers to be closed down and forbade arbitrary arrests. He ordered the release of thousands of political prisoners, including the members of the Muslim Brotherhood. For the first time in twenty years, censorship was lifted. "Speak up. Speak out," Anwar urged the people who had been stifled by fear for too long. In a highly popular move, he also ordered all the tapes of private conversations that had been recorded during Nasser's time and stored at the Ministry of the Interior to be burned.

A trial of the conspirators was held, and all were sentenced to life imprisonment. The only sadness was from General Nassif, the commander of the Presidential Guard. He had done his duty perfectly, dispatching his men immediately when Anwar had called him to arrest the ministers involved in the plot. But his heart had been anguished. Shortly after the coup was foiled, Nassif went into such a deep depression that he was sent to London for medical treatment. While there, he fell from a fifth-floor balcony to his death.

Everyone in Egypt believed he had committed suicide, unable to reconcile his duty to the President and his loyalty to Nasser and his followers. But I believe that the medication General Nassif was taking for his depression either made him so weak and dizzy that he fell by accident or so disoriented him that he jumped without being conscious of what he was doing. My husband was very, very sad about Nassif, for he had been a most brave and principled man.

With the help of God, Anwar had survived the first crisis of his presidency. Now he had the clear opportunity to surround himself with people who would work with him and not against him. Thanks to God, Anwar had been saved. Egypt had been saved. Now my husband could get on with what he wanted to do for our country. But first I had to keep a promise I had made to God during these terrible seven months. "Please, Lord," I had prayed, "if you rescue Egypt and my husband, I will fast for one month in gratitude and make the pilgrimage." God had answered my prayers. Now it was my turn to honor Him. Two weeks after the successful completion of the Corrective Revolution, I left for Mecca.

Chapter 9

damm ibrahim

The Blood of Abraham

abayka, Allahumma, labayka! La sharika laka! Here I am, O Lord! Here I am. I am here to do Your bidding. You have no partners. I am here to do Your bidding. Praise, bounty, grace and sovereignty are Yours. You have no partners. Here I am!"

On the airplane to Mecca and now in my hotel room, I repeated the pilgrim's traditional chant to God while visiting Mecca on pilgrimage. Millions of Muslims gather in Mecca every year, arriving by plane, by bus, by car, a few still by camels across the desert. So sacred is Mecca that for fourteen hundred years only believers have been allowed to enter it. And during the month of Dhu el-Hijja, when Muslims make the Hajj, or greater pilgrimage, in fulfillment of one of the five Pillars of Islam, as many as two million pour into the holy city at once, making the pilgrimage the single biggest international gathering in the world.

I was not in Mecca to make the greater Hajj, but the Umrah, or lesser pilgrimage, which can be undertaken at any time of the year. I had made this lesser pilgrimage once years before, having flown to the holy city and back in one night while Anwar was meeting with King Faisal in Riyadh. And I would make it two more times, taking a group of seventy volunteers after the 1973 war to thank them for their dedication, going again with my children and a small group of friends after a health scare I had in 1984. But this pilgrimage after the dangers in the spring of 1971 was especially moving and significant to me. God had anwered my prayers by sparing my husband's life.

"Here I am, O Lord! Here I am! I am here to do Your bidding!" I unpacked the Quran I always carry in my suitcase. "They will come to Thee on foot and mounted on every kind of camel, lean on account of journeys through deep and distant highways," I read from the "Pilgrimage" Sura, repeating aloud God's charge to Muslims to visit Mecca. Putting all thoughts of myself out of my mind, I concentrated instead on thoughts of love and peace. Worldly concerns and affectations were not to be brought to the pilgrimage. Neither were the enmities and conflicts I had experienced over the last few months. I was in Mecca, as was every other pilgrim, to commune with God, to meditate on His oneness and to feel the strength of our communal prayers.

I had begun the rituals of the pilgrimage before leaving Egypt, readying myself by entering Ihram, the state of purity. After removing my makeup and jewelry and taking a long bath to symbolically cleanse myself of my impurities, I had dressed in the long white dress of the pilgrim and placed a clean white scarf over my hair. To dedicate myself for the sacred journey, I had performed a prayer of two prostrations, then appealed to God, "Allah, I intend to perform the rites of the Umrah, so facilitate it for me and accept it from me."

Now, in Mecca, I saw many moving through the streets in

Ihram garments, threading their way through the stalls that sold Qurans of all colors and sizes, and the taxis, buses and cars which twenty-four hours a day carry Muslims to the Holy Mosque to begin their pilgrimage. The garments of men on pilgrimage, too, are traditional, sandals and two loose white togas made without seams. After visiting the Holy Mosque, men and women both often bring their white robes home with them, to be used in life as reminders of their sacred journey, and in death as their burial shrouds.

"Here I am, O Lord! Here I am!" Outside the Great Mosque I met our *mutawwif,* the official guide who would lead us through the rituals of the Umrah and act as our imam during the prayers. All around me the pilgrims called out their fulfillment of God's charge as we surged together up the broad marble steps of the Holy Mosque, leaving our shoes at the entrance. As the wife of the President of Egypt, I traveled with an entourage of security agents and my secretary, but still I was swept along with the crowd, calling out to God myself.

"Allah, You are the peace, and from You peace proceeds. O Lord of ours, greet us with peace," I and all the other pilgrims prayed as we reached the Gate of Peace that leads into the Haram, the vast white marble courtyard of the Holy Mosque. The Prophet had always begun his movements with the right side of his body, and now we too entered the Haram by stepping through the gate with our right feet first.

The scope of the Haram took my breath away. Seven main gates led into the massive oblong courtyard, big enough to hold half a million people. On all sides, arches and colonnades of white marble rose two stories into the air. Seven intricately carved minarets towered above the broad, flat roof over the colonnades.

As if struck dumb, the thousands of pilgrims who had shouted their praise of God before entering the Haram now fell suddenly silent. For thousands of years, even before Islam, the Haram had been a sanctuary, a place of peace. Still the atmosphere is one of total calm and quiet. Even the birds who flock to Mecca, it is said, dare not fly over the Great Mosque for fear of disturbing the spirit of harmony below. Only the occasional cries or laughter of children whose mothers had no one to leave them with at home could be heard through the silence—sounds I loved, for they were sounds of life.

Many pilgrims sat on the red silk carpets running the length of the Haram, meditating or reading silently from their Qurans. At the muezzin's call to prayer from the high minarets, all of us lined up in disciplined rows, the men in the front lines, the women behind or in the section of the Haram reserved just for women. As one we joined the rest of the Muslims of the world in prayer, following the lead of the imam as we rose and fell in the prostrations familiar to Muslims no matter where they had journeyed from or what languages they spoke.

Nowhere have I felt the power of belief so strongly. Praying along with the others, I was at once humbled and uplifted. Before God there are no distinctions between races, classes, or even sexes. In the Haram, women were forbidden to cover their noses and mouths with veils or their hands with gloves. In the true spirit of Islam, carpet weavers from Pakistan were bowing down beside oil executives from Bahrain, engineers and architects from Egypt, factory workers from Russia and Indonesia. Housewives from Afghanistan were praying next to teachers from Sri Lanka, doctors from Iran and the wives of Arab sultans and emirs. There were pilgrims, too, from America. On one Umrah I saw the boxer Muhammad Ali leaving the Haram as I entered it.

After the prayers, many of the pilgrims streamed forward as I did toward the Kaaba, the stone structure fifty feet high and thirty-five feet long in the center of the Haram. Here our patriarch Ibrahim, whom Christians and Jews call Abraham, had raised the first house of worship dedicated to a single God over three thousand years before. "The first house of Allah built for people is the one in Mecca," God says in the Quran. The Kaaba is very, very simple—little more, really, than a huge cube with a single door set six feet from the ground. But the power of this building is boundless. It is toward the Kaaba that Muslims everywhere, one fifth of the world's population, turn five times daily and bow down in prayer.

To actually see the Kaaba with my own eyes, to be close to the one object that binds Muslims all over the world, was a profound sensation. Draped over the entire building was the famous Kiswa, an immense black velvet cloth embroidered in gold with verses from the Quran. When I was young a new Kiswa had been woven and embroidered each year in Cairo, and the day the camel caravan bearing it began its journey across the desert toward Mecca had been a national holiday in Egypt. Now the Saudis weave the Kiswa every year in their own mills in Mecca, but it is no less beautiful. At the conclusion of the Hajj, when the old Kiswa is removed and replaced by a new one, pilgrims pay great sums to take bits of this beautiful cloth home with them as mementos of their sacred mission.

In the southeastern corner of the Kaaba was the Black Stone, the symbol of our concentration in the love of God. Only eight inches in diameter and framed in silver, the Black Stone has a great place in our tradition. According to the Hadith the Prophet Muhammad himself had honored the stone, kissing it as he helped to place it in the Kaaba. Now, in the next sacred rite of pilgrimage, called the *tawwaf,* or circumambulation, I and thousands of others moved forward to do the same.

Seven times we circled the Kaaba keeping it always on our left, beginning each circuit abreast of the Black Stone and reciting, "*Allahu Akbar,* God is most Great," as we passed it. I walked carefully, making sure not to jostle those who walked around me or those who, too weak to walk, were being carried around the Kaaba on litters. "O our Lord, grant us good in this world and good in the hereafter, and protect us from the torment of the fires in hell," we all recited as we passed the southern wall of the Kaaba, repeating the prayer said by our Prophet, may Allah grant him peace and mercy. Each time we reached the Black Stone, hundreds rushed forward to glimpse it, to touch it, even to kiss it as the Prophet had done. Because the crush made this extremely difficult, I and many others simply nodded and raised our arms in greeting to the stone as we passed around the corner of the Kaaba in which it was set.

The most fortunate pilgrims are invited by the Saudi royal family to pray inside the Kaaba itself. Twice I have been so honored, climbing a portable stairway rolled up to the structure to enter through the door inscribed in silver with verses from the Quran. As I stood above the white-robed worshipers swirling around and around in waves, it seemed that the Kaaba was the sun around which the whole earth turned, the center of the universe. Watching the pilgrims circling like angels, I felt a great sense that religion is indeed the center of our lives.

The feeling inside the Kaaba was one of the greatest spirituality. I felt so fortunate to be in the most sacred place any Muslim could dream of. As I prayed in all four corners of the

Kaaba, asking God to help my husband restore the land taken from us by Israel, to be with my husband in his search for peace, for the health and well-being of my family and friends, I felt that He was very near. The inside of the Kaaba was very dark, and was kept empty as a reminder that Ibrahim's temple was once filled with pagan idols. The Prophet and his army of ten thousand believers had driven the pagans out of Mecca in A.D. 630, smashing their idols and reestablishing the belief in one God, the God of Ibrahim. It was then that the Prophet had banned all non-Muslims from entering the city, and charged all Muslims who could afford it to honor God by making the pilgrimage once in their lifetime.

After the completion of the *tawwaf* we all went to the Station of Ibrahim in the Holy Mosque and there performed two prostrations. Bowing down before God in this way, we reminded ourselves that the circumambulation was not a worship of the Kaaba itself, but a worship rendered to Allah, the One and the Only One, the Eternal and the Absolute, none except Him deserving to be worshiped. We then left the Haram to move on to the sites of the next rituals: the Well of Zamzam and the Mas'a, the Running Place.

It was here, in the plains surrounding Mecca, that Ibrahim placed his second wife, Hagar, and his eldest son, Isma'il, before going on to Palestine with his other wife and son, Sarah and Isaac. Isaac's descendants in Palestine would develop the faith of Israel and that of Christ, while Isma'il's descendants in Arabia would perfect the faith of Islam. Because Isaac and Isma'il were both sons of Ibrahim, we say that Sarah is Mother of the Jews and the Christians while Hagar is Mother of the Muslims, and that all of us, Muslims, Christians and Jews, are cousins.

Left in the desert with only a bag of dates, Hagar had searched desperately for water to quench her thirst and the thirst of her young son. Seven times she ran between the two hills of Safa and Marwa, hoping to find a well from which she and Isma'il could drink. At last the Angel Gabriel replenished a dry well at the feet of Isma'il, fresh clear water, God's mercy, to save the life of Hagar and her child. The well was named Zamzam, and it still runs fresh and clear.

Pilgrims can drink from the Well of Zamzam anytime after the completion of the rituals in the Haram, but I and many others moved first to perform the *sa'ay,* the "running." Seven times we followed our *mutawwif* back and forth between the hills of Safa and Marwa, continuously reciting verses from the Quran and chanting "*Allahu Akbar,* God is Great." Along the way were signs telling the men when to run and when to walk, while the women were asked only to walk. The conditions were far easier for us than they had been for Hagar, the path now being enclosed in a very wide air-conditioned marble corridor whose center was left free for those on litters or in wheelchairs. But the lesson of patience and perseverance was still powerful. Like Hagar, we cried out for God's mercy. And, like Hagar, we then refreshed ourselves at Zamzam, which was now covered with a beautiful marble vault and equipped with hundreds of taps to quench the thirst of the faithful.

"In the name of Allah, render it for us useful knowledge, bountiful livelihood and a cure for every illness. Wash with it my heart and fill my heart with awe toward You," those of us gathered at the well called out to God, drinking a few sips of the holy water and sprinkling it on our bodies and garments. Many of the pilgrims filled jars with the water from Zamzam to carry home with them, for the sacred water is considered by many to have healing powers. Our guide then cut off small locks of our hair, symbolically ending our state of dedication. The Umrah had been completed. But though the time was shorter, only a few hours instead of the four days spanned by the Greater Pilgrimage, the spiritual renewal was the same.

"The visitors of God," the Saudis call the two million *hujjaj,* or pilgrims, who come to Mecca to make the Hajj each year. All two million of the *hujjaj* must arrive in Mecca by the seventh day of the month of Dhu el-Hijja. To welcome them the Saudi royal family has built a special airline terminal at the Jedda airport fifty miles away on the Red Sea. The largest enclosed space in the world, the Hajj terminal provides every foreseeable service for the *hujjaj:* tent rentals, guides, interpreters, food, transportation, the seamless white garments of the Hajj, even a hospital for those who are elderly or sick. The government and people of Saudi Arabia consider dedication to the welfare and well-being of the pilgrims a duty before God, and a heavenly omen.

Once in Mecca, the *hujjaj* perform the same rituals I did during the Umrah, praying at the Great Mosque, circling the

Kaaba seven times, performing the symbolic run between the knolls of Safa and Marwa. On the second day of the Hajj and the eighth day of the month, the hujjaj set off on busses or on foot for the Valley of Mina, about six miles north of Mecca, where they halt and stay the night. The next morning they proceed another five miles north to the plain and hill of Arafat. It was here that Adam and Eve had united after their wandering. It was here also that Ibrahim had been ordered by God to sacrifice his son Isma'il. And it was here that the Prophet Muhammad had delivered his final sermon four months before he died in 632.

"Ye shall have to appear before your Lord, Who shall demand from you an account of all your actions," Muhammad charged his followers over fourteen hundred years ago. "Know that all Muslims are brothers. Ye are one brotherhood; no man shall take aught from his brother unless by his free consent. Keep yourselves from injustice. Let him who is present tell this to him who is absent. It may be that he who is told this afterward may remember it better than he who has now heard it."

To the millions of believers streaming into the plain and up the steep sides of Mount Arafat on the ninth day of Dhu el-Hijja, the meaning of Muhammad's last message is clear: There is only one God. All Muslims are brothers. All will have to face the Day of Judgment. To prepare, do not steal or lie or cheat, but always be charitable and fair. And tell others the message so that they too may see the light.

"Here I am, Oh God! here I am!" the *hujjaj* call out on this, the most important day of the pilgrimage, the day on which God cleanses all of us of our sins and bestows His forgiveness. All *hujjaj* must arrive at Arafat by noon, for the pilgrimage is invalid for those who fail to properly perform the "standing ceremony" that takes place here. For six hours the pilgrims stand, many remaining bareheaded in the heat of the desert which often reaches 120 degrees, praying and reading from their Qurans. The *hujjaj* are allowed to shield their heads with umbrellas or to seek shade, but the strongest embrace the suffering as testimony of their faith. At dusk all move on to an open plain between Arafat and Mina, where they rest and pray and gather small stones through the night in preparation for the rituals on the fourth day of the Hajj and tenth day of the month.

"In the name of God Almighty I do this, and in hatred of the

Devil and his pretense! *Allahu Akbar!"* the pilgrims chant the next morning, each casting seven sets of pebbles at the stone pillars symbolizing the Evil One which stand along the road to Mina. At this same spot Ibrahim drove Satan away when the seductive Devil tried to convince him not to sacrifice his son Isma'il as God had ordered. Now, symbolically, the *hujjaj* also drive off the Devil, each pebble thrown relieving them of a burden, a bad thought, or a temptation to sin.

Thus cleansed, the pilgrims continue on to the vast plain at Mina to celebrate the 'Aid el-Adha, the Feast of the Sacrifice. In the final ritual of the Hajj, the pilgrims butcher over a million sheep, goats and camels in commemoration of Ibrahim's willingness to sacrifice his son to God, and God's compassion in allowing Ibrahim to substitute a ram instead. For four days Muslims all over the world share in the pilgrims' celebration, closing their businesses, buying their children new clothes and taking vacations to the parks or the countryside. Every family that can afford to also buys a sheep to sacrifice so that they, like the *hujjaj* at Mina, can remind themselves of the lessons of the pilgrimage: sacrifice, obedience, mercy and faith.

In Egypt I usually bought two sheep, for we shared the sacrifice not only with our relatives but with the poor. Egyptian sheep were expensive, about £E100, but they had fatty tails that could be melted down for cooking fat, and a delicious taste from grazing on our rich Egyptian clover. Somali sheep were cheaper, only around £E60, but they did not have tails and tasted much less rich. In the days before the 'Aid el-Adha, all Cairo was filled with both kinds of sheep, every street filled with their baaing. Our children and everyone else's delighted in playing with the animals tethered in villa gardens, on the roofs and balconies of apartment buildings, even in bathtubs!

"Aywa, gazzaar," the butchers cried out in the streets on the morning of 'Aid el-Adha. "Yes, a butcher!" For a small amount of money the roaming butchers faced the animals toward the Kaaba and slit their throats in accordance with the instructions in the Quran, allowing all their blood to drain before skinning them. *"Bismillah! Allahu Akbar!* In the name of God! God is Great!" the butchers prayed as they sacrificed the animals. The skinning process was a ritual in itself, the butcher cutting a thin slit in the thigh of the animal, then pumping air through it to separate the skin from the flesh. I used to watch in fascination

when I was a child, seeing the sheep get bigger and bigger while the butcher hit the animal's body with a stick to distribute the air evenly. But some found this process gruesome, like my daughter's mother-in-law, who refused to eat the meat at the Great Feast and later became a vegetarian.

Nothing of the sheep was wasted. On the morning of the Great Feast, every family prepared a special breakfast made out of the sheep's liver and other organs, and while Anwar took Gamal to pray in the mosque my daughters and I stayed at home to ready this delicious meal. Even the skins of the slaughtered animals were salted and put on roofs all over Egypt to dry. After the feast was over in Cairo, government ambulances would circle the city with bells clanging to pick up the skins and take them for tanning and distribution to the poor.

In the afternoon, the Great Feast began. Thirty or sometimes forty of our relatives would gather at our house in Giza to celebrate the 'Aid, all bearing traditional small presents of money for their nieces and nephews. In my father's day, he told me, the presents were pieces of gold, much nicer, I thought, than the paper money the children now were given. But my children, especially Gamal, didn't care what form the money came in.

It was during 'Aid el-Adha that we discovered what a shrewd businessman Gamal was to become. Parents too gave money to their children to buy sweets and fireworks for the four days of the feast of the Sacrifice. Instead of giving each a pound all at once, I gave them a little each day to spread out the treat. Gamal was not satisfied with that arrangement at all and used to collect worthless bottles from our kitchen and then sell them to his gullible sisters. With their holiday money in his pocket, he would rush off to buy all the firecrackers and cherry bombs he wanted.

At two o'clock, after praying together, we sat down, as did families all over Egypt, to feasts of *fatta,* a delicious baked lamb with rice, or lamb shish kebab. So did the millions of pilgrims in Mina, who had made ready for the feast by having locks of their hair cut to end their dedication to the pilgrimage and exchanging their white robes for their most joyous, brightly colored clothing. As in Egypt, those too poor to have bought an animal to sacrifice for themselves on the Plain of Mina ate freely of the meat of others. What meat remained after the pilgrims had finished their feast was sent to giant cold-storage warehouses provided by the Saudi government, and was later distributed to the needy in other Muslim countries. Such a feeling of rejoicing and of sharing was a fitting way to end the formal ceremonies of the Hajj in Saudi Arabia. The pilgrims would pray and repeat several of their rituals for the next two days of Tashriq and then begin their long journeys home, deeply satisfied that they had fulfilled the Hajj before being overcome by death. For those old or sick people who had died while on the trip to Mecca, there was rejoicing, not sadness. To die on Hajj, Muslims believe, is to go straight to Paradise.

The trip to Mecca is far safer now than it was before the jet age, when hundreds of pilgrims perished during the grueling journey across the desert. But for many, making the pilgrimage successfully is the dream of a lifetime, and returning *hujjaj* are greeted with the greatest enthusiasm and respect. In Egypt's rural areas, the whole village celebrates the return of a pilgrim, hanging brightly colored lamps in the streets and dressing in their finest clothes as if going to a wedding. With great pride, the pilgrim then strings lights around his door, paints the story of his pilgrimage on the outside of his house, and receives those who come to wish him *Hajj mabruk,* or pilgrimage congratulations. For the rest of his life the pilgrim is entitled to place the title of "Hajji" before his first name. This term of utmost respect reminds all that he has fulfilled the fifth pillar of Islam, and in this way has pleased God.

I felt refreshed and calmer after returning to Cairo from my lesser pilgrimage. Anwar, however, was becoming increasingly frustrated. Egypt's economy was almost bankrupt. Our land was still occupied by the Israelis. Egyptian soldiers and freedom fighters continued to be killed in the sporadic fighting along the Suez Canal. The windows of all the houses and the headlights of all the cars in the Canal Zone continued to be painted dark blue to stop any lights from showing during air raids. In Cairo sandbags were still piled in front of buildings, while the windows on museums and stores were taped to minimize damage from bombs. The atmosphere was very depressing during this time that the historians were to call "no war, no peace." We all hated it and wanted it to end. Especially Anwar.

Nineteen seventy-one was to be the Year of Decision, he

proclaimed over and over, the year in which he would vindicate Egypt and regain our land either by negotiation or by force. Again and again my husband stated publicly that Egypt would resume the war with Israel if we had to, this time to win. He said it so many times that people began not to believe him, thinking he was merely blustering. But I knew he meant it. Hardly a day went by that Anwar did not meet with his military advisers. Every night he studied old war films on a movie screen he set up in the basement. The only barrier to Anwar's pledge to avenge our honor was the Russians.

Anwar had always said that the suspiciousness and the broken promises of the Soviets toward Egypt had helped break Abdel Nasser's health. Now it was my husband the Russians were making sick with rage. Anwar's highest priority after becoming president had been to rebuild our military and increase our weapons strength. With the greatest reluctance, he had signed a treaty of friendship with the Soviets in 1971, expecting the Russians then to fulfill their promise of modern weapons and missiles. But in spite of the treaty, the weapons Anwar wanted were not forthcoming.

Time and again in 1971 and 1972, Anwar traveled to Moscow. And time and again he came home rebuffed. "The Israeli weapons from America are twenty steps ahead of ours," he would fume, "yet still the Russians refuse to help us climb even one more step." I never went with him to Russia, for his trips were very short and I didn't like the idea of going to a country where there was such repression and lack of privacy. I had had enough of wiretapping in my own home in Egypt. But I shared his distrust of the Russian leaders, who promised much and delivered little.

By the spring of '72, Anwar's patience with the Russians was wearing out. Once again Leonid Brezhnev had promised him a shipment of arms, scheduled to arrive well before the upcoming United States presidential elections in November. The timing was critical, for Anwar wanted to ensure Egyptian military readiness against Israel in case the new U.S. President would prove reluctant to negotiate a settlement in the Middle East. But while Anwar waited through the spring for the weapons, Brezhnev and President Nixon held a summit. In May the two superpowers announced a new policy of "detente." Not wanting to alienate Nixon or strain the new spirit of detente, Brezhnev once more delayed sending the promised Russian arms to Egypt.

At home in Cairo, Anwar grew increasingly preoccupied and silent. Often he retired by himself to meditate in the garden of the Barrage Rest House, a government residence just outside the crowds and noise of the city. I didn't ask him what action he was considering, for it was not my place to interfere in his work. Instead, I tried to make the atmosphere as calm as possible for him, sending the children away to our residence in Giza. Day after day through the early summer, he sat in the garden. Day after day the weapons did not arrive from the Russians. In July, two months after the announcement of detente and only three months before the U.S. elections, Anwar received a new message from the Russians. There was no point arming Egypt, the Soviets informed Anwar, because Egypt was not capable of winning a war against Israel in any case.

Rarely have I seen Anwar so angry. At our summer house in Ma'amoura, his face was dark with rage. "I must make a speech to the country," he told me, leaving to go to the television studio. He often made speeches, so I didn't pay too much attention. But this speech was to be different. "I am going to expel the Russian military advisers from Egypt," he said to me on his way out the door.

Expel the Russians? I felt a moment of panic. There were more than fifteen thousand Soviet military personnel living and working in Egypt. If Anwar angered Russia by ordering them out of the country, the Communist superpower might choose to crush my husband's government. The dramatic move might be counterproductive, too, to our already strained relationship with the United States. America, I felt sure, would use the expulsion of the Russians to exert more pressure on Egypt in favor of Israel.

"Anwar," I said quickly. "Are you sure that's wise? What will the Russians do to you? And what about the Americans?" But he was gone. And the more I thought about his decision, the more I felt it right.

What good, after all, was an ally who didn't stand beside you, to whom you turned for help only to find that the help wasn't there? Whenever I had gone through difficult times, I needed my friends. If they were not there, I no longer needed them. And so it was with Russia, who had broken one promise after another and was certainly not with us during this critical time of no war, no peace, with Israel.

While I watched Anwar's announcement on television, I heard the first sounds of celebration in the street outside our house as the people began to sing and dance. Wherever I went in my car for the next few days, people would surround it to make the sign of victory. No one in Egypt liked the Russians. No one. Though Anwar's objections to the Russians were political ones, the Egyptian people disliked them just as much on the everyday level. Aloof, moody and stingy, the thousands of Russians in Egypt were very, very unpopular.

Never did they mix with Egyptians, to share a meal or even a cold drink, but kept only to themselves. Save for the Russian ambassador and his wife, I never met a single Russian in Cairo, nor, for that matter, in Alexandria, where there was a large Soviet colony. Friendliness and hospitality are strong parts of our tradition and religion, but the Russians were interested in neither. They did not care about our culture. They did not share in any of our celebrations, nor did they invite us to their homes. They drank beer in public in spite of our religious beliefs which forbid alcohol, and they had no religious beliefs of their own. They were not even lighthearted. In the streets and the marketplaces Egyptians always laugh and joke, but the Russians wore only frowns.

The shopkeepers hated them most of all, for of all the foreigners who had lived in our country the Russians were the most miserly. Every single item they bought, from food to clothing, had to be haggled over, the Russians refusing to give one piaster of profit to our people who were so poor. Rarely did they buy anything of quality, like our beautiful works in copper and brass or our intricately carved furniture inlaid with ebony and mother of pearl; they looked only for what was cheapest. Except for gold. They couldn't get enough of our gold, which was much cheaper than it was in Russia. They bought so many bracelets and necklaces and blocks of gold that people used to joke that the Russians even bought gold teeth!

It was no wonder, then, that the people were so ecstatic after Anwar expelled them. "Tell the President that he is our hero for kicking out the Russians," a taxi driver told a friend of mine when she asked him to take her to our house. She was puzzled by his fervor. "The Russians weren't occupying us. Why do you hate them so?" she asked him. "Ah, madam, you don't understand," the driver chided her. "In the markets, in the restaurants, even in my taxi they were always bargaining the price down, down, down. The Communists always want the cheapest thing and have no generosity at all."

And so in July of 1972 the Russians left, leaving Anwar in the position he most wanted for Egypt: beholden to no one. Had the Russians supplied the military experts in the war Anwar was preparing for, he told me, our hoped-for victory over Israel would be claimed by the Soviets. Anwar wanted the world to know that Egyptians could stand up for themselves. The expelling of the Russians also created the smokescreen Anwar wanted. Now the superpowers and Israel herself decided that Anwar must have given up his plans to fight for the return of our land.

No sooner had Anwar's frustration with the Soviets subsided than a new source of frustration arose: Colonel Muammar el-Qadaffi of Libya.

The first hint of Qadaffi's erratic behavior had come at the Arab summit conference Nasser had convened in 1970, where Qadaffi had called King Hussein of Jordan a madman who ought to be put into an asylum. Shortly after Anwar became president, another meeting was held at which Qadaffi had claimed that he wanted union among Libya, Egypt, Syria and Sudan, only to deny his own claim twenty-four hours later. Now Qadaffi decided again that he wanted Egypt and Libya to enter into a union and become one country. What Anwar or the rest of the Egyptians wanted was of no concern to him.

In August 1972, without even consulting us in Egypt, Qadaffi announced his intention of creating a new Egyptian–Libyan republic. Anwar would be the president of the new state, he declared, while he, Qadaffi, would be vice-president and commander in chief of our collective armed forces. Anwar laughed when he heard of this outrageous plan, for he would never consider giving Qadaffi control of the Egyptian military. How could he have announced such a union without even asking the Egyptians' permission?

Anwar had first met Qadaffi just after the Libyan revolution in 1969. He had been a young visionary then, wanting the best for his country, and had looked often to Anwar for advice. In turn, Anwar had respected the idealism of this young leader who had modeled the Libyan revolution after that of the Free

Officers in Egypt. Calling Qadaffi "my son," Anwar frequently invited him to our home in Cairo and to Mit Abul-Kum. "You are like a father to me," Qadaffi told Anwar many times in the first year of my husband's presidency. "If I make mistakes, advise me."

Only months after his proposed plan for a merger, Qadaffi acted irresponsibly again, this time in a far more dangerous manner. Honoring Qadaffi's request for increased naval protection, Anwar had agreed to lend Libya two submarines manned by Egyptian crews. With Qadaffi's first orders to the Egyptian vessels, the world came close to disaster. "Steal into the international waters of the Mediterranean and sink the *Queen Elizabeth II* before it gets to Israel," Qadaffi instructed the Egyptian commanders of the submarines. Sink the *QEII*? That was insane. The ship was filled with civilians, British and American tourists en route to Israel.

Only because the commander of one submarine radioed his orders back to our naval command in Alexandria, which in turn relayed them immediately to Anwar, was Qadaffi's mission discovered. Anwar could not reach Qadaffi personally to make him cancel the orders, the Libyan leader having retreated, as usual, to a tent in the desert to wait out any sort of crisis. So Anwar himself ordered the submarines to return immediately to our base in Alexandria.

I had never seen my husband look so relieved as he did when he received word that the submarines were back safely in Egypt. "Qadaffi has the mentality of a small child," Anwar said. "The tragedy is that the toys he plays with are real weapons." A rational man would have considered the consequences of sinking the *QEII*. Not only would our own submarines have been sunk by the American Sixth Fleet, but world opinion would never have forgiven the Arabs for murdering innocent men, women and children who had nothing to do with Arab–Israeli conflict. And during this period in 1973, it was this conflict which was uppermost in Anwar's mind. I didn't know it. Qadaffi didn't know it. The Americans, the Russians and the Israelis didn't know it. But Anwar was just about to go to war.

"Jehan, prepare my suitcase for me, for I will be spending tomorrow night away from home. And be sure to pack my military uniforms."

"Are you going outside the country?"

"No."

"Are you going to visit the military outposts again in the Canal Zone?"

"Perhaps."

"Then one uniform will be enough."

"No. Pack all of them. I may have to be away for more than one night. In an emergency you will find me at the military headquarters in el-Tahrah Palace."

El-Tahrah Palace? Military headquarters? I said nothing. Anwar had that calmness in his voice, that brooding look in his eyes I had come to know very well and to respect. As we walked in our garden in Giza on October 5, 1973, ninth Ramadan, I knew this was not the moment to tease him or to question him further. If he wanted to tell me why he was moving into military headquarters, he would. There was no real reason for me to question him, anyway. My heart knew. My instincts knew. Anwar was about to launch war against Israel.

For months, I had been noting the signs: Anwar's increased meetings with the Minister of Defense, his unusually frequent trips to the front, his withdrawal into longer and longer periods of meditation. In August, a woman had brought me a letter she had received from her husband, who was stationed on the Suez front. "He has written me to look after the children carefully," she said anxiously, showing me his letter. "Doesn't this mean we are about to go to war?"

"Perhaps your husband was referring to some secret military exercises," I calmed her, not knowing any more than she did.

I had told Anwar about the letter, but he had just shrugged. "Rumors, rumors," he said. "One letter from a husband on the front to his wife does not mean Egypt is about to go to war." But I was increasingly sure we were. One afternoon in September I had happened to overhear part of a conversation between Anwar and the Minister of Defense. "I want all this to be recorded on film for history," Anwar said to Ahmad Isma'il as he saw him out the door. Wanted what to be recorded? It had to be an Egyptian attack. At least, I consoled myself, this time we would be prepared. The Soviet Union, in spite of the expulsion of the Russian military advisers, had finally delivered some of the weapons Anwar had been waiting for.

I was frightened. And so was everyone else. Three times I

and those of my generation had suffered through the anguish of war, waiting for the bombs to fall, listening to the noises of death skimming over our heads, seeing the pain and mutilation of our young men and the devastation of our cities. Each time —the Palestine War in '48, the Suez War in '56, and the '67 war —we had been humiliated by the Israelis and their powerful allies. Defeat after defeat after defeat had demoralized us and robbed us of confidence. The Israelis seemed unbeatable.

From birth we had been taught to hate the Israelis, and from experience to fear them. In school our children drew pictures not of flowers but of missiles, tanks and planes. Israel, they were being taught, would stop at nothing to expand her borders, wanting to possess all the land from the banks of the Nile to the Euphrates in Iraq. Already they had taken Palestine, the Sinai and pieces of Syria and Jordan. Would Egypt be next?

Defiant posters plastered the walls of buildings: "Free Occupied Palestine!" and "Free Sinai!" But we felt very insecure. We knew that the Israelis with their American military equipment were stronger than we were. How could we not be frightened? In all ways, the Israelis were larger than life, clever, ruthless and unstoppable. The myth surrounding them was compounded by the fact that most Egyptians, including me, had never seen one. How could we have confidence that we could ever defeat them?

"Anwar, I know you are trying your best to restore our land," I told my husband as we walked in the garden on October 5. "No one will condemn you if Egypt goes to war and fails. All the leaders of the world will understand our right to our land and appreciate that you have tried." I searched for words to let my husband know that I supported him in spite of the military defeat I felt was inevitable. "We live once and we die once," I told him. "Let us face our fate bravely, for there is no point in living without dignity. It is far better for you to do something even if you do not succeed than to continue to accept the humiliation of the Israeli occupation."

Anwar stopped abruptly and turned to face me. "Jehan, I know I am going to win the war," he said.

I was shocked. Here I had been encouraging my husband like a good wife, encouraging him when he had needed no encouragement at all. How could Anwar be so sure, so confident? I knew then that his confidence must come from God. At that moment I myself became confident, knowing that God must be with him.

Early the next morning, October 6, tenth Ramadan, I finished packing Anwar's suitcase. "Should I let the children go to school today?" I asked him, searching for a clue as to when the war would begin.

"Of course. Why not?" he replied.

I hugged him at the front door, once again not knowing whether this was to be our last farewell. I did not let him know my feelings of apprehension. "The children get out of school at one o'clock. Will that be all right?" I asked him in a matter-of-fact way.

"Let them go to school normally," Anwar said.

I waved as he got into his car. "God bless you and be with you," I called.

One o'clock. Anwar had as much as told me the war would not begin before 1 P.M. I cancelled all my appointments scheduled after that hour. I wanted to be alone during the afternoon to listen without interruption to the radio. I sat distracted through my morning appointments, hearing hardly a word during my last one, an appointment with Nahla, the wife of the singer Abdel Wahhab. When she finally left, I rushed upstairs to our living quarters.

"Have you heard the news?" I said abruptly to Noha, who had just arived home.

"What news?" she said, looking puzzled at my intensity.

"Oh, nothing," I said lamely, regretting the slip of my tongue.

Upstairs in my bedroom I turned on the radio, but heard only the soap operas. I put aside my inclination to alert the heads of the various women's committees in the Red Crescent to start preparing to receive the wounded. If Anwar was being so secretive, a sudden burst of activity around our hospitals would be a clear signal to the Israeli spies always in our midst. I did not even share my thoughts with my daughters, who found it very odd that I was sitting with my radio held to my ear. "What are you so concerned about, Mother?" they kept asking. I did not reply.

Suddenly, just after 1:30 P.M., the news bulletin I had been waiting for interrupted the normal programming: "Attention: Enemy forces have started an attack against our forces in the

Gulf of Suez. Our forces are now engaged in repelling the aggressors."

I suspected immediately that the announcement was a feint to give us the excuse to begin our assault. And I was right. Shortly thereafter came another bulletin: The Egyptian Air Force was striking at Israeli positions in the Sinai! Our troops were crossing the Suez Canal! The war, which we would call the October War and which the Israelis would call the Yom Kippur War, had begun.

The mood was electrifying as I alerted the heads of the women's committees in the Red Crescent and issued an appeal to the public for contributions of blankets and medical supplies for our fighters. The unbelievable was happening. Egyptian soldiers were overcoming all Israeli resistance along the 110-mile-long Bar Lev Line on the eastern bank of the Suez Canal, the $238 million forty-seven-foot-high Israeli line of defense that the Russians had told us only an atom bomb could destroy!

"*Allahu Akbar!*" our troops were crying out as they stormed across the Canal during Operation Badr. "God is most Great!" To give our troops courage, Anwar had chosen the code name "Badr" for the secret military crossing, a reminder of the Prophet's heroic siege against the enemy Meccans in 624 in which three hundred followers of Muhammad and a thousand angels sent by God had overcome close to a thousand heavily armed unbelievers. Our troops were now achieving the impossible again.

It took our Air Force only twenty minutes to successfully bombard 90 percent of the Israeli targets. Simultaneously our field guns began to pound other Israeli targets along the earthen barrier of the Bar Lev Line. Our infantry, eager to avenge the loss of Sinai in '67, rushed to cross the Canal in rubber boats ahead of schedule, then immediately scaled the Bar Lev Line, letting down rope ladders so that other troops might quickly follow. Pipes that the Israelis had set in the embankments to spew napalm on approaching soldiers were quickly plugged with cement. Ropes were lowered to haul up antitank missiles and medium artillery. And in a move that stunned the world, the Egyptian Engineer Corps cut "passes" in the sand of the Bar Lev Line with high-powered German water pumps and then laid down pontoon bridges over which our tanks could roll.

In six hours, the Israelis were off balance. The surprise had been complete, right down to the trick of printing articles in our papers saying that our generals were preparing to go to Mecca to make Umrah, and having Egyptian soldiers relax on the west bank of the Canal in full view of the Israeli forces, chewing sugarcane as if they were on holiday. Within twenty-four hours, Israeli resistance was broken. Within four days the Canal would be back in Egyptian hands. The myth of Israel's invincibility was shattered, while Egypt's credibility in the eyes of the world soared.

"We crossed! We crossed!" crowds of people chanted outside our house. "God bless Sadat!"

As our wounded began to arrive in the hospitals, the difference between the soldiers' attitudes toward this war and the '67 war was dramatic. The psychological cases were far fewer, our biggest struggle this time being to persuade the wounded to remain in the hospital until they were well enough to get back to the front. Many soldiers refused to exchange their soiled, bloody uniforms for clean hospital pajamas. One soldier with a deep head wound was so determined to return to the fight that he went on a hunger strike. In desperation, his doctor finally asked me to see him.

"When you are cured you can return to the front," I told the soldier, "but what good would you be now? We need our soldiers to be fit and not weak like you." I held a spoonful of rice to his mouth, and for the first time in five days he ate.

I was in the recovery room another day when a young soldier regained consciousness. "Mother," he whispered to me, "do you know that I was the one to first plant our flag on the east side of the Canal?" Weakly he took my hands in his and kissed them.

I was very moved. Without thinking, I kissed his hand in return. "Your hand is the one to be kissed, not mine," I told him, tears coming to my eyes. "You have put the flag back where it belongs, on our land."

The next day a photograph of my visit with this soldier ran in the newspaper, but with no mention that I had kissed his hand. Such an act was felt to be undignified for the wife of the President. But I didn't care. This boy and thousands like him were the heroes of Egypt.

Our soldiers were fighting with the utmost courage and intelligence. Hoping to avoid the disastrous mistakes of '67, their commanders had ordered them to make their own decisions in the field. "Don't be afraid of making mistakes," Anwar had told the troops when he visited the front before the war. "Simply fight with all your might and die honorably, if you must. I will assume responsibility for any mistake which is made." And they were fighting superbly against our occupiers. During the '67 war I had been called "Um el-Shuhada'," Mother of the Martyrs. Now I was given a new title: "Um el-Abtal," Mother of the Heroes.

Fearing total defeat, the Israelis were doing everything they could to break the self-confidence of our troops. "We shall turn your days into nights and show you the stars at high noon" the Israelis broadcast in Arabic to the Egyptian soldiers on the front along the Canal. "We shall put your faces and noses in the mud. We shall crush your bones."

This time the Israeli propaganda didn't intimidate anyone. Many soldiers were convinced that God had taken their side in a jihad, or holy war, against Israel. In Cairo, the fundamentalists were distributing pamphlets insisting that angels were once again fighting on the side of the Muslims in Operation Badr, adding momentum to the rise in fundamentalism which had begun with our defeat in '67. This interpretation grew so prevalent that Anwar would eventually have to remind the country that General Fuad Aziz Ghali, one of the first Egyptian military leaders to cross the Canal, was not a Muslim but a Copt.

For days I felt as if I were flying, working day and night without feeling tired. The joy inside me made me light. Anwar was just as excited at el-Tahrah Palace, where I had moved to be with him. The first cloud to dampen my exhilaration came from a wounded pilot who had flown in the first wave against Israel. Only five minutes after the assault had begun, he told me, he had seen the Mirage jet of Anwar's twenty-six-year-old brother 'Atif shot down in flames. I sucked in my breath. Who could have survived such a crash? I felt the truth immediately. 'Atif was dead.

I didn't tell Anwar right away. I couldn't bear to. Neither could Husni Mubarak, the commander of our Air Force. No one wanted to break my husband's spirit, to upset him as he worked night and day at military headquarters.

" 'Atif is missing," I told Anwar four days after the crossing.

Two days later, I told him they were checking all the hospitals. Little by little I gave Anwar the news so that he could adjust to the shock. They had been very close, 'Atif visiting us for a few weeks every year and often sharing in our religious observances. Anwar had been 'Atif's hero, the twenty-nine-year age difference between them so great that Anwar referred to him not as his brother but as his son. Finally, eight days after the assault began, I told Anwar the truth, that his brother was dead.

Anwar looked as if he had been struck. For a long minute he just stood in front of me, shaking his head. "I felt it," he finally said. "I felt it." For the second time in my life I saw tears fill his eyes. Anwar had cried only once before, when his mother had died in his arms. Now he tried to compose himself. "All those who died for our country, who sacrificed themselves, are my sons," he said. "Even now my own brother." And with his sadness he went right back to work, not wanting his personal grief to be more than the grief of any other who had lost a family member.

Our forces pressed on in the Sinai, in spite of calls for a cease-fire from the Soviet Union and from the United States. I worked all day in the hospitals and took the phone calls for Anwar from foreign governments that came during the night in our bedroom, one from the British Foreign Secretary coming in at five in the morning. But Anwar refused to accept a cease-fire unless Israel agreed to withdraw from all the occupied Arab territories.

For the first time Egypt was dealing from a position of strength. Our planes had destroyed one third of the Israeli air force on the Egyptian front in the first three days of the war. Syria, who had joined Egypt in the attack against Israel, had destroyed much of Israel's airpower to the north. On the fourth day of the war Egyptian forces destroyed over 120 tanks in Israel's most important armored brigade. The unbelievable was happening. The road to Tel Aviv, if we wanted to travel it, was now wide open to Egypt. In Israel, Defense Minister Moshe Dayan broke down and wept in front of the foreign press corps.

But just as suddenly the news turned ominous. "Please save us!" Israel was begging the United States. When a Pentagon report confirmed that Israel was in fact losing the war, the results were immediate. In the hospitals along the Canal Zone, we watched the numbers of Egyptian casualties swell and the nature of the wounds change in ways none of us had ever seen before. To keep up with the new rush of wounded our doctors had to take pep pills, while the other volunteers and I gave up all thoughts of sleep. Over the radio we were hearing what we feared the most. American ships and planes were delivering military supplies to the Israelis at el-Arish in the Sinai. The most modern American technology, including the new cluster bombs, was now being used against our troops.

How could we defend ourselves? The U.S. shipment of arms to Israel, we would find out later, was bigger than the famous Allied airlift to Berlin after World War II, with the Americans giving the Israelis arms worth more than $2.2 billion. For every Israeli tank our Army destroyed, another was immediately taking its place. Some of the tanks we captured were so new that their odometers read "120 kilometers," the distance from el-Arish to the Canal. The rumor spread through our hospitals that America was sending even more modern weapons, to be handled by American Jewish volunteers. American rockets soon destroyed two of our missile stations. We were not prepared for these unfamiliar new weapons.

As the war raged on, our friends and allies rallied to our defense. President Tito of Yugoslavia sent Egypt 140 tanks, President Boumédiene of Algeria 150. The Shah of Iran sent tankers loaded with 500,000 tons of oil. Other Arab countries, led by King Faisal of Saudi Arabia, mounted a war of a different sort. To punish the United States for her blind support of Israel, eleven oil-producing Arab states imposed an oil embargo on America, causing gasoline shortages all over the country and forcing the price of fuel there to skyrocket.

But in Libya, the behavior of Muammar el-Qadaffi was incredibly cruel. Instead of helping Egypt, he had done everything he could to sabotage us. Before the war, he had promised Anwar spare parts for our twenty-five Mirage planes, as well as four million tons of oil to compensate for the Egyptian fields Anwar had had to shut down for safety, and the use of the Libyan port of Tobruk in case our port at Alexandria was destroyed. Luckily we did not need to use Tobruk, for Alexandria survived intact. But neither the parts nor the oil ever arrived, Anwar said.

Even our early success in the war had brought Qadaffi no satisfaction. Angered that Anwar had not told him exactly when the war would begin, Libya's radio had declared two days after Egyptian forces had crossed the Canal that we had no chance of winning. "The Egyptian soldiers are cowards who are used to defeat, who will be defeated for a fourth time by Israel," came the radio broadcast, the words shocking and discouraging our troops.

The Libyan invective continued when, on the tenth day of what would be an eighteen-day war, the Israelis succeded in forcing open a gap in our lines at the Deversoir, allowing some Israeli forces to cross to the western side of the Canal. More than ever Egypt needed the support of her Arab neighbors, but from Libya there were only more insults. "When I heard the radio broadcasts I assumed the propaganda was coming from Israel," Ahmad Badawi, commander of our troops at the Deversoir, would tell me later. "When I realized the broadcasts were coming from Libya, I admit I wept. How could one of our own brothers stand against us?"

With the increased support of Israel from America, there was only one course of action for Anwar to take. On October 19, he announced a cease-fire. "I have accepted, with a heart that bled, the call for a cease-fire," he cabled to President Assad of Syria. "I am willing to fight Israel no matter how long, but never the U.S.A. . . . I won't ever again allow my armed forces to be destroyed." But the Israelis did not honor the cease-fire, instead launching a new attack two hours after it had supposedly gone into effect. Anwar could only respond cautiously, not wanting the Americans to intervene again.

He looked terrible, seeing all his dreams of regaining the Sinai slipping away. "Eat something," I begged him every evening when it came time to break the Ramadan fast. But Anwar only shook his head, saying that he had no appetite. I suffered from his suffering. For weeks this man who usually slept eight or nine hours a night had been working for eighteen or twenty hours a day. Even when I brought him a bowl of clear soup, he would not eat. He was living totally on juice. Watching him grow pale and gaunt, I worried about him in silence. By November he was urinating blood. And the cease-fire was breaking down, Egyptian forces skirmishing with Israeli forces on the west bank of the Canal.

It was the Americans who had escalated the war, and the Americans now who would end it. On December 11, the U.S. Secretary of State, Henry Kissinger, came to see Anwar in Cairo for the second time in four weeks. On this second visit, he brought a chilling ultimatum from the American government. From aerial photographs, the Pentagon knew that Egyptian tanks and artillery had the Israeli troops on the western side of the Canal surrounded. They also knew that Anwar was prepared to liquidate them. If Anwar started such an action, Kissinger now told him, the United States would be forced to attack Egypt. U.S. global policy could not permit the possibility of American arms being defeated by Russian arms for the second time. U.S. forces all over the world had been put on military alert.

In January of 1974, the first agreement on the disengagement of Egyptian and Israeli forces was signed, the United States acting as the mediator between our country and Israel. Egypt would reoccupy the east bank of the Suez Canal, while Israel agreed to withdraw from the west bank. Another war between us was uneasily ended, leaving thousands of Egyptians dead or wounded. Our casualties were five times higher than those of the Israelis.

Was there to be no end to the suffering? Many Israeli prisoners of war were lying wounded in our hospitals. Their cries of pain were no different from those of the Egyptian wounded. Their mothers and fathers, their wives and children, cried for them no less than Egyptian families were crying for our own losses. How cruel for all of us.

A few days after the first cease-fire I had received a letter from an Israeli mother, Mrs. Ruth Lys, whose son had been killed in battle:

MADAM,
From beyond the camps of the fighting I stretch out my hand to you asking you to unite all women who, like you and me, wish to put an end to all hostile actions—to form a union prepared to collaborate with the women of Israel. We women, if united, have great power. Don't hesitate, every day counts, for every day brings about new and unnecessary victims. . . .

I agreed with her entirely. What difference did it make what nationality we were, what religion? Our suffering in war was the same.

"I wish that the word 'war' could be cancelled from the dictionary of human relations," I replied to Mrs. Lys in a letter that was printed, to my astonishment, in the Israeli press.

> I firmly believe that women, as mothers, wives, daughters and sisters, can play an active role in protecting humanity from the horrors, dangers and damages of war. The motherly instinct urges us to have a happy family and to raise our children to grow up in a joyful atmosphere based on love, sympathy and peace. The young generation has a right to dream of a wonderful future in which they can devote their creative energies to a better life. . . .
>
> I wish the leaders of Israel would direct their efforts toward peace, for strength will not solve the human problem. That is my firm belief and that is my husband's call. We have to know that love and friendship are better than enmity.
>
> I support your call for friendship and love. I wish that all women would devote their time to hard and constructive work to realize peace.

Eight years later, my husband would answer the call for peace with his life.

Chapter 10

maktab el-sayyida el-'ula

The Office of the First Lady

nwar, please, you have to mention family planning in your speeches. At least just mention it.''

"Anwar, today will you meet briefly with the foreign cancer experts here for my conference? All you need do is say hello. I promise.''

"Anwar, I am sorry to miss dinner again. But today there are delegations here from the Sudan and Lebanon to visit the Wafa' wal Amal. I must be there.''

From dawn to dusk after the October War, I was on the run. There were new projects to launch, established ones to further, ideas and issues for which I became the advocate. By defeating the Israelis, we had begun to set things straight on Egypt's border. Now finally the government could turn its attention toward solving the domestic problems which continued to plague Egypt.

As president, Anwar could do much to guide Egypt through social change. Egyptians had always been passionately involved with their leaders, whether his title was caliph, sultan, king, or, most recently, president. Our leaders' attitudes became our attitudes, good or bad. If the leader was a weak one, the people felt powerless. If the leader was strong and innovative, as was Anwar, the people felt strong and courageous. And after the October War the timing for social change was ripe.

Anwar had never been so popular. Wherever he went, all over Egypt, the people spoke their gratitude with one voice. *"Yahya batal el 'ubur,"* the crowds shouted, rushing to greet the presidential car as it moved through the streets: "Long live the Hero of the Crossing." The reaction of the peasants in the villages was even more emotional. *"Bil-ruh, bil-damm, nifdik ya* Sadat! With our soul, with our blood, we would sacrifice ourselves for you, Sadat!" they called, struggling to get past Anwar's bodyguards to touch him, to hug him, to lift him triumphantly on their shoulders. There was no question but that he was deeply loved by Egypt's population. But the problems facing him were formidable.

Over twenty years had passed since the Revolution, but the goals of the government had not been reached. In the rural areas, where over half the population lived, many of our farmers were still using the short-handled hoe from the time of the Pharaohs, while blindfolded water buffaloes, not engines, turned the water wheels. Though education was now compulsory for children, adult illiteracy remained high: 43 percent for men, 60 percent for women. Our people were still poor, making on the average only ninety dollars a year. In the cities hundreds of lawyers, engineers and other university graduates sat idle in the jobs the government had guaranteed them, assigned to offices so overstaffed that half the employees were unnecessary.

Anwar knew that something drastic needed to be done. And he was ready to be as daring with our economic problems as he had been with our military ones. In 1974 he took a radical step away from the isolationist policies of Nasser, declaring a new economic policy of *infitah,* or open door. Tourism from the West and Europe increased. More important, so did the number of jobs available for our population. For the first time, Egypt was opened to foreign investors, who began to join Egyptian entrepreneurs in joint ventures, building new factories, banks and luxury hotels. Egyptians were also producing ceramics, washing machines, television and stereo sets. Even Italian Fiat automobiles were now being manufactured in Egypt, by Egyptians. Heavy industry in aluminum, oil, and chemicals sprang up all over the country.

Unlike Nasser, Anwar also encouraged Egyptians to find employment abroad. Thousands who had never before left Egypt now went to countries less advanced than ours to work as accountants, doctors, lawyers and technicians. Our Ministry of Education placed nearly thirty thousand Egyptian teachers in Arab and African schools in 1974 alone. Our professionals welcomed the greater work opportunities outside Egypt, as well as the higher salaries. And our economy benefited tremendously from the almost $1 billion they sent home to their families every year.

If Anwar could influence the people as president, I hoped as his wife that I could as well. After the October War I threw myself into social work, eventually heading some thirty charitable organizations. I chaired the Egyptian Red Crescent, the Egyptian Blood Bank Society and was honorary chair of the Supreme Family Planning Council. I also headed the Egyptian Society for Cancer Patients, the Egyptian Society for the Preservation of Egyptian Antiquities, the Scientific Association for Egyptian Women, and the Society for the Welfare of University and Higher Institute Students. "Anwar, there is no point in offering a free university education," I would tell my husband, "if the students cannot afford the books or even the clothes they need to wear to class."

Sometimes my husband grew impatient with my enthusiasms, my constant nagging at him to officially support family planning and to speed up women's-rights legislation. "*El-sabr gamil,* Jehan," he would say to me, using one of our most common proverbs: Patience is beautiful. I would try hard to retain my composure when he made the Egyptian sign for patience, putting his fingers and thumb together and drawing his upturned palm downwards. "God took seven days to make the world," he would tell me. "How do you expect me to change it in one? *El-sabr gamil.*"

My bedroom became littered with research papers and proposals for new projects. My car too was filled with folders and files. I converted one of the bedrooms in the Giza house into an office and hired a staff of three. I also had to hire a press secretary, for my public endeavors were beginning to attract the curiosity of the international press. I was nervous about their attention at first, knowing it would fuel criticism from the most traditional in Egypt. It was embarrassing, too, that foreign newspapers and magazines concentrated more on me than on the projects with which I was involved. But the more publicity there was about my new projects and those already under way, the more money came in to fund them. Already the impossible was beginning to seem possible.

In 1972 I had established a rehabilitation center for the disabled, a project inspired by the many crippled war veterans I had seen in my work during the '67 war. "Mother, mother, what shall we do?" men on crutches and in wheelchairs had called out to me again and again after the war, clustering around my car whenever I visited the military hospitals. "The doctors have dismissed us, telling us to go back to our villages. But we having nothing to do there and will only be a burden on our families." For four years the complaints of these men had haunted me. They were as recovered as they were going to be, but they had no training which would help them support themselves. Egyptian soldiers were being forced to live without their dignity, relying on the charity of their families, or on what little money they could make selling pencils and tobacco on the streets because their pensions were meager.

I did not want Egypt to be like so many other countries, welcoming their soldiers home as heroes from battle and then forgetting about them. Our men had served Egypt. In turn we had to serve them. After discussing what was needed with the directors of the veterans' hospitals, I decided to create a training center which would help the disabled return to society as self-supporting members and not charity cases. The Governor of Cairo had given me some undeveloped land in the desert near Cairo, and the Ministry of Social Affairs had provided some money to build housing, workshops and health clinics designed especially for the disabled. I had named the center el-Wafa' for the faith our country had in the disabled, and Amal for the hope the disabled would now have in the future. Madinat el-Wafa' wal Amal—the City of Faith and Hope.

In the positive attitude toward my husband and Egypt following our victory over Israel, Arab money for the center began to pour in from Saudi Arabia, Qatar, Abu Dhabi and the other newly wealthy countries of the Gulf. At last I could realize my dream of expanding el-Wafa' wal Amal to include not only war veterans but also disabled civilians. The response to my plea for funding was overwhelming. One Saudian man pledged £E120,000 to the Wafa' and promised the same amount to be paid from his estate after he died. I couldn't believe such generosity, and when I heard he was in Cairo I sent for him, thinking he must be elderly and near death. To my great surprise, I found a young man, Mr. Saleh Kamel, standing in front of me.

"I approve totally of what you are trying to do," he told me. "I also feel a debt to the country which gave me such a fine education." To this day he still donates £E10,000 a month.

Donations to the Wafa' were coming in, too, from Italy, England, France, even the United States. "I understand you are involved with a project to rehabilitate the wounded," U.S. Secretary of State Henry Kissinger said to me politely one day during a visit after the October War.

"Yes, I am trying to raise money from everyone, Dr. Kissinger," I told him, "thanks to the American people."

"The American people?" he asked in surprise.

I smiled. "We may have been fighting the Israelis, but their military equipment came from the United States," I said. "It was American tax dollars that caused our soldiers to lose their arms and legs and to need rehabilitation."

He laughed, realizing he had fallen into my trap. "Well, then, we'll have to help you," he said. The United States contributed £E6 million.

All in all we would raise £E10 million for the Wafa', the project of which I am most proud. We expanded the original concept to include special housing, office buildings, a hospital, and a school for handicapped children. We designed and equipped a factory for manufacturing artificial limbs which was so advanced that doctors from all over Africa and the Arab world came to study our methods and to be trained in amputee physiotherapy. Many of the Arab countries began to send us their disabled to be rehabilitated and trained in a skill.

Soon we set up training centers at the Wafa' for the retarded as well, receiving mentally handicapped people from Oman, from Lebanon, from Jordan, from the Sudan. All of the patients who stayed with us took jobs in the offices, shops or restaurants of this city designed especially for them. Thousands went through our program, for which I insisted we charge fees scaled to the income of the participants. By paying even the smallest amount on installment for their wheelchairs, their artificial limbs or their specially designed cars, the people could maintain their self-respect.

Wherever I traveled with Anwar on official visits, I asked to be taken to see the latest equipment for the handicapped in the hospitals, to see what advances had been made in the care of premature babies, to tour kindergartens and schools. It would have been nice just to go sightseeing to please myself or to visit a few museums, but I did so rarely. There was too much we needed to learn to help the people of Egypt.

In Rome I had seen the way the Italians had preserved their ancient monuments, restoring them and lighting them at night in a very striking manner. Our monuments were much older than theirs, but we had neglected them. The aqueduct running from the 12th century Citadel to the Fum el-Khalig in Cairo, for example, was cluttered with abandoned cars and garbage. Why would tourists want to visit it if they were going to see only rusted cars? I founded the Committee to Preserve Egyptian Antiquities and as its head launched a campaign to clean up and light some of the greatest treasures from our past, including the Muallaqa Church, built in the fourth century in Coptic Cairo, and the thousand-year-old Ibn Tulun Mosque, which many consider the finest example of Islamic architecture in the world. We were not up-to-date on the most modern techniques of preservation and restoration in Egypt, so I invited experts in this field from all over the world to a conference in Cairo. Many came, offering us invaluable advice.

I invited experts, too, whom I had met at the American Cancer Society in New York. Our own doctors and research scientists were well known all over the world for their work in cancer, Egypt being a member of the International Cancer Society. But many Egyptians did not have an awareness of cancer or the preventive steps they could take to avoid succumbing to this dreadful disease. We mounted a massive campaign all over Egypt, holding conferences and running informative messages on television and in the newspapers about cancer prevention. Older women should have mammograms annually, we pointed out, because breast cancer could be cured if detected early enough. The risk of lung cancer also could be greatly reduced if Egyptians would give up one of their favorite habits—smoking.

"Don't be weak. Be strong and give to your country by giving up cigarettes," I pleaded in one television message. "The money you spend on cigarettes disappears into the air like smoke. And your health is being ruined. A surgeon told me that he has seen with his own eyes the black lungs of those who smoke, the pink and healthy lungs of those who do not smoke." I felt very strongly about the threat of cigarette smoking. My son-in-law smoked. My husband had smoked until he had a heart attack and even then had continued to smoke a pipe. "Please, Anwar, please won't you give up your pipe at least during the antismoking campaign?" I begged him. "How can I try to convince millions if I cannot convince my own husband?"

But Anwar just stubbornly lit his pipe. "Jehan, I spend hours in meetings, devoting my life to the people. I can't go out to a meal just to relax, even to take a walk without bodyguards. My pipe is one of the few pleasures I have and I won't give it up, even for you." And he kept on smoking.

To care for those who were nearing the end of their fight with cancer, we started a network of hospices like those I had seen in Europe, homes for terminally ill patients where they could spend their last weeks in a peaceful atmosphere. Our first hospice was in the basement of a mosque, which startled a few people until I pointed out how appropriate it was. There those close to death could hear the Quran being read aloud and thus increase their serenity.

The more I traveled, the more ideas I got for improving the lives of the people in Egypt. For me these ideas were like dreams, and though I knew that not every dream could become a reality, many did. There were not enough dormitories for students to live in at the universities, for example, and few students could afford to pay rent in a private home or a boardinghouse. Egypt's future lay in the young, and we had to do everything we could to make their education possible. After founding the Society for University and Higher Institute Students, I met with the Ministers of Education and Social Affairs as well as with the deans of our universities. All agreed we had to provide affordable housing for the students. Between subsidies from the government, private contributions and proceeds from the bazaars students themselves held, money was raised to build student housing at the universities in Cairo, Assiut, Zagazig, Tanta and Alexandria for which the students paid only £E5 a month, the equivalent of seven dollars. Creating living facilities for our students became a very popular project with the people, and many contributed regularly to encourage education.

Contributions and expertise for the people of Egypt were also flowing from abroad. On a visit to Germany and Austria, for example, I had asked to see the famous SOS Villages for orphans which had been established by Mr. Gameiner. I had brought presents for the children, small toy camels and *ta-qiyyas*, the skullcaps worn by many in Upper Egypt. But the present of love and hope that the children in the SOS Villages gave me was much greater. Our orphans in Egypt were well taken care of, but they did not enjoy the same warm, family atmosphere that these orphans had. In the SOS Villages the children all lived in small houses with a "mother" as if they were in a normal family. The "mother," who had been specially trained, treated them like her own children, disciplining them, training them, cooking meals for them, loving them. "How lucky your children are," I told Mr. Gameiner when it was time for me to leave. "We have nothing like this in Egypt."

Mr. Gameiner called me three days after I returned to Cairo. "Would you like to have an SOS Village for orphans in Egypt?" he asked me.

My hopes rose as my spirits sank. I could not add another burden to the Ministry of Social Affairs by asking for any more money, having already appealed to them for help with the disabled, with students, with educating women, with everything. "I would love to have an SOS Village, Mr. Gameiner," I said, "but the government cannot afford another project right now."

There was a silence. Then: "Well, if you are as sincere about our SOS Village as you seemed during your visit, we will build you the exact same village in Egypt."

I could not believe my ears. "You will pay all the expenses?" I asked incredulously.

"On two conditions," he said. "You provide the land. And you consent to be chairman of the village."

My mind raced. The Ministry of Social Affairs would gladly contribute land to anyone with a worthwhile project, and there was still some undeveloped land in the Wafa' wal Amal. Chairman of the SOS Village? Of course. "When can we begin?" I asked him.

I could feel his smile over the telephone. "I will be there in two days," he said.

Anwar inaugurated the first SOS Village we built for 300 children in Cairo, then two more—for 120 children in Alexandria and 70 children in Tanta. From advertisements we had placed in the newspapers for women over thirty years of age, we selected and trained Muslim women to be mothers to the Muslim children and Christian women for the Christian children so that both groups would be raised properly in their own religions. Each mother started with just four children in her village home, the number of children growing to a maximum of nine. When a mother wanted to leave on vacation or to see her own children, an "aunt," whom we had also trained, would take her place.

To oversee the mothers and aunts, we hired one man per village to be the "father." It was his responsibility to supervise the finances of the village, to make sure all the mothers were keeping clean houses, to take the children to the hospital if they were ill or had an accident, to make sure they were attending the government schools outside the villages with the other neighborhood children. In the summers we took the children in groups to the seashore at Marsa Matruh, to Isma'iliyya or to a camp we had set up in Abu Kir not far from our home in Ma'amoura. Every New Year, we also took groups of orphans to celebrate at the big hotels in Cairo, the Mena House, the Hilton, the Sheraton.

To support the children when they were old enough to leave the villages, we started a sponsorship program. Every month my own children and I, as well as many other families both in Egypt and abroad, paid ten pounds into an account for the orphans so that each would have a nest egg to get started outside the village. And with such attention, the children began to flourish. Where before these orphans had had sad looks on their faces, and smiles that were obviously forced, now in the family atmosphere of the SOS Village their voices grew naturally gay with excitement and happiness.

While I worked on all these projects, I also began to campaign seriously—and with much opposition—for women's rights. As a result of our work with the wounded in the last two wars, women all over Egypt were being shown a new respect, having finally been recognized as the partners of men in our national struggle. Now was the time to advance what the Revolution had begun. We had won the vote in 1952, as well as the right to equal education and the opportunity to participate with men in government, in industry, in every field. Yet women were still greatly discriminated against in private and were underrepresented in all public sectors.

To emphasize education for women, I enrolled in Cairo University at the age of forty-one. I loved my subjejct, Arabic literature, even though there was an enormous amount to study: the difficult grammar, the linguistics, the archaic vocabulary used by the pre-Islamic poets, the history of the Umayyad and Abbasid periods.

"You are much too busy," Anwar would chide me when I joined him for an after-dinner film in the basement only to sneak away to study after the credits. Not surprisingly, he felt the same way when we drove in the car and I clamped earphones on my head to listen to the tapes of my professors' lectures. "You can't combine the study of Arabic literature with all your other obligations," he would insist. "Change to an easier subject like history which will give you knowledge and just require reading."

But I refused to give up Arabic literature. "Please, God, I have started this course and can't get out," I often prayed before exams. "Please help me. I just have to graduate."

I wished very much I could blend in with the other students at the university. But of course that was impossible. The professors and my fellow students expected me to be perfect in all my exams and in my papers. Three of my children, Loubna, Gamal and Noha, were in university with me at the same time, and they too had the highest expectations—and competitiveness. "What mark did you get on your exam?" my children would ask me constantly, working to outdo me. Before a test I got up at 3 A.M. to prepare. I felt I had to set an example for everyone, including my own children. If I didn't do better than they did, they would have no reason to respect or obey me.

At times my spirit faltered. But then I would remind myself of the perseverance of my university adviser and friend Professor Suheir el-Kalamawi. She had been one of the first women in Egypt to get a master's degree, a feat considered so controversial and threatening in 1939 that a large crowd of men had gathered to prevent her from entering the examination hall. The men had screamed at her as she made her way through the crowd, then had hurled stones through the windows of her examination room, finally forcing her jury of professors to move her oral examination to another location.

To make sure a woman could have absorbed such complicated material, the professors had grilled Suheir on her subject, Arab Romantic poetry, for six solid hours, an exam that other candidates usually took three hours to complete. Her examiners had included her academic supervisor, Dr. Taha Hussein, Egypt's foremost scholar of Arabic literature, who, although blind, had received a Ph.D. from the Sorbonne and would later become the dean of Cairo University and our minister of education. Suheir's brilliance during the exam had been without contest. She would go on to take her Ph.D. with honors and to become a full professor herself. If Suheir could overcome such a challenge, I kept telling myself, so could I.

I would graduate in 1978, then go on to take my master's. When I sat for my own oral exams for the M.A. in 1980, I would consent with great trepidation to have the entire three hours carried live on Egyptian television. I would draw confidence throughout the ordeal from remembering the story of Professor el-Kalamawi. And I would be very proud when, after my examination, I was invited to lecture twice a week at the university, and to stay on there for my Ph.D.

I was very anxious about taking my exams on television. But I was willing to do whatever was necessary to encourage other women to educate themselves. Besides, I wanted people to know that I had actually earned my degree, not just been given it on a silver platter because I was the wife of the President. There were too many ready to criticize any woman who tried to better herself with education and leave the old, subservient ways behind.

Few women had taken full advantage of the opportunities the Revolution had provided for them. So in 1974 I decided to demonstrate the political role women could assume by running for an elected office. I did not run for Parliament, but for a seat on the powerful People's Council of Munufiyya, which oversaw the province's 301 villages, including Mit Abul-Kum and Talla. I did not run as a party member, but as an independent, for I was not interested in a career in politics or in a position of power. I wanted only to pave the way for other women to participate in rural politics.

"*Ma sha'a Allah*," Anwar said when I told him of my decision to run soon after the October War. "What God has willed." But still he cautioned me. "Whether you run or not is up to you, Jehan," he said quietly. "But remember that the more you work outside the home, the more you will be criticized. You are taking a big step. Very few women have served on the People's Councils. And there has never been a woman on Munufiyya Council."

"That is why women's concerns have been totally ignored in the rural areas," I told him. "In Cairo there are almost as many female students in the university as there are male. Yet in Mit Abul-Kum most of the women cannot read. In Cairo I see women lawyers and doctors going to their own practices each day dressed practically and comfortably in skirts and blouses. In Mit Abul-Kum the women wear cumbersome long dresses, and they work in the fields for no wages at all. The rural women do not even bother to send their daughters to school, seeing no future for them except to repeat their own lives and those of their grandmothers before that. In Cairo, eight women are in the Parliament, and you yourself have appointed 'Aisha Rateb the minister of social affairs. But what about women in the rural areas, Anwar? There almost none take an active part in politics."

"You do not need to give me a speech, Jehan," Anwar said. "Run if you like and see if the men will vote for you."

"You are forgetting something, Anwar," I reminded him. "The vote of the women."

But would the rural women vote? They were not political and did not consider themselves as an important part of the democratic process. Around the waterwheel in Mit Abul-Kum they still talked only of men—their husbands, their sons, the village boys their daughters would marry. Besides, unlike men, who were required to vote under the election law, women had merely been given the option.

"Woman must be regarded equal to man, and she must shed the remaining shackles that impede her free movement," the 1962 charter drawn up by the Revolutionists had proclaimed. Yet in 1974 most village women could not read the ballots they cast during elections. Candidates had to be represented by symbols—a sun, a lion, a palm tree—instead of by their names. Many women could not even write their own names and had to sign all documents with their fingerprints instead. This had to change. To achieve any sort of democracy in Egypt, the women had to wake up, to be motivated to take part in the workings of our country, to help form decisions instead of just accepting them. I was sure that once the rural women saw they had the opportunity, they would be off.

"O women, listen!" Once a week I rose with the egrets and the peasants in Mit Abul-Kum and went to ask the help of women in Talla and other nearby villages. "You have praised me for the work that I did during the wars," I called out at the village waterwheels, at mills, at pumps where the women gathered. "But now I want to talk not of the past, but of the future. I want to talk of women's role in government." Soon men joined the women in the crowds, partly out of curiosity to see their President's wife, but mostly to see the phenomenon of a woman speaking out so strongly in public.

I was known already in the governorate, and cries of welcome greeted me everywhere. "Twice welcome, Mother of the Heroes. Come, a glass of tea!" "You bring light to our house, Um Gamal. Come to us more often!" "Allah! Is that your face, or the face of the moon? We have missed you!"

I may not have had the technical training of the engineers, farmers, teachers and lawyers who made up the thirty-six members of the council. But I must admit my campaign was very easy. I had the great advantage of being married to the very popular President. Not only did the villagers think I could do more for them than the other council members, but I had Anwar's approval. If he had allowed his wife to run, the villagers reasoned, then he must think I was qualified.

People's acceptance of the idea of women in rural politics

rose even higher when another woman, Su'ad el-Najjar, decided that she would run for the other vacant seat on the council. Su'ad was highly respected in Munufiyya, for she had begun the first project for women in the province, establishing a kindergarten program for girls and a workshop to train young women to sew. A wealthy woman, Su'ad for years had donated money and land to social activities, spending all her time and energy in helping the people. There was no question that she, like me, made up in new areas of interest for what she lacked in technical training. Unlike the other council members, we both had taken our training at the waterwheel.

On election day in September of '74, the women of Mit Abul-Kum lined up at the school to vote, the first time they had had the choice of voting for a woman. And, in what had become a village tradition, they came afterward to my home to offer a show of their support. Each time Anwar's name had appeared on a ballot in Munufiyya province, the men and women of the village had gathered in our front garden on election day to play music and sing for him. While the women beat on the *tabla,* our Egyptian goatskin drum, the men had taken turns composing rhymes about my husband's attributes, calling him Ibn-el-Hayy, the Son of the Neighborhood. "Anwar, Anwar *ya* Sadat! *Ihna ikhtarnak bizaat!* Anwar, Anwar O Sadat! We chose you and no one else!" they would call out while the women applauded and broke into the *zaghreet.* "*Ya* Sadat, *seer, seer, ihna waraak fil ta'meer!*" others would respond. "O Sadat, forward, forward, we're behind you in the reconstruction!" Late into the night the celebration would continue, the men hiking up their galabiyyas to dance, shouting out while performing their complicated kicks and circles. Only after Anwar invited the men inside for many cups of tea, and I entertained the women in a separate room, would the crowds go home.

On my election day too, the front yard filled with people singing and dancing. This time, though, there were more women than there had ever been before. All over the province, I would find out later, women had come forward to assume a new level of participation in the election. "Look! Look! Watch! Watch! Here comes the Mother of the Heroes!" the women of Mit Abul-Kum sang to me in their song of victory. Later, when it was announced that both Su'ad and I had won positions on the council, they took their song to Shebbein el-Kum, the capital of Munufiyya province, where they surrounded the People's Council building and continued their celebration.

I would serve on the Munufiyya People's Council for four years, donating my salary every month to the Talla Cooperative. After my re-election in 1978, I would serve three more as the first woman council chairman in Egypt. Following Anwar's death in 1981, I would resign, being too upset to carry this responsibility. But I would be extremely touched to learn that the council members had voted to honor me by leaving my position of Chairman unfilled for the year remaining of my term. We had made great gains together.

When first elected, though, I found work with the council frustrating, for I was not accepted by the other council members. No matter what I said, no matter how provocative, none of the men would ever challenge me. "I agree with Mrs. President. Mrs. President is absolutely right" each would say reverently. It made me furious. "I am not here as the wife of your President, but as a member of this council," I responded time and again. "Do not treat me with such deference. It is in fact unkind, for it shows that you are not taking my opinion seriously." Finally, one morning a month after my election, one council member slammed his fist on the table, shouting, "Mrs. Sadat, you are wrong!" I smiled at him, knowing that now we could all begin to work together.

Some of the meetings grew truly stormy, especially after my husband increased political freedom in Egypt by creating three opposition parties in 1976. During my tenure as council chairman, an American television crew was taping one of our meetings when a council member from the opposition Labor Party started shouting at me. At issue was the money I had allocated from our budget to build and upgrade the main roads in the province. All agreed that money had to be spent on the roads, but my critic accused me of deciding on the sum without the democratic consent of the council.

"How dare you allot eight hundred thousand pounds for paving the Shuhada'–Manouf road?" he said in a very loud, angry voice. "You have no right to make such a decision for all of us."

The other council members murmured to one another uncomfortably at this man's seeming lack of respect, especially in front of foreign television cameras. But I was not upset; I was pleased.

"You are right," I told him. "Please tell us your opinion." And the man's shouting continued.

"You should be ashamed," one of the other members finally yelled at the man challenging me. "Mrs. Sadat is being too fair in letting you speak this way."

"Let him continue," I insisted, knowing that one always learns from those who disagree.

After the meeting the man came up to the podium. "This is a true democracy," he said to me. "Thank you for giving me the opportunity to explain my position."

As a result of the debates, we brought many improvements to the province, building a bridge between the east and west banks of Shebbein el-Kum at a cost of £E2 million, spending £E2.2 million on the construction of new roads and the paving of old, rutted dirt ones, bringing electricity to all villages in the province which had never received it. To improve the health of the people we built new hospitals, installed new pumps to bring potable water, and new pipes to carry it. To encourage industry and lessen our dependence on foreign factories, we allotted desert land for the construction of three factories, two for spinning cotton and one for weaving it. To encourage education, we established Munufiyya University, opening several branches in the province which offered degrees in agriculture and technology, education and sciences. By 1979, thirteen thousand students had enrolled, and plans had been made to open schools of medicine and commerce.

Many of Munufiyya's concerns were agricultural, and my office became even more cluttered with blueprints for egg and poultry farms, calf-fattening facilities, even fish-farming factories. We experimented with increasing the productivity of our crops, growing tomatoes, beans and peas on trellises rather than on the ground, where many rotted—an experiment which increased the yield tenfold. We experimented with the resulting new surplus of tomatoes and other fruits and vegetables by placing them in solar ovens to dry out the moisture and preserve them. The sun-dried tomatoes were especially successful. They did not lose their vitamins and kept for a long time, so the women no longer had to go to market to sell them every two days.

Unlike other provinces, we did not keep these experiments quiet, but photocopied the plans and the results to send to all the other councils as suggestions. And we went ourselves, for the first time, to meet with council members in other provinces so that we could share ideas and information. What point was there in each province acting as a separate fiefdom when there was so much to learn from each other?

Wherever I went, I used my position on the council to raise women's issues: the need to elevate women's status through education and work, and to achieve financial independence from our traditions of paternalism. There was a shortage of public transportation in Munufiyya province when I took office, for example, limiting the ability of the fellaheen to sell their produce in nearby larger markets. The rural women, especially, were handicapped by being forced to sell their cheese and eggs only locally. Our council soon set up bus routes so that the peasants, including the women in the smallest villages, could take their wares to larger, more lucrative markets.

I also worked closely with 'Aisha el-Rateb, the Minister of Social Affairs, in solving the problems of women throughout the rural areas. There were only 140 day-care centers scattered throughout the farming areas in 1974, for example, a paucity which severely curtailed the possibilities for mothers of young children. To make it possible for more women to work, the Ministry of Social Affairs established a nationwide program to increase Egypt's day-care facilities, insisting that each province set aside a percentage of its budget for the construction of nurseries. I lent my support to the ministry's program by touring the governorates with 'Aisha each week and visiting the new centers. And the program was very successful. By 1981 there would be sixteen hundred day-care centers throughout Egypt. But even so, there would be far too many children for the centers to keep up with.

The problem that surpassed all others in Egypt was our exploding population. No matter what new support services we provided, what charities we funded, or what advances we made in education, all our accomplishments would be hollow if we did not attack our greatest enemy: the birth rate. I was seeing the population crush with my own eyes at Cairo University. Eighty-five thousand students swarmed over the campus; as many as one thousand jammed into a single lecture hall. In some of my classes the students spilled off the benches onto the floor and wedged themselves onto the windowsills. A whole row had been cleared for me when I first came to class, but I had refused the gesture, preferring to squeeze on to the benches like everyone else.

Things were no better in the rest of the city. The buses were so overcrowded that passengers hung out of the windows and the doors, even rode on the roofs, as they moved through the streets. The streets were so congested that it was common to be caught in a traffic jam for three or four hours. Cairo had been designed for three million people, but there were nine million living there. The city's facilities were overwhelmed. Every time it rained heavily, the city sewers overflowed. The telephone circuits were so overloaded that it took ten or fifteen minutes just to place a call from one side of Cairo to the other. "Allo? Allo? Alloooo?" I and millions of other Egyptians would shout again and again into the telephones in our offices before hanging up the receiver and redialing.

Migration from the villages made Cairo's problems especially severe. Fellaheen seeking a better life for themselves and their families were streaming into the Ramses railroad station so constantly that the number of people living in the city went up by one person every ninety seconds. Many of the new arrivals could find no place to live, and they built makeshift sheds on rooftops or in alleyways. More than half a million others moved permanently into the City of the Dead, setting up entire communities complete with shops and cafés among the mausoleums. The housing shortage was affecting middle-class families as well. Many young couples in Cairo were forced to postpone their marriages indefinitely because they could find no apartments in which to begin their new lives together.

Our country was running out of food. Throughout the sixties Egypt had enjoyed an agricultural surplus, exporting grain, fruits and vegetables all over the world. Now we no longer had enough even for ourselves, having to import large quantities of wheat and rice from abroad. With so many migrating from the countryside to the cities, our agricultural problems were getting worse and worse. Faced with labor shortages in the rural areas, some farmers were finding that they could make more money by selling their topsoil to brickmaking factories than by raising crops. More and more farmland was being lost, too, as Cairo grew to accommodate the thousands of new inhabitants.

But Anwar, who had come from a family of seventeen himself, resisted endorsing birth control. "Anwar, every week you delay, another twenty-five thousand Egyptians are born," I would remind him. "Family planning is not so simple, Jehan," he would respond. "Too many think it is against Islam."

"But, Anwar, you know as well as I do it is not," I would say again and again in frustration. "Muslim conferences all over the world have approved birth control short of abortion or sterilization, and even these when the doctor says that having another baby would endanger the health of the mother."

"I know that, Jehan," Anwar would reply again and again, "but I have to work with the religious conservatives who do not agree."

Time after time our discussion would end unresolved. And Egypt's population grew at ever-increasing speed.

The Supreme Family Council was doing what it could. But many of the villages, where Egypt's birthrate was highest, were distrustful of all forms of birth control. Ignorance and misinformation abounded. "I have given my husband the pills from the Family Planning Center every day, but still I have gotten pregnant," one village woman said to me in bewilderment. Others complained that the birth-control devices the clinics gave them made them dizzy and weak. "It is not the birth-control devices that make you sick. Pregnancy makes you much weaker and dizzier," I would tell them, pointing out that my own married daughters and I used birth control.

The village women, however, saw no advantage in limiting the size of their families. The more children they had, the greater the free work force in the fields. The larger the family, the greater the woman's status in the village. Children were not only insurance for the parents' old age, but insurance, too, for a marriage. The women knew that the more sons they had, the less apt their husbands would be to divorce them or to take a new wife. And with six, eight, even ten children from a first marriage to support, the father would be much less attractive to another woman than a father with two or three children. It was not surprising, then, that the message of family planning was falling on deaf ears, especially in the rural areas, where, after a dip in the birthrate during the '67 and '73 wars, the rate was now climbing back up.

We had to be clever to circumvent the resistance to family planning. "One woman after another has said she is too embarrassed to go to a male doctor for such intimate matters," I told the Family Planning Council. "Let us train women in the methods of birth control and send them into the villages."

We turned first to the Country Pioneers, a corps of educated young girls recruited by Nasser to spread the socialist ideas of the Revolution throughout the villages. The Country Pioneers helped to spread the message of birth control. But our greatest messengers, whom we turned to next, were the *daya*s, the roving rural midwives who were already intimately involved with the women of the villages.

Before the medical clinics had come to the rural areas, it had been the *daya*s who had officiated at the birth of the women's babies. It had been they who had performed the circumcision of little girls before we banned this barbaric practice, who had ringed the babies' eyes with kohl to ward off eye sickness, and washed out the babies' mouths with butter three days after birth so that they would never choke. In 1974, Dr. Mamdouh Gabr, the Minister of Health and chairman of the Supreme Family Planning Council, suggested that we start a program to train the *daya*s in modern contraceptive methods. No matter how many trained doctors and nurses we sent to the rural areas, he pointed out, they could do nothing unless they had a link to the people. The *daya*s proved to be that link, for they, above all others, could have frank conversations with the women and encourage them to ask questions without shame.

For the first time we also gave women an incentive to restrict the size of their families. We set up training workshops at the family-planning centers to instruct women in making jams and pickles to sell, to teach them to sew, weave and crochet. I had noticed at the women's cooperative at Talla that few of the women had more than four children, because they knew that they could not earn money and bear one baby after another at the same time. If we trained more women to work, then they too would listen to our message of family planning that doctors and nurses delivered during the jobs program once or twice a week. A room was set aside at the new village medical centers as well, and lectures on birth control given to the women coming in for their own health problems or those of their children. To draw as many women as possible to the lectures, we offered them free flowers and cooking oil and tried not to let them leave without birth-control pills or an IUD.

Still our birth-control program seemed lopsided. "Why do we concentrate only on the women? We must have a program, too, for men," I suggested to the Family Planning Council. It was the men, after all, who held the final power in family decisions, who often discarded their wives if they did not bear sons, who were guarding the notion of male supremacy. We had to change their engrained notion that the more children they had, the better off they'd be. "Think of how much further your salary would go if you were supporting only two children instead of four or five," members of the council lectured at the police and army recruiting centers around the country and at the nighttime classes held to eradicate illiteracy. "Your wife's health would be much stronger and she could work harder to better the lives of your families." We did not offer birth control to the recruits, many of whom were uneducated fellaheen from the villages. They would not have accepted it or used it. Instead we tried to educate them to the possibilities of a better life if they had fewer children to support. And I continued to pressure the one village man who played the most important role of all in slowing Egypt's growing population. My husband.

"Anwar, the Sheikh of el-Azhar has publicly approved birth control. The Minister of Religious Endowments has approved it. Why will you not do the same?"

But no matter how I tried to convince him, Anwar was reluctant to promote or even support family planning. "I have many priorities, Jehan," he would snap at me. "I have to feed the people, to find housing for the people. I have to find these solutions first."

I refused to be discouraged by his stubbornness, pointing out to him while he was shaving or getting dressed that the population of Egypt had tripled between 1900 and 1970, that in another twenty-five years we'd have thirty million more people. "The solution, Anwar, is family planning," I kept insisting quietly. "If there were not so many people you would not have the problem of housing and feeding them."

We argued about the issue unceasingly in private, even once

publicly during the taping of the American television program *60 Minutes* in 1977.

"President Sadat, do you think your wife tries to do things too quickly?" the interviewer, Morley Safer, asked.

I watched Anwar's face darken with temper. "Family planning and family planning!" he fumed as the television tape rolled. "What can I do for this family planning when I have the villagers who think this is against religion? Some of the philosophers, and my wife is one of them, are urging me every day, 'Family planning. Family planning. The explosion is coming.' Yes, I know this, but what am I going to do? It can't be done by law at all."

"Why can there not be a law?" I responded quickly, drawing from Indira Gandhi's population-control effort in India. "There must be one. Anyone who brings more than three children must pay a fine."

I knew that this was unrealistic, of course. But I wished we could have such a law. I had just met with a foreign family-planning group who had told us that in China families were limited by law to one child. But what was possible in totalitarian China was not possible in democratic Egypt, where the people had a right to say no. The Family Planning Council had considered levying a fine on families who had more than three children, but had decided it would be counterproductive. "Instead of paying the fine, the family just won't send the child to school, and illiteracy and ignorance will rise," the Minister of Education had argued. "Education is the answer."

But our population crush was crippling us. And our foreign creditors knew it. At a 1978 meeting in Paris, the Western European consortium known as the Paris Group cited Egypt's overpopulation as a greater issue than our external debt. Foreign financial support for Egypt would cease, they implied, unless the government seriously tried to curb the birthrate.

Anwar had to act. And he finally did after an American family-planning group came to our home to show us a presentation prepared by the Agency for International Development. As slide after slide flashed on our screen showing the statistics of the population explosion threatening Egypt, Anwar's face grew more shocked. He could no longer deny or avoid what would happen to our country if his government did not put its full attention to curbing Egypt's population. The statistics were terrifying, but I was secretly pleased that Anwar was finally going to have to face the full scope of our population crisis.

"Our principle problems are interrelated," Anwar said in a speech celebrating Suez National Day in October 1978. " . . . Food, security, clothing, housing, prices and wages need an integrated policy reflecting our change to a peace economy. However, thorough planning cannot disregard the hurdles that encumber our masses, both psychologically and economically, like illiteracy and overpopulation. For the sake of every family in Egypt and the entire Egyptian family, we have to curb our overpopulation."

At last Anwar had spoken publicly. And he acted as well. Families of all sizes had long been allowed to buy inexpensive government-subsidized food. Now food allotments were restricted to families with no more than five members. Larger-sized families had to pay for extra food at retail prices.

A new, nationwide campaign was launched to convince people to have fewer children. Posters appeared in the Nile Centers in every governorate showing a happy family with only two children in a nice house surrounded by many geese and chickens, next to a large frowning family jammed into a tiny house with no poultry at all. Whole communities were invited to attend birth-control seminars at the centers. The Supreme Family Planning Council sponsored contests to see who could come up with the best family-planning jingle, and it commissioned songs about the healthy family of fellaheen who had only two children and the unhealthy one that had nine. On television, *Look Around You,* a short film supporting family planning, ran three or four times a day. Millions watched this film of a father whose family grows bigger and bigger every time he turns around until at last he is shouting and crying in despair, while a father of two sits quietly smiling. And slowly, very slowly, I watched the rate of Egypt's population growth begin to drop.

Anwar would provide an even more important birth-control incentive with the "Sadat Pension" he began in 1980. Under this program, people over sixty years of age were granted a small monthly pension from the government, allowing our older people for the first time to live out their lives independent of the support of their children. This program was implemented slowly in the rural areas, governorate after governorate, and my husband dreamed of the day when his pension plan would cover the whole country. On the first day the pension was distributed in a new province Anwar would always go himself to give the money to our senior citizens personally and thank them for all they had done for Egypt. I often went myself, proud not only that our senior citizens would be able to live out their lives with dignity, but that, with this guaranteed income from the government, husbands and wives would no longer have to have so many children to look after them in their old age.

Looking back, I do not know how I survived the pace. Every morning I rose at five to bathe and say my prayers, then drink a cup of coffee for breakfast, read the newspapers, prepare for my classes at the university and study my council and charity projects. From eight to nine I tried to exercise, either walking three miles or playing tennis or squash. Soon after nine I would wake up my husband, opening the shutters in his bedroom, bringing him a morning cup of tea and the newspapers and turning on his radio. Then I would be ready to begin the official schedule of the day, allotting ten days a month for my organizations, one day every other week for my council meetings and one and a half days for receiving diplomats and meeting with other dignitaries. Before taking my degree at the university, I had classes to prepare for and attend five days a week, and afterward I had to prepare for my twice-a-week lectures. In between I sandwiched meetings with my other projects, often running late into the night. And I was the mother of four teenaged children.

At the most I had six hours to sleep. When people asked what I hoped for or dreamed of, I always wanted to answer, "To sleep seven hours." I used to laugh at the journalists who declared after one day of following me around that they would need a week in bed to recover. I just kept going, paying no attention to the pace I had set for myself until I got home at night. Then the pain would start in my legs and feet, pain which no aspirin or soaking in hot water could dispel. I tried mixing in the water a powder put out by Scholl's which helped a little, and finally I settled on an ointment which I spread on my legs after soaking them for ten minutes. While I slept the pain went away, and in the morning I felt fit to start again.

Unless I had a headache. My migraines grew more frequent, blurring my vision and making me ill. But I could not change one moment of my schedule. During the ten days a month I met with the board members of my organizations, for example, I held one meeting in the morning and two in the afternoon. It was impossible for me to miss even one meeting, for a whole month would have to pass before meeting again. Often the pain would be so severe I couldn't see clearly who was talking or follow exactly what was being said. "Perhaps I am just a little tired," I would admit.

But we were all tired. The armies of volunteers with me were devoting long hours working in the hospitals, in the schools, the family-planning centers, everywhere there was a need. They encouraged me as much as I encouraged them. Without their help and dedication I could have done nothing. We were achieving much for the people of Egypt.

But increasingly I wondered what activities and programs the wives of other leaders in our area were pursuing for their countries' problems. What solutions had we discovered in Egypt that they did not know? And what could they teach us? It was ridiculous for us to remain isolated from one another when together we could share information and help one another. Men came together in international conferences. Why shouldn't women?

In the summer of 1974, the women members of Parliament and I convened a conference of African and Arab women in Cairo. The members of Parliament invited their counterparts in other governments as well as women active in social programs, while I issued personal invitations to the wives of the African and Arab leaders. All in all we invited over two hundred women from thirty different countries in an atmosphere of great excitement. It was to be the first conference of its sort ever to be held in Egypt, and the first time many of the women we invited would travel outside their countries. Their response was as enthusiastic as it was heart-warming. Delegations came from Kenya, Ethiopia, Uganda, the Ivory Coast, Burundi, Togo, Chad, Ghana, Nigeria and Zaire, as well as from Mauritania, Morocco, Algeria, Yemen, Qatar, Kuwait, Bahrein, Oman, Lebanon, Syria and Iraq. Mrs. Ahmadou Ahidjo, wife of the leader of Cameroon, accepted my invitation, as did Mrs. Moussa Traore from Mali, Mrs. Julius Nyerere from Tanzania, Mrs. Ahmed Sekou-Toure of Guinea, and the wives of the leaders of Tunisia and Somalia. Queen Alia, the wife of Jordan's King Hussein, had a perfect excuse for not attending, having given birth to her second child just two weeks before, but even as a new mother she did not want to miss this gathering of so many women.

With great pride I introduced the women to Egypt, taking them to see our project for the disabled at the Wafa'wal Amal and to visit our SOS Villages for orphans. I took them to the Egyptian Museum in Cairo, then on to see the antiquities in Upper Egypt on a Nile river boat, as well as to our new factories where women were working side by side with men. I took them also to see the Bar Lev Line in the Sinai so that they could better understand our pride in our victory. I wanted them to see our past, our present and our future, to show them that Egypt was both a part of the Middle East and a part of Africa, to increase the understanding among our different countries. And, of course, we shared information.

"What is your program for the blind? How did you raise money for the Wafa? What resistance did you get to your projects?" Queen Alia asked me, eager to know details. I was delighted to share what I knew, and in turn I learned much from Queen Alia and the other women. Each delegation presented a paper on the role of women in their respective countries, and a lively and informative dialogue followed.

Friendships grew among all of us, Queen Alia and I becoming especially close. After the conference we corresponded with each other and called each other frequently on the phone. Years later, when she returned with King Hussein on an official visit, she and I would spend many happy afternoons gossiping on the terrace of the Cataract Hotel overlooking the Nile in Aswan. Slim and elegant, a personification of the modern Arab woman, Alia was also a very good mimic. I laughed until I gasped one afternoon while she described a meal she had attended in Oman with the mother of Sultan Qabus. " 'You must eat more. You look too thin and weak,' " Alia mimicked the Sultan's mother, poking me in the ribs. " 'Eat. Eat. Eat. Then you will be healthy.' "

Two months later Alia would be dead, killed in a helicopter crash in the desert. She had insisted on going to visit a hospital, even though it was windy, and her helicopter had gone down in a sudden sandstorm. I was shocked that someone so young, so full of life, could so suddenly be gone. I grieved for her husband, for her two young children, and left for Jordan immediately to pay my condolences. What a sad reason for my first trip there. On my way to the palace to sit with the Queen Mother and other women connected with the court, many shop windows were displaying Alia's wedding photograph.

King Hussein was informed that I was in Jordan and asked me to come pay condolences to him as well after I had visited with Alia's mother. On my way to the palace we passed Alia's tomb, which the King had ordered built for his young wife where he could see it from his balcony. My sorrow increased when I entered the palace and I saw a huge painting of Alia on the wall beside a portrait of the King. I found it very hard to control myself and wept as the King entered. He looked stricken, as if he were ill. I could find no words to console the husband of this lovely young woman and the father alone now of a very small boy and girl.

"I know that she loved you," the King said to me. "We shall both miss her very much."

Queen Alia had done much for her country, and would have done much more. Like so many other wives of Arab and African leaders, she had become increasingly involved in the social affairs of her country. From the moment of the first conference of Arab and African women in Cairo, a new spirit of cooperation and support had sprung up among all of us. The emergence of Egyptian women into public and professional life since the Revolution had sparked great curiosity, igniting a growing consciousness throughout the Middle East. Muslim women were ready and eager for change.

Chapter 11

el-mar'a fil islam

Women in Islam

Women. All my energies and projects kept coming back to advancing women. Stemming the birthrate. Eradicating illiteracy. Educating the young and, by my example, the older. Providing health care, nutrition and child care. Creating jobs. Raising the standard of living. Urging women to become more involved. Women. In them lay the future of the world, for it was women everywhere who were the ones to pass down their values and principles to their children, who raised their sons to manhood, who set the example for their daughters to follow. As it is said: "The hand that rocks the cradle rules the world." Women were capable of much, but, in many Muslim societies, were allowed to do little. What a waste. And all because of the way men had interpreted Shari'a, the set of laws set down in the Quran and the Hadith, or collected sayings of the Prophet.

For centuries the ulema, the Muslim religious scholars, had debated the meaning of Shari'a and its application to new situations. When coffee was introduced into the Muslim world in the 15th century, for example, ulema from all over the Arab world had convened to debate whether Muslims should be allowed to drink it. Some had argued that coffee, like wine, was intoxicating, and therefore forbidden by the Quran. Others had argued, successfully, that coffee was a stimulant which would give the believers more time to pray. And coffee was condoned. Five hundred years later, when every Arab country made its laws independently in accordance with its own interpretation of Shari'a, the radio was approved by ulema throughout the Muslim world for similar reasons. Since the Quran could be broadcast over the radio, bringing the word of God to a large audience, they declared the instrument beneficial to Islam and not an invention of Satan as some had originally claimed.

On women's issues, though, the ulema of different countries were sharply divided. In Saudi Arabia, where legal experts used a most conservative interpretation of Islamic law, women were not allowed to drive cars, to work alongside men, or to travel without a male relative. At the United Nations International Women's Year Conference in Mexico City in 1975, to which I led the delegation of women from Egypt, the "women's delegation" from Saudi Arabia had been all men, as would be the Saudi delegation to the similar conference in Nairobi in 1985. Saudi women had to pay strict adherence to an ultraconservative dress code, and any woman seen in public without her head and legs covered was reprimanded by the religious police. When the wife of our own Vice-President, Magda el-Shaf'ei, was seen in Mecca during pilgrimage without a head covering, the police smacked her legs with sticks.

Boys and girls did not study together in Saudi Arabia, but at separate universities. When the first university for women opened in 1973, only women professors, mostly from Egypt, were allowed to teach the students. When male professors were permitted, the segregation of sexes was preserved by not allowing the professors to be in the same room with their students;

the young women had to listen to their professors' lectures on closed-circuit television and ask questions over a direct phone line. It must have been very difficult for young women not to be able to meet with their professors and discuss their work face to face.

In Egypt, our laws toward women were more moderate, a blend of secular and Shari'a law which Anwar called a combination of science and faith. Our universities were coeducational, women making up one third of the student bodies. Our factories were filled with women workers sitting side by side with men. By 1976, thirty percent of medical, pharmacy and dentistry school graduates were women, a far cry from the first days of the Revolution, when 91.3 percent of Egyptian women were illiterate. But, for all our progress, we still shared much with the more repressed women in the Arab countries.

Whether the women covered themselves in the heavy black *abayyas* of the Gulf States or walked bareheaded as many of us did in Cairo, whether they fought in the Army in Libya or fought for their right to drive a car in Saudi Arabia, one bond united us all. We all wanted to loosen, if not to break, the traditional patriarchal bonds that prevented us from contributing as much as we could to society. Men liked to say that it was our common religion of Islam that demanded strict restraints on women's activities. But they were wrong. Freedom and progress for women were in fact at the very heart of Islam.

At its inception, Islam had been positively revolutionary toward the status of women, correcting much of the discrimination of Jahiliyya, pre-Islamic times. The Quran forbade the killing of female infants, for example, a practice common among the Arabs and continued until recently by the Chinese. More than fourteen centuries ago Islam had also given women the right to equal education, the right to work and open their own businesses, the right to initiate legal action and the right to buy and sell property. It would take hundreds of years before women from the more "enlightened" countries of Europe were given the same privileges. Not until the beginning of the twentieth century could a French wife sell or transfer properties without the written approval of her husband.

I was always amazed by the depth of misunderstanding about women in Islam. In Europe and the West, people would always question me about what they saw as our primitive and debasing marriage traditions which allowed men to take four wives and parents to "arrange" marriages for their daughters. But their information was not complete. Yes, parents tried to arrange good marriages for their daughters. But the Quran expressly requires the consent of the woman before such a marriage can take place, a great improvement over the pre-Islamic, tribal tradition which forced women automatically to marry their cousins.

A man's right to take four wives, though shocking to some in modern times, had also been a great step forward for women fourteen hundred years ago. Before Islam, a man could have up to forty wives, and could treat them as he chose. The Quran not only severely limited the numbers of wives a man could take but further protected women by charging men who practice polygamy to treat all their wives equally. "If you fear that you cannot do justice (to so many), then marry (only) one," reads the Fourth Sura, "Women." "Thus it is more likely that you will not do injustice." All over the Arab world the taking of multiple wives was the exception rather than the rule. In Egypt, polygamy was practiced by only three percent of the population. In Tunisia, polygamy had been banned since 1963, the ulema there having decided that it was impossible to treat more than one wife fairly.

Even the Quran's unequal allocation of a parent's estate between a son and a daughter was not such an injustice as it appeared. True, a daughter could inherit only half the share of her brother. But the daughter, no matter how rich she might become, was not required by the laws of Islam to help support her parents or even her own children. What money or property she acquired was hers alone. Furthermore, her brothers were bound to support her if she needed money. Islamic laws of inheritance as detailed in the Quran were in fact very advanced. At least the daughter was entitled to a share. Only a century ago in England the oldest son was the only one to inherit his family's title and wealth.

Yet in Europe and other countries in the West, the stereotype of the shrouded and oppressed Muslim woman persisted. On my first official trip abroad without Anwar in 1975, the first official trip ever taken alone by the wife of a Muslim leader, hundreds of people gathered to greet me at the airport in West

Germany. They were convinced, I am sure, that they were going to see a Muslim woman covered from head to toe in veils and surrounded by male guards. But that was not Islam. It was amazing to me how many people needed to be educated about the status of women in Islam.

In Egypt, the women's groups and I were not campaigning for radical changes, knowing that asking for too much all at once could result in a damaging backlash. Instead we were working slowly and carefully to gain one little freedom after another, quietly creating new and reasonable opportunities for women. In the Western countries, the fight for women's rights during the 1970s was being called the "Women's Revolution" and the women who participated were called "feminists," but we resisted such labels in Egypt and were not strident at all. We moved cautiously, believing that if we took away the opposition to women's liberation piece by piece, in the end we would remove the wall.

Many Arab leaders, though, felt very strongly about women's place in society, especially in Libya, where President Qadaffi clung to a severe interpretation of a woman's proper role in Islam. "To demand equality between them [a woman and a man] in any dirty work which stains her beauty and detracts from her femininity is unjust and cruel," the Libyan leader had written in his *Green Book,* the manifesto in which he discusses the details of his "third universal theory" of history and social development. "Education that leads to work unsuitable for her nature is unjust and cruel as well."

Qadaffi was entitled to his views, of course, however extreme. But I was increasingly uncomfortable with the way he passed judgment on the behavior of women throughout the Arab world. Especially me.

In 1972 I had visited our troops along the front in Port Sa'id and on the islands of the Red Sea. The life of our soldiers was a harsh one, the men living in trenches in the desert and seeing their families only every few months. As a mother, I wanted the troops to know that all Egyptians appreciated the sacrifice they were making for our country, that they were not alone or forgotten.

The weather had been terrible when I left the mainland in Suez to travel by military launch to the islands, through waves whipped up by a fierce wind. It was worse on land. When we disembarked on Shadwan Island, we were enveloped in a sandstorm so fierce that it all but obliterated any vision and made it very difficult to breathe. Luckily I had worn a pantsuit, so my skin was not torn too badly by the sand blasting across the desert. "Do not worry about me," I reassured the soldiers. "What about you? While we are comfortable in our homes and offices in Cairo, here you must live exposed to sandstorms like this one. To share the discomfort of this for one day with you is an honor for me. It is nothing compared to the discomfort you must continually face."

The morale of the troops, I was told later, was strengthened by my trip. But my visit to the front had enraged the reactionaries in Libya. "The wife of the Egyptian leader is too forward," Libyan newspapers and radio stations blared the next day. "Visiting the troops is the President's responsibility, not hers. Instead of meeting with men, she should restrict her activities to meeting with women and children." For days the criticism from Libya continued. "Why should Mrs. Sadat call for women's rights? Women already have many rights and are satisfied. She is a troublemaker."

I tried my best to understand why Qadaffi's attitude was what it was. He had always been very warm and very polite to me whenever we had met. And he seemed to respect many of my social activities with the poor, the sick and the disabled. But he could never accept my work with men or for women's rights.

At times he took his conservatism to the absurd, especially about the proper dress for women. One hot summer day in Libya, where I had traveled with my daughters in 1970, he had chided my youngest daughter, Nana, for wearing a sundress. "Your back should not be so exposed," he had reprimanded her, though at the time she was only nine years old. He was just as strict in his attitude toward his second wife, Safiyya, whom he had met in a Tripoli hospital during his recuperation from an emergency appendectomy. Safiyya had been his nurse in the hospital, and they fell in love. After he was released from the hospital, he married her. I could understand his attraction for Safiyya, for she was witty and full of life. For her part, she adored him and obeyed his every wish.

On her wedding day, Safiyya told me, her relatives had made

up her face, applying eye shadow, lipstick, powder and rouge. But her bridegroom had stared at her as if she were a stranger. "Go and wash your face," he had told her right after the ceremony, an order she hurried to obey. At his insistence, she had never again worn makeup, only a little kohl around her eyes. And she had followed his wishes to dress conservatively in long dresses and to cover her hair, though occasionally she had gotten around them by wearing long pants and throwing a scarf over her head.

In spite of her husband's attitude toward women, Safiyya was very progressive. One time when I was in Libya as her guest, she invited me to a luncheon meeting with Mrs. Anaizi, the leader of the women's movement in Benghazi. I was very impressed with Mrs. Anaizi, an old woman who was still fighting to raise the legal age of marriage for girls to sixteen, still actively involved in programs for women, training girls to use sewing machines, and teaching them to read and write. Safiyya was a fighter as well, wanting to learn, to improve herself and do more to help the people. In 1972 I invited her to Cairo so that I could show her the various social-welfare programs and women's associations we had in Egypt, and she came, traveling alone for the first time. Her husband laid down only one condition: to preserve her modesty, her photo could not appear in the newspaper.

I met many interesting women in Libya, Qadaffi's mother, Um Muammar, among them. Um Muammar was a Bedouin who had moved with her husband from the desert to Tripoli to be near her son. She could neither read nor write, but she had skills I and others who had been brought up in cities would never have. Um Muammar had done everything for herself and her family, raising her children with only the most primitive means, planting and grinding the wheat with which to make bread, shepherding the family sheep and goats, making cheese and yogurt from their milk. I admired her and women like her greatly. In the spring the Bedouin women spun the wool from the sheep to weave blankets for the cold of winter, and made their own long black dresses, which they embroidered with colorful thread. Like Um Muammar they had had no formal schooling, but were entirely self-sufficient. And their faculties were very sharp, especially their hearing from living so long in the silence of the desert.

Um Muammar's wit too was sharp, and, like so many peasants and people of the desert, she loved to tease. "Are you ill? Doesn't your husband feed you?" she often goaded me, concerned that I was so thin. She was also full of spontaneous warmth and compliments. "You are so beautiful," she often told me. "It must be from the love your husband has for you."

Always Safiyya was a gracious hostess, taking me to see the monuments left from the time of the Romans, and to the museums, where I saw ancient Greek statues, ceramic bowls, carving tools and paintings from the Greek period. In Tripoli she once gave a lovely party for me in the garden of her home, inviting the wives of the Revolutionists as well as the wives of the government ministers and those of the foreign diplomats, while a group of Bedouin sang and danced for us. On the wall of her house I noticed she had hung pictures of Abdel Nasser, of Anwar and of me torn out of magazines. When I returned to Egypt I sent proper photographs to her with inscriptions of thanks.

Safiyya had eight children to whom she was devoted. My heart went out to her when America bombed Libya during the antiterrorist raids in 1986, killing her fifteen-month-old adopted daughter, Hanah, and severely wounding her youngest sons. Despite the political differences between Egypt and Libya, I could not condone the bombing of civilians or the use of force to solve a political problem. But I was particularly distressed to see Safiyya on television, wild in her grief and anger. I would have liked to go to comfort her, but the relationship between our two countries had ended long before 1986.

Before that, I had managed to adjust to Qadaffi's severe criticisms of my activities, knowing they were not directed personally at me but were his general attitude about all women. I had adjusted also to his irritating habit of flying to Egypt without telling us beforehand of his plans. The first notice of his arrival would come from the airport controllers, who would phone us when his plane entered Egyptian airspace. If Safiyya was with him, I would have to drop everything and rush with Anwar to the airport to greet her. We never knew when Qadaffi was coming—or when he was going. Once, in Alexandria, he had said his farewells to Anwar and me after an informal dinner at our home, but when we went for a drive an hour later we found his car at the end of the garden and Qadaffi playing soldier with Gamal and a friend in the military tent the boys had set up.

It was on one of Qadaffi's many trips to Egypt to promote the idea of an Egyptian–Libyan federation, that he lost me forever. Time and again Anwar had explained to Qadaffi that Egypt was a democratic society and that he would have to seek popular approval for a formal union between our two countries. "When you are in Egypt, you are free to go anywhere and to attend any meeting you like," Anwar had told him. "Put your views to the people. Should they want a merger with Libya, then I will carry out their wishes." In the spirit of our new democracy and free expression, I had invited Qadaffi, on one of his trips to Cairo in 1972, to address a meeting of the Cairo Women's Union.

With the greatest anticipation, one thousand women crowded into the auditorium at our party headquarters to hear the young revolutionary leader of our neighbor Libya speak of his hopes for Arab women. "I will need a blackboard and some chalk," Qadaffi said. Immediately, the building staff rushed to fill his wish. My husband introduced Qadaffi, and a silence fell as he strode to the center of the stage and began to write on the blackboard. And the murmuring began.

I could not see what he was writing, because I did not have my glasses on. "What is it? What has he written?" I asked my daughter's mother-in-law, Suad Mare'i, who was sitting on my left.

She blushed. "I cannot tell you," she said in embarrassment.

I fumbled for my glasses in my pocketbook, all the while patting Safiyya el-Qadaffi, who, sitting on my right, was obviously upset at all the murmuring. "Oh, my God," I blurted out when finally I found my glasses.

"VIRGINITY. MENSTRUATION. CHILDBIRTH," Qadaffi had written in big chalk letters on the blackboard.

"You women are asking for equality, but you can't be equal," Qadaffi started his remarks. "A young boy can travel to his work in the fields, in a factory, in construction. But a young girl cannot safely travel alone and still protect herself." I couldn't believe my ears or my eyes. Nor could the other women in the room, whose muttering was turning now into a deep rumble.

"How can women be equal to men if you cannot work during your time of the month or when you're nursing your babies?" Qadaffi continued. "From the point of view of nature, there can be no equality between men and women in character or temperament, in moral or physical strength." Ignoring the rising sounds of protest from the audience, Qadaffi went on to describe women's role in society as being no different from that of cows, who are destined to do no more than become pregnant, give birth and suckle their young. And the meeting erupted.

"Mr. President, I am a physician. Nothing you have written or said prevents me from working," cried out Dr. Zenaib el-Soubky. "I have children. I am head of the Blood Bank. I share in social activities. And I have never missed a day from my work."

But Qadaffi remained stubborn. "I insist that I am right," he said. "Can you work all day in construction, digging a road, carrying heavy loads on your back, while you are menstruating?"

"*Na'am! Na'am!* Yes! Yes!" the women cried out. "If we have the opportunity."

On the stage my husband was staring at Qadaffi in amazement. In the audience, woman after woman was leaping to her feet.

"Perhaps you have forgotten, Mr. President, that at the time of the Prophet women were sharing the burden of the struggle and fighting side by side with men," said Amina el-Sa'id, our distinguished journalist. "How can you say that after so many centuries women no longer have equal footing?"

"I insist I am right," Qadaffi said, his voice rising. "Can you work all day in a factory, standing in front of the furnaces like men? Can you bear the heat? I believe not. The heat would spoil your beauty. It would be too hard on you. There are certain jobs for men and certain jobs for women."

"*La! La!*" the women shouted. "No! No!"

"Don't worry," I whispered to Safiyya who couldn't help but feel the women's fury at her husband. "Let the women express themselves. Perhaps your husband's clarifications will soften his position." But the meeting only became more stormy.

I waited for my husband to bring the session to a close. But he didn't. From the look on his face I realized he was enjoying this confrontation, leaving Qadaffi to say whatever he wanted. My husband was in fact trying to keep himself from roaring with laughter, laughter that he could finally release as we drove together to the Barrage Rest House after the meeting.

"Oh, Jehan, if you could have seen the faces of the women," he said, laughing until tears ran down his cheeks. "If I had been Qadaffi, I would rather have faced the entire Israeli Army."

We were taking a nap after our lunch when one of Anwar's aides telephoned us to say that Qadaffi was on his way to see us. I dressed hurriedly and arrived downstairs before Anwar, to find a furious Qadaffi with two of his fellow revolutionaries, Muhammad Galloud and Omar Mehashi.

"I don't like to tell you this, madam, but some of those women are not good women," Qadaffi said to me angrily.

"Like whom, Brother Muammar?" I asked the highly agitated man.

"Amina el-Sa'id. Do you know that she smokes?" he replied, so sarcastically that smoking a cigarette sounded like a sin.

"Why not?" I said to him. "That is her choice."

"Well, there is something more. I hate to say it," he said.

"What, Brother Muammar?" I asked.

There was a pause. "I have heard that she drinks beer," he said in a deep voice.

I steadied myself. "So do the revolutionaries around you," I said to Qadaffi. "That is a personal matter between them and God."

Qadaffi glared at me.

"I'm sorry if you were upset by the women at the meeting," I said to him as Anwar came into the room. "But it is very difficult for women to sit quietly while you compare them to cows. Even a cow would have felt insulted by your description and rejected it. She has something more to do in life than just nurse a calf."

But Qadaffi never changed his mind. And I would become increasingly worried about his erratic behavior.

After Libyan radio criticized our troops so severely during the October War in 1973, Qadaffi asked Anwar's permission to address our National Assembly. My husband agreed, thinking he wanted to apologize for Libya's harsh accusations and to reconcile our two countries. Qadaffi would apologize indirectly to Parliament, claiming that the remarks had stemmed from the shock of Israel once more crossing the Canal and his feeling that it was over for all of us. But it was his second request to Anwar, soon after his arrival with Safiyya in Cairo, that was most startling.

"With your permission, Mr. President, I would like to speak to your wife in private," Qadaffi said in Qubbah Palace, where we had escorted the Libyan leader and his wife from the airport.

In private? My heart beat wildly. There were four of us there. Why single me out? Anything he told me I would tell Anwar anyway. And what would his wife think? This was most unusual, unheard of really, for a Muslim man to ask to be alone with a woman. My God, I thought in a panic, is he going to kill me?

I led Qadaffi into a private room at Qubbah Palace, making sure to leave the door open. Remain composed, I said sternly to myself. Do not let him know how frightened you are. I could not take my eyes off the revolver Qadaffi always carried in a holster on his hip. I was convinced he was going to take it out and kill me on the spot.

"I wish to arrange a marriage between my cousin and your daughter," he said.

My mouth almost fell open in astonishment. This was his secret message? "Which daughter?" I asked incredulously.

"Your youngest daughter, Nana," he replied.

I couldn't believe my ears. Nana had just had her twelfth birthday! "She is not yet the legal age for marriage, Mr. President," I told him, not wanting to be rude by abruptly saying no.

But he had thought of that. "Just the intent of their marriage will be acceptable," he said. "When she is old enough and has gotten to know and admire my cousin, they can be married."

"Let us think about a marriage then, Mr. President," I sputtered. "There is much time ahead of us."

But he seemed not to hear me. "My cousin is of impeccable character and is as close to me as a brother," he continued. "You and your daughter will be extremely satisfied."

I understood then why he had wanted to talk to me in private. He thought that as a mother I could convince my daughter to agree to this marriage, that together we could convince the father. But a marriage such as this was out of the question. After all his insults, how could he expect me to welcome a union between our two families? He was using his tribal ways to bind Egypt and Libya. But his ways were not our ways. I would never even consider letting my daughter marry a foreigner. Nor would I allow her to be used as a political pawn by anyone.

"Thank you, but no," I said politely to Qadaffi. But still he persisted. "It is customary for the father to give his daughter's hand," I finally told him, trying to end our discussion, "so why don't you go and ask her father, President Sadat?"

But he demurred. Later Qadaffi would try to arrange a similar marriage between either this cousin or another and the adopted daughter of President Bourguiba of Tunisia. But Qadaffi would get no further with Bourguiba than he had gotten with me.

No scheme, no maneuver, seemed too farfetched to Qadaffi in his goal of uniting the Muslim world. Two years after he had failed to cement a union between Egypt and Libya through marriage, he would try the most bizarre action of all. "March on Egypt! Let the Egyptians know how much you want unity," he exhorted his countrymen, reasoning that if the Egyptians would not listen to him, perhaps they would listen to the Libyan people. Our newspapers and television in August of '75 were filled with the story of thousands and thousands of Libyan civilians poised on the border to drive their cars and trucks across the Western Desert to Alexandria. No one could believe this, including Anwar, who laughed heartily at the absurdity of it. "What kind of unity would that be?" he said. "No one can achieve unity by force, not even Qadaffi." But our government had to take the threat seriously, knowing what eccentricity Qadaffi was capable of. To prevent the Libyans from making the trek, the Minister of the Interior ordered railroad cars to be laid across the desert road as a precaution. The Libyan march never materialized. Nor did a formal union between Egypt and Libya.

In spite of Qadaffi's confusing behavior, women activists in Libya fought on courageously for their rights. And so did the women in the rest of the Muslim world, who were making increasing gains in their quest for freedom. Though our struggle was not as public as that taking place in the West, and our demands were not as extreme, nonetheless great progress was being made. A new sense of pride and purpose was sweeping the women in the Middle East.

"How do you convince the peasants to send their daughters to school?" asked Farah Diba, the wife of the Shah of Iran, soon after Anwar and I arrived in Teheran in June of 1976. "How do you draw women to your vocational programs?"

I was accompanying Anwar on a round of official visits to Iran, Saudi Arabia and the Arab emirate of Abu Dhabi. And everywhere we went, I was extremely gratified to see how much women's consciousness had grown. In Teheran, Farah's questions, like those of Queen Alia, never seemed to stop. And I never tired of answering.

During the four days Anwar and I spent as guests of the Shah and Farah, a mutual respect and understanding developed between Farah and me. Both of us were struck by how similar the history of women was in our two countries, and how many of the same challenges we still faced. In the early 1900s, Farah told me, Iranian women had demonstrated against the Russian and British troops in Iran in much the same way Hoda Sha'arawi and her friends had demonstrated against the British in Egypt. Like Hoda Sha'arawi and her friends, these women had begun to educate girls in their country shortly thereafter, selling their jewels to build the first Iranian school for girls. And like me and many of the women I knew in Cairo, Farah and a group of highly motivated women in Iran had tried to continue that tradition, turning old houses into kindergartens, opening schools and centers for women to learn crafts and to read and write.

In addition to sightseeing trips in Teheran to view the breathtaking Mirror Palace, where tiny prisms of glass covering the walls and columns sparkled like solitaires, Farah took me also to the museums. She was very fond of the arts and inaugurated many art exhibitions. She had also traveled around the world buying back Persian antiquities which belonged to Iran, and these too we saw in the museums. I was personally stunned by the museum's unbelievable collections of royal jewels: the golden throne of the Emperor encrusted with precious stones; life-sized peacocks of gold with tails of rubies, emeralds and sapphires; the huge bowls filled with unset stones blazing red, blue, green and diamond white. Farah also took me to see Iran's most modern hospitals, schools and new kindergartens. And what I saw was very impressive, especially her dedication to education.

At one educational institute, I was shown a film of Farah's efforts to educate the Bedouin tribes cut off from the mainstream, even from this century, by their isolation in the desert. Whereas many of the Bedouins in Egypt had settled down and had permanent schools in the desert, the Bedouins in Iran were still nomadic. I was impressed by Farah's dedication as I watched schoolbooks being loaded into a truck in Teheran for their journey first along paved highways, then onto more primitive roads and finally into the desert, where the car track ended. The books were then reloaded onto pack horses to complete the journey to the teachers who circulated among the Bedouin camps.

This was only my second meeting with Farah, the Shahbanu having visited Egypt with her husband shortly after Anwar, as the new President of Egypt, had moved to reestablish normal relations with Iran. But the Shah and my husband had known each other for years. Anwar loved to remind the Shah about the first time he had seen him, during a military parade in Cairo in 1938 to celebrate the Shah's marriage to the sister of King Farouk. "You were on a raised platform and I passed before you in the parade," Anwar would laughingly remind the Shah. "The distance between us was very small, yet in reality it was great. You were the heir to a throne, and I was a minor officer from a village you had never heard of."

It would be another thirty years before Anwar would actually meet the Shah at an Islamic summit in Rabat, where their relationship began with a quarrel. After the burning of el-Aqsa Mosque by a deranged tourist in 1969, Nasser had sent Anwar as Egypt's representative to discuss with other Muslim leaders what steps to take to protect the holy places under Israeli occupation. My husband had found the Shah's suggestions on the matter weak and, in Arabic, told the leaders so. The Shah had responded angrily. The quarrel was defused when Anwar, realizing that his remarks had sounded more inflammatory when translated into French so that the Shah could understand them, had addressed the Summit members in Persian. The Shah, who was known never to laugh and only rarely to smile, on this occasion had risen to his feet with a smile to applaud Anwar. The seeds of a lifelong friendship had been sown. "There can be no love except after enmity," Anwar was fond of telling the Shah, quoting one of our Arabic proverbs.

Though their backgrounds were very different, my husband and the Shah coincidentally shared much. Both were born in 1918. Both were graduated from military academies in 1938 with the same rank, second lieutenant. And both led the oldest countries and most ancient civilizations in the region, the Iranian Empire dating back 2500 years and Egypt's civilization going back seven thousand. This bond between our two countries lent a special significance to the alliance between the two men. Now, on our visit to Teheran, we were coming to know each other as couples.

We laughed and joked one day while the Shah drove us in his convertible from his country palace to the hotel in Ramsar on the Black Sea where Anwar and I were staying. "Slow down or I will lose my hair," I pleaded with the Shah from the back seat, trying to keep my false chignon attached to my head in the wind.

"Don't you wish we had problems like that," the Shah said laughingly to Anwar.

How well I remember that trip, my only one to Iran, not only for the flowering of my friendship with Farah, which remains to this day, but for the surprise of the slightly premature birth of our first grandchild, Sherif. I was resting in the hotel before a large dinner being given in our honor, when a sudden pounding came on the door. "You have a phone call from Cairo," the excited porter told me. "*Mabruk.* Congratulations." Noha! A grandson! I hugged and kissed my eldest daughter, Loubna, who had come to Iran with us, tears of joy streaming down our faces while Anwar fell to the ground in prayer.

"My Lord, arouse me to be thankful for Thy favor wherewith Thou hast favored me and my parents, and to do good that shall be pleasing unto Thee and include me in Thy righteous slaves," he prayed in a loud voice while he prostrated himself over and over on the floor of our suite.

Only one shadow was to hang over our trip to Iran. For all the modern advances we were seeing as the guests of the Shah, we were also seeing the gap that existed between the very rich and the very poor. Though both the Shah and Farah were highly intelligent people and genuinely trying to enact social reforms, not enough of their efforts were reaching the people who needed them most. To my dismay, for example, Farah had shown me the small school she had built in the garden of their remarkably modest palace in Teheran so that children from all backgrounds could attend school with her own children. I had made a mental note that though her intention was good, her actions were not in touch with the times. The imperial children should have gone out to school like everyone else in a democratic way rather than having a hand-picked few come into the palace to be schooled.

I was further distressed by a lavish farewell dinner party given for us and the Shah by a high government official at his ranch outside Teheran. I had been in many palaces around the world and had been entertained at many extravagant parties, but never had I seen such overindulgence as I did that night in Iran. The setting was beautiful. The people were charming. The presentation of the food was exquisite. But Iran was a poor country. And all in all, it was too much.

The steps leading into the very large house were made of crystal. Crystal! Never had I seen that before—nor have I seen it since. Liquor and wine as well as soft drinks and fruit juices were being served in the marble reception hall. A full orchestra was playing in a tent through which we entered the garden. In front of us was an elaborate buffet, the tables not laid out in rows but grouped in circles under the trees like intricate mosaics. Under one tree were different meats, under another vegetables and salads, another an assortment of fish, smoked, grilled, poached. The presentation of the food was an artform in itself, whole fish laid out in fish-shaped platters, crystal bowls of black caviar, gray caviar, golden caviar, nestled in ice and lit from below.

Anwar would eat only fruit, and even he was astounded when he went to fill his plate. Compotes of fruits were presented in intricately carved bowls of melon. Peaches, grapes, mangoes and fresh figs were woven into the boughs of the trees and draped across the tables. Nothing was ordinary. Chocolate mousse was offered as one of the desserts in swans made of spun sugar and presented against a backdrop of a huge aquarium filled with tropical fish. Fountains splashed, the guests strolled between the food tables and the dining tent on a bridge over a small pond, and we ate off place settings of gold.

"There will be a revolution. I feel it," I said to Anwar after we had flown back from the party to Teheran in the Shah's helicopter. "The rich here are too rich and the poor too poor without enough of a middle class to provide stability. The Shah must do something quickly to calm the people, give more of his land away, perhaps drop the title of emperor and call himself president. There are no other emperors in the world now except in Japan, and Hirohito is only a symbol like the Queen of England. The world is changing and there is no place anymore for an emperor. I am going to tell this to the Shah."

Anwar exploded. "Jehan, you will tell him nothing! This is none of your business. Why do you interfere?" he shouted at me. "The Shah is an emperor. He was born to be an emperor. And you, Jehan, want him to change his title to president? Don't you dare tell him this, do you hear me? Don't you dare!"

"But, Anwar," I protested, "I love the Shah. I want to tell him. He and Farah are our dear friends. Perhaps they do not see Iran as others see it, or perhaps they are ill advised."

"If you tell them how to run their country, perhaps they will not be our dear friends any longer," he said to me in his loudest voice. "You must not stick your nose into other people's affairs. The Shah will listen to you out of politeness and then he will not change anything. So what's the use?" Anwar was glowering at me. "I forbid you to say anything of the sort to the Shah," he said.

"Still, there will be a revolution," I insisted. "You will see, Anwar."

The next morning we flew on to Saudi Arabia. And I said nothing to the Shah.

"*Hamdillah 'alal-salaama.* Thank God for your safety," King Khalid greeted me at the airport in Jedda, shaking my hand and using the traditional Arabic greeting for one coming from a long way off. "*Hamdillah 'alal-salaama,*" he said also to Anwar, embracing him and kissing him on both cheeks.

"*Allah yisallimak,*" we each responded. "May God keep you safe also."

King Khalid and at least twenty of the Saudi princes were lined up to greet Anwar at the airport, dressed in their immaculate white robes and headdresses. *"Hamdillah 'alal-salaama,"* each of the princes greeted me politely. The television cameras whirred while waiters circulated among us with trays of fruit juices and iced yogurt whipped with mint. The journalists knew, Anwar knew, and certainly the Saudi princes knew, that this was an historic moment of sorts. I had chosen to enter the kingdom not behind my husband, but by his side.

There had been no gasps from the Saudi princes when I appeared at the door of the plane beside Anwar, nor did I sense any hostility. The princes were far too diplomatic to display any emotion that would offend me or, more important, my husband. Still, it was well known that in such a conservative and deeply religious society as Saudi Arabia's, a Muslim woman did not appear in public in the company of men. The Saudi Embassy in Cairo had made that quite clear before we began our journey, suggesting that on arrival I remain behind on the plane for an hour or so until my husband and the King and the princes had completed the official greeting and had left the airport. The embassy had pointed out that that had been the solution chosen by Mrs. Tito, the wife of the President of Yugoslavia, who had accompanied her husband on a state visit to the kingdom just the week before. But I had resisted.

"Anwar, on this trip I am deaf," I had said to my husband after receiving the message from the Saudi Embassy. "I don't need anyone to tell me or to teach me what it means to be a good Muslim woman. I respect my religion very much. Nothing I do is against Islam. My work with women, with children, with the poor, is, in fact, the very essence of Islam. Why should I be invisible just because I am a woman? I do not hide from the sight of men in Egypt. Nor will I anywhere else. It does not matter to me if we are in Japan, in Saudi Arabia, or on the moon. I will not change."

Anwar had looked bemused throughout my tirade. "I am not surprised to hear your reaction," he said. "I gave in to your attitude long ago and now support you. But others may take just a little longer."

Now the Saudi television cameras followed me as I left the airport reception with the Saudi princes, followed me again as I was escorted to the limousine of the King's brother, Prince Fawwaz ibn Abdel Aziz, the Prince of Jedda, while Anwar rode ahead with the King. I did not display the slightest surprise at riding alone with a man into the city, nor did Prince Fawwaz display the slightest surprise to be riding with me. En route I asked him many questions about the services the royal family provided so well for their subjects, their care of orphans, the disabled and the blind. I also asked him about the status of women. "I was delighted to find women serving as air hostesses when the King kindly offered me the royal plane to fly from Jedda to Mecca on my first pilgrimage," I told Prince Fawwaz. "At last, I thought, Saudi women are being allowed to work. But as soon as I heard their accents I knew that the hostesses were not Saudis but Lebanese. I hope soon they will be Saudis."

"Soon," the Prince said enigmatically. "Soon."

I wondered how soon. Women in Saudi Arabia had only recently begun to exercise their rights, and they still had very far to go. But there was no doubt that they had gained much in only fifteen years. Not until 1960 had the Saudi government established the first school for girls, and even then so many men had rioted against the school that the National Guard had been called out to maintain order. King Faisal had stood firmly against opponents of women's education, insisting that women too had the right to schooling, and pouring millions and millions of riyals into female education. It had been he who had built the first university for women in 1973, a great step forward in a country where tribal beliefs about women's status were so deeply engrained. In Saudi Arabia, the tents of the nomads had two parts, one for women and the other for men. And even the most highly educated Saudi women found their opportunities severely limited by the restrictive traditions which "protected" them by forcing them into a world apart.

I had heard all this before coming to Saudi Arabia, knew also the heritage of the Saudi royal family which had handed down such a conservative legacy. The Saudis were descended from Muhammad Ibn el-Sa'ud, founder of the dynasty that has ruled parts of the Arabian Peninsula for more than two hundred years. Sa'ud, a Bedouin famed for his clever diplomacy, had joined forces in 1744 with Muhammad Ibn Abdel Wahhab, a puritanical legal scholar who was calling for a return to the strict Muslim practices of the fourteenth century. Together these two men had won the allegiance of hundreds of nomadic tribes scattered throughout the peninsula, enabling them to set up the power base which would, in 1934, allow the modern ruling family of Sa'ud to control the country. Still the royal family continued to practice this legacy of diplomacy and fundamentalism, keeping the Quran as their only constitution, following the strictest codes of Islamic law while trying to balance their traditions with more modern ways.

That night, while Anwar attended a banquet at one of the royal palaces with the King and the princes, I attended another at the Queen's palace with thirty or so of the royal princesses and their friends. One after another the guests arrived in limousines whose windows were darkly tinted to ensure their modesty. All the princesses were beautifully dressed underneath the simple black *abayya*s which they wore to pass from their cars to the palace. And all of them were well-traveled and well-educated. Though cinemas, theaters, concert halls and even many books were not allowed in Saudi Arabia, many of these women had brought stereos, books, music and films back with them from abroad.

As we took our places in the Arab-style square of chairs and sofas in the salon, it was difficult for me to sort out who was who. Each guest seemed to be the cousin, aunt, sister or daughter-in-law of the others, for the royal family married often within itself. And, unlike Egypt, there was no protocol to the seating. In my country, the wife of the Minister of Defense knew exactly where to sit in relation to the wife of the Vice-President, for example, while in Saudi Arabia and all the other Arab countries, everyone sat wherever they pleased.

Our dinner was delicious, a first course of warm pita bread to dip into the appetizers of chickpeas mashed with sesame oil, richly seasoned eggplant puree, bowls of yogurt, tomatoes, olives, cucumbers and cheeses, then a whole roasted lamb, chickens, and pigeons along with bite-size balls of rice seasoned with saffron, dill or simply salt. When they dined alone, the Saudis ate their meat and rice with their right hands, but tonight we all used flatware of gold.

The conversation flew easily after our dessert of fruit and honey-drenched pastries and over cup after cup of rich Yemeni coffee, spiced with cardamom to aid digestion.

"What is your latest project, Mrs. Sadat?" the princesses and their guests asked me as we moved outside into the walled gardens scented with jasmine and lemon trees behind the palace. "What you are doing is not just for the women in Egypt, but for all of us." They were fascinated, they told me, by the pictures they had seen of me in the newspapers at inaugurations of charities or working at my various projects. No Saudi woman could have her photograph appear in public. Nor could any Saudi woman appear on television, even as an actress. The women in Saudi Arabia did not know what it was like to live in a society that did not discriminate between men and women.

The next night, at a dinner given at the home of the Queen's brother, more and more women joined me to ask questions about Egypt. "How lucky Egyptian women are," one university graduate said. "They can go out freely without wearing *abayya*s. Here we are hidden. No one knows who is who. We have no identity. And we are restricted. Egyptian women can pursue any course of study. Here we can enroll in the department of humanities, but not enter the schools of engineering or law. And if we practice medicine, we can only be pediatricians or obstetricians."

"You have to start fighting for your rights yourself," I told her, just as I told every group of women. "No one is going to present them to you, saying 'Here are your rights, women.' That will never happen. Unless we fight for ourselves, nobody is going to fight for us. Remember our proverb: *Ma tibkee 'alayna ghayr aynayna*. Only our own eyes will cry for us."

"But how can we start?" asked another guest of the royal family. "We do charity work, yes, but we have many empty hours. Our possibilities are very limited. No one dares be involved in man's work, because we are afraid we will be ostracized from our society and not be accepted. Does this happen in Egypt?"

"I have never found that," I reassured the young woman. "Men and women work side by side in Egypt. Men accept this. I have found it no different working with a man or a woman."

"But we are frightened," said another woman. "We don't know what it would be like to go out without a veil or to mingle with men at a job."

"You would do your job as God wants you to," I told her. "Remember His words in the Quran: 'Never will I suffer to be lost the good works of any of you.' But let us be practical. If men do not want you to earn money of your own, continue to work for charities. But make more of an effort. Go to your charities three or four times a week. Let the men feel that you have a responsibility. Then go out even more often. Let them get used to it. Ask for concessions slowly. Start with the smallest things at first, but never rest in your demands for progress. Someday you'll find that you are driving yourself to work, your pride in your accomplishments infinite."

The next morning when Anwar and I were leaving, I saw my husband and King Khalid laughing together. "What was so funny?" I asked Anwar as we flew on to Abu Dhabi.

"King Khalid was telling me how amused he was by your visit," Anwar said. " 'I'd better watch out,' he told me. 'Jehan is trying to make a revolution among the women.' "

"I wish I could," I said.

But, tiny step by tiny step, women were gaining ground. At the airport in Abu Dhabi, we were met by Sheikh Zayyid, the leader of that Gulf state. "*Hamdillah 'alal-salaama*, madam," he told me, shaking my hand. "We enjoyed watching your arrival in Jedda yesterday on television. All the women were very happy about it." I looked at him, startled, not knowing whether he was speaking genuinely. But he seemed to be. "Your wife is a revolutionary just like you, Mr. President," Sheikh Zayyid said to my husband, smiling.

Sheikh Zayyid glanced over his shoulder and carefully lowered his voice. "Today for the first time my wife has come to the airport to greet a foreign guest," he said to me. "She regrets she cannot come forward to greet you in front of the press, for it would be immodest. But she will meet you when the men have gone and ride back with you in the car."

I was delighted. Another breakthrough. Silently I cheered for his wife, Sheikha Fatima, of whom I was extremely fond, having met her on a prior trip to Abu Dhabi. "I'm honored by your hospitality and that of your wife, Sheikh Zayyid," I responded. "*Katar khayrku*. May your goodness grow even greater."

And it did. The traditional dinners were held for us that night, Anwar dining with the men, and I with the women. Sheikha Fatima had arranged a very large reception for me, inviting the wives of all the foreign diplomats and the wives of the government ministers as well as the women from the big families in Abu Dhabi. Even the servants were women, Indians and Pakistanis who made up much of the labor force in the

Gulf. This was very unusual because in our country, even in Saudi Arabia, it was men who traditionally served the guests at any official reception. But what happened next was even more unusual, in fact unique.

We were listening to a singer after dinner when there was a stir at the door. As the women all stared in disbelief, Sheikh Zayyid strode into the room.

"I have come to say hello to Mrs. Sadat," he said. "May I join you and listen to the singing?"

"Of course, with pleasure," I said. "Why not?"

The women looked even more amazed when he circled the room, shaking hands with each of them.

"Come. Let us hear some songs," Sheikh Zayyid then said, settling himself down beside me and applauding the singer on.

I didn't realize what an extraordinary event had taken place until the evening was ending. "Thank you so much for giving us this opportunity, Mrs. Sadat," one woman after another whispered in my ear. "This was the first time I have ever met Sheikh Zayyid." It seemed incredible even to me that the women, especially the wives of the foreign diplomats, had never before been face to face with the Arab emirate's leader. But it was true. "I have been here with my husband for three years," the wife of the Swedish ambassador told me, "and this is the first time I've ever shaken hands with Sheikh Zayyid. I thank you."

"How have you done so much in Egypt?" the women of Abu Dhabi asked me the next day at a large meeting which Sheikha Fatima had arranged. Fifty or so had gathered, women who were already active and women who wanted to be. And the list of their frustrations began.

"We have one woman lawyer, but she is from a prominent family and has not been allowed to join the Ministry of Justice for fear of dishonoring them," they told me. "We have one woman engineer, and she has gotten a job only because her brother works in the same department. We cannot even work as secretaries, because we are not permitted to appear in front of men."

"That is unfortunate. In Egypt, many women are secretaries," I told them. "In the end I believe this will make it easier for women to rise to positions of greater responsibility. But if you can't work with men, find things that you can do without making the men furious. Help in the hospitals. Hold bazaars to raise money for charities. Start off slowly. But start."

"What if our husbands refuse to let us go out in public?" one woman asked me.

"Then of course you must obey them," I told her. "Go in a car with dark glass. Or work at home instead. Invite other women to come in to help. You can sew hospital gowns for the sick or make handicrafts for the bazaars. There are many things you can do to earn respect. The point is to begin."

I knew it would be difficult for these women, because in Abu Dhabi, as in many of the smaller Gulf States, there was not yet a university. For men this was not so important, since generous government scholarships made it possible for all who wanted to study abroad. But for women, who needed their families' permission to leave the country, the situation was very hard. Fewer than two hundred women from Abu Dhabi had so far received higher education, most of them graduating from universities in Egypt. Still, I was confident that many of those gathered around me would soon realize their aspirations. The first university in the country was due to open in 1977. And with Sheikha Fatima as their leader, the women of Abu Dhabi were in good hands.

I knew of no other leader's wife in the Gulf States, perhaps even in the Muslim world, who was working more or fighting harder for women's rights than Sheikha Fatima. To set an example for others, she was continuing her own education, studying English and perfecting her Arabic. All over Abu Dhabi she had started literacy programs for women in the rural and urban areas. And in 1973, with the support of her husband, she had started the Abu Dhabi Society for the Awakening of Women, an organization which had quickly expanded and opened branches in four of the other emirates to eradicate illiteracy and train women in trades.

Education of the next generation of women in Abu Dhabi was particularly important to Sheikha Fatima, who had had little education in her own childhood. She arranged for television programs to be aired encouraging the people to send their girls as well as their boys to the country's newly constructed primary and secondary schools. Those whom she could not reach through television she went to in person. When she heard that the Bedouins in the south had suddenly withdrawn all their daughters over eight years old from the new school, she flew to the region and begged each family to reconsider. Out of respect for her, they agreed.

My own respect for Sheikha Fatima grew even greater when that night I attended the open meeting, or *majlis,* she held weekly for all the women in her country. Though the male leaders of many Gulf countries regularly held the *majlis* to hear the problems and grievances of their subjects, only Sheikha Fatima held one just for women. I admired this custom, which we did not have in Egypt but which continues to this day in many of the Arab countries.

Never does one need to call ahead for an appointment or apply for an audience during the *majlis.* Everyone from shepherds to high-level officials is welcome to come. And hundreds do, praying together with their leaders before the *majlis* and sharing a meal with them afterward. For hours the petitioners sit patiently on the floor waiting for their turn to speak while servants pass trays of food and cups of mint tea among them. Some come only to give advice to the leader, and always the leader listens. It is part of Islam not to be a dictator, but to always take into consideration the advice of others.

Most petitioners, however, come to ask for favors: the help of the government to send an ill family member abroad for medical treatment; a loan to help the family through the year if their crops failed; the leader's help to investigate a wrongdoing or to mediate a dispute. If the leader can grant their wishes, he does. If he is not knowledgeable enough to deal with a specific petition, a question of taxes perhaps, he directs the query to an expert in that field. All petitions are answered, in keeping with our Islamic tradition. It is said that during the Prophet's time, any person who petitioned the Prophet Muhammad or his helpers was assured of support, just as these petitioners at the *majlis* in Abu Dhabi were now being helped. If a favor is asked of any Muslim and he can give it, he has to, be it money, advice, food or lodging. If the petitioner is later able to repay his debt or return a favor, he does.

At Sheikha Fatima's meeting, the fifty women sitting in her big salon spoke their minds openly and made their requests known—the need for money to send a sick husband abroad, a request for her intervention in a dispute between a husband and a son. "They are fighting bitterly," one woman told Sheikha

Fatima. "My husband wants our son to work with him in his shop. My son wants to work for the government." The family's name and address were taken down and Sheikha Fatima said she would send her son or a personal representative to mediate a reconciliation.

The women who had to wait for hours to speak expressed no disappointment at all, for the *majlis* was as much a social gathering as it was a political one. Here was a community of women learning from one another and expressing their views. Wives of the foreign diplomats were invited to attend as well, and Sheikha Fatima's secretary, an Egyptian graduate of the American University in Cairo who spoke both French and English, translated for them. I went home to Egypt greatly impressed by the *majlis*. The leaders and the people prayed together. They ate together. They solved their problems together. There was no barrier between the rich and the poor, those in power and those whom they ruled. The custom continues in spite of the risks of such openness. In 1975, King Faisal was killed by a relative while holding a *majlis* in Riyadh.

I was always treated with the greatest respect and consideration wherever I traveled. And I, in turn, urged the women whom I met abroad to come to Egypt to visit me. Many did, Sheikha Fatima becoming the first wife of a leader in the Gulf to travel alone when she visited me soon after I had visited her. Sheikh Zayyid asked only that her photo not appear in the newspaper. Farah Diba of Iran came several times to Egypt, as did Iris Ferengia, wife of the Lebanese leader, and Bouthaina el-Numeiry from the Sudan.

Always I took my guests to see my projects, to meet with the Cairo Women's Union and to visit the Talla project. I took them to factories and to the workers' cooperatives in the villages, where women from the Arab countries could see Egyptian women working side by side with men to make something better for themselves. But, for all our progress in Egypt, there was one critical area where women remained at a cruel disadvantage.

Since 1929, women in Egypt had been subject to the Personal Status Laws, laws which made it very clear that women's status was inferior to men's. For years women's groups like the Egyptian Women's Union had been fighting to reform some of these humiliating laws, especially those concerned with marriage and divorce. Ninety-eight percent of the women in Egypt were married, yet the laws governing marriage and divorce were cruelly discriminatory. In 1977 I joined the fight to give women greater justice and security within the family. For the next two years, the reform of the Status Laws was to be the most important issue in my life.

Some laws we could do nothing about. The Quran allowed men to repudiate their wives at will, for example, making this right unquestionable. But highly questionable was the way men were abusing this privilege. "Divorce may be pronounced twice, and then a woman must be retained in honor or allowed to go with kindness," reads the Second Sura, "The Cow." Many ulema recommended that men wait at least a month between each pronouncement, although it was permissible for a man to simply repeat the words "I divorce you" three times in a row to end his marriage. All too often men in Egypt took this hastier option, some men not even saying the words of repudiation in front of their wives. As long as divorce was pronounced in the presence of two witnesses, it was considered valid. Some Egyptian wives were never even informed that their husbands had divorced them, a cruelty of the worst sort.

While it was easy for a man to divorce his wife, it was very difficult for a woman to divorce her husband. Though the "Women" Sura of the Quran exhorts men to treat their wives with kindness, "for even if you do not love them, it may well be that you dislike a thing which Allah has meant for your own good," a woman had to petition the court to end her marriage and had to prove her husband impotent, incapable of supporting her, insane, terminally ill with a contagious disease or dangerously abusive. Divorce was not granted to her because her husband beat her short of permanent injury, took another wife or treated her like a slave, though these were certainly not acts of "kindness." And while she waited for the court to hear her petition, sometimes for three or four years, she was still bound by law to give her husband total obedience.

I had seen this inequity in divorce myself with one of my own relatives. Women from better families did not petition the courts for a divorce, such a public forum not being considered respectable. Instead, like my family member, they had to plead with their fathers or other male relatives to intercede. My relative had been so miserable in her marriage that she had gone to her father, threatening suicide if he refused to order her hated husband to divorce her. Under the law, her grounds would not have held up anyway, her husband being such a miser that he counted the pieces of chocolate in every box of candy she bought and scolded her severely if she ate more than her share. But my relative had been so desperate that her father had agreed to order his son-in-law to divorce her. If her father had refused, she would have been forced by the Status Laws to stay with her husband. At that time, she would not even have been able to leave her husband's house.

Until Anwar became president, a woman who moved out of her husband's house without his permission or approval from the court was running the risk of arrest. Under the Beit el-Ta'a, the House of Obedience Law which Anwar revoked in 1976, a husband could have the police return his wife to him by force, and could then legally keep her under lock and key to prevent her from fleeing again. Even worse, the husband could later use the wife's attempted escape as proof in court that she was *na-chez*, disobedient. This would ensure that she was never granted a divorce at all.

With such sorry possibilities looming in marriage, a few women insisted on including the right to divorce their husbands as part of their original marriage contracts. But very few. No man would agree to it unless the woman was extremely rich and he had nothing. Even at that, the future groom was quite naturally suspicious about the motives of his bride. Such a woman was also looked down upon even by other women as being shrewd and undesirable. The cost of the right to divorce came high to these few women. But under the current Status Laws, many women were paying too high a price for their marriages.

Men were allowed to take more wives than one, multiple marriages being allowed by the Quran. And the few men in Egypt who did practice polygamy were not required by law to tell their first wives that they had taken another wife. Even when the first wife was informed, there was nothing she could do about it. Under the current Status Laws, polygamy was not considered grounds for divorce. The result was often cruel.

"Mrs. Sadat, please help me. My husband took another wife three years ago but has refused to divorce me," a pretty woman carrying her little daughter petitioned me one day at a bazaar I was opening in Cairo. "Now he has left the country and though the court has sent him many letters asking him to divorce me, he refuses even to answer." For months, wherever I went to speak, at school inaugurations, hospital fund-raisers, anywhere my appearance had been announced, this same young woman and her little daughter would come, too. She haunted me, her face always streaked with tears, pleading and pleading for my help. But under the present laws there was nothing I—or the courts—could do. She had none of the legal grounds for divorce. The courts could not order him to divorce her, as he was out of Egyptian jurisdiction. And I couldn't send for him to try to change his mind, for he was abroad, moving from one destination to another to avoid his responsibilities. I was heartbroken for her because she was young and should have been able to marry again. But she couldn't.

Other women were being treated just as badly, it being perfectly legal for a husband to keep a different wife in every quarter of town without ever telling the others. One well-known story went around about the man who kept two unsuspecting wives on separate floors in a large apartment building, one the mother of his children, the other a younger, secret wife. If he met someone he knew in the elevator, he went to the mother of his children. If not, he went up three floors to his other wife. And neither one knew until "their" husband died. Friends and relatives coming to pay condolences to the "widow" met in the elevator and discovered the intrigue.

Unfortunately, such a discovery was not that rare. Some new widows found strangers at their doors on the day their husbands died, showing the birth certificates of their children to prove that they too had been legally married to the husband and were therefore entitled to a full share of the widow's already small inheritance, only one eighth of the estate. The shock at the husband's deceit sometimes mitigated the widow's grief.

I loved the famous story of one such widow who, upon receiving a surprise visit from her late husband's second wife, immediately went into the bedroom to exchange her black mourning clothes for a bright-red dress. "Don't waste your time paying condolences to me," she told the women who had come to sit with her in her sorrow. "I'm not crying anymore for this man who cheated me all these years." I admired her spirit and agreed with her totally. I could never have tolerated such deceit. If a woman loved her husband, lived with him and shared with him, then he was bound by honor to at least tell her the truth. He should also have been bound by law.

•

"The fundamentalists will be strongly against us," Minister of Social Affairs 'Aisha Rateb cautioned me when I met with her to discuss the women's strategy for reforming the Status Laws. "When I proposed changing the laws before, the fanatics staged demonstrations against me."

I was not surprised. To the religious fanatics, a woman's role was clear: to serve men without questioning and with complete obedience. "But we are not straying from the Quran," I said to 'Aisha. "Rateb, there are four schools of Islamic law, not just the ultraconservative school to which they belong. Do they ignore the story in the Hadith of the woman who was told by the Prophet Muhammad himself to leave her husband if she was unhappy with him?"

'Aisha shrugged. "It is very difficult to argue successfully with them," the Minister said.

My frustration rose. "But the fundamentalists must see that the present laws encourage rather than discourage men to divorce," I told her. "And the Quran itself has told us that 'of all lawful things, divorce is the most hateful to God.' "

"I agree with you totally, Mrs. Sadat," 'Aisha said. "And we will continue to fight for reform. But the fundamentalists are very convincing in their interpretation of Islam. To change the laws will be very delicate."

Petitions were circulated at meetings of different Egyptian women's organizations, many of whose members, like Karima el-Sa'id, the Chairwoman of the Egyptian Women's Organization, added their voices to the call for reform. So compelling were the arguments in favor of new laws that three of the highest religious authorities in the country—Muhammad Abdel Rahman Bisar, Sheikh of el-Azhar, Minister of Religious Endowments Sheikh Muhammad Abdel Mun'em el-Nimr, and Mufti of Egypt Sheikh Gad el-Haqq—agreed to serve on the committee responsible for recommending the reforms to Parliament. Minister of Justice Abdel Akhar Muhammad Abdel Akhar, too, sat on the committee.

Purposefully I kept my name off the committee, feeling that the reforms would find more support in Parliament if they were seen as having the backing of a broad cross section of Egyptians. I was quite content to work behind the scenes with the women and to publicly support their goals. But at first, my desire to participate had made the women's groups uneasy.

At the first meeting I attended in support of the reforms, Amina el-Sa'id rose to caution me. "Madam, I am afraid that being the wife of the President will make it difficult for you to back us, because we are ready to demonstrate and to be very aggressive in our demands," she said. "We will have to go to extremes, which may mean that some of us may go to prison. You would not be able to do that."

"If you go to prison, I will go with you," I replied quickly. "Indira Gandhi once said, 'It is true that women sometimes go too far, but it's only when you go too far that others listen.' But let us not think of such extremes as prison. My husband is a very progressive man and will not move against us. Our opposition will not come from the President, but from the religious reactionaries. And I wish to help."

To defuse what the committee knew would be emotional and irrational resistance to the reforms, they had collected as much hard evidence as possible to support them. They did not need theories. They needed facts. And the committee had them in the work of a highly respected professor of sociology at Cairo University whose published study had shown a correlation between juvenile deliquency and the high Egyptian divorce rate, as well as in the research of Aziza Hussein, one of the founders of the Egyptian Family Planning Association and the first woman appointed to the Egyptian delegation to the United Nations. Aziza's research showed clearly that the high birthrate in Egypt represented a woman's only insurance against divorce, ranging from a low divorce rate of 4 percent among women who had four children up to 62 percent for divorced women who were childless. No wonder our birthrate was so high. Under the current Status Laws, bearing child after child was the only leverage a woman had against her husband's divorcing her.

The committee researched the proposed reforms carefully, making sure none of the proposals contradicted the Quran, the Hadith or Shari'a. The members knew that the religious fundamentalists, though a minority, had a growing influence, especially among the young. They had to proceed very cautiously in selecting and wording the reforms that would best serve women while remaining in compliance with Islamic law. Despite the need for caution, I felt a great urgency to press quickly for reform. I wanted nothing more deeply than to achieve security for women and their children. And I knew that Anwar supported our efforts. If we had ever had a chance to win reform, it would be during his leadership.

Atheist! Petty Dictator! Enemy of the Family! These were just a few of the names Islamic extremists began calling us in the spring of 1978 when the committee released the list of proposed and really quite mild reforms: the court to appoint arbiters, preferably relatives, to try to reconcile the differences between a divorcing couple; the requirement that a husband promptly inform his wife he had divorced her; the requirement that he inform his first wife of his intent to take a new wife; in such cases, the first wife's right to seek a divorce within twelve months; the right of a divorced mother to retain custody of the children at least until her sons reach ten and her daughters twelve, or longer if the court found it beneficial to the children; the right of divorced women in certain cases to collect not only alimony from their ex-husbands, but also a lump sum whose amount increased in proportion to the length of their marriage; and, most controversial of all, the right of the wife to retain the family home for the children.

The committee members knew that this list of proposed amendments was in total accordance with Islamic law. They had not questioned our laws of inheritance, nor a man's right to take four wives, for both were written in the Quran and were thus deemed untouchable. The issue of a woman's testimony in court being worth only half that of a man was also not raised, for this too was a law based on a Quranic injunction. The right of a man to remarry immediately following divorce while a woman had to wait three months to ensure she was not carrying his child had also been left alone, as this too was in the Quran. Nor had the proposed reforms challenged a man's right to repudiate his wife at will. Nonetheless, our call for just these simple reforms spread like a firestorm around the country.

"These are Jehan's laws, not Islam's laws," roared one of the most vocal fundamentalist sheikhs, who railed against the reforms every week after the Friday prayers. "These laws she wants will turn men into women and women into men! They will cause the breakdown of the Egyptian family structure and move hundreds to godlessness! These laws are against the Shari'a, the word of God as revealed in the Quran!"

None of us was surprised by the sheikh's reaction, though I was startled that the reforms had come to be known as "Jehan's laws." A professor at the American University who wanted to interview me on a book he was writing about Egyptian women had been the first to tell me.

"I want to talk to you about Jehan's laws," he had said to me one day.

"Jehan's laws? What laws are those?" I asked him.

He looked at me amazed. "Don't you know?" he said. "Everyone all over the country is calling the proposed Status Law reforms 'Jehan's laws.' "

It was my turn to be amazed. "Well, that makes me very proud," I told him. "If I accomplish nothing else, this will be enough."

Soon the newspapers, the magazines and the television news shows were flooded with editorials and stories about "Jehan's laws." "Alimony need only be paid to a woman for a single month unless arranged for in the marriage contract!" a well known sheikh was quoted as saying, having based this argument on the Hanafi school of Islamic law. "Alimony must be paid until the husband's legal debt has been fulfilled," countered the Minister of Religious Endowments Sheikh Abdel Mun'em el-Nimr, citing the Shafa'i school. "Women cannot ask for a divorce even if their husband harm them in word or deed, with force or with slander," cited the fundamentalist sheikh. Countered Sheikh Bisar, the Sheikh of el-Azhar Mosque and perhaps the most prestigious and influential member of the committee for reform: "The Malaki school says that women may ask for a divorce whenever their husbands harm them in word or deed. Certainly marriage to another without their consent is something harmful."

By May of 1979, there were articles for and against the reforms in almost every Egyptian periodical. The debates grew hotter, the pressure more intense. I spoke out at every opportunity in support of the reforms, as did all the committee members. And the fundamentalists counterattacked. "The Prophet has told us that 'men are in charge of women because Allah hath made the one of them to excel the other,' " one after another challenged us from the text of the Quran. "The Prophet was a crusader for women's rights," I would respond, citing the Quran's directives outlawing female infanticide and granting women rights to property and education.

Speaking to a student summer camp in Alexandria about the need for reform, I found myself in a debate with a young fundamentalist sheikh. Though I had not planned to argue with him, I had no choice, for he challenged me from the audience.

"How can you say, Mrs. Sadat, that a man cannot marry more than one wife?" the young sheikh cried out. "It is our right."

"We are not denying your rights at all," I replied. "We are merely putting obstacles in the way of polygamy because, as the Quran tells us, it is very hard for a husband to be fair to more than one wife."

The young man pressed on. "Why should I have to inform my wife if I plan to take another wife?" he asked. "She has to obey me. It is her duty. If I keep a home for her and give her everything she wants, that is enough."

"No, that is not enough," I said. "You certainly have a right to remarry, but she also has a right to know about it. Maybe she would choose to leave and marry someone else."

With each question and answer, the students applauded more. They knew that nothing I was saying was against Islam or Shari'a. My husband would never have approved of reforms that were. Nor would I.

Soon, the fundamentalist sheikhs began to defame 'Aisha Rateb, Amina el-Sa'id and me, though never by name. "These women calling for their rights are imitating Western women," the sheikhs called out to the men praying in the mosques on Fridays. "They are going around like men. A good Muslim woman's place is in the home." Magazines put out by extreme Islamic groups resorted to publishing long articles about the weaknesses inherent in women's character. We were too emotional to use the laws responsibly, one of these articles claimed. If a woman was told that her husband had taken other wives, she would be too quick to get excited and would demand divorce immediately without taking time to contemplate or reconcile.

But it was the fanatics who seemed to be getting overexcited, leaping to their feet at meetings to scream their approval of any antifemale diatribes. "A woman has to stay at home to cook, to wash, to clean, to care for the children. Nothing else. This is her Paradise," they cried. "If a woman works among men, she will seduce them. It is a sin for her to show her arms, her legs, her head." Their charges were revealing and ultimately depressing. They demeaned the image of men.

So explosive did the issue become that one day rioting broke out at el-Azhar, the seat of Islamic orthodoxy. What started as a demonstration against "Jehan's laws" soon broke down into chaos. "One! Two! Three! Four!" hundreds of male students screamed, marching around the university courtyard in the white robes and skullcaps of the devout. "We want *one, two, three, four* wives!" It did not seem to matter that in no way had we challenged a man's right to polygamy. In the protesters' religious fervor, truth was not a factor. When the demonstrators spilled out into the street, the police had to disband the highly agitated crowd.

The women working against the laws and I received many letters of support in the mail, as well as many letters of disapproval. Amina el-Sa'id said she could fill an entire trunk with the hate mail. Threats against me—and her—became common, but I was used to that and paid no attention. Mostly, the actions against us were petty. Cartoons began to appear on the bulletin boards at the university of me dressed as a man in a military uniform. As soon as the students who supported women's rights took the cartoons down, new ones would appear.

The complaints I was hearing from my friends about the reforms were just as petty. At almost every social function I attended, the husbands took me aside to whisper that though they wholeheartedly supported most of our divorce reforms, they objected vehemently to one: the family home going to the women and children. In overcrowded Cairo, finding a decent place to live in was at a premium. But the men's concern for their own comfort smacked of the double standard in our society, which had always favored men. "You know that women who wander the streets are not considered respectable," I would chide them. "As a man you can sleep anywhere. But not your wife and children."

Often men joked with me about the reforms, though underneath I knew they were not really joking. "What are you doing to us, Mrs. Sadat?" they would say, always with a laugh. "We are going to have to call for our rights now, too."

I would smile back and answer in my sweetest voice: "You don't have to call for your rights, because you've had them for thousands and thousands of years. Now it's our turn."

Still Anwar continued to insist that his other priorities for Egypt took precedence over our fight for women's rights. At home I did everything I could to advance our cause, launching a one-woman campaign myself.

"What do you want for your birthday?" he asked me in 1977 and again in 1978.

"Women's rights," I responded.

"What do you want for Mother's Day?" he asked me just as often.

My answer became a predictable one: "Women's rights."

I must confess I nagged him, though he believed as strongly as I that women had earned the right to equality in Egypt. Whenever Anwar and I were the subjects of a news interview, I seized the opportunity to face him with the issue in public.

"Egypt is a democracy, Jehan," he would say to me afterward in exasperation. "I do what the people want me to."

"Over half our population are women, Anwar," I would press him. "Egypt will not be a democracy until women are as free as men. As the leader of our country, it is your duty to make that happen."

I began to plant questions about our proposed reforms among the audiences wherever Anwar was speaking. The wider the support for women's rights, the more likely Anwar was to respond. At one political meeting in Cairo, I sent a note with my bodyguard to Emtethal el-Deeb, a prominent member of the women's movement, who was sitting on the other side of the room: "Ask him, 'Mr. President, if you were told that 90 percent of the minors who commit crimes in our country come from divorced families, would you consider reforms that would strengthen the family and discourage divorce?' " When Emtethal asked the question, Anwar measured the distance between us with his eyes before answering.

I even took my campaign for women's rights abroad. "President Sadat, the women of Egypt are suffering and their children are suffering from the insecurity fostered by the unfair Status Laws of 1929," read the note I passed along the long row to Dr. Afaf, the Egyptian counsel in Washington, D.C., where Anwar was talking with Egyptians studying in the United States. "If the woman feels secure, her family, the nucleus of society, will also be secure. When are you going to correct what is presently an unfair and destabilizing situation for the Egyptian family by granting women their rights?"

"Where is Jehan?" Anwar said immediately, searching for my face in the audience.

Innocently I smiled up at him, making sure he noticed how far away I was sitting from Dr. Afaf. But Anwar was not fooled.

"My wife has become the women's lawyer," he said, laughing, to the audience. "She nags at me all the time, calling for women's rights. Well, they will have them, but not now. I have other priorities first, to feed the people, to provide housing, schooling, medical care. I will get to women's rights, but later on."

Anwar may have had other priorities, but during the fight for reform, I did not. Nor, it appeared, did members of the press, especially in America, who asked me the same questions time and again: "What rights, if any, do women have in Islam?" "It is true a man can divorce his wife just by saying 'I divorce you'?" "How do women feel about being forced to marry a man by their parents?" Over and over I would answer the same questions in thirty-minute interview after thirty-minute interview, until both my throat and my brain felt parched. But rarely did I turn down such opportunities to explain our society and to advance our cause for women.

Nor did I let up on Anwar. Women were still greatly underrepresented at all levels of government, allowing many women's issues to be ignored. From my work on the People's Council in Munufiyya, I knew that we needed women, many more women, to sit on the councils in every governorate. From my work with the few women members of Parliament, I knew that we needed many more women represented at the national level of government as well. On a trip to the Sudan that I had made with Anwar in 1976, I had learned that a number of seats in the Parliament there were set aside for women. "If they respect women so much in the Sudan, why do you not in Egypt?" I told Anwar. "We are half of the population. We have to be represented at the policy-making levels with far bigger numbers."

Anwar agreed. "Many groups should be guaranteed representation, Jehan," he said. "The fellaheen are already represented in government, but what about young people and students?"

"There should be quotas for them, too," I concurred. "Why not set aside seats for youth. And for women."

In March of 1979, Mother's Day drew near again. "Anwar, there is just one special gift that I am longing for this year, a present which I would love to have," I said to my husband.

"What is it?" he asked.

I stalled. "Will you give it to me?" I asked him.

He laughed. "If I can afford it," he said.

"Yes, this time you can afford it," I told him.

"All right, Jehan. What is it?" he said.

I took a deep breath. "Women's rights."

He threw back his head and shouted with laughter. "Yes, Jehan, yes," he said. "This year I will give it to you. The women deserve it."

On June 20, 1979, Anwar issued the first of two presidential decrees about women. Thirty seats earmarked for women were to be added to the Egyptian Parliament, and 20 percent of all the seats on the twenty-six People's Councils as well were to go to women. With one bold stoke, Anwar had multiplied the number of women in national government fivefold and raised the number of women in rural politics from seven to more than thirty. Where for eight years there had been only two women on the Munufiyya Council, now there would be ten.

The second decree was even closer to my heart: the reforms of the Status Laws were to be voted on in Parliament in July.

Nothing could diminish my happiness. But one obstacle remained: the vote in Parliament. We were sure of our support, knowing that the Status Law reforms expressed the opinion of the majority. But the vote would give the fundamentalists one last chance to block us. We had to head off the fundamentalist lobby before they dragged out the debate long enough for them to give themselves additional time to mount opposition. 'Aisha called all the women in the Parliament, and mapped out a strategy.

"When the fundamentalist members start voicing their opposition to the reforms, say nothing," 'Aisha suggested to them. "Don't let the debate degenerate into men versus women, both using the same old religious arguments. Let the male members of Parliament who support the reforms defend them. That will make a much better image for the people, the men being for us this time and not against us."

On the day of the debate, 'Aisha and I held our breath. The women in Parliament held their tongues. And on July 3, 1979, after four hours of noisy discussion, the reforms of the Status Laws were approved by an overwhelming majority, as were the new quotas for women representatives in government.

The next day the women members of Parliament came to my house to celebrate. "We made history," we all cried together, hugging each other. "We are no longer inferior."

"I wish I could have spoken out in the debate," said one woman, "but it was better listening to the men defending the rights of their mothers, their sisters, their daughters."

Our greatest hopes had been realized. And there were more to come. During the general election held a few weeks after the quotas were approved, three women beyond the thirty guaranteed by the new decree were elected to Parliament. In our country which so many in the West considered backward, we now had 5 percent more women in the national legislature than there were in the United States Congress and 10 percent more than in France's National Assembly.

Egyptian women had finally gained a political voice. And in their personal lives they were far more secure. In the first year of the new Status Laws, the divorce rate would fall 25 percent, due mostly, the women's groups felt, to the men's reluctance to move out of their apartments. Among those granted a divorce under the new laws was the young woman who had followed me at public functions for so many years, seeking the help that then I could not give her. I pray that she found a new husband who would give her and her daughter the happiness they deserved.

"Jehan's Laws," as the reformed Status Laws continued to be known long after the debate about them had died down, would make their mark all over the Arab world. The last time I prayed at the Kaaba in Mecca, a Saudi woman came up to me and whispered her thanks for all I and the other women of Egypt had done for women all over the Arab world. Though by then her government and the governments of many other Arab countries had long since broken their diplomatic ties with Egypt, still the actions of my husband toward the status of women were being held in the greatest respect.

How courageous my husband had been. At the time he issued the presidential decree raising the status of women in 1979, fundamentalists in Iran had toppled the government and sent the Shah into exile. The forces of fundamentalism were rising in other Muslim countries, as well. For Anwar to elevate women in Egypt in the face of this reactionary political atmosphere was a bold and daring action. But Anwar had never shrunk from enacting reforms and initiating policies that other leaders avoided. My husband was not one to pander to political polls or to court popularity by compromising his convictions. Broad-minded and independent, Anwar would brook no interference in his vision of democracy for Egypt. Or in his quest to end our country's problems.

By 1979, Anwar had embarked on a daring new crusade. It had all begun two years before with a single but extraordinary journey. I had not accompanied Anwar on this particular journey. He had gone alone. But regardless of the great danger I knew he faced, my husband had traveled with my blessings and the prayers of people everywhere who yearned for peace. If he were to succeed, he would change forever the history of Egypt and the entire Middle East.

Chapter 12

BETTMANN NEWSPHOTOS

el-tariq ilal salaam

The Road to Peace

i knew from the moment my husband announced his willingness to go to Jerusalem to make peace with Israel that he would be killed for it. I did not know when his death would come, where it would occur, or who would kill him. I only knew that my days on earth with my husband were now numbered. From that moment in November of 1977 until his assassination, the headaches that had plagued me for years became constant. I would not know a day without pain.

Few people knew beforehand of Anwar's intention to visit Jerusalem. I was not one of them. Had Anwar discussed this decision with me, I would have supported him 100 percent. Though I knew it would eventually take his life, I also knew that peace with Israel was the only path open to Egypt.

Future wars would accomplish nothing. The Israelis were able to control the Sinai, an area of sand and Bedouin tribes, but never could Israel, a nation of two million, hope to occupy Egypt and subdue her 42 million inhabitants. At the same time, we could not conquer Israel even if our troops reached Tel Aviv, for the United States would not allow it. "It's ridiculous going through war after war with Israel," Anwar had often reflected. "There is nothing to win."

It was for peace that Anwar had gone to war with Israel in 1973. He had had to. There could be no peace with the Israelis, he had said over and over, until they believed that Egypt could inflict as much harm on them as they had inflicted on us. Our stunning victory in the '73 war before the United States intervened had proved his point. From that time he could say to Israel, "I am here. I am not weak. Now let us talk." This moment could be postponed no longer.

Anwar was being torn apart by the misery in Egypt. He wanted to build new schools and hospitals, to establish new industrial centers and jobs, but the cost of everything was going up. Anwar's economic policy of *infitah* had brought new profits to Egypt from foreign investment, but it had brought a high inflation rate as well. The cost of living was rising steadily, and more and more of our people could not afford decent housing for their families or even to feed their children. By 1977, our foreign debt totaled close to $15 billion.

Our country was in desperate financial straits with no end in sight. The four wars we had fought with Israel had already cost Egypt billions of pounds. Yet, because of the continuing threat from Israel, Anwar was forced to continue spending one third of our annual budget on defense instead of on services for our people. The cost of the wars had been even higher in human terms. Many thousands of Egyptian soldiers had lost their lives. And our land was still occupied.

Someone had to do something to stop this catastrophic spiral, to take the first step toward a solution. It did not surprise me that it would be my husband.

I had awakened a little late on November 9 and had to hurry to complete my homework for my class at the university before going into Anwar's bedroom to wake him.

"*Sabah el-khayr,* morning of goodness," I said to him, throwing open the shutters.

"*Sabah el-nur*, morning of light," he replied.

As I handed him the morning newspaper, I noticed how serene his face looked. "You slept well?" I said.

"Very well," Anwar said, his eyes clear and without the puffiness that signaled a restless night.

I wanted to stay with him, to share breakfast with him and together to read the newspapers, but I was already behind schedule. "I will not be home until late tonight," I told him regretfully. "I have an important meeting with the women's group."

"You set such a pace, Jehan," Anwar teased me. "I have nothing to do today except address the opening session of Parliament."

"What a lucky man you are to have so little on your mind," I teased him back. "God bless you."

In the car that evening en route to the meeting, I studied the blueprints for the new overpass we were trying to get funded in Munufiyya province. I tried not to get depressed as my car inched its way through the Cairo traffic past the burned-out shells of movie theaters, restaurants and cafés destroyed by riots ten months before. The government had followed the International Monetary Fund's advice in January of 1977 and had ordered government subsidies to be cut on such basic commodities as bread, meat, sugar, oil, rice and soap. To accountants, these cuts had made sense: the subsidies were costing the government over $1 billion a year. But to the millions of Egyptians who depended on the subsidies to feed their families, the cuts had been the final outrage.

"Tea Subsidy Canceled! 10 Millime Increase per Kilo of Rice and Sugar! Tank of Butugaz to Rise to 95 Piasters!" I had known as soon as I read the front page of *el-Ahram* on the morning of January 18 that there would be trouble. What I did not anticipate was how great the trouble would be. From my balcony in Giza I saw clouds of smoke begin to billow over Cairo. "What is burning?" I anxiously phoned Anwar's secretary Fawzi Abdel Hafez at his office, wishing that Anwar were in Cairo instead of in Aswan to receive President Tito of Yugoslavia.

"Downtown shops and nightclubs along the Pyramids Road," Fawzi told me. "What began as a peaceful demonstration against the subsidy cuts is turning into riots. Agitators are inciting the crowd to set fires."

Rushing back to the balcony, I had heard one explosion after another as more shops and automobiles were ignited. It was a terrifying sound, bringing back memories of the riots before the Great Cairo Fire in 1952. No one was sure who had caused the violence then, but this time I suspected the Communists, who continued to oppose Anwar's opening of Egypt to foreign investors; more and more stores carrying foreign goods or catering to tourists were being torched. I turned on the television set and checked with Anwar's office every twenty minutes. The riots were speading to Alexandria, even to Aswan, where angry mobs were destroying the Western symbols of affluence they were unable to afford.

"*Ya batal el-ubur, fein el-futur?* O Hero of the Crossing, where is our food?" the crowds had chanted. "Jehan, Jehan, *el-sha'ab ga'aan.* Jehan, Jehan, the people are hungry." For three days the rioting had continued, leaving over one hundred people dead and wounded. "Are you all right?" Queen Alia of Jordan had called me from Amman. "We are very concerned for you." Empress Farah had called as well. "I hope it will soon be over, Jehan," she phoned me from Paris. "We are with you in our hearts." I was touched by their concern, but alarmed at the picture of Egyptian unrest that was going out all over the world when it had been started by a such a few.

The riots had caused President Tito to cancel his state visit, and on January 19 Anwar had hurriedly returned from Aswan.

"What are you going to do?" I asked him.

"I am going to restore the subsidies," he said.

"But you will be going back on the orders of your own government," I said.

"Which is better," Anwar had replied, "to continue to enforce something that is wrong or to admit that the economic committee made a mistake?"

"You are right, Anwar," I said.

As soon as Anwar had announced the resumption of the subsidies, the people had become calm. But we all knew we were living on borrowed time. Our economy was almost bankrupt. So was our spirit.

"Mummy! Mummy! Have you heard the news?" my youngest daughter, Nana, cried out in great excitement when I got home from my meeting with the women's group on that evening of November 9.

My heart stopped. My daughter Noha was nearing the end of her second pregnancy. Had something happened to her?

"What is it, Nana?" I said sharply.

Her voice was incredulous. "Pappi is going to visit Israel!"

"Your father is going to what?" I asked.

"He announced it in his speech to Parliament this morning," Nana said rapidly. "He has offered to go to Jerusalem."

Go to Jerusalem? Anwar? "Where is he, Nana?" I said.

"Upstairs in the bedroom," she said.

I rushed up the stairs. "Anwar, is it true what Nana has told me?"

Anwar nodded. "Yes," he said. "For too long we have been sitting in our own capitals issuing warnings to Israel to return the occupied lands or else. Our image before the world is laughable and ugly. We have been calling for the return of our land but refusing to ask it of those who are occupying it. I have decided to go to the Israelis directly. What other choice do I have?

"If we do not regain the Sinai peacefully, then we must make good on our threat and once more go to war with Israel. Many more will lose their lives. Is this what we want for our people? To sacrifice the lives of our sons on wars that neither country can win, to spend our money on arms instead of using it to rebuild our country and to help the people? It is a waste, Jehan, a waste that will only continue. I must explore every avenue for peace between our two countries."

"But why must you go there yourself, Anwar?" I asked him. "Can't you wait for the peace conference in Geneva?" Anwar shook his head. "Who knows what will come of the peace conference, or even if it will take place?" Anwar said. "Months, maybe even years will be wasted while everyone argues about the agenda, about the delegates, about the participation of the Palestinians. No, Jehan. The only way to begin to search for peace is for our two countries to talk honestly and frankly with each other. And I am ready to do that."

Peace. Peace with Israel. I shook my head in disbelief. No Arab leader had ever been to Israel. But my husband was not an ordinary man. "Oh, Anwar," I said, throwing my arms around him and kissing him. "To think that there could be peace with Israel. But what if Prime Minister Begin refuses to meet with you?"

"That will be his problem," Anwar said. "The next step is up to him."

I felt dazed. To bring myself back to earth, I turned on the television set to watch the news show carrying Anwar's historic proposal. "I am willing to go to the ends of the earth if this will prevent one soldier, one officer, among my sons from being wounded, not being killed, just wounded," Anwar was saying calmly, as if he were discussing the weather. "I say now that I am willing to go to the ends of the earth. Israel will be astonished when it hears me saying now, before you, that I am ready to go to their house, to the Knesset itself, to talk to them."

The members of Parliament seemed stunned, as if they too couldn't believe their ears. How could any of them so quickly absorb such a dramatic and visionary idea? Never had anything but suspicion and hostility flowed between Egypt and Israel. We had never even officially spoken to each other. In Egypt it was against the law for an official to deal with an Israeli in any capacity whatsoever. We had refused to even acknowledge the existence of Israel. On maps of the region, Israel was demarcated simply as "Occupied Palestinian Land." And that was where my husband had just announced he was willing to go.

I watched as the members of Parliament clapped politely, even Yasir Arafat, in Cairo for a visit, joining in. Many would later insist that the leader of the Palestinian Liberation Organization had sat stone-faced through the surprise announcement. But, like the other politicians present, he had applauded before the implications had set in. The words of hope to so many Egyptians would be taken as words of betrayal by the Palestinians. After Anwar's speech, Arafat would stride out of the Parliament and leave Egypt, never to return.

For a week, the country was in shock. No one believed Anwar. No one except me. While Anwar awaited a reply from Menachem Begin, our phone at home never stopped ringing. "Is it true that the President is actually willing to go to Jerusalem or is he just saying so?" one friend asked. "Surely if he goes it will cost him his popularity."

"You do not understand my husband," I replied. "He is not concerned with popularity, but with what is right for our country."

"Tell me that Anwar is not really going to Jerusalem," another phoned.

"He will if Begin agrees," I replied.

"Oh, don't say that, Jehan," my friend said.

"Why not?" I said. "Someone has to pave the way to peace for others to continue."

Our Arab neighbors were just as stunned. Anwar knew they would resist his proposal and so had made his decision alone, consulting none of them. He was most hopeful, however, that he could persuade his comrade-in-arms Hafez el-Assad of Syria to support his position. A few days after his address to Parliament, Anwar flew to Damascus, only to return shaken and disappointed. "I argued with Hafez until four in the morning," he told me, his face drawn with exhaustion. "I told him that I was taking full responsibility for my actions. If I succeeded and peace was assured, then it would be a victory for all of us. If I were to fail, I alone would bear the consequences of failure."

But Hafez was to remain dead set against Anwar's peace initiative, even turning against Anwar himself. Immediately upon Anwar's return from Syria, Radio Damascus started broadcasting a campaign of invective against my husband and anyone who planned to accompany him on his proposed journey. Whoever set foot in occupied Jerusalem, Radio Damascus threatened, was betraying the Arabs and would bear the brunt of all the Arab blood spilled to liberate Palestine. I was chilled by Hafez el-Assad's attacks. He had been very close to Anwar, had eaten at the table with my family, had laughed with us and told us jokes. Now he was threatening his old friend with death. Not until after Anwar's assassination did I learn that the Syrian government had even considered arresting Anwar in Damascus to prevent him from pursuing his quest for peace. Only at the last minute had Assad ruled against such a futile and dangerous action.

Some Egyptian politicians too were against Anwar's peace proposal. On the eve of Anwar's departure for Syria to meet with President el-Assad, Isma'il Fahmy, our Foreign Minister, had resigned so abruptly from office that his baggage had gone on to Damascus without him. I was shocked at his resignation, though I understood that not everyone could be expected to be as farsighted as my husband. Still, I was hurt and suspected that Isma'il might be opportunistically protecting himself in case Anwar's mission for peace failed. I felt a personal loss as well. Anwar and I had always been close friends of the Foreign Minister and his wife, 'Affaf. Whenever I met 'Affaf again after her husband's resignation, I would shake hands with her but never visit with her as a friend again.

Anwar had expected many to disagree with his mission. He was also well aware of the risk he was taking, both politically and personally, and so was I. "If the people do not agree with your desire for peace, you will have to resign from office," I warned him. "I know and accept that, Jehan," he told me. "But peace has to be more important than politics. Surely I will have to pay a price. But in the end Egypt will gain."

On November 15, Prime Minister Begin extended a formal invitation to Anwar. Representatives of Israel and Egypt worked out the details. In deference to the Jewish Sabbath, Anwar chose to land in Israel after sundown on Saturday, November 19. The following day would be 'Aid el-Adha, our most important religious holiday. Anwar would perform his morning holiday prayers at el-Aqsa Mosque in Jerusalem, then visit the Christian Church of the Ascension. In the afternoon he would address the Knesset.

"Anwar, please, will you wear a bulletproof vest in Jerusalem?" I pleaded with him.

He refused. "There has been too much suspicion between Egypt and the Israelis for years," he said. "A soldier may enter the home of his enemy prepared to be attacked, but I am entering Israel in the spirit of peace."

Not for the first time I was frustrated by Anwar's serenity. He knew as well as I did that there were those who were as vehemently against such a peace as he was for it. The Zionists could kill him. Islamic fundamentalists could kill him. The Palestinians could kill him. I was convinced my husband would not return from Jerusalem alive.

I could not take my eyes off Anwar when our whole family gathered in Isma'iliyya for a few days before he left. We took one family photo after another, Anwar laughing as he threw our little grandson Sherif into the air time and again, Anwar pulling Sherif away from the water the little boy was determined to throw himself into. I drank in every detail of Anwar's face, his every gesture, committing them to memory. None of us said anything out loud, but we all knew these might be the last moments we would ever have together.

"Come, Nana. Come, Noha. Another picture," Anwar said. "Come closer. Squeeze together."

The phone never stopped ringing, the plans changing every minute. Anwar would fly from the airport in the desert at Janaklese. Would he take the small helicopter to the airport? The big helicopter? His entourage arrived, including Prime Minister Mustafa Khalil and Butros Ghali, his third Foreign Minister in a week; Isma'il Fahmy's replacement, former Minister of State Muhammad Riad, had resigned only twelve hours after his appointment. And still the telephone rang, continually taking Anwar away from us. I wanted to cut the cord, but of course I couldn't. Never have I felt so torn. I was extremely happy that he was making this mission for peace, terribly worried for his life.

And then it was time. "*Rabbina ma'ak,* Anwar," I said to him at the steps of the helicopter. "*Rabbina yibarak feek. La illaha illa Allah.* God be with you, Anwar. God bless you. There is no God but God."

"*Wa Muhammad rasul Allah,*" he said to me "And Muhammad is the messenger of God."

My children and I stood in the desert while the helicopter lifted off, the wind stinging our eyes and skin with hot sand. Only then could we let our tears fall.

"What's wrong, Granny? What's wrong?" Sherif kept asking me. When I didn't answer, he turned to his mother. "What's wrong, Mummy?"

Noha couldn't answer him, either.

I stare at the television screen, my body so tense that for days afterward I cannot move my neck. The Egyptian 707 jet carrying Anwar to Israel is coming in for a landing at Ben Gurion Airport, the announcer is saying, himself unable to keep the tone of disbelief out of his voice. The President is scheduled to land at 8:00 and is right on time.

"Shhh, Sherif," I soothe my grandson who has fallen on our front steps and cut his lip badly in the rush home to Cairo to watch Anwar's arrival. I have sent my daughter Noha, whose second child is due in just two weeks, home to rest, and have kept Sherif with me. Now Sherif and I watch Anwar's plane draw to a stop on the runway, watch as an El Al ramp is wheeled to the forward door. Sitting on my lap, Sherif still cries from discomfort. My own tears are those of fear and disbelief. My husband in Israel. It cannot be.

Trumpets strike a fanfare. The door of the plane opens.

There he is! My heart pounds as I watch him walk down the steps. He looks so serene and confident. What must he be feeling underneath? "I felt that God had sent me on this mission of peace," he will tell me later. "When I first set foot on Israeli soil I felt I was not of this world but as if I were flying." Watching him, I too feel I am dreaming, but on the brink of a nightmare. How I wish my eyes were television cameras so that I could scan the crowds for suspicious characters, so that I could spot the bulge of a revolver or the gleam of a gun barrel before it is too late. Anwar is well protected, of course. Extra security men had flown to Israel the day before to double-check the arrangements, Many more security agents have accompanied him. But I have more at stake than any of them. He may be their President, but he is my husband.

I cannot believe my eyes. Anwar is shaking hands with Ephraim Katzir, the President of Israel, with Premier Menachem Begin. There they are on the same television screen, the leaders of two enemy countries for whom tens of thousands have given their lives. I hear the familiar strains of our national song, "Biladi, Biladi," My Country, My Country, being played by an Israeli military band, see Egyptian flags waving side by side with the Israeli Star of David. How can this be?

The last time I had seen the Egyptian flag flying next to the Israeli flag had been fourteen years before in Germany, where Anwar, then Speaker of the Parliament, and I had gone on vacation. When we returned to the hotel one afternoon from a walk, I saw to my horror that the Israeli flag as well as our own was flying in front of the hotel. "Come quickly, Anwar," I had said to my husband in panic. "We must pack." "Where are we going?" he had said. "There are Israelis staying here. We must leave immediately," I had insisted. "We cannot leave unless we know exactly where we are going," Anwar had said. "We'll make a plan and leave tomorrow." "But they will kill us if they see us," I had protested. But Anwar had refused and I had been left to lie awake all night, sure we were going to be murdered in our beds.

As our anthem draws to a close in Jerusalem, shots ring out. I knew it! Anwar! I grip Sherif so tightly that momentarily he is distracted from the pain in his lip. My eyes must be boring holes in the television screen. But my husband does not fall and I realize that the shots are coming from a twenty-one-gun salute. I begin to count the segments of time my husband has survived. He has made it through the first ten minutes. Now we will take the next ten minutes.

Dimly I hear my telephone ringing and ringing, but I do not answer it. I will not relax my concentration for even one minute. "We don't want to disturb her, but tell her please that we are with her and are praying for the President," the messages mount up from our friends. "We are deeply moved by what we are seeing."

Moshe Dayan. Ariel Sharon. Golda Meir. Mordechai Gur. There they are, all of them, in the receiving line of government officials, past and present, at the airport. Anwar is moving toward them, shaking their hands, laughing. Laughing! I strain to read his lips and theirs. What are they saying to each other? They seem to be greeting each other like the oldest of friends. If war is absurd, then this scene of peace makes it even more so. Ariel Sharon, the dreaded general who had broken through our defenses in the '73 war and led Israeli forces across the Canal, is pumping Anwar's hand with the enthusiasm of a reunion between two old partners in battle.

"I was going to block your break through our lines completely, but I couldn't catch you," Anwar later told me he joked to the now Minister of Culture.

On the screen I see Sharon throw back his head in laughter. "I am glad to greet you as a guest in our country," he replied.

As Anwar turns next to Golda Meir, I hold my breath. "Please, Anwar, make a special effort with Mrs. Meir," I had asked him just before he left for Jerusalem.

He had looked at me with astonishment. "Oh, Jehan, as if you do not know me," he had said. "Do you think I will make less of an effort because she is not a man?"

"No, no, Anwar," I had assured him. "But I know you. Sometimes people misunderstand you. You keep your feelings to yourself and sometimes don't even speak at all. People like Mrs. Meir who do not know you well might think you are cold and distant."

"You will see what an effort I will make with Mrs. Meir, just for you, Jehan," he had teased me.

I had felt a bit embarrassed, remembering how many times in my quest for women's rights I had held the examples of Golda Meir and Indira Gandhi up to Anwar as two very brave and successful women. Both had led their countries during wars, Mrs. Meir in the '67 war between Israel and Egypt, Indira Gandhi in the war between India and Pakistan. And both women leaders had won. Now Anwar was about to greet Mrs. Meir, for whom I felt both dislike and respect.

On the television screen I see Anwar holding Mrs. Meir's hand, see her listening intently to him. My ears burn with tension and curiosity. Suddenly her face creases into a huge smile. Instinctively, I smile also.

"You are very well known in our country, Mrs. Meir," Anwar later reported their conversation to me. "Do you know what you are called?"

"No. What?" she had asked.

"The strongest man in Israel," my husband had said. It was then that Mrs. Meir had smiled. "I take that as a compliment, Mr. President," she had replied.

My own smile trembled a bit when Anwar told me what he had said, for I was not sure he had meant it as a compliment. But he probably had. As soon as he was face to face with her, he told me, he had decided to forgive and forget. Instead of harping on the past, he wanted to open a new page between Egypt and Israel, to start a new era for peace. And it looked as if he was succeeding.

All along the road into Jerusalem enthusiastic crowds are chanting, "Sa-dat! Sa-dat!" Many people have tears streaming down their cheeks. The people of Israel seem to be having as much difficulty believing that the leader of their enemy has come to them in peace as had the people in Egypt when Anwar announced he was going. Some in the crowd are holding up newspapers. "WELCOME, PRESIDENT SADAT," read the huge headline of the *Jerusalem Post*. There are women, many women, in the crowds, mothers who are holding up their babies to see this man of peace. The sight of these women and children would turn out to be the most moving sight of all to Anwar, he would tell me later. "It was as if each mother was saying to me: 'Your message of peace has reached us and we agree. Look at our children and know that we do not want any more wars.' "

In Cairo I hug Sherif and give him another Novalgin. Anwar has now arrived safely at the King David Hotel, where the Egyptian delegation is staying. I can relax my vigil for the moment, for I will need all my strength in the morning. For Anwar to pray at el-Aqsa Mosque, the third most holy shrine in Islam, will be an act of the greatest spiritual significance, for the Hadith say that one act of worship in Jerusalem is worth a thousand acts of worship anywhere else. But it is also a great risk. To kill the first Muslim leader to pray on Temple Mount since the formation of Israel, to kill my husband as he prostrates himself in this sacred place, will be the highest temptation for the zealous enemies of peace with Israel. "Please, God, look after my husband," I pray and, still hugging Sherif, fall sound asleep.

Just after midnight I am awakened by an emergency phone call from my son-in-law Hassan Mare'i. Noha's anxiety over her father's trip to Jerusalem has sent her into premature labor. She has been taken to the hospital.

Noha! I rush to the hospital, where Hassan's mother and aunt are already at Noha's side. Anwar and I had missed the birth of Sherif, our first grandchild, because we were in Iran. Now I, at least, am in Cairo. "Relax," I say to Noha, stroking her hair. "Soon it will be over." After a difficult labor, a beautiful girl is born at dawn. "She is very ugly," I laughingly tell her mother, "but she is a good omen. She must be a herald of peace."

I call Anwar in Jerusalem, where he is just about to leave the hotel to pray at the mosque. "We have a granddaughter," I tell him. "She is dark-skinned and not very beautiful. She looks just like you."

He laughs. "If she is as dark as I am, then she must be very good-looking indeed."

In the hospital we watch Anwar's visit to Temple Mount. I feel dizzy with exhaustion and conflict. The birth of a grandchild should bring me the utmost joy, yet once again the moment is clouded by anxiety.

Be careful, Anwar. Look to see who is praying to the right and left of you. I know that the security forces in Israel have screened the Muslim worshipers who will pray on 'Aid el-Adha with Anwar, but I also know that the fanatics are very clever. I scan the worshipers while Anwar prays. Ten minutes pass and nothing happens. But while I am sitting rigid with tension in Cairo, in Jerusalem Anwar is fulfilling a dream.

"I couldn't believe that I was actually touching the ground of el-Aqsa during the prayers. I felt close to tears," he would tell me. "Was this really happening to me? I wished it could be happening to all Muslims." Ten more minutes pass. I see my husband emerge safe and begin to walk across the square toward the Dome of the Rock, from which we believe the Prophet Muhammad ascended into heaven on his famous night journey and where the Christians and Jews, it is said, believe Ibrahim prepared to sacrifice his son Isaac. Look out, Anwar! I see a group of Palestinian demonstrators waving their fists at him and yelling curses. The security forces chase them away down the alleyways of Old Jerusalem. Anwar has survived another ten minutes.

I jolt myself back to the reality of Cairo. I have an appointment to take tea this afternoon with my official guest, Madame Bourguiba, wife of the President of Tunisia. Her visit has been planned for a long time, well before my husband announced his trip to Israel. Already I have been rude enough, canceling my meeting with her the night before so that I could see Anwar's arrival in Jerusalem. I cannot be rude again, and quickly I dress to go to the reception, which has been scheduled to begin shortly before Anwar addresses the Knesset. "Look after Sherif," I say to my youngest daughter, Nana. When I arrive at the reception, I find that all there, including Madame Bourguiba, want to watch Anwar's address. Gratefully, I hurry back home.

When Anwar enters the Knesset at 4 P.M., he is greeted by a standing ovation. Will the Israelis be as enthusiastic when they hear what he has to say? "Peace and the mercy of God Almighty be upon you and may peace be with us all, God willing," Anwar begins his address. "Peace for us all, of the Arab lands and in Israel, as well as in every part of this big world which is so beset by conflicts, perturbed by its deep contradictions, menaced now and then by destructive wars launched by man to annihilate his fellow men." I am struck by how handsome he looks in his dark suit, standing erect and fearless in front of the Israeli parliament. "Look at your grandfather and be like him," I tell Sherif, who is squirming in my lap.

For the next hour I am just one of a world audience of millions watching and listening to the impossible: the leader of Egypt offering the branch of peace to the governing body of Israel. "I come to you today on solid ground to shape a new

life and to establish peace," Anwar is saying in Arabic while
the translator struggles to keep up in Hebrew. "We all love this
land, the land of God. We all, Muslims, Christians and Jews,
all worship God. . . . God's teachings and commandments are
love, sincerity, security, and peace."

I am moved, as are countless others, by his eloquent plea to
end war. "Any life lost in war is a human life, be it that of an
Arab or an Israeli. A wife who becomes a widow is a human
being entitled to a happy family life, whether she be an Arab or
an Israeli. Innocent children who are deprived of the care and
compassion of their parents are ours. They are ours, be they
living on Arab or Israeli land. . . . For the sake of them all,
. . . for the generations to come, for a smile on the face of every
child born in our land, for all that, I have taken my decision to
come to you, despite all the hazards, to deliver my address."

The camera moves across the impassive faces of the Israeli
leaders. Abba Eban, the former Foreign Minister. Bar Lev, the
designer of Israel's supposedly impregnable line of defense.
Ezer Weizman, the current Defense Minister, whose face seems
very pale. Later I learn that Weizman had insisted on leaving
his hospital bed, where he was recovering from a fractured leg
and several broken ribs suffered in a car accident, to be present.
"You're going to take your instrument cases, fill them up with
heroin, cocaine, hashish or anything else you like," he had told
his doctors, "then you'll come along with me and make sure I
can stay on my feet for at least twenty-four hours." It has taken
a helicopter, a wheelchair and a walking stick to get him to the
Knesset. But he is there. And what he is hearing, what everyone is hearing, is comforting the Israelis while sending shock
waves throughout the Arab world.

"You want to live with us in this part of the world," Anwar
is saying to the Knesset. "In all sincerity I tell you we welcome
you among us with full security and safety. This in itself is a
tremendous turning point, one of the landmarks of a decisive
historical change. . . . We used to reject you. We had our reasons and our fears, yes . . . Yet today I tell you, and I declare
it to the whole world, that we accept living with you in permanent peace based on justice. We do not want to encircle you
or be encircled ourselves by destructive missiles ready for
launching, nor by the shells of grudges and hatreds."

These are the words the Arab countries have been dreading:

the recognition of Israel's right to exist. I admire my husband greatly for his courage to face the reality of Israel, but I cannot help but feel a chill. Already the price he will have to pay has begun. The moment his plane had landed on Israeli soil, Qadaffi had broken diplomatic relations with Egypt while enraged Libyans burned the Office of Egyptian Relations to the ground in Tripoli. At the moment Anwar set foot on Israeli soil, muezzins in Damascus had called Syrian worshipers not to pray for peace but to send prayers of hate and anger. The Palestinians in the camps near Damascus had burned Anwar's pictures, and a bomb had been thrown at the Egyptian Embassy. The fever of hate was spreading all over the Middle East and the Mediterranean. In Greece, a group of Arab students had stormed the Egyptian Embassy before being shot and wounded by the police. In Spain, Palestinians succeeded in occupying our embassy and temporarily holding prisoner our ambassador, the uncle of one of my sons-in-law. And the storm was just beginning, not only in the Arab countries but in Israel as well.

Tension is flickering over the faces of the Israeli leaders while Anwar outlines the conditions for the peace. "Let me tell you without the slightest hesitation that I have not come to you under this roof to make a request that your troops evacuate the occupied territories," Anwar says firmly. "Complete withdrawal from the Arab territories occupied after 1967 is a logical and undisputed fact. Nobody should plead for that . . . there is no peace that can be built on the occupation of the land of others. Otherwise it would not be a serious peace."

I see Ezer Weizman, who speaks fluent Arabic and does not have to wait for the Hebrew translation, quickly scribble a note and pass it to Menachem Begin and Moshe Dayan. They read it and nod in agreement. "We must prepare for war," I later learn the note reads.

Anwar does not shrink from the Palestinian cause either. "Here I tell you, ladies and gentlemen, that it is no use to refrain from recognizing the Palestinian people and their right to statehood as their right of return. . . . You have to face reality bravely, as I have done. There can never be any solution to a problem by evading it or turning a deaf ear to it. Peace cannot last if attempts are made to impose fantasy concepts on which the world has turned its back and announced its unanimous call for the respect of rights and facts."

I have tears of pride in my eyes when, in conclusion, Anwar turns to the Old Testament of the Bible and our own Holy Book to show our similar beliefs. "I repeat with Zachariah: Love, right and justice," Anwar is saying. "From the Holy Quran, I quote the following verses: 'We believe in God and in what has been revealed to us and what was revealed to Abraham, Isma'il, Isaac, Jacob and the thirteen Jewish tribes. And in the books given to Moses and Jesus and the prophets from their Lord, who made no distinction among them.' " Anwar looks around the Knesset. "So we agree," he says. And he delivers a benediction: "*El-salaamu aleikum.* Peace be upon you."

"*Kan 'albi ma'ak tul ma inta hinaak!* My heart was with you all the time you were there!" the people cried out in the streets when Anwar returned to Cairo forty-four hours after he had left. Millions of Egyptians lined the twelve-mile route from the airport to our home in Giza, cheering, whistling, throwing white flower petals, trilling the sound of the *zaghreet.* "*Bil ruh bil damm nifdeek, ya* Sadat! With our souls and our blood we would sacrifice ourselves for you, Sadat!" Soldiers had to link their arms to keep the crowds from engulfing Anwar's car, but still the car's progress was in inches. "The President is now in Heliopolis," the announcers on the radio and television said, charting his route. "The people will not let him through."

If they had balconies, the people crowded onto them. If they didn't, they stood on parked cars, clung to trees, hung off traffic signs. "SA-DAT! SA-DAT!" Helicopters hovered over the motorcade, one carrying Gamal, who was videotaping this momentous welcome for his father. Rather than attempting to get through the crowds myself, I was watching at home on television. And never had I seen such an outpouring of emotion. So massive was this spontaneous demonstration of joy that the journey between the airport and our home, which normally took twenty minutes, today would take Anwar almost three hours. The streets near our home in Giza were completely blocked by crowds playing flutes and drums.

I could not restrain my relief when finally Anwar was standing in front of me in our home. I rushed to him, putting my arms around him and kissing him right in front of the Cabinet ministers who were accompanying him. After dinner, when the ministers had left, I could tell him at last how worried I had been for his life every minute he'd been in Jerusalem.

Anwar smiled. "It was worth the risk," he told me. "If I hadn't gone then my dream of peace might never have become a reality. Now at least we can talk directly with the Israelis."

Together we prayed the last prayer of the day, thanking God for the successful completion of this first step toward peace. We did not know how difficult the next steps would be.

As 1978 dawned, the American newsmagazine *Time* named Anwar as its Man of the Year in recognition of his daring quest for peace. But there was no peace and few prospects for a resolution. I do not know where Anwar found the patience to continue the negotiations. The Israelis refused steadfastly to agree to return the Arab territories they had taken during the '67 war along the Gaza Strip and were actually expanding their settlements on the occupied West Bank.

"Begin has such a complex from the Holocaust. He is the most suspicious man I've ever met," Anwar had said to me after their second summit meeting, this one on Anwar's birthday, December 25, 1977, in Isma'iliyya. "I respect him for his concern for his country, but he is very frustrating to negotiate with." Still, Anwar refused to give up.

"God must have chosen such a patient man as you to deal with such a complicated man as Begin," I told him. "I would have given up long ago."

The peace process with Israel was stalemated. And so were our relations with many of our Arab neighbors. Because of the Palestinians' attacks against my husband and their violent protests in foreign countries, Anwar had ordered all the PLO offices in Egypt closed down two days after he returned from Jerusalem. He had then called for peace talks with all our Arab brothers to be held in Cairo in December at Mena House. But the PLO, Syria, Iraq, South Yemen, Algeria and Libya refused to attend. Instead they had held their own summit in Tripoli on December 2, voting to freeze diplomatic relations with Egypt. Angered by the Arab refusal to even consider peace, Anwar had responded by ordering three hundred of their diplomats to leave Egypt. The Soviets had boycotted Anwar's peace talks as well, and my husband ordered them to shut down their consulates all over Egypt as well as the consulates of their satellites. Poland, Czechoslovakia, Hungary and East Germany. Meanwhile, American Secretary of State Cyrus Vance was shuttling between the cities of the Middle East, trying to broker peace.

Only one lone voice in the Middle East was speaking up in support of Anwar. "I will be coming to Aswan for just one night," read the unexpected cable from the Shah of Iran in January. When Anwar met him at the airport, the Shah told Anwar he had come to reinforce his support for Anwar's peace initiative not only to the whole word, but specifically to the Arabs. "I will go to Saudi Arabia to ask King Khalid and the Saudi princes why they are delaying their support for you," the Shah told my husband. "They must recognize that you are working for the whole area, for a comprehensive and just peace and for the return of Arab rights." The Shah's trip to Jedda would prove to be futile, but Anwar would never forget the lengths his friend, unasked, had gone to for him.

And the violence continued. In February of '78, one of Anwar's oldest friends, Yusif el-Seba'i, chairman of the largest newspaper in Egypt, was shot in the back and killed by Palestinians in Nicosia, Cyprus. Yusif's only crime was that he had accompanied Anwar on his trip to Jerusalem. I felt sick to my stomach when I went to pay my condolences to Yusif's wife and their two children in Cairo. How cruel. And how senseless.

Why were the Palestinians taking out their bitterness on us, their friends? Why couldn't they sit down with us to plan a strategy to secure their homeland? We must excuse the Palestinians many things, for their homeland was—and still is—occupied. Many have grown up in the horror of refugee camps or with few rights in the land still occupied by Israel. But at the same time the Palestinians have to know that they have missed many opportunities for a resolution. Even now Yasir Arafat could say, "I am willing to go to Israel to say to the Knesset and to the whole world that we are ready to make peace on the condition we regain a homeland." If he announced this willingness, he would put Israel in a corner, forcing the Israeli leaders to either invite him to make his address or be condemned by the whole world for rejecting his offer of conciliation. But no. The violence started at the beginning. And it continues to this day.

The Arab countries were being just as stubborn. Over

and over Anwar explained in his speeches that peace with Israel would not be just a treaty between Egypt and Israel but a treaty covering all the Arab territories. Such a peace would benefit the whole area, not just Egypt. But his Arab brothers remained deaf. "If you have a better alternative, tell me and I assure you I will follow it," he said to them time and again. But, not surprisingly, no one had one. The Arabs knew as well as we did that we could never regain our land by force. The United States would never allow Israel to be defeated, and none of us could defeat the United States. Our only option was to regain our land through peaceful negotiations, an option Anwar had earned by his victory over Israel in the '73 war. Now, finally, Egypt could negotiate from a position of strength and confidence. But the Arabs would have no part of it.

I clung to my studies at the university, immersing myself in preparation for my final exams before graduation in June. My first four-year term at the Munufiyya People's Council was drawing to an end, and I decided to stand for election again. I worked hard raising money for my charities and organizations, and campaigned for the proposed new Status Laws. I was also planning a most important event in our family: the marriage of our son Gamal. It was a marriage that had caused me much conflict.

Gamal had met Dina Erfan at the Gezira Preparatory School when he was fifteen years old, and he had been in love with her ever since. But I was against their marrying. In his first year at the university, Gamal was too young to even think of marriage. I forbade him to see Dina, in the hope of diminishing their adolescent love. But their feelings for each other had only grown stronger. Even when Anwar and I sent Gamal to London for the summer, nothing had changed. "Please, Mummy, I love Dina and want to marry her," Gamal kept pleading with me. But I refused to give my consent, refused even to meet her. She was the first girl in his life. I hoped for his sake he would meet other girls instead of tying himself down so young to just one. He was still a student, far too young to take on the responsibility of a wife and children. It took Gamal five years to change my mind.

I was startled one day after a meeting with the board of the Wafa' wal Amal to find Gamal in the doorway of my office, tears streaming down his cheeks. "You spend all your time listening to the problems of the people, solving the problems of the people. But you do not help your own son," he said to me.

I was shocked. Perhaps he was right.

"I love Dina," he said, "and I love you. I'll never marry unless you approve. Please, Mummy, please."

I felt terrible. "Why don't you finish your studies and then we'll see," I said.

But Anwar had followed Gamal into the room. "Jehan, they truly love each other," he said. "Why don't we give them the opportunity to become officially engaged? Then they can marry in a year after Gamal's graduation."

I still thought Gamal was too young. But I questioned my objections. This was, after all, the same predicament I had found myself in when I fell in love with Anwar. Was I just reenacting my own mother's stubbornness? And was Anwar being as sympathetic and supportive as my own father had been? I looked at Gamal's anguished face, and saw my own face twenty-eight years before.

"Get your girlfriend on the phone, Gamal," I said to my son. "Tell her I wish to speak with her."

His face had gone white with shock. "No, Mummy, no. I don't want you to be forced quickly into changing your mind."

"It is not so quick, Gamal," I said gently to him. "I have been testing your love for Dina, but if after all these years you still have not changed your mind, then you must really love her. Get her on the telephone."

Dina had been almost speechless when I spoke to her. "Dina, my husband and I would like to come this afternoon to meet with your mother and father," I told her.

She sputtered that her mother, Nicole, was away in Paris, but that her father and grandmother were there.

"Fine," I said. "Then my husband and I will take a cup of coffee with them." Immediately Dina had phoned her mother, who, at this unexpected news, went straight to the famous Notre Dame to give thanks. "I bowed and kissed the floor of the church," Nicole, a Lebanese Christian who would become my dear friend, later told me. "At last my daughter would be happy."

Happy. Never had I seen a face as happy as that of Gamal's

when his father and I left to go to the home of his love. Once there, I kept sneaking looks at Dina to see what had made her so fascinating to my son, as did my daughters who had come with us. Dina looked lovely in a dress she had hurriedly borrowed from her aunt, for evidently she was quite a tomboy and dressed ordinarily in blue jeans and a t-shirt. Even so, our meeting was quite awkward. Dina's father seemed overwhelmed when Anwar told him that he had come with his wife and daughters to ask if Dina would become Gamal's wife. "It's an honor, Mr. President," was all he could say. "It's an honor."

Dina and her aunt had also been too excited to speak, leaving just me and Dina's grandmother. "Your granddaughter is very lucky to be marrying my son," I said to her. "Yes, Mrs. Sadat," she had quickly replied. "And your son is also lucky." I liked her spirit. "They are both lucky," I agreed. I had brought a watch to give to Dina for an engagement present and I put it on her wrist, kissing her. The wedding, we all agreed, would take place in a year. We did not know, as we sat rather stiffly together, what significance that wedding would have.

"I am going to America," Anwar told me on a hot August afternoon in Alexandria during Ramadan in 1978. "Cyrus Vance has just brought me an invitation from President Carter to attend another summit there with Begin, and I have accepted." Once more, my hopes for peace rose. Almost nine months had passed since Anwar had called for peace in Jerusalem. If any country could bring pressure on Israel to be reasonable, it was America. Anwar also liked President Jimmy Carter very much, knowing him to be a moral man and a religious man as well.

"When will you go?" I asked Anwar, for Gamal's wedding was just a month away, on September 24.

"As soon as possible," Anwar said. "But don't worry. Do you think I would miss my own son's wedding?"

"In early September I will be in Paris with Sherif," I reminded Anwar. Our little grandson had bad asthma, and our doctor had made an appointment for him with a specialist in France some months before.

"I will be at Camp David," Anwar said.

"Anwar, how are you? How are the talks going? There is a news blackout and I have heard nothing," I phoned Anwar from Paris on September 5, 1978.

"Begin is being very difficult," Anwar sighed. "That man is so complexed."

"But you understand him, Anwar," I encouraged him. "You must keep trying."

"I am trying and trying and trying, Jehan," he said. "But it is discouraging."

"It will change tomorrow, Anwar. Just wait and see. We have to have hope," I told my husband. "God is with you in your endeavor. I am praying for you and know that God will help you."

Every night I called Anwar from Paris. And every night his news was more discouraging. President Carter was meeting separately with my husband and Begin, trying to mediate their broad differences, while the foreign ministers of the three countries, Cyrus Vance, Moshe Dayan and Muhammad Ibrahim Kamel, were trying to work out the details. But there were few details to work out.

"You sound so tired, Anwar," I said to my husband two days later.

I could hear his sigh all the way across the ocean. "It is exhausting to have to fight so hard for peace," he replied.

The news from the rest of the world was just as discouraging. Rioting had broken out in Teheran, and every evening the television news in Paris showed films of the violence. It was terrifying, really, to see the glazed eyes of the religious fanatics so filled with hate, to hear the mobs shouting death threats against the Shah.

"Farah, are you and your husband all right?" I phoned Farah Diba in Teheran. "I have been watching the demonstrations on television and I am concerned for you."

Her voice sounded remarkably calm. "We are going through a very hard time," Farah said. "We are praying it will soon pass." But it didn't.

Night after night the news in Paris carried stories of the troubles in Iran—films of women crying at the tombs of their relatives who had mysteriously disappeared, interviews with Iranians in France who had fled the abuses of Savak, the Iranian secret police, stories of corruption and abuse in the government. I was shocked by how black and white the complex situation in Iran seemed to the French, shocked even more by the flattering stories about the Ayatollah Khomeini and his followers, who were living in France.

"I talked to Farah in Teheran," I phoned Anwar.

"How are they?" he asked.

"Farah said they were well, but of course the times are very hard for them."

"I am very worried," said Anwar, who had been following the trouble in Iran at Camp David. "I have called the Shah myself, and told him that I was praying for him."

"I am praying also for you and for peace," I said to my husband.

In Paris I was spending the mornings with my daughter Noha and Sherif in the clinic where he was undergoing treatment, most of the rest of the time following the news about Iran on television. I had no desire to go out to visit friends or to eat at restaurants, for the news was becoming more and more ominous. I distracted myself by making last-minute arrangements for Gamal and Dina's wedding.

There was to be a huge green-and-white tent set up in our garden, the same colors as the Egyptian flag before the Revolution. The tablecloths were to be green, while all the flowers on the tables, Gamal and Dina's bridal thrones, even the crowns of roses on the flower girls' heads, would be white. We had invited 2,500 people, including all the women from my work cooperative at Tella, the women members of Parliament, women who were working with me in my social activities, everyone.

Many singers had asked to come perform at the wedding, but we could accept only four or so. Otherwise the wedding would have gone on for a week. I was thrilled that Sabah, a beautiful Lebanese and one of the most popular singers in the Middle East, would be there to sing for our guests. Gamal was the last of our children to marry, and I wanted the wedding to be perfect. Every afternoon I called my office in Cairo from Paris: Were the dancers were ready, the members of the Rida folkloric troupe, the comedians who would tell us jokes, the beautiful white horses who would dance in our garden? By phone I checked, too, on the seven-layer wedding cake. At the moment Gamal and Dina cut it, white doves would be released to soar over their heads. Would these beautiful white birds be the doves of peace as well? On the night of September 15, ten days after Anwar had arrived at Camp David, I put in my usual call to my husband.

"What is it, Anwar?" I said, knowing as soon as I heard his voice that something was wrong.

"I am leaving Camp David," he said.

"Leaving Camp David? Anwar, don't tell me this. What has happened?"

"Begin is being totally unreasonable. He refuses to return the West Bank to Arab rule. And Moshe Dayan told me last night that the Israelis have no intention of signing any agreement now. There is no point in continuing. All that we have worked for is finished."

"Anwar, please. You have been a patient man for so long. Try just a few more days."

"Jehan, there is no point."

"But, Anwar, then there will be no chance of peace. You must stay. You must."

"My bags are packed and we have called for a helicopter to take us to the airport in Washington."

"Does President Carter know this?"

"Yes. He has asked to meet with me privately, but I see no reason to."

"Anwar, you gave President Carter your word that you would do everything you could to bring peace. Now you are walking out. He is a man of morals and principles. And so are you. You cannot do that to him."

"I have no choice."

"Yes, you do. You can hear at least what President Carter has to say. Please, Anwar."

"All right, Jehan," Anwar said, his voice strained.

At that moment I regretted that I was not by my husband's side at Camp David. Had I been there, I could have soothed him, joked with him, encouraged him. I found out later that Rosalynn and President Carter had wanted the wives of both leaders to accompany their husbands to Camp David to defuse the tension and make them more reasonable. Aliza Begin was there at Camp David. I had to play my part over the transatlantic phone.

Two hours later, Anwar called me back. "I will stay, Jehan," he said. "But I can promise nothing."

"Oh, God bless you, Anwar," I said. "God bless you."

I was in my room two days later when the phone rang. This time Anwar's voice was jubilant. "We have reached a solution," Anwar said.

I couldn't believe it. "Say it again, Anwar, so that I can believe you," I yelled happily into the phone.

"Oh, Jehan, I have said it once, and I meant it," Anwar said. "Israel has promised to stop all further settlement on the West Bank, and a timetable has been set to negotiate Palestinian autonomy. We are leaving now for Washington, where it will be announced."

"My prayers are answered," I said.

Anwar spoke rapidly. "I am flying tonight to Morocco. "Come and meet me there." "I shall be there of course," I told him. "With this news I could probably fly even without a plane."

Peace. Finally peace. I threw my arms around my daughter and a friend who was with us. "Today we are going out to celebrate in the best restaurant in Paris," I said. "Choose wherever you want to go. It's on me."

Miraculously in the street we ran into dear friends from Cairo, Amin Shaker, a government minister, Zinna, his wife, and their daughter, Mona.

"Have you heard the good news?" I asked them. Amin and Zinna were dumbfounded when I told them. "Come," I said. "Join us for a celebration. I invite you."

"You must be my guest," Amin insisted. "I am the man." And together we celebrated the courage of my husband, and the relief he must be feeling.

When I met Anwar in Morocco, he cautioned me that the agreement had only been initialed, that there were still details to work out. "How long will it take?" I asked him.

"Perhaps three months," he said. And we flew home together to the wedding of our son.

"*Mabruk,*" one guest after another told Anwar. "Congratulations." In the streets, crowds gathered to send their goodwill, both to Gamal and to Anwar for bringing peace to our country. The garden had never looked so beautiful: the colors of green and white had become the colors of peace. Tears ran down the cheeks of many of our guests when the doves were released. Peace. And now the marriage of our son. "Come, Gamal. Come, Dina," Anwar had said that morning as we sat on our balcony watching the people dancing in the street below. He had put out his hands to us and drawn us all into a circle. Then, unbelievably, he had begun to dance, leading us in the steps of the *dabka*. I had danced and laughed till my sides ached, filled with wonder at the happiness on Anwar's face. It was the first and only time I ever saw him dance.

On October 27, 1978, the Nobel Peace Prize was awarded jointly to my husband and Menachem Begin. In the West, in Europe and in Egypt, my husband was being regarded almost as a saint, a martyr who was willing to sacrifice himself to end the centuries of strife between Jew and Muslim. In the Middle East, however, many Arabs were calling Anwar a devil and such a peace with Israel a heresy. Six months after my husband's return from Camp David, the Arab countries would even offer him $5 billion a year for ten years to break off negotiations with Israel. Anwar flatly refused the bribe. Egyptians, he said in an emotional speech to the People's Assembly, held morals and values all-important. Egypt was "not like other countries, with a hundred million dollars making it decide one way, a hundred million another . . . No, not all the billions of this world could buy the will of Egypt."

I was astonished with our former friends in the Arab countries with whom we had shared so much. I also knew that the majority of the Arab leaders agreed privately with Anwar's peace initiative but didn't have the courage to say so publicly. When a foreign diplomat came back from a meeting in the Gulf States, he told me that a government official there had privately praised Anwar for taking the only possible avenue to liberate our land. The very next day, this same government official had told a journalist right in front of this diplomat that Sadat was not right, that all Arabs were against any kind of solution with Israel because the Israelis were occupying Palestinian land.

King Fahd, who as a prince had often been a guest in our home in Giza, was now allowing the Saudi press to print personal attacks against my husband. I too was being attacked, even though I had always been received so affectionately by the royal princesses. The Syrian press was also being merciless, though our friendship with Hafez al-Assad and his wife went back long before he had become president of Syria.

I felt hurt by these attacks, saddened, too, by the criticism of Anwar's vision of peace from the wives of Arab leaders. Madame Wassila, the wife of President Bourguiba of Tunisia, had given a lovely party for me when Anwar and I visited the Bourguibas at their beautiful palace by the sea in Tunis, and she had been my official guest in Cairo during Anwar's trip to Jerusalem. Then she had seemed very supportive of Anwar's quest for peace, but now she sent me a personal letter protesting the Camp David agreement. I sent her an appropriate reply, and luckily my friendship with her survived. But most of the wives of the other Arab leaders cut off all communication with me. I resented deeply the fact that my personal relationships had to depend on politics. What unnecessary losses.

How well I remembered the discomfort of the wife of Ahmad el-Khatib, who happened to find herself in Cairo on a day when her husband, Prime Minister of the short-lived United Arab Republic, had attacked Egypt in the newspapers. None of the Egyptian women at a luncheon we were attending agreed with her husband's criticism, including me. But it was her husband who angered us, not she. When I made a point of going to sit next to Mrs. el-Khatib she had burst into tears. "Dear Jehan, my sister, please, these are only political statements," she had wept. "Of course," I had soothed her. "We all know that politics is made up of quarrels which eventually get patched up. This is not our concern. Let us set aside the work of politicians and instead enjoy our happy and personal ties as women and friends." Always I have felt this way. But not everyone else has agreed.

"Auntie Jehan, I must speak with you privately," Mona Nasser, one of the daughters of Gamal Abdel Nasser, called to tell me in the summer of 1978. "I have just returned from Libya with a message for you from Qadaffi."

"I can't see you now, Mona. Anwar is just about to leave for the Sudan and I must see him off," I told her. "I will call you back."

A message from Qadaffi? I felt a chill as I hung up the phone. Qadaffi had been threatening Anwar's life for months now. Was he going to have Anwar assassinated in the Sudan? I rushed downstairs to tell Anwar that I had changed my mind and wanted now to go with him on his trip. I told him nothing about the call and stuck close to his side during the two-day visit to the Sudan as if daring someone to try to harm him.

As soon as we returned, I invited Mona to come and see me. She confirmed my intuition. If I refused to use my influence to make my husband give up the Camp David Agreement, Qadaffi had told her, he would be forced to kill him.

I was outraged. "Please convey a message back to President Qadaffi for me," I asked Mona, who seemed very upset. "Tell him that he knows full well that as a wife I would never interfere in any political or state decision of the President. As for his threat to murder Sadat, let him know also that God alone holds sway over a man's life."

I got no reply. Instead the Libyan press stepped up its attacks. "Jehan Sadat wants to rule Egypt," the papers there declared. "Her husband does anything she says, obeying her blindly!"

The Israelis too continued to act shamelessly. Only three months after the initialing of the peace agreement at Camp David, the Israelis had begun to go back on their word. Instead of dismantling their settlements on the West Bank, they continued to enlarge them and even announced plans for new ones. Anwar was so furious at these blatant moves against the spirit of the peace accords that he refused to go to Oslo with Menachem Begin to accept the Nobel Peace Prize in December. My daughter's father-in-law, Speaker of the Parliament Sayyid Mare'i, went in his place. Anwar did not accept the money from the Peace Prize either, directing instead that it be given to his village of Mit Abul-Kum to replace the houses made of mud with houses of brick. On December 25, 1978, Anwar spent his birthday brooding in Mit Abul-Kum while the children and I tried in vain to cheer him up.

I was extremely frustrated by the violations of the Israelis, as were many others. From the moment of Anwar's trip to Jerusalem, millions of Egyptians had embraced the possibility of peace with Israel, the possibility of turning enemies into friends. When the first group of journalists and other Israelis had come to Egypt after Anwar's visit to Jerusalem, Egyptians had warmly called out "*Shalom*" to them, offering them presents and refreshments. With some degree of nervousness I had even consented to be interviewed by an Israeli journalist. Uri

Avneri, I had been told, was sympathetic to the Palestinian cause and had been a spokesman for the Peace Party in Israel until his expulsion from the Knesset by Golda Meir. Now, with no hope for peace in sight, I consented to meet with Uri again.

"What has come over your country?" I asked him. "You started off wanting peace, wanting our recognition. My husband made your impossible dreams come true. Now all you do is put obstacles in the way of peace. Why?"

Uri couldn't disagree. "Our people are ridden by complexes," he explained. "The history of the persecution of Jews in Europe has taught us to regard everything with deep suspicion. Peace will come, but it will take time."

"So you don't really need a brave leader to bring peace," I teased him. "What you need is a panel of psychiatrists to rid you of these complexes."

"This is so," Uri had to agree.

How discouraged we all felt as 1978 drew to a close. More than a year after Anwar's visit to Jerusalem, and three months after Camp David, there was still no peace with Israel. And the news from Iran was worsening. Students were demonstrating against the Shah. Women were demonstrating against the Shah. Even children were being organized to demonstrate against the Shah. At the funerals of rioters killed by the police, the Shah's opponents were inciting new demonstrations. They would whip up more violence during the fortieth day of mourning ceremonies, when ever more people would be killed. These well-planned cycles of violence were coming closer and closer to toppling the Shah.

"Farah, we have read in the papers here that you are planning a vacation. Why don't you and your husband come visit us in Egypt?" I phoned the Shabanu in Teheran just after the New Year in '79.

"Thank you, no, Jehan," Farah replied. "We are not planning a vacation right now."

I was puzzled when I hung up. I had known when I read about their intended holiday for rest and convalescence that it really meant they were about to be forced into exile. Their lives were in extreme danger in Iran. Didn't Farah understand that? And why would she turn down our invitation? Certainly she and the Shah must know that Anwar and I thought of them as our dear friends regardless of the politics of the situation.

"Anwar, will you phone the Shah and see if you can change his mind about coming to Egypt?" I asked my husband. "For some reason, they have declined our invitation."

Anwar soon told me why. "The American ambassador in Teheran has been urging the Shah to leave the country for some time so that a new government can try to stabilize the country. But the Shah does not want to leave and suspected when you called that the United States had made a deal with me to get him out of Iran. When I assured him that we were extending a personal invitation, not a political invitation, he changed his mind. He and Farah will be arriving next week."

"That is wonderful news, Anwar," I said. "They have both suffered terribly."

"We will do everything we can to receive the Shah with the greatest possible welcome," Anwar said. "I will never forget how he helped us during the October War and supported my peace initiative with Israel. It is our duty now to stand by him."

On January 17, 1979, I stood beside Anwar at the airport in Aswan as the Shah piloted the *Falcon,* his own silver-and-blue jet, to a stop. Anwar had ordered a full military reception, for although an interim government had been installed in Iran, the Shah was still the official head of state. All our Cabinet ministers were assembled at the airport to greet him, as was the Iranian ambassador to Egypt, Abbas Naieri. Ambassador Naieri knew, as did we all, that the Shah would never return to Iran and that he himself would be severely criticized by the new regime for receiving him. But, like my husband, Naieri was a man of principle. And the Shah was still the Emperor of Iran.

How drawn the Shah looked as he stepped down onto the red carpet and stood at attention while the Egyptian honor guard fired a twenty-one-gun salute, and the military band played the anthems of both our countries. I did not know then, nor did Anwar, that the Shah was mortally ill with cancer. I ascribed his frailty to the terrible strain he had been living under, and my heart went out to him. Anwar kissed the Shah warmly on both cheeks, even though his aides had advised him against such an enthusiastic welcome, knowing that the picture would be on the front pages of newspapers all over the world.

But my husband was not one who would abandon a friend just because the political tide was running against him.

"Rest assured, Muhammad, you are in your country and with your people and brothers," my husband said to the Shah, whose eyes were brimming with tears.

I walked with Farah behind Anwar and the Shah while they reviewed the military guard. What a lovely woman Farah was —and is—and how much she had tried to do for her country. If only she had had more time. She hadn't been able to become too involved in social activities while she was having her four babies. But afterward she had become an essential link between her husband and the people, listening to their problems. I put my arms around her and hugged her while we all drove together to the Oberoi Hotel. Along the route were photographs of the Shah that Anwar had ordered to be hastily mounted, left over from a former state visit. But I doubt the Shah noticed anything, he was so distraught.

Tears poured down his cheeks in the car while he told my husband about the emotional farewell he had just had with the Iranian military at the airport in Teheran. "My bodyguard grabbed my arm and pleaded with me to stay. 'Don't leave us,' he begged me. 'Iran will be lost without you, and the future is dark.' I feel like a leader who has deserted the battlefield."

Immediately my husband offered sanctuary to the Iranian armed forces, who through all the chaos had remained loyal to the Shah. "Why don't you withdraw the aircraft of your Air Force and your naval units?" he suggested. "Egypt will host them until the conditions stabilize in Iran."

But the Shah's reply revealed his hopelessness. "The Americans will not allow it," he said sadly. "They forced me to leave, the ambassador even looking repeatedly at his watch at the airport, saying that every minute I delayed was not in my interests nor in the interest of Iran."

I saw the shock on Anwar's face. Later he told me he could not believe that any leader, especially the Shah, could have allowed the affairs of his country to be controlled by a foreign government. In that moment, he knew the Shah was lost.

The newspapers in Egypt and in Iran continued to call the Shah's stay with us a "vacation." And so did Farah, who had brought very few clothes with her. "We will return soon to Teheran," she said to me over and over during the next five days we spent together at the Oberoi Hotel in Aswan. The

Shah, though more realistic, also spoke longingly of returning to his country. Besides the Americans, his own advisers had urged him to leave temporarily, he told us, thinking it would calm the people. He and Farah were waiting for the "perfect time" to go home, they kept telling us. But every day the news from Iran grew worse.

We talked of nothing else. The Shah could not contain his anguish over the mistakes that had been made, mistakes that had not necessarily been his. Members of his family and the government had been corrupt. The secret police, the Savak, had been too cruel with the people. Much information had never reached the Shah, leaving him ignorant and helpless to act. His advisers had kept him too isolated. "Thank God, you are here safely with us," we kept trying to soothe him. The Shah and his wife had come out of a nightmare, really, and could easily have been killed anytime.

Every morning the Shah walked for an hour around the beautiful grounds of the Oberoi, which we had chosen because it was so secluded, on a manmade island in the middle of the Nile. From one side of the island you could see the lights of Aswan, from the other the tomb of the Aga Khan, the Imam of the Isma'ilis, a small sect of Shiite Muslims. Though the old Aga Khan, grandfather of the present Aga Khan, was not Egyptian, he had asked to be buried in Aswan.

In one of the mysteries that cannot be explained, the Aga Khan, who had been confined to a wheelchair, could walk without pain in Aswan. Perhaps his relief came from the weather, so dry that before the construction of the High Dam no one in Aswan had ever seen a cloud in the sky. Who knows the secret of the desert? But every winter the Aga Khan had come to Aswan to relax and walk before having to spend the rest of the year in a wheelchair. I was hoping the magic of Aswan would take the paleness out of the Shah's cheeks as well.

On the fourth day of their visit, when Anwar had to excuse himself to go to an important meeting in the Sudan with President Numeiry, I arranged to take the Shah and Farah on a river trip along the Nile. They seemed more relaxed now, and ready for distraction. We packed sandwiches and soft drinks and sweets, and for three hours or so we cruised in the calm waters of Lake Nasser above the High Dam to the Greco-Roman ruins of the Philae temple.

"Welcome," the people shouted to the Shah and to the Empress Farah as our boat passed close to the shore. "Welcome in Egypt." Farah and the Shah waved back to the crowds, deeply touched by their friendliness and goodwill. But I could see in the Shah's eyes that their enthusiasm hurt him as well. His own people in Iran had shouted curses at him.

On January 21, Farah and the Shah, looking rested and relaxed, prepared to fly on from Egypt to Morocco. "You must come back to Egypt whenever you wish," I said to Farah when I kissed her goodbye. "Call us at anytime, from anywhere. You will always be welcome."

On February 1, the Ayatollah Khomeini returned to Iran.

When I returned to Cairo, I found that the fires of fundamentalism which had swept Iran were smoldering now in the university. As I hurried to a lecture, I was dismayed to find that Islamic groups had covered the walls with posters hailing the Iranian revolution. Bearded young men and veiled young women were handing out leaflets warning that all governments that did not implement Shari'a, Islamic law, could expect the same sort of popular uprising.

I was disturbed, though not to the point of alarm. I knew that what had happened in Iran could not happen in Egypt. There was no similarity at all between the circumstances in the two countries. In Egypt, we Sunni Muslims were moderate in our beliefs. The Shiites in Iran were more political and prone to violence. From the seventh century, after the murder of their Imam Hussein in Iraq by Sunni forces, the Shiites had inherited a passion for rebellion and uprising against authority. They had also glorified those who sought out martyrdom, a trend which continues to this day in the carnage of the Iran–Iraq War. In Iran, those who fall in battle against the Iraqis are buried in a special cemetery reserved for martyrs, and their families are given special privileges and the highest respect.

The Shiites in Iran also perceive the Ayatollah Khomeini and Iran's other religious leaders much differently than we Sunnis in Egypt perceive our own. Sunni Muslims believe that all men are equal in the eyes of God, the greatest sheikh being no closer to Him than the poorest man. But in Iran the Shiites elevate their Islamic scholars to the highest spiritual and political positions, accepting the word of their Ayatollahs as law. This hierarchical belief had allowed Khomeini, whose word was unquestioned, to rise up to the head of the new government in

Iran. In Egypt, even the most fanatical Sunni would never believe that one man could speak for God.

Still, the religious extremists at Cairo University and throughout Egypt were sobering. Though they represented only the smallest fraction of our population, the fanatics were well organized and not to be ignored. "The young are drifting into the hands of the fundamentalists," I told Anwar, relating to him what I was seeing in the university. "You have brought Egypt many steps forward, but there are those who want to take us back."

Anwar agreed, though he thought that perhaps I was making too much out of the fundamentalist influence on campus.

"Anwar, I can only tell you what I am seeing with my own eyes," I persisted.

To my great relief, Anwar traveled to the university in Assiut in February to address the students. "We will allow neither religion in politics nor politics in religion," he declared. "I believe that we must return to religion as a culture . . . not at all in the way that some are now advocating. No. We must approach it as a culture that will restore to the world spiritual peace and social peace within a single homeland." After my husband's speech, the demonstrations calmed down.

Political peace with Israel, however, continued to be elusive. Six months after Anwar returned from Camp David, he and Begin remained deadlocked in their negotiations on the fate of East Jerusalem, which had been occupied by the Israelis since the '67 war, the ownership of the oil in the Sinai, and, as always, the question of Palestinian self-determination. Israel was continuing to expand her settlements on the West Bank in violation of the agreement reached at Camp David. The peace process was on the verge of collapse.

"Jehan, President Carter has decided to come here to talk to me, then to go to Israel to talk to Begin," Anwar told me early in March. "Otherwise he does not see any chance for peace."

I did not dare get my hopes up again. "That is good news, Anwar," I said cautiously.

"Mrs. Carter will be coming with him," he went on.

That *was* good news. I had grown very fond of Rosalynn. When I first met her in Washington soon after her husband was elected in 1976, we had found much in common: our work with the mentally handicapped, the elderly, the disabled. She had held a reception for me at the White House, inviting the heads of several organizations with interests like mine, the disabled and the education of the illiterate among others. Personally, Rosalynn was very warm and sensitive. During the Camp David negotiations, she had arranged for the American delegation to have American food, the Israeli delegation to have kosher meals, and Anwar to have his simple diet of boiled chicken, vegetables and tea of boiled mint leaves. One building at Camp David, Anwar told me, had even been set aside as a mosque.

But Rosalynn and I had one bond that truly united us. She wanted her husband to negotiate a peace settlement between Egypt and Israel just as I wanted my husband to achieve the same peace. Our husbands were very courageous men. And both were at risk.

The Carters arrived in Cairo on March 8, 1979, to an overwhelming reception. President Carter was only the second U.S. President to visit Egypt, and he would be the first to address our Parliament. Most important to the Egyptian people, however, was his personal dedication in our search for peace. As we drove from the airport to the Qubbah Palace, where the Carters would be staying, millions of cheering Egyptians lined the streets. "Welcome, Kartar" read some of the hand-lettered signs along the route, "We Love President Kartr," "God Bless You, Qatr." "Perhaps we should move to Cairo," Rosalynn joked in the car.

Anwar and President Carter had much to talk about, but we were also anxious to show our American friends as much of Egypt as was possible in two days. Together we rode in the antique train from Cairo to Alexandria the next morning. Looking out at the farmland in the Nile Delta, Rosalynn expressed envy at our dark and rich soil, which was such a contrast to the red soil that her husband had farmed in Georgia. When we returned, I went with Mrs. Carter to the National Assembly to listen to her husband speak eloquently of the desire for peace, drawing from the Quran, the Old Testament, and the Sermon on the Mount from the New Testament. Over and over the members of Parliament interrupted President Carter with applause. He wanted peace as much as we did. And he was as religious as we were.

The next day, with only fifty minutes to spare before the Carters had to leave for Israel, we sped to show them the Pyramids. The Khamsin, the fifty days of wind and sandstorm weather we have in Egypt each spring, had started on the day the Carters arrived. But though the wind stung us with sand and filled our eyes with grit, the Carters seemed to feel the mysterious power of the Pyramids as much as we did. "We feel humbled," President Carter said as he and Rosalynn left to go on to Israel.

The Carters' arrival in Jerusalem was shocking. Only one thousand greeted them at the airport. The signs held by the crowds read, "Go Home, Carter" and "Welcome, Brother of Billy." How could the Israelis truly want peace? During the presidential motorcade to the King David Hotel in Jerusalem where Anwar had stayed sixteen long months before, hostile demonstrators got close enough to throw eggs at President Carter's car.

Nothing, however, prepared me for the rude way President Carter was treated during his speech to the Knesset. He had been cheered at the National People's Assembly in Cairo. At the Knesset his initial remarks were met with silence, but even silence was better than the heckling that erupted after his speech. The outbreak was so loud that Prime Minister Begin could barely deliver his own speech.

"It is finished," Anwar said to me as together we watched the hostile display on television.

The Egyptian press was also deeply disturbed by the Israelis' behavior. "If peace is not born," said *el-Gumhuriyya,* "the whole world and the U.S. in particular should give chase to the culprit who committed this crime against humanity." American news agencies declared that the prospects for peace were now almost nonexistent.

On March 13, the Carters flew back to Cairo, making a brief stop at the airport because President Carter wanted to discuss with Anwar what progress he had made, if any, in Israel. I was as deeply depressed when I went with Anwar to meet them as my husband was angered. "My people in Egypt are furious at how the Israelis have treated our friend Jimmy Carter," Anwar greeted the American President. While the two leaders went into a private room to talk, I sat with Mrs. Carter, who was just as depressed. An hour passed. Then another. As we sat in the reception area at the airport, Rosalynn and I prayed together.

I knew that something incredible had happened when the men emerged. President Carter had looked very grim when he arrived. Now he was smiling. I searched my husband's face for a sign. "Anwar, what is it? What has happened?" I asked.

Only then did he permit himself a smile. "President Carter and I have just spoken to Begin in Jerusalem," he said. "We have reached an agreement."

I must have cried out. I must have hopped up and down with joy. I cannot remember, the moment was so blinding. I turned toward Rosalynn, but we could barely see each other for the tears in our eyes. "God has heard our prayers," I said to her as our husbands walked out of the terminal toward the waiting microphones and television cameras of the international press. Peace had been declared. Our enmity with Israel which had consumed us for thirty years was over. As President Carter made the historic announcement, I looked at the strain on my husband's face that the arduous peace process had made permanent.

Anwar el-Sadat. Menachem Begin. Jimmy Carter. These men, these leaders, are shaking hands, embracing each other. The sight is too much to readily absorb. It is March 26, 1979, ten days after the joint announcement of peace at the airport in Cairo. We are at the White House, where these three men have just signed the Camp David Peace Accords. I cannot believe this is actually happening.

All day I have been disoriented, starting with a quiet lunch with the Carters in their private quarters in the White House. The table is set for six: President and Mrs. Carter, Prime Minister and Mrs. Begin, President and Mrs. Anwar el-Sadat. For the first time, I am going to be face to face with the Prime Minister of Israel, a man whose face I know only too well from Egyptian television and newspaper photos.

"Mrs. Sadat, how nice to finally meet you," he says when we are introduced, offering me his hand.

Automatically I take it, this hand that I had always thought belonged to the Devil. "It is my pleasure," I respond. But inside I am shaking. Will this man who has caused us so much pain and frustration go through with the signing or will he change his mind again?

My apprehension almost proves to be true, not because of any last-minute suspicions from Begin, but because of his wife's health. Halfway through the meal Mrs. Begin begins to cough and choke. We all sit stunned as she gasps for air, her face turning purple. Is she going to die right here, in front of us? Oh God, please God, save her, save her, I prayed. Struggling to breathe, Mrs. Begin reaches into her bag and pulls out an atomizer. I pray with all my strength while she puts it into her mouth, and sprays and sprays and sprays. Please, God! Slowly her cough subsides, her fit of asthma passing. *El-hamdu lillah.* Thank You, God. Thank You. Thank You. Her attack has probably lasted only a few seconds, but they are the longest seconds I have ever known.

Now on the dais set up on the White House lawn, each leader is speaking eloquently of lasting peace. I hope no one notices the tears coming down my cheeks. I try to regain my composure, to keep my attention on the speakers. But on this day I cannot. Out of the corner of my eye, I become aware of a familiar figure sitting near me. I sneak a look.

My God! Moshe Dayan! Here! In person! Quickly I lower my eyes, but not before I have seen another familiar figure, Ariel Sharon, the former Minister of Defense. My heart is pounding so hard it must show through my dress. All of them are here, these Israeli legends who have played such a huge and dreadful role in my life. Now suddenly these men who have been our enemies for thirty years are our friends.

My sense of unreality continues through the White House dinner to celebrate the signing of the peace accords. The tables are set up in a green-and-white tent, the same colors I used for my son's wedding. Egyptians, Israelis and Americans are seated at each table, not separated but all mixed up together. I look around the tent, trying to take it all in. Since 1948 these men have fought one another, wounded one another, killed one another's brothers and sons. Now they are sitting together and sharing bread. Many look as stunned as I feel. Am I able to talk politely to these people? Am I allowed to? Is this possible? So many years of mutual suspicion and fear are hard to quickly reverse.

I am seated between President Carter and Prime Minister Begin. The talk is not of war, not of military preparedness, but of our children and grandchildren. Begin's daughter, Hasya, he tells me, is the same age as my daughter Loubna. "You must come visit us in Israel soon with your husband," Mr. Begin says. "And bring your children." Come to Israel? During the after-dinner entertainment provided by musicians from Egypt, Israel, and America, I look around the tent, to see Israelis and Egyptians cautiously coming to know each other. I close my eyes and when I open them everyone is still there. My son Gamal is having a good laugh with Moshe Dayan. They must be trading jokes.

From the moment the peace accords were signed, everything was different. Everything. When Anwar and I left the White House the next day, it was as if to a new world. On a trip to the United States in 1974 when Anwar had been visiting the United Nations, the mayor of New York, Abraham Beame, had refused to meet him. Like many people, Mr. Beame was equating the political conflict between Egypt and Israel with a religious conflict between all Jews and all Muslims. But he was wrong. Though obviously some religious sympathy existed, a Jew in the United States was an American, not an Israeli, and between us there was no quarrel. I had wondered at the time if Mayor Beame had thought he was the mayor of Tel Aviv or the mayor of New York.

I had met hostility myself on that same trip from an officer of protocol in Los Angeles. In the car from the airport, she had barely responded when I asked her her name, whether she had children, whether she enjoyed the sunny weather in southern California. "What is the matter with this lady?" I had asked the city official who was escorting Anwar, when we arrived at the hotel. He had looked embarrassed. "At first she refused to greet you at all, claiming she was sick," he explained. "I told her that as a protocol officer it was not her business to approve or disapprove of our guests. But she is Jewish and it was difficult for her."

Now all that was past, and indeed the opposite was happening. We were being flooded with invitations to parties and receptions all over America, to receive honorary degrees at universities, to accept keys to at least twenty different cities. From that moment, the people who would be the warmest to me wherever I went in the world, who would speak of my husband with the greatest affection, often with tears in their eyes, would be Jews. The contrast was most startling in New York. On the evening of the day the peace accords were signed, the Empire State Building was lit up with the colors of Egypt and Israel.

The mood was very different in the Arab countries. Even as Anwar was signing the accords which would bring peace to our region, the Palestinians were calling for an oil embargo against Egypt and the United States. Demonstrations against my husband broke out in Syria and Lebanon. In Iran, frenzied mobs seized the Egyptian Embassy, displaying banners that showed Anwar hanging from a scaffold. Even King Hussein in Jordan, who was the most moderate Arab leader, was threatening to break off diplomatic relations with Egypt. Peace had won new friends for Egypt, but had turned our old friends into enemies. Not surprisingly, the most hateful was Muammar el-Qadaffi. He would not rest, the leader of Libya declared, until Anwar was dead.

How sorry I felt for their shortsightedness. And how proud I felt of the Egyptian people who lined the streets of Cairo to greet Anwar when we returned to Egypt. They, who had suffered so in the wars, truly knew the value of peace. "*Bil ruh, bil damm, nifdeek, ya* Sadat!" they called out to Anwar. With our blood and souls, we would sacrifice ourselves for you, Sadat! *Bil ruh, bil damm, hankamil el-mishwar!* With our blood and souls, we shall complete your journey!"

One ceremony remained, a ceremony that would mean more to Anwar than any other. On May 25, 1979, two months after our return, we flew to el-Arish with his cabinet ministers to celebrate the first stage of the return of the Sinai. Never had my heart been so full. Anwar had fulfilled his promise to the Egyptian people to regain our land. And he had done it without bloodshed.

How beautiful and peaceful el-Arish seemed that day, the palm trees waving on the bench, and, beyond, the blue sea. There were so many memories. It was here that Anwar and I had started our married life together twenty-eight years before. And it was here that Egypt had suffered her worst humiliation, losing this land for eleven years. Now, in peace, it would be ours again. When the honor guard carried the Egyptian flag to be hoisted once more over the Sinai, Anwar bowed before it and kissed it, as did all the ministers. Many of the war veterans who had gathered with us in el-Arish to witness the return of the land they had fought so bravely for had tears in their eyes, as did I. It was for this moment that my husband had prayed and worked for so long. Who could have believed that it would actually happen?

I felt the same suspension of belief when in September my family and I accepted Mr. Begin's invitation to visit Israel. A twenty-one-gun salute greeted us when we arrived by ship in Haifa. On the shore waiting to greet us were people so tightly packed together that you could not throw salt between them. "Welcome, Sadat," their signs read. "Welcome." "Welcome." There was such excitement in their eyes, in their smiles, that we knew this was not a welcoming ceremony ordered by the government, but one of genuine warmth.

"Why did we spend so many years fighting these lovely people?" I teased Anwar as we prepared to step onto Israeli soil.

Anwar laughed. "This is not the moment, Jehan, to discuss it," he said.

Aliza Begin was most gracious, taking me to visit hospitals, a center for the disabled, nursery schools, even to deliver a speech to the university about our work in Egypt with the handicapped. With great ceremony in one hospital I was shown a newly acquired CAT scanner, of which the Israelis were most proud.

"We have one ourselves in the Wafa' wal Amal," I couldn't keep myself from saying.

Anwar glared at me. "Don't say that," he muttered. "This is new for them and they are very proud of it."

"Well, so am I proud of our own CAT scanner," I muttered back, adding emphatically, "which we have had for years."

"Just don't talk about it," Anwar said.

I was most pleased to meet Leah Rabin, the wife of former Prime Minister Yitzhak Rabin, at a luncheon. We had been together once before, in 1975 at the United Nations International Women's Conference in Mexico City, but I had not spoken to her, had refused even to shake her hand, because her country was occupying our land. Now we hugged each other.

"I apologize for my rudeness in Mexico City," I said to her.

"You don't have to," she replied.

But I wanted to tell her the relief I now felt. "As a woman I wanted to sit with you, to discuss the problems we had in common, but politics prevented it," I told her. "Let us sit down together now." And we did.

My daughter Jehan was just as charmed by the people of

Israel. Wherever she went sightseeing, people came up to her in the streets to welcome her. In one shop where she stopped to buy souvenirs, the shopkeeper refused to take any payment. "Please accept these as gifts from our country to your family," the shopkeeper insisted.

Still, there were moments of shock. I couldn't help shuddering a little every time I saw an Israeli helicopter, reliving the terror they had brought during the wars. The shock was the greatest when we actually flew in a helicopter with Ezer Weizman on the way to the airport to fly home.

"Would you like to come up front and sit by the pilot?" said this wonderful man whom my husband loved very, very much. "You can see much better from there."

I kept glancing at the pilot in his military uniform as he pointed out the agricultural areas we were flying over, the industrial areas, the areas populated by both Jews and Arabs. This very officer in this very helicopter could have been one of those killing Egyptian soldiers just a few years before. Now he was proudly taking me sightseeing.

Back in Cairo, I discounted the criticisms that were beginning to appear in the Egyptian press, charges that Anwar had traded too much for peace with Israel. Did they not care about the return of the Sinai? I was also not surprised by the sporadic demonstrations against the government by the fundamentalists. On the night when my husband and President Carter had jointly announced that an agreement with Israel had been reached, the police had had to disperse a demonstration at Assiut University with tear gas. I knew that the fundamentalists would never agree with the peace. But I thought that soon enough they would see that Egypt had had no alternative.

Only the actions of Qadaffi were disturbing me. As Anwar and I left the White House after the signing of the peace accords, President Carter had kissed me goodbye. He had known, of course, that such intimacy was forbidden between men and women in Islam, but it was a spontaneous gesture. "Oh, Jehan, we've been through so much together," he had said to me at the door of the helicopter while the news cameras recorded the moment. Now a blowup of that photograph, I was told, was hanging in the airport in Tripoli over the legend "Can this woman call herself a true Muslim?"

The fires which were to consume my husband were spreading.

Chapter 13

bismallah

In the Name of God

i am late again for class. I hurry through the gates of Cairo University toward the department of Arabic literature, but I am blocked by a wall of people. "It is the fundamentalists," someone whispers. "They are praying in the central courtyard." Praying in the central courtyard? It is ten o'clock. The next prayer is not until twelve. Besides, the central courtyard is the path to the classroom buildings, not a mosque.

I cannot get through. No one can get through. As I join the crowd of students I see several hundred young men in white robes rising and falling in prayer, several hundred keeping thousands from their classes. "We must call the police," a girl in front of me says. But I remind her no police can come. To encourage a free atmosphere at the university, Anwar has forbidden them on campus.

It is almost two hours before I am able to take my place in the Master's Seminar. Even then the interruptions continue. Thump! A fist bangs on the door of the classroom next to mine. The professor pauses, then continues talking. Thump! Thump!

Thump! The noise at the door grows so loud that the professor cannot continue.

"Stop studying now," scream the religious extremists through the door. "It is time for prayer!" The voices belong to men and women both. The professor does not open the door, waiting instead for the crowd outside to move on to the next classroom. But I can see them in my mind. The men wear beards and galabiyyas. The women are in long dresses and veils. Their eyes are gleaming.

For years I had watched the influence of the fundamentalists grow stronger and stronger at the university. It had been in 1974, the year I entered as an undergraduate, that Anwar repealed Nasser's ban on the religious groups, insisting that they too had a right to speak if Egypt was to move toward democracy. And slowly the religious extremists had formed a small but well-organized core of opposition to my husband's policies. In 1977, three months after Anwar returned from Jerusalem, the militant Islamic groups had surprised everyone on campus when their delegates swept the student elections. Now, starting on my master's degree in the fall of 1979, I wondered where the power of the extremists would end.

To an extent, I was sympathetic with those embracing the message of the fundamentalists. Our problems in Egypt had remained chronic, with no relief in sight. Too many of our people were poor. Too many couldn't find decent housing. Too many were uneducated. Too many could not even buy clothes, making it far more economical for them to have just one galabiyya to wear or one long dress. But all these conditions stemmed from just one fact: the government could not afford to support so many people.

The increasing strain on our social structure was leading many to confusion and despair. The poor especially, and the thousands who moved every day to Cairo from the rural areas, felt lost in the overcrowded, noisy urban neighborhoods where it was difficult to find a place to live or a job. Naturally they were susceptible to the strict guidelines of the fundamentalists, which gave them an identity and a purpose.

The family structure, which had always been the backbone of Egypt's stability, was also being weakened. Generations who had lived together in the villages and in the cities were beginning to split up. The housing shortage made it difficult for married couples to live near their parents, at times causing not only neglect of the elderly but neglect of the young as well. Instead of leaving their children in the care of their grandparents when they went to work, some mothers now had to leave their children with strangers. Many fathers worked not one but two or even three jobs every day. Everybody was busy. Everybody was working or looking for work. No one had enough time to tend to the family.

I could see this sense of neglect spilling over into the schools, where the sheer number of students was overwhelming what had always been a supportive system. Where once our teachers had known all their students' families and had acted as the link between the school and the home, now they hardly knew their students' names. At the overcrowded universities, those with problems, perhaps the death of a parent, a divorce, even learning problems, were being lost in the masses. Even students with no particular problem found they had to hire private tutors in order to get a passing grade. There was no way the professors could teach so many at once. And the students felt lost at that critical time in their development when they needed attention the most.

I tried my best with the students, talking with them after class, inviting them to my home to talk about anything they wanted to. But of course I alone could not make up for their feelings of alienation. Nor could I compete with the fundamentalists, who arranged for the poor, including many students, to be housed in mosques where they were given food, clothing, money for their schoolbooks, even tutoring. Outside the university, the Muslim Brothers and their splinter groups were working to help others, too, setting up health clinics in the poorest neighborhoods, organizing reading workshops for children who were in the overcrowded public schools, building shelters for those who could find no homes. Their campaign was well organized—and well funded, though no one was sure where they got all the money. Some said it came from the religious conservatives in Egypt. Others suspected Qadaffi, the Muslim Brothers in Saudi Arabia or the Shiite fundamentalists in Iran.

Whoever was supporting the fundamentalists, I was sure that they were satisfied with the results. Each time the Brothers gave their services, they gave religious lectures as well. Shari'a must be the only law in our society. All imports from the West must be eliminated. Peace with Israel is forbidden by the Quran. The Copts are the Muslims' enemies, and want Egypt for themselves.

At the university, I could not walk ten steps without seeing another one of the booths from which the members of the fundamentalist groups sold books for low, low prices and tried to recruit others to their ways. They distributed free galabiyyas to the young men who stopped to listen to them, and gave veils and long robes to the young women. And each year more and more students were accepting, greater numbers wearing beards or putting on veils rather than taking them off.

It surprised me that so many, including some of the best and brightest young women in my class, were choosing to wear the *hegab,* the light veil that leaves the face exposed but covers the back of the head and the shoulders. One of my students chose to wear the veil because she was deeply religious, a choice I respected. But others in the university were making more of a political statement, especially those who were taking the *niqab,* the heavy veil, almost like a mask, that covers a woman's entire face and leaves only two slits for her eyes. These most extreme girls shielded their bodies entirely, covering their hands in gloves even on hot summer days, and wearing thick stockings. To see them walking down the halls of the university made me sick at heart. This was not Islam.

The fundamentalists, in turn, criticized my own dress. Time and again, they sent well-spoken girls to try to persuade me at least to adopt the veil. "Why don't you take the lawful dress?" the envoys would urge me, using the name that Islamic groups had coined for the veil and long robe they considered essential for women. "Should not you, the wife of Egypt's President and a model for our women, set an example?"

"I always wear long sleeves and conservative, respectable clothes," I would counter firmly. "But more important than your clothing are your deeds. When it is time for God to judge us, He will not put you in heaven first because the dress you wore was longer."

"*Inna el-a'mal bil niyyat,*" says the Hadith: Deeds are weighed by their intention. I could not blame the fundamentalists for following what they believed. But they should not have tried

413

to impose their will, the opinion of a minority, on everybody else. They were taking advantage of Anwar's move toward freedom of expression, and noncensorship. My husband's openness had given possibilities to Egyptians they had never known before. But the religious extremists saw only the bad side of everything, feeling threatened by every new development. Their list of complaints was endless.

They hated the Western rock music most students were listening to, charging that any music except the chanting of the Quran was sacrilegious. The blue jeans worn by both boys and girls at the university offended them. Western television programs were popular all over Egypt, but the Islamic fundamentalists wanted them banned. Immoral, too, was the celebration of nonreligious holidays such as Mother's Day. To the most extreme fundamentalists, even Western scientific methods were suspect, some medical students refusing to learn about certain aspects of the anatomy of the opposite sex.

I did not understand these fanatical viewpoints at all. And it was obvious the fanatics did not understand me. With increasing frequency they waited outside lecture halls to chide me about what they saw as Egypt's sinful new policies. "Your husband is letting in corruption from the West," they would say. I told them: "Take what you find good in Western ways and disregard the rest. We cannot afford to isolate ourselves any longer. As educated people, we must find out as much as possible about the world around us, and use that knowledge to improve ourselves." But my arguments fell on deaf ears.

Most threatening to the fundamentalists was the breakdown of the barrier between the sexes. I believed that coeducation was the first step toward women gaining equality with men, but it made the extremists furious to see boys and girls talking and studying together. The fundamentalists funded special all-girl school buses and wanted segregation of the sexes in the classrooms and the cafeterias. They objected to putting out the lights during slide shows in the classrooms, insisting that it was improper for men and women to be together in the dark. " '*Lakum Dinukum wa Liyya Dini,*' " I would quote endlessly from the Quran to those who now demanded to know how I could support coeducation and the reforms in the Status Laws while still calling myself a Muslim. You have your religion and I have mine. Deeds are weighed by their intention.

The situation was not helped by an interview I had given

along with Amina el-Sa'id to an American journalist who had assured us her article would appear in a family magazine like *Parade*. I couldn't believe my ears when the Egyptian Ambassador in Washington phoned to prepare me for the fact that the article had been published not in *Parade*, but in *Playgirl!* The interview with Amina had in fact appeared on the same page as a picture of a naked man! There was nothing we could do about it, for the magazine was already in circulation. But for days the newspapers and magazines all over the Arab world were full of the story, and the criticism from the fundamentalists in Egypt was unrelenting.

I tried to reason in my debates with the fundamentalists, but in my heart I was appalled. They wanted to take Egypt back hundreds of years, to ignore all the progress we had made. They did not want the joint ventures the government was making with foreign investors which had brought us new hospitals, schools, hotels and clinics. They did not want the new Status Laws. They did not want ties with the West, or peace with Israel.

I wondered whether Anwar knew how deeply they were against him. My husband had advisers and intelligence reports, but I had more access to the people. While Anwar traveled through Egypt by helicopter, I went almost everywhere by car. Anwar visited the governorates with a large entourage, but I often went alone to the rural areas. Anwar occasionally visited the universities, but I saw the fundamentalists with my own eyes every day. And unlike some advisers, I was not afraid to pass on an unfavorable report.

"Fundamentalism is growing, Anwar," I cautioned him during the fall of '79. "If you do not act soon they may gain the political strength to overthrow everything you stand for." And Anwar did act, going as he had a year earlier to address the extreme Islamic groups and ask them to stay out of politics. At the same time, he tried to better the situation of all university students, increasing government subsidies for student housing and textbooks and starting new programs to improve conditions for graduates who took jobs in government offices. More than this he could not or would not do. "I know that the fanatics are dangerous, Jehan," he told me, "but I cannot throw them into jail simply because they do not like my policies."

I had to agree. It was against the principles of democracy to arrest those who opposed you. But what would be the consequences of the bigotry and prejudice the fundamentalists were spreading all over Egypt? It worried me even to see the cover of the Muslim Brothers' magazine, *The Call*. "Warning: The Jews are Coming!" proclaimed an article in a September 1979 issue of this magazine, whose cover showed a cartoon of a Jew hanging a man with a beard and a galabiyya. The article offered advice on how to deal with Israelis following the normalization of our relations with Israel, scheduled for February 1980. "Buy Egyptian products even if they are worse than those made by Jews," it advised. "Never work for a Jew, even if he gives you twice as big a salary. Don't put your money in non-Islamic banks."

Even more disturbing were the fanatics' attacks against the Copts. In Egypt we had never thought of this person as Muslim, that one Christian, always looking on one another simply as Egyptian. Islam fully recognized the right of the Copts to observe their religion, the Quran honoring both Christians and Jews as monotheistic "People of the Book," like the Muslims. Even the Prophet himself had a Christian wife. But ever since the peace with Israel, the fundamentalist groups had ignored all this, instead fanning new religious tensions. "The Copts should have no voice in Egypt's policies," claimed the pamphlets distributed by the Islamic groups. "The Christians are in conspiracy with the imperialists abroad. Do not befriend a Copt."

Few people read the fundamentalists' literature. But it was hard to avoid the message of intolerance the fanatics were preaching from the mosques all over Egypt. And gradually the opposition to peace with Israel, to the Copts, and to my husband grew stronger and stronger.

Opposition was also growing among our Arab neighbors. For the first time in my memory, Egypt no longer had to fear the enemies along her Eastern border. Our new opponents were those we had thought were our friends.

To punish Anwar for having made peace with Israel, the leaders of the Arab countries had met in Baghdad in March of 1979 and had voted to cut off all new aid to Egypt. Millions of Egyptians were suffering from the sudden loss of funds, which before the peace had been more than several hundred million pounds. Even more cruel to a country as poor as ours, the Arab leaders had also voted to impose a total economic boycott on Egypt. Thousands were losing their jobs as multimillion-dollar Arab companies closed their Egyptian branches. Cairo's biggest hotels and riverside nightclubs, ordinarily filled to overflowing with summer tourists from the much hotter Gulf, had stayed empty this past summer. So had the thousands of luxury apartments Egyptians normally rented to the Arab visitors. Some Arab airlines had suspended service to Cairo the moment Prime Minister Begin's plane touched down in Isma'iliyya on December 25, 1978. The rest had followed suit the moment Anwar signed the Camp David Peace Accords. To ensure that no one traveled to Egypt, the Arab governments had even barred Egyptian planes from Arab airspace.

We had also been cut off politically at the Baghdad Conference by the Arab leaders trying to teach Anwar a lesson. It was Egypt which in 1945 had proposed and founded the Arab League, the group of twenty-two Arab countries which functioned much like a small United Nations. But in Baghdad the Arabs had voted to revoke Egypt's membership and to move the headquarters of the Arab League from Cairo to Tunis. Egyptian representatives would not be invited to attend any future Arab summits. By 1980, the embassies of all the Arab countries in Cairo would be closed down, every Arab country except Oman and the Sudan having severed diplomatic relations with Egypt. Even scholars from el-Azhar Mosque would be banned from attending international conferences on Islam.

But Anwar was not one to be bullied into submission. These attempts to break his will only made him firmer in his resolve for peace and more bitter toward those who were hurting Egypt. Over and over in his speeches, he rebuffed his Arab critics and insisted that he would maintain the peace. I was sorry the Arab countries were acting so harshly. Soon, I hoped, the Arabs would see the benefits of peace with Israel and end their feud against Egypt. In the meantime, I tried to help my country in any way I could.

It was no longer so simple. There had always been those who opposed me and the role I had taken outside the home. But there had never been the kind of opposition that I was finding in the fall of 1979. Under Nasser the people had had to repress their anger and their resentment toward the government, afraid of arrest. Now, as Egypt entered one of her most difficult phases economically, Anwar's policy of free expression allowed their tension and frustration finally to spill out. Anwar's political opponents, the fundamentalists, the Communists, certain members of the opposition parties, were banding together to denounce everyone and everything connected with the government. And I seemed to be one of their favorite targets.

"She has thirty-five Mercedes of her own. She got them through customs by saying they were for her charity."

"Coca-Cola Company gave her a hundred thousand dollars to help the handicapped. She kept it for herself."

"She has taken a big piece of land outside Alexandria. Just put her name on it and took it."

What was going on? Suddenly everywhere I turned I heard another rumor of my "corruption." At one time, Ibrahim Loutfi, the chairman of the Nasser Bank of Egypt, offered to join forces with the Wafa' wal Amal by jointly investing in a small fleet of limousines to be rented by tourists, half the profits to go the Wafa'. But when the bank sent the limousines and the drivers to the Wafa' for the board of directors to review, the drivers mistakenly told people that they were delivering the cars personally to me. The word was immediately spread by the oppositioners that I had bought the cars for my own use. Even when Wafa' wal Amal's board of directors decided not to go ahead with the project at all, that it was not worth it financially, the rumor did not die. The talk continued about "Jehan's cars," spreading so rapidly that I had to dispel it during an interview on television.

It was a terrible time. People I had barely met started using my name to justify their own illegal actions. One former employee of the Wafa' wal Amal filled a big truck with television sets and other appliances from the duty-free zone in Port Sa'id and told the customs officers he was bringing the goods to the charity on the orders of Mrs. Sadat. Luckily the man was arrested while trying this trick for the third time, when one of the officers called my office to check on his credentials. If no one had called, I would never have known what had been happening.

Another incident was even more disturbing. "I am shocked and disappointed," read a letter I received from a navy officer in 1980. "I always admired your work with our soldiers. But neither that nor your marriage to our President gives you the right to claim the land I bought for my family in Alexandria." I was totally confused, for the only land I owned was the twelve acres I shared with Anwar in Mit Abul-Kum. My confusion only increased when I sent someone from my office to investigate the story. "The officer is right," he announced. "There is a billboard on his land saying that it now belongs to Jehan Sadat."

Quickly I discovered the truth. The sign had been put up by Jehan Talaat Sadat, the daughter of Anwar's brother Talaat. Her husband had bought the land with the naval officer, and the two co-owners had then quarreled over the size of their plots. My niece had tried to solve the problem by intimidating the officer, making the billboard and purposely omitting the "Talaat" from her name on it. When the officer realized that the President's wife was involved in the dispute, she had reasoned, he would give up.

I was infuriated, as was Anwar. Anwar ordered Talaat's daughter Jehan to settle her land dispute immediately, in court. Legally the issue was cleared up, but the rumors remained.

Anwar was much more philosophical than I was about most of the attacks being launched against him, and against me. "These oppositioners are *ahl el-la-at,* People of the No-Nos," he would tell me. "Pay no attention to them. No matter what you are involved in, they will find something to reject or be suspicious of." He was right, of course. I knew I couldn't please everybody. But I also knew that I hadn't taken from any of my charities. I tried to ignore the irrational charges against me, but they still hurt. And the attacks continued.

In September of 1979, the American actress Elizabeth Taylor asked if she could come to visit Egypt. I was thrilled. Elizabeth Taylor was my favorite actress, for she was not only beautiful but filled with tremendous spirit. I had always wanted to meet her. But like all those who had been to Israel, Miss Taylor had for years been banned from entering our country.

After the Camp David Accords, of course, it made no difference who had been to Israel. The Arab blacklist no longer applied to us. And so it was with the greatest pleasure that I invited Elizabeth Taylor for a cup of tea at my home in Cairo. All of my children arranged to come and see her, and we had a lovely time together. But Miss Taylor was very disappointed not to see Anwar, who was away in Isma'iliyya. "Perhaps I can arrange a meeting before you leave Egypt," I told her.

"I have someone here who wants to meet you," I phoned Anwar in Isma'iliyya.

But Anwar said he was too busy to see anyone.

"What a pity, Anwar," I replied. "Elizabeth Taylor will be so disappointed."

There was a pause. "In that case, let her come. Welcome," he said, laughing.

His office arranged for the presidential helicopter to take Elizabeth to Isma'iliyya on her way to Israel. Anwar loved the opportunity to see her. But the oppositioners hated it, criticizing us both for wasting our time with a Western actress who was a known Israeli sympathizer.

Another "scandal" involving an American celebrity followed shortly. Not long after Anwar signed the peace accords, our embassy in the United States had received a letter from Frank Sinatra offering to sing in a charity gala being organized for the Wafa' wal Amal. I was excited by the idea, and grew even more enthusiastic when the U.S. benefit committee, headed by Michael Bergerac, chairman of Revlon, decided to hold the benefit in Cairo in the fall. Who could ask for better publicity for our country than the television pictures of Frank Sinatra singing in front of the Pyramids? Many Americans would see it in their homes and want to come visit Egypt themselves.

For the gala itself, the foreign businessmen would pay $2,500 dollars a ticket, which included a three-day stay at a hotel with their families plus tours to attractions like the Cairo and Islamic museums. Having come so far, we hoped, the foreigners would probably stay in Egypt longer, spending their dollars in our markets, restaurants and hotels. What a gift. The gala would cost us nothing. The money would come from abroad from those who could afford it, and the profits would go to Egypt. Frank Sinatra and his entire entourage of musicians would even play for free, only the cost of their transportation to Egypt to be borne by the benefit.

As soon as word of the benefit got out, however, the People of the No-Nos attacked. Egyptians would be excluded from their own party, they claimed, for too few would be able to afford the price of a ticket. "They are right," I agreed. "Let us set aside tickets for our own people." Ten percent of the tickets were then reserved for Egyptians at the price of £E100. But, for the oppositioners, this was not enough. The committee had planned a fashion show at the Mena House Hotel before the concert. This too, was denounced by the oppositioners, who insisted it was shameful for women models to parade in front of men, especially wearing Western clothes.

The underwriting of the benefit by Revlon and our welcome of Frank Sinatra himself drew even more vehement criticism. Revlon had been banned from the Arab countries for having had business dealings with Israel. Frank Sinatra had himself been personally blacklisted for his well-known support of Israel. Why did that matter? Frank Sinatra was helping our country, not harming it. If he had sung for Israel, fine. This time he would sing for Egypt. And so he did, until 1 A.M. on September 27, 1979, one night that was like one thousand. Floodlights played on the Pyramids, and Sinatra was superb. I was only sorry that Anwar could not attend with me and the children, though luckily Sinatra had met him earlier at our house. "He really is a great cat," Sinatra had said to the newspapers, using a jazz musician's expression neither Anwar nor I understood until the children explained it to us.

The gala was a great success, raising over $100,000 for the Wafa'. The next day Frank Sinatra came to the Wafa' itself, singing to the young boys and girls and the war veterans in their wheelchairs, who tried to sing along with him although they didn't know the songs. It was very moving to see them all so happy and excited, bringing tears to many eyes including my own. I was so proud that others were supporting our project, that the gala had brought so many foreigners to see our ancient monuments found nowhere else in the world, and to learn more about the Egyptian people.

I ignored the criticisms of the benefit. If the critics could have contributed that much money to the Wafa' I would have listened to them, but of course they couldn't. From the beginning I had decided to accept contributions for our charities from anyone who offered to help. If others saw a conflict, that was their problem.

"Mrs. Sadat, would you like me to raise money for your projects?" a Jewish friend had recently asked me when I was in the States.

"Of course. I would love it," I told her.

"I have one condition," she warned me. "If I'm going to raise money for the Wafa' wal Amal, then I'm also going to raise money for the Hadassah in Israel."

I had laughed. "What's wrong with that?" I said. "Help ten organizations in Israel if you like. I don't mind. If you are going to help us as well, that's wonderful."

But the oppositioners refused to recognize that peace meant more than just an end to war. "We must stop the Israeli invasion of Egypt!" declared the Unionist leftist party, burning paper Israeli flags and flying the black-and-white flag of the Palestinians in February 1980 on the day the first Israeli ambassador arrived in Egypt. The Socialist Labour Party reacted similarly, flying the Palestinian flag over its headquarters and printing it on a page of its newspaper. The Muslim Brothers, of course, had been making their attitude clear for months. Normalization of relations with Israel, said *The Call*, was "a cancer in Egypt's body" that would bring to Egypt ideas "contradictory to Islam and destructive to the Egyptian family."

Anwar refused to give in to these narrow attitudes. Only a month before normalization began he had quoted the Prophet in a speech to our Parliament: "Even if they place the sun in my right hand and the moon in my left to change my mind about this matter [of peace], I will not change it until God makes my message prevail or I die . . . " I supported my husband, staying as calm as possible in the face of so much opposition. Neither of us knew that the most severe test of Anwar's courage and principles was only a month away.

"Jehan, our situation is desperate," Farah phoned me from Panama in March of 1980. "My husband's cancer has spread to his spleen and if he does not have an operation immediately, he will die. But I cannot trust anyone here."

"Why, Farah, why?" I asked.

She sounded close to tears. "It is difficult to explain over the phone," she said, letting me know that her telephone was bugged. "But we must leave Panama immediately. There are ominous reports."

I knew right away what she was referring to, for I too had heard rumors that Panama might be bargaining with Khomeini to return the Shah to Iran and to certain death.

"But what about the Shah's operation, Farah?" I asked her.

"Oh, Jehan, I don't know what to do. I must get him out of this hospital." I knew exactly what Farah couldn't say, though I didn't want to believe it. Would Khomeini go as far as having the Shah killed on the operating table?

"Can you not get American doctors there to perform the operation?" I asked her.

"The government of Panama has refused them permission," she said, her voice breaking.

"Surely the U.S. government can intercede on your behalf," I said.

"The U.S. government?" Farah said bitterly. "We have had enough of their help to last a lifetime."

Tears came to my own eyes as I listened to her. Her voice, once so strong, was now strained, her former confidence broken. How cruel the last fourteen months had been for the Shah and Farah. From the time they had left Egypt they had gone from Morocco to the Bahamas to Mexico to the United States looking for sanctuary, but they had found none. The cruelest blow had come from their supposed ally, the United States, which had hurried the ailing Shah out of the country after militant students had stormed the U.S. Embassy in Teheran in November 1979 and taken fifty American hostages. "If the Shah is not returned to Iran, the hostages will be tried," Khomeini was threatening the Americans.

Anwar was disgusted by Khomeini's actions and attitudes. "Islam teaches love, brotherhood. It does not teach what this man is doing," he said to the foreign press. He was upset, too, by the sorry way the Shah was being treated. Mexico, which had accepted the Shah before his trip to America, refused to take him back. Finally the Shah and Farah had found temporary shelter in Panama. Now they had to move again. Quickly.

"You must come to Egypt immediately, Farah," I told her. "I will call you back with the arrangements." What more punishment could she take? Farah had lost her country. Now she might lose her husband as well. Even if I had not known the Shah personally, my reaction would have been the same. A man was lost, sick and surrounded by enemies. Not to help him would be inhuman. If we give this man shelter, God will never leave us, I thought to myself. This was not a matter of politics. It was a matter of principles.

I contacted Anwar at his office, telling him the gravity of the situation. "I have just told Farah that she and the Shah should come immediately to Egypt," I said. "Was I wrong?"

"There is no question, Jehan," he said. "Tell Farah I will send the presidential plane for them immediately."

"You are sure? You know there will be trouble," I said to him.

But he was sure. "It will please God," he said.

Farah could not believe it when I called her with the good news. "You will allow the American doctors to operate?" she asked disbelievingly. "You are sure?" She had been afraid for so long that she did not know whom to trust.

"Yes, Farah, yes," I said to her again and again. "We have many Egyptian specialists here to help you if you need them. But it is up to you."

In fact it would not be Anwar's plane that took Farah and the Shah out of Panama the next day, March 23. For political reasons, the United States insisted that a commercial airline bring the Shah to Egypt. They even pressured Anwar not to accept the Shah at all. "Do not take in someone who could jeopardize your own security," the American ambassador to Egypt advised my husband. But Anwar remained unmoved by the Americans' political pressure. Egypt made her own decisions. No one else. And my husband was not one who abandoned his brothers. In spite of Egypt's problems, he was telling the world, we had not lost our principles.

I was shocked when I joined Anwar at the airport to greet the Shah and the Shahbanu. The Shah walked down the steps of the plane with difficulty, so thin that his suit seemed two sizes too big for him. His face was deathly pale. If any man ever needed friends, it was he. Looking at him, I was struck again by the callousness of the Americans. Thank God my husband had the courage to treat the Shah with humanity, welcoming him to Egypt personally.

As the four of us flew together to Ma'adi Military Hospital in a helicopter, the Shah could not keep his tears from overflowing. "I have done nothing for you," he said to my husband, "yet you are the only one to accept me with dignity. The others whom I have helped have offered me no help in return. I cannot understand."

"Please, Your Majesty," I said to him, "my husband hasn't done anything for you that you wouldn't have done for him.

If we were in your shoes, wouldn't you treat us the same way?"

Later, Anwar would offer the Shah one of our most beautiful residences, Qubbah Palace, to live in with his family.

Four days after the Shah arrived, the American surgeon Michael Debakey arrived with seven other doctors, nurses and technicians to remove the Shah's spleen. Egyptian surgeons and specialists assisted the American team in the successful operation. I was relieved that the Shah's life had been saved. But I was sickened by the events that his arrival had set in motion.

Down with Sadat! Out with the Shah, the alcoholic, the dictator, the adulterer! On the campuses of Egypt's universities, the fanatic minority had been demonstrating steadily since the Shah's arrival. Anwar had expected some reaction, for the Muslim extremists admired greatly the Ayatollah Khomeini, but he had refused to compromise.

After taking the Shah to the hospital, Anwar had given a beautiful speech broadcast on television explaining his reasons for giving refuge to the Shah. The Egyptian people had responded with an outcry of support for my husband, fellaheen from the countryside offering to come into Cairo to stand guard over the Shah. The People's Assembly, by a vote of 384 to 8, had overwhelmingly approved my husband's decision to accept the former Iranian ruler. But the fanatics had not.

Rumors of terrorist actions caused armed guards to be stationed at the American University in Cairo, where the Shah's son Rida was a student. In Assiut, the center of Egyptian fundamentalism, trouble had already begun. As the Shah was being prepared for surgery in Cairo, more than two thousand people had gathered there to denounce my husband. Taking advantage of the unrest, the most devious fanatics had begun to preach against the Copts as well, turning the antigovernment demonstration into an anti-Christian one. The angry crowd then turned on the Copts, killing several. Riot police armed with tear gas had to be called in to stop the violence.

Was there no limit to the fanatics' inability to understand? Helping a brother in need, as my husband was helping the Shah, was a basic principle of Islam. "Show kindness unto your parents and kindred, to the orphans and the needy, to your near and distant neighbors," reads the Fourth Sura of the Quran. From the time of Jesus Christ, whose family fled to Egypt for a refuge, Egypt had always offered asylum to political refugees. Former President Salal of Yemen is living as a guest of the government in Cairo, as was the wife and family of Kwame Nkruma of Ghana. Former King Paul of Greece and King Zog of Albania had both lived as exiles in Egypt, as had the current presidents of Tunisia and Algeria, Habib Bourguiba and Houari Boumédiene. King Idris of Libya and King Sa'ud of Saudi Arabia had both been welcomed to Egypt after they were deposed. Anwar had even given Egyptian passports back to the family of King Farouk, and some of his relatives had returned to live in our country.

Yet now the fanatics were calling my husband a *kafir*, an infidel, for continuing this tradition of hospitality and support. How wrong they were. No one had a deeper faith than Anwar. He knew the Holy Book by heart, and every Ramadan he read it again three times, recording it once for our children. He slept with a Quran under his pillow, kept another on his bedside table, and had a verse from the Quran inscribed on the back of his watch. He missed none of the day's five prayers, prostrating himself so often that he had the mark of the devout on his forehead, the small circular bruise Egyptians call *el-zebiba*, "the raisin." On Fridays Anwar went without fail to a mosque, changing his place of worship often to hear different sheikhs give the *khutba*. Most importantly, Anwar lived his faith, abiding always by the principles of Islam.

The Islam of the fanatics was one of hate. Their attacks on the Copts in Assiut made me sick. They were using the Shah controversy to achieve what they had often sought by other means: the destruction of the harmony between Muslims and Christians. For over a year now I had heard rumors that members of the radical Islamic groups were harassing Copts in Minya and Assiut, the two Egyptian provinces with the highest percentage of Coptic inhabitants. In January of 1980, a group of fanatics calling themselves Jihad, Holy War, had bombed two churches in Alexandria. No Copts had been killed, and the members of the group had been arrested.

Reports of violence against the Christians began to pour into Cairo. In the same week as the demonstration in Assiut, several students had been wounded when Muslim and Coptic students clashed in a hostel in Alexandria. On March 30, the Coptic Patriarch Shenouda protested the incident by canceling all

Easter celebrations, including the traditional exchange of greet-
ings between him and my husband. On April 3, five thousand
Muslim students marched in demonstrations against both the
Shah and the Copts. And on April 8, two Copts were killed
and thirty-five wounded when they were attacked by Muslims
in Minia.

By May, rumors were running wild. "The religious fanatics
are kidnapping Christian girls and forcing them to marry Muslims," one Coptic friend in Cairo told me. "Churches are being
burned down all over the country," said another. Pamphlets
put out by the fundamentalist groups in Cairo claimed, completely falsely, that government forces had fired on the Muslims during the Minya incident. Coptic extremists were
exaggerating the rumors in an effort to force the government
to pass new laws protecting Christians. Muslim extremists
were exaggerating the rumors to turn people against the government. No one knew whom to believe.

A shocking event involving the United States was making
the situation even worse. Although Anwar knew that the fundamentalists would disapprove, he had agreed to let a U.S.
rescue team use our air base at Qena as the springboard in its
April attempt to save the American hostages in Iran. The mission was a disaster. The Americans were unused to the tricks
of the desert, and in a sandstorm one helicopter went down and
two planes crashed, killing eight men. I was stunned, we were
all stunned, that a military mission mounted by such an advanced country as America could end in such chaos. Now the
zealous followers of Khomeini in Egypt had new ammunition
to level against Anwar. He had to move quickly.

Within a month, Anwar hammered out a political solution
to our religious strife. He appointed a committee of Muslims
and Copts from the Parliament to investigate reports of religious tensions. And after considering the committee's findings,
Anwar took an evenhanded approach to the problem of sectar-
ianism. To reassure Egypt's six million Christians, he ordered
a clamp-down on all organizations spreading religious fanati-
cism, including the fundamentalist groups at the universities.
As a concession to the Muslim extremists, Anwar proposed a
change in the wording of Egypt's constitution. Our constitution said that Shari'a, Islamic law, was "a major source of
Egypt's legislation." Now Anwar suggested making Shari'a

"the major source of Egypt's legislation." This move was opposed by the most extreme Copts, but it was approved by 98 percent of the Egyptian voters in a referendum held in May 1980.

The government too supported Anwar wholeheartedly, so wholeheartedly that they refused to believe him when in the spring he announced his decision to step down as president in 1982, two years short of the end of his term in office. I was at the annual meeting of the Central Committee of the Nationalist Union Party, at which Anwar made the announcement. "For life! For life!" chanted the members of the party in response. "You must stay for life, Sadat!" All around me, the audience began to clap and join the chant. Anwar laughed at his party's insistence and enthusiasm, obviously pleased. But the momentum was growing. Shortly after the congress, a constitutional amendment was passed lifting the limit on the presidency to two terms. Now Anwar had the right to seek another six-year term, something he had no intention of doing.

"They don't believe you are going to resign," I warned Anwar. "You must really step down, not just say you are going to."

"Don't worry, Jehan," he told me. "As soon as we have regained all of Sinai, I will hand the government over to Mubarak. I know my time. I will not be like an old actor who stays on stage long after the audience is sick of him."

For now, my husband's constituents seemed very pleased. Appeased by Anwar's new attitude toward the Muslim fanatics, Pope Shenouda and his followers lifted the ban on Coptic celebrations. Even the constantly complaining fundamentalists could not hide their satisfaction with the new amendment to the constitution.

As the religious crisis eased, Anwar began to move against our economic one. He granted special bonuses to government employees and raised their wages by ten percent. He cut import duties, raised the Egyptian minimum wage by almost a third, and continued government subsidies on such staples as bread, gasoline, cooking oil, electricity and sugar. The gloom that had settled over the poorest and most dissatisfied began to lift. But nothing Anwar did could satisfy all of the factions in the increasing chaos of the Middle East.

"Another threat has come by mail," Anwar told me one day in June of 1980. "The Palestinians say they will kill or kidnap you if you appear at the women's conference in Copenhagen."

I was silent.

" I will not stop you from going, Jehan," Anwar continued. "But you have to decide if it is worth the risk."

"Well, Anwar," I said after a moment, "better to die that way than to die in bed."

There was no way I was going to miss the United Nations Conference for Women in July. I had learned too much at the first one, held five years before in Mexico City. Meeting with Prime Minister Bandaranaika of Sri Lanka, Nusrat Bhutto of Pakistan, and others working to improve the status of women in their countries, I had heard many things that helped me with my work in Egypt. I had refused to meet with Mrs. Rabin of Israel in Mexico City, but this year in Copenhagen the Israeli delegates and I would be able to talk as friends. It was the Palestinians this time who had declared themselves my enemies.

The airport was filled with security men when I landed with the other Egyptian delegates in Copenhagen. A Danish newspaper had published an article about the plan to kidnap me, and the Danish government was determined to avoid any catastrophes. Many bodyguards were stationed at our embassy where I was staying, and in front of the rooms I went to in the conference, the hospitals and the home for the aged that I visited, even the Tivoli Gardens. In the four days I spent in Denmark, I was alone only when I went to the restroom.

Since it was so difficult for the Palestinians to get at me physically, they chose other methods to attack me. Though they had no country, Palestinian women had been invited to the conference as "observers." I had met several of the women in the Palestinian group in Cairo years before, including the delegation's leader, Laila Khalid. Laila had seemed a nice, almost shy woman then, but that was before she took part in the hijacking of two American airliners. In Copenhagen now, she was very harsh, wearing camouflage battle fatigues. While I gave a press conference at which I discussed the Arabs' obligation to make peace with their neighbors, Laila was telling reporters that because Israel did not recognize Palestine, the only language that Israel had left for them was violence.

During my speech to the assembled delgates, Laila and her group became openly hostile. I had barely adjusted my microphone and begun to speak when half the Palestinian women stood up and noisily walked out of the conference hall. I continued to speak, ignoring their rudeness. But it was harder to ignore the Palestinians who stayed behind to heckle me. "Down, traitor!" one woman shouted at me in Arabic. "Your husband betrayed the Arabs!" I continued speaking as if I were the only one in the conference hall. "Traitor! Traitor! Sadat is a traitor!" other Palestinians began to shout, their voices so loud that it was almost impossible for me to continue. Pretend you are deaf, Jehan, I said to myself, the others in the hall do not know Arabic. But the shouting grew even louder. Only when the chairwoman of the conference signaled me to stop did I fall silent. But the Palestinians did not.

All I could think of was a line from Shakespeare. "When I open my mouth let no dogs bark," I quoted from *King Lear* into the microphone, speaking in English so that everyone could understand me. But I doubted that the Palestinians heard a word I said, for now they were fighting with the police who had come to quiet them. The meeting was disrupted again moments later, when the Iraqi and Iranian delegations stood up and walked out in sympathy with the Palestinians. The conference was dissolving into chaos. I finished my speech.

How disgraceful the attitude of these Arab women at the conference was. I thought we had come to Copenhagen to discuss our similarities, but they were dwelling only on our differences. It was any delegate's right to walk out of a speech she did not like. I had almost left the speech of an Iranian woman who claimed that Khomeini's new law requiring women to take the veil was an advancement for women because it saved them money on makeup and encouraged them to take a needed rest at home. But I would never have been as rude as the Palestinian delegation. It was shameful that these Arab women had had to be dragged from the room by the police while all the world watched.

Their behavior made me furious. I had always tried my hardest to be charitable toward the Palestinians, no matter how many times they threatened or attacked me, for I was in sympathy with their cause. But at times it was difficult. Once, for example, while I was on my way from Cairo to Alexandria on the Desert Road, I had come across an overturned car. The driver had fallen out onto the pavement and was covered in blood. A woman passenger was sitting next to him in shock, crying.

"Stop the car," I said to my driver, reaching for the first-aid kit I always kept in the car and rushing to help them.

"God bless you, sister Jehan! God bless you, my mother!" the wounded man cried out in a Palestinian accent when I wiped the blood from his face and washed the ugly wounds on his neck with antiseptic.

"Shhh. Don't worry. It is nothing," I said to calm him.

"God keep you, sister Jehan!" the man cried again, this time with even more emotion. Cleaning the blood away from his eyes and mouth, I could finally see his face clearly. It was Yasir Arafat's brother Fathi, a physician working in the Palestinians' Red Crescent in Heliopolis.

Quickly I turned to the passenger. Ena'am, Arafat's sister. For weeks the Palestinians and Yasir Arafat had been threatening to kill my husband, publicly condemning Anwar to death for making peace with Israel. Now these two were in front of me, needing my help. I decided to forget what lay between us and to remember only the human way of helping. "My bodyguard will take your brother to the hospital," I told Ena'am after I had calmed her and given her some smelling salts. "You will be fine, and your brother needs only a few stitches."

When they had gone, I called ahead to make sure that the doctors saw them promptly. I did not hear what happened after that, for neither Fathi nor Ena'am ever contacted me. It did not matter. All I cared about was that I had not let my politics deprive me of my humanity.

Maintain your dignity in times of hardship: this was the lesson God was teaching me constantly in 1980. As soon as I returned to Egypt from Denmark, I learned it again. Anwar had called me at the conference to tell me that the Shah was sick again. And when I went with Farah and her children to visit him, I knew that his time was near.

The Shah was thinner and paler now than I had ever seen him. He breathed only with the greatest difficulty. Yet there was nothing pathetic about him, nothing at all weak. On the contrary, you could tell even by the way he sat against the pillows on his bed that he was still a fighter. The doctors had said that he was in great pain from his cancer. But never did the Shah complain. God must have loved this man to give him the strength to bear hardships so gracefully, I thought as I stood by him in the intensive-care unit.

"Soon you will be better and we will spend a lovely time together in Alexandria," I said to the Shah. I looked at the tears in Farah's eyes. "Be brave. Don't show him your feelings," I said to her. "He is very intelligent and will understand."

Two days later, on July 26, 1980, the Shah was dead.

No state funeral was grander. Anwar organized it all himself, overseeing even the smallest details. Thousands of students from our military academy led the procession, all playing instruments and dressed in uniforms of white, yellow and black according to their rank. Next marched soldiers carrying wreaths of roses, irises, followed by officers mounted on horseback. Then came a squadron of men carrying the Shah's military decorations on black velvet pillows, preceding the coffin itself, which was wrapped in the Iranian flag and drawn by eight Arabian horses on a military caisson. We followed behind.

It was very, very hot that summer day in Cairo as we marched the three miles from the 'Abdin Palace to el-Rifa'i Mosque, where the Shah would be buried. The Shah's father too had been buried here before the Shah took his remains home to Iran. At Anwar's direction I marched with Farah, the first and only time I have ever marched in a funeral procession. "Do whatever Farah does," Anwar had told me. "We must help her get through this most sad and difficult day." And so I stayed beside her, marching with my children and her children.

Behind us for as far as we could see stretched the rest of those who honored the Shah's memory. All the ministers of the Egyptian government marched with us, as did former President Nixon of the United States, former King Constantine of Greece, ambassadors from the United States, West Germany, France, Australia and Israel, and countless Egyptian citizens. People lined the streets, the balconies and the rooftops to watch the procession pass. The music was louder than any they had ever heard. There were more flowers than anyone had ever imagined. It was the most spectacular funeral that any of us in Egypt had ever seen, and the last chance to show the world that the Shah deserved better than the way he had been treated. Egypt, at least, had not turned her back on a friend.

Four days after the Shah's death the next calamity struck, when
the Israeli Knesset declared Jerusalem the "united and indivis-
ible capital of Israel." It was bad enough that the Israelis had
broken the Camp David Accords by continuing to build their
settlements on the West Bank, bad enough that the deadline for
the Palestinian autonomy talks had passed two months before
with no progress. But it was a sacrilege for the Israelis to claim
the sacred city of Jerusalem as theirs alone. Jerusalem was the
home of 70,000 Muslims and was sacred to almost 800 million
more. If the Israelis wanted part of the city, they should have
left Jerusalem divided as it had been before the '67 war. This
move stunned us all.

In Saudi Arabia, the King called for jihad against the Zionists, as did all the other Arab leaders. Anwar could hardly contain his rage at Israel. "Whose side are they on?" he said to me
in anguish. "Instead of working with me, the Israelis are putting me in one corner after another. It is as if they have joined
with the Arabs to fight against Egypt and peace."

The Israelis would erode support for the peace process again
in 1981, when Israeli jets bombed the nuclear reactor in Iraq
only two days after a summit between Prime Minister Begin
and my husband in the Sinai. Begin had told Anwar nothing of
this move, but of course Anwar's opponents in Egypt assumed
that he had. Stunned by Israel's betrayal, my husband immediately summoned the Israeli ambassador to our house in Alexandria to protest this latest provocation. Never have I heard
Anwar so enraged, his anger so strong that his voice reached
me on the third floor. Then, as now, the newspapers and magazines put out by the Egyptian opposition parties would be
filled with anti-Israel editorials. For every step my husband was
taking for peace, the Israelis were taking two steps backward.

"We must liberate Jerusalem from the Zionists! We must
regain el-Aqsa Mosque, by force if necessary!" preached imams
in their Friday *khutba*s all over Egypt after the annexation of
Jerusalem. The *khutba*s given by fundamentalist sheikhs were
especially well attended. In mosques, in meeting halls, in university classrooms and auditoriums, the fundamentalists were
massing. And their campaigns were winning over more and
more of those disillusioned with the peace with Israel.

By fall, students were buying tapes of a fundamentalist
sheikh's sermons as if they were hit songs. So many mosques

aimed their loudspeakers at the campus that at prayer time the muezzins' cries drowned one another out. The fanatics never pounded on my classroom door to demand that the students stop studying to pray, but I could hear them up and down the hallways. And they were becoming increasingly militant and violent, one time bursting into an auditorium where students were rehearsing for a play and driving them off the stage with knives. I was horrified when the next day several of the students came to show me the ugly red gashes on their arms and legs. One boy, the head of the students' union, was wearing a cast. The fanatics had broken his arm.

At campuses outside Cairo the news was even worse. In Alexandria, men in galabiyyas and beards had stormed the office of the dean and threatened him with death unless he banned coeducation, Western music, and classes held during the times for prayer. "Kill me if you want to," the dean had told his assailants, "but I will not yield to your threats." After hours of negotiation the fanatics had given up their hostage, but only on the promise that boys and girls be seated on opposite sides of every classroom.

In Assiut, the fanatics had practically begun a revolution. "Show us your marriage license!" they were demanding of men and women they saw walking together in the streets. Bearded men with sticks started to beat the legs of girls whose skirts did not come to their ankles. Students in the radical Islamic groups had even joined forces with fundamentalists outside the university, destroying a television shop in town, scrawling the words "Sin Shop" across the windows of hair salons and camera stores, and ordering all businesses to close during the call to prayer. Night after night, the news reported some new horror the Assiut fanatics had committed.

Each morning in the fall of 1980, I read the opposition newspapers at dawn and told Anwar about them when I went to wake him. Anwar himself had long ago stopped reading the opposition press. "I know what they are going to say, so what is the point in reading their lies and exaggerations?" he told me. "When they use their freedom responsibly, then I will read." Though he was well aware of the danger from the fundamentalists, he still refused to move against them. "What is the use of democracy if I put everyone opposed to me in prison?" he said during one of our walks in the garden, torn between his beliefs and the mounting danger. "At the right time I will act and prove my way best, Jehan."

But what was his way? All through this difficult period, the more agitated I became, the calmer Anwar grew. As calm as he had been during the Corrective Revolution. As calm as he had been before our surprise assault in the '73 war. As calm as he had been before his trip to Jerusalem.

The danger of the civil war was mounting, calling for swift measure. But Anwar wanted to move democratically, step by step. Already there were signs of his new attempts to satisfy the fundamentalists. A station on the radio now broadcast the Quran nonstop. Television programs had been ordered to pause five times daily for the call to prayer. Classes in the Quran and the Hadith now were offered in the government schools, and £E250 million had been allocated to build new mosques in many of the poorest Cairo neighborhoods. But in every mosque in downtown Cairo, and on many street corners as well, bearded men with bullhorns were still asking for private donations.

Anwar began to spend more and more time at home, praying and meditating in the garden. I immersed myself totally in my work at the university. "Why do you work so hard for just a small salary?" my friends, my children, even Anwar asked me. "My job brings me great satisfaction. I love teaching," I answered them. "Remember that I will not be the wife of a President forever." Secretly, I cherished the thought of the day when Anwar would step down and take me on the vacation in the Black Forest he had promised. Only eleven months remained before the last phase of the return of the Sinai, and his retirement. With relief I welcomed the start of summer recess at the end of May. At least I would have a rest. But the violence continued.

Early June saw the worst clashes between Muslims and Copts in Egypt's history. Muslims had laid claim to land on which some Copts had planned to build a church. An ordinary quarrel between neighbors turned into an armed battle. The residents of Zawiya el Hamra' the neighborhood in which all this had taken place, were tense and polarized. The news made me tense, too. This time the trouble was not in Assiut. This time it was in Cairo.

Five days after this first incident, the Muslims and Christians of Zawiya el-Hamra' clashed again. The toll rose to ten killed and forty-five wounded, this time because a Coptic family allowed some dirty water to fall onto the balcony of a Muslim family living below. The two families fought first with words, then with bricks and guns, and passersby of both religions joined in. It seemed unreal, unbelievable. The religious extremists on both sides were worse than children. They let more than a thousand years of common history and goodwill dissolve in a few drops of dirty water.

Anwar was infuriated by the violence, as was I. We had lived among Copts in Cairo all our lives. Never had religion been a cause for violence or even disagreement. Copts were our neighbors and friends, in every way accepted. We joined with them for secular holidays like Sham el-Nessim, and on religious holidays we honored our differences. As children, yes, we had at times teased our Coptic schoolmates, eating our meat sandwiches in front of them during Lent when they were forbidden to eat anything with a soul. The Copts could have only *ful* or salad, for even cheese came from a cow, and eggs from a chicken. Still, we Muslim children thought they were lucky to be able to eat anything at all during their religious observance. And when we had fasted during Ramadan, our Coptic friends had teased us back, eating their lunchtime sandwiches and drinking fruit juices in front of us when we could eat or drink nothing at all.

Now the careless actions of the extremists were threatening an age-old trust. "Why are people wasting their energies fighting each other over such a nonissue?" Anwar stormed. "What difference does it make—Copt, Muslim? We are all Egyptians, Egyptians who should be spending our time celebrating together the return of the Sinai. We have more important things to do than worry about who is a Copt, who a Muslim."

But the tension did not abate. Police were stationed at the door of every Coptic church, and 113 people were arrested in connection with the incidents. In one village in Upper Egypt, undercover agents seized more than three thousand weapons, including an antiaircraft gun at the headquarters of an Islamic cell. The religious fever of a few was turning into an epidemic among the many.

Muslims started displaying Qurans on the dashboards of

their cars, and on their bumpers they stuck our testimony of faith: "There Is No God but God, and Muhammad Is His Messenger." Copts rolled up their sleeves to show the crosses some had had tatooed on their wrists at birth, and on their bumpers they stuck pictures of Shenouda, the Coptic Pope.

Even Pope Shenouda was acting recklessly, overstepping his role as a religious leader to preach politics. Other Coptic priests too seemed to be going out of their way to enflame the strife rather than calm it. "As the minority, you are in danger. Have as many children as you can, and keep a pistol in your home," they proclaimed, raising the Copts' tension further. Anwar was furious at the Coptic extremists, as furious as they were at him.

"Please, Jehan, do everything you can to reconcile the Pope and your husband," a message came in from one of my dear friends, a Copt. "The situation is getting dangerous." I tried to persuade Anwar to sit with Shenouda and talk reasonably with him, but he refused. At the same time, Mousa Sabri, the editor of the newspaper *el-Akhbar,* who was very close to Anwar and was himself a Copt, was trying to persuade Shenouda to make peace with my husband. But the Coptic Pope too refused. "It is impossible," Mousa Sabri said to me with regret. "Shenouda will not be flexible."

In the summer heat, the people's anger rose. In August, just before Anwar and I left to go to America for our first meeting with President Reagan and his wife, Nancy, it boiled over. A bomb killed some guests and wounded others at a Coptic wedding in Shubra, a mostly Christian neighborhood in Cairo. I was horrified at another of these senseless acts of terrorism. And Anwar was livid, vowing to punish all involved on our return.

In the meantime, the Copts punished us. I could not believe my eyes when, on the second day of our U.S. visit, I opened the *Washington Post.* "Coptic men have been burned alive," proclaimed a half-page "letter to President Sadat." "Children have been thrown off balconies. Christians have been forced to abandon the religion of their forefathers. The Christian religion has been attacked and ridiculed by the state-controlled media." The list of complaints, signed at the bottom by the Coptic Associations of America and Canada, seemed to go on forever. "Mr. President," it concluded, "you have often condemned state-sponsored fundamentalism as exemplified by Qadaffi and

Khomeini. *Why do you not put an end to this same madness in Egypt?"*

If the Copts had wanted to win sympathy with their exaggerations, they had succeeded only in making Anwar angrier. *"Kefaya!"* Anwar snorted after reading their advertisement, his face growing dark with rage. "Enough!" By the end of the day, however, his calm had returned. He was cheerful as he chatted with President Reagan over dinner at the White House. I too had a pleasant evening, enjoying very much my talk with Nancy Reagan about our children and our projects. But that night I got little sleep, being kept up by a headache that was even worse than usual.

What was going to happen in Egypt? What were we going to do? My worries only grew worse when Chancellor Kreisky of Austria called Anwar in Washington, advising him not to stop in Vienna on our way home as we had planned. Two Palestinians had been arrested at the airport carrying automatic weapons and hand grenades Kreisky said. For our own safety, the Austrian government was suggesting, we should go straight to Egypt.

Our enemies were everywhere. But was this really so unusual? We will be fine, I told myself, remembering how many times we had been threatened in the past. Safely back in Egypt, Anwar seemed calmer and more confident than ever. For the next few days he consulted his advisers, getting the latest information on the status of the Muslims and the Copts. He spent even more time at home, sitting alone on his balcony and walking in the garden. I knew this pattern well, and I did not disturb him. Anwar had listened carefully to the advice of others. now he would make a decision of his own.

On September 5, exactly one week after our return from America, Anwar moved boldly to restore order to Egypt: he ordered the police to detain in one night all those who might have had a tie to the recent religious violence. Fifteen hundred were taken into the custody of the state, including many fundamentalist sheikhs and a number of Coptic priests known for their extremist views. Hundreds of those belonging to the Muslim Brothers were held for questioning. Their magazine was banned, as were two radical Coptic publications. Even Pope Shenouda was restrained from making any further inflammatory political statements. Stripping him of his power and appointing a council of five to serve in his place, Anwar banished the Coptic Pope to Wadi el-Natroun, a Coptic monastery in the western desert.

The activities of the fundamentalist student groups too were curtailed, for Anwar outlawed galabiyyas and the *niqab,* the total covering of the whole body save for the eyes, on campus. Many of the professors were very relieved. Finally the universities could return to their role of educating the people. Anwar had taken well-known members of the opposition parties into custody and temporarily suspended publication of their newspapers.

What a crucial time for Egypt, a very dangerous time. For all those opposed to Anwar whom he had taken out of circulation, others had eluded arrest. One potential conspirator particularly worried him. Some weeks before, the Minister of the Interior had sent Anwar a tape of a transaction between an arms dealer and a man who said he needed to buy arms to kill Anwar el-Sadat. The man had been trailed to the home of one Abboud el-Zoumor, a military-intelligence officer. But when the police had moved to arrest el-Zoumor along with all the others on September 5, he had vanished. So concerned was Anwar about the potential danger from el-Zoumor that he even mentioned him in one of his speeches. "I know that there is one officer left at large and he must be watching me now," Anwar said. "I warn him that we shall catch him too."

My husband's ministers and the members of his party fully supported Anwar's move to finally detain the agitators. Nothing was more important than preventing any civil strife during the last phase of the return of the Sinai. In April, just seven months away now, the return of our land would be completed. I was counting the days, clinging to the moment when Anwar would step down as president. We had the rest of our lives to look forward to, to travel, to enjoy our family, even just to go shopping, without this terrible burden of responsibility. Seven months. What a short time to ask for. But what a terrible time.

The European press and the press in America were criticizing my husband sharply for holding so many political subversives, calling him a dictator rather than a supporter of democracy. Anwar was deeply hurt by their attacks. "Pay no attention," I tried to soothe him. "If they knew the situation better here, they would understand what you have done."

But still Anwar was troubled. "I need time. Time!" he said,

restlessly pacing up and down his bedroom. "Don't they understand that? Egypt is at the boiling point. I had no choice but to try to cool the situation by temporarily immobilizing those who would bring the country down. We must not upset the return of the Sinai. We must not!"

"You are right, Anwar, and the foreigners are wrong," I tried to calm him.

But he continued to feel bitterly betrayed. "There is nothing I would rather do than release all those I have had to hold," he said. "And soon I will, for most will soon come to their senses about what is best for our country. The religious extremists, I'm afraid, I can do nothing about. With them there is no point even arguing."

But the slander against Anwar from the West and Europe continued, along with the threat of one plot after another against him from within.

"Please Jehan, be very careful," he said to me each morning during September. "Restrict your activities for a few months until I feel the situation is controlled. There may be people who are upset by the detentions."

He doubled the numbers of my bodyguards and those surrounding Gamal, knowing how tempting a target our only son was. I, in turn, begged him to restrict his own activities. But he refused, instead exposing himself more and more to the people. In late September he visited the pilot farming projects at Salihiya and Nubariya and toured the new housing projects at el-Salaam City in an open car.

There was not a morning I said goodbye to him that I expected to see him alive that evening. "Please, Anwar. If you won't cancel your trips, at least drive in a closed car or wear a bulletproof vest," I pleaded with him.

Our children were just as anxious. "The majority of the people love you. We know that, Pappi," Loubna said to him one morning. "But it will take only one crazy man to kill you."

Anwar only became more resolute. One morning he showed me a letter he had received from the man who had hidden him from the British forty years before during one of his escapes from prison. The man, a truck driver whom Anwar hadn't seen since, was now inviting him to be his guest at the wedding of his daughter in Mansoura. Anwar was very touched by the invitation and the opportunity to repay such a great favor after so many years. "Why not send a gift instead?" I asked, hoping to dissuade him from making another perilous journey.

"You know sending a gift is not the same as being there, Jehan," Anwar said. And so Anwar accepted the invitation, making plans to travel in an open-balconied train and to stop briefly in the villages along the way and, after the wedding, tour the city in an open car.

"At least reduce the number of train stops," Husni Mubarak pleaded with him before he left. But Anwar refused to listen even to his own Vice-President, wanting to take his own poll about the people's reaction to the detentions. He returned safely from Mansoura, extremely happy that the people there seemed so supportive of his measures to combat civil strife.

But I was very worried. Increasingly, Anwar was refusing advice from anyone, spending more and more time alone. It was as if he were set on some sort of divine mission that no one could interrupt. He seemed distanced, not in the state of solitude he had always sought when he was making important decisions, but in a more spiritual way. He became more like the Sufis, relating to God in an intimate, loving and open way. He even looked like a Sufi, thin, very thin, from denying himself food and taking only soup now and boiled vegetables for his meals. He also began to talk repeatedly of death.

Three times in September he had told me he was going to meet God. "How interesting, Anwar," I teased him the first time while we walked together in the garden. "When did God tell you He was coming to meet you?" I teased him the second time as well, though I was getting upset. This was not the Sadat I knew, the realistic, tough Sadat who never lived in illusion. The third time, I said nothing at all.

"God has granted me more than I ever dreamed of," he told me during another walk at the beginning of October. "We have been victorious in war and victorious in peace. I have laid the foundations for democracy in Egypt and set out the landmarks of economic prosperity. What more could any man want? I have fulfilled my mission set out for me by God."

"Why do you think you have fulfilled your mission?" I argued. "God never reveals His secret to any human heart."

But his answer was ready. "I have never claimed to know the secret of the heavens, Jehan. But I do feel that my life, by God's grace, has made its contribution to destiny."

He began to talk about his burial place, his desire to be buried at the foot of Mount Sinai. But the more he talked about his premonitions, the more I talked about the life ahead we had both looked forward to.

"Where will you take me first? To the Black Forest in Germany or to Venice, where you can sing to me in a gondola?" I mused.

"Ah, Jehan," he said. And we kept walking.

I refused to give in to his intimations of mortality, refused to let him go. I was on this earth, and I wanted him to be, too. "Anwar, you are spoiling Gamal," I scolded him on October 2. "Why are you letting him go to America? You should tell him no."

Anwar smiled at me. "I want to do everything I can for him while I am still living," he said. "You will see he is not spoiled. When I pass away he will show you he is a true man and will carry his responsibilities."

"How can you promise me that?" I demanded. "You will be gone and I'll be left with him."

"You will see, Jehan," he said. "You will see."

On October 3, Gamal left for California. He hugged his father and me goodbye and went downstairs to get into the car, only to be told his flight would be delayed half an hour. He came back upstairs to pass the time sitting with his father.

"Pappi is acting very strangely," Gamal said to me when he prepared to leave again. "When I left him I said, '*La ilaha illa Allah*,' but he did not respond as usual '*wa Muhammad rasul Allah*.' He didn't say anything, Mummy. He just smiled and said, 'Don't stay long in the States, Gamal. Hurry back.' "

"What else did he say, Gamal?" I asked.

"He said, 'Take care of your mother,' " Gamal replied, his face worried. "He's never said that before. He's always just told me to take care of my sisters."

"That's just what you're going to do," I said to ease his worry. And off he went.

On October 5 I spent the morning working on my Ph.D. dissertation. As always I had not a moment to spare, and I envied Anwar sitting in the garden trying to read while Gamal's two-and-a-half-year-old daughter, Yasmin, crawled all over him. How peaceful and happy Anwar looked from my window. He was looking forward, I knew, to the military review the next day. In preparation, I had seen to it that his new uniform and his grand marshal's sash were ironed and had sent his boots to be polished. Except for Gamal, all our children and grandchildren would come to celebrate with us the eighth anniversary of our victory against Israel. There would be no threat from the members of the armed forces at the review. None. October 6 would be a holiday for all of us, a respite from the tension seething in Egypt. On this one day, there would not be a cloud in the sky.

Chapter 14

AP/WIDE WORLD PHOTOS

el-huzn bila nihayya

Sorrow Unending

ay turned into night, night into day. Mechanically I went through the formalities following Anwar's death, receiving condolences from my friends, from my colleagues at my charities and projects, from the members of government in Cairo and in Munufiyya, from the world leaders who had come to Anwar's funeral, including three former U.S. Presidents, the Prince of Wales and Israeli Prime Minister Menachem Begin.

"It is very sad, but I am glad my husband died on his feet and not on his knees," I told Begin, whose face was gray with shock and grief.

"I have lost not only a partner in the peace process, but also a friend," he said.

Hundreds of people came to pay their respects during the three days of visiting, while thousands of letters of sympathy began to arrive. The doctors gave me sedatives to rest, but sleep would not come. I kept thinking of something I had to tell Anwar, of something I wanted to share with him. But then I would remember. Anwar was gone.

Every day, at first, I slipped away from our house to visit his tomb, to feel close to him and to calm his soul. At least Anwar was in Paradise, I consoled myself. By dying so violently from an assassin's bullet, Anwar had become a martyr, and martyrs in our religion are welcomed directly into Paradise. By being taken so quickly by God, Anwar was twice blessed. Lesser men are often made to suffer, but God spares pain to those whom He loves the most.

But even though I had always known that my husband would be killed for his courage and his visions of peace, I was not prepared. My heart was broken.

"God bless you, Mrs. Sadat," said the people who, like me, stood in shock and sadness at my husband's tomb whenever I went, even late at night. Some were praying, some crying, some just staring in disbelief. "God be with you, Mrs. Sadat."

Our children were devastated. "If only I had been with him," agonized Gamal, who had always sat right behind his father at the sixth of October ceremonies. "I would have pushed him immediately to the ground and thrown my body over his."

"No, Gamal," I tried to soothe our son. "His life was not in your hands, but in God's. Nothing anyone could have done would have postponed his time."

But Gamal was inconsolable and for months afterward would remain in a deep depression, feeling he had failed his father.

Our youngest daughter, Nana, also suffered terribly. Every day for months she would visit her father's tomb, coming home each time with tears streaming down her cheeks. She could not let go of her grief, and I was afraid it was beginning to make her ill.

"Don't go every single day, Nana," I urged her gently. "Your father would not be pleased to see you so sad."

But she continued her vigil until we had to prevent her

for her own sake. Now, whenever I am home in Cairo, the children and I go once a week. And still Nana's tears come down.

A memorial service was held at the United Nations in New York. "His earthly frame, the cage, may no longer remain with us," spiritual master Sri Chinmoy prayed before the delegates and staff in the Dag Hammarskjold Auditorium. "But his heavenly soul, the bird, will remain with us here until it inundates the length and breadth of the world with peace, peace, peace." At a meeting of the Commonwealth of Nations in Melbourne, Australia, the leaders of forty-one countries observed a moment of silence as they opened their session, and they passed a declaration of sorrow which Malcolm Fraser, chairman of the Commonwealth, sent to me. "I regarded him as one of the world's great leaders," the Prime Minister of Australia added in a personal note at the end of the declaration. "We grieve with you."

Spiritual leaders around the world mourned Anwar, including Pope John Paul II, who himself had been shot and wounded just five months before, and His Holiness the Dalai Lama. "The unexpected tragic death of Mr. Sadat was a great loss to you as well as to millions of people including us in the world," wrote Tsering Dorjee, the Dalai Lama's representative in Europe. "He will remain in our memory as a great man of world peace."

Official messages of condolence came in from governments all over the world, as well as personal messages to me. President Gregorio Álvarez and his wife of the Republic of Uruguay sent their sympathy, as did the Prime Minister of Finland; François Mitterand, the President of the French Republic; Zia el-Haqq, the President of the Pakistan Republic, and Mrs. Haqq; President Kenneth Kaunda of Zambia; Helmut Schmidt, Chancellor of the Federal Republic of Germany, and his wife, Hannelore. "May Allah give you and the members of your family the strength and fortitude to bear this tragic loss. Amen," wrote Justice Abdus Sattar, Acting President of the People's Republic of Bangladesh. "We pray to God Almighty that his soul may rest in peace," cabled President and Mrs. Soeharto from the Republic of Indonesia.

Most moving letters came from our friends in the state of Israel. Yitzhak Navon, Israel's President, wrote:

Offira and I were deeply shocked by the heavy blow which has befallen you. Your late husband was not only an illustrious leader of international stature but also an extraordinary person. He combined in his being a warm, human heart and the mind of a great thinker. We admired and loved him at one and the same time . . . His memory will for ever serve as model for generations to come.

Aliza Begin also wrote to me from Jerusalem, regretting she had been unable to accompany her husband to the funeral.

Dear Madam, I was extremely proud of you when I watched you in your sorrow and pain. Your noble behavior is a measure of love for your husband. Life is composed of very few bright moments, the rest is an uphill struggle. Standing by your husband's side for so many years, you helped him realize his dreams. I feel close to you and your children because all of you showed me and my daughters so much friendship and warmth. Hasya and Lea join me in expressing our sympathy to you and all your children, their dear friends.

Letters poured in from America, from members of the U.S. Senate and the Cabinet. President and Mrs. Reagan sent me a photo album of our last visit to America, along with a special photo of Anwar which showed, their letter read, "his very soul." It was the second communication I had gotten from the Reagans in two days. Shortly after Anwar was shot and before the news of his death was released, I had received an urgent and very thoughtful message from Mrs. Reagan through the American ambassador in Cairo. Having experienced an assassination attempt on her husband just six months before, she had wanted me to know that she knew personally what I was going through and that she was praying for my husband's recovery.

What kindness so many showed. A month after Anwar died former President Richard Nixon would send me his personal copy of Churchill's *Great Contemporaries,* which he and I had discussed briefly after the funeral because it contained a quotation pertinent now to my family. " 'His children are his best memorial and their lives recount and revive his qualities,' " President Nixon wrote, citing the page on which I would find the quote. "Your children can be *very* proud of their heritage."

I received a lovely handwritten note from Jacqueline Kennedy Onassis, whose own husband had been cut down by an assassin.

President Sadat was one of the most visionary statesmen who has ever lived. His legend will grow through the ages. I count it as one of the greatest privileges of my life that my children and I were fortunate enough to meet him —and you, who added so immensely to his lustre. Knowing that your husband's loss changed the world, that his life changed history, is a proud and shining thing, but I think it makes your loss harder to bear. May you find solace in the closeness of your family. And may the feelings of all the world that grieves with you somehow have the power to help you heal, you who have inspired so greatly and who deserve so much.

The many friends we had made in Britain wrote to me, among them Prime Minister Margaret Thatcher, former Prime Minister James Callaghan, Lord and Lady Carrington and the Queen of England, who had entertained my whole family in 1979 at Buckingham Palace. "I was very shocked to hear the dreadful news about your husband," wired Queen Elizabeth. "Prince Philip and I send you and your family our heartfelt sympathy in your tragic loss."

Prince Charles, who had come to Cairo for my husband's funeral, wrote to me of his shock at the suddenness of Anwar's death. It had been just two months since Anwar and I had joined him and his lovely new wife, Diana, for a very happy dinner on the royal yacht *Britannia* when they put in to Cairo harbor at the end of their honeymoon. "One of my greatest regrets will be that we never have the opportunity to go with your husband, as he suggested, to some of the interesting, historic sites in Egypt," Prince Charles wrote to me from the British Embassy in Cairo. "But nevertheless, I shall always remember his warmth and humanity—qualities that seem to be all too rare amongst many of the world's leaders." Diana, he wrote, was "bitterly disappointed" that she could not accompany him to Cairo, but he enclosed a lovely handwritten note from her. "All my thoughts and prayers are with you and your family at this lonely and tragic time," wrote the Princess of

Wales. "I am desperately sorry not to be able to accompany Charles to Egypt and this is the only way I can think of as being near to you during your loss. This comes with deepest affection from your devoted Diana."

Often I had to fight back tears reading these letters. Fadila Ahmad Fu'ad, the daughter-in-law of King Farouk, wrote:

> I offer you and the rest of your kind family all my condolences upon the death of the beloved hero of Peace Muhammad Anwar el-Sadat, calling upon the Almighty Lord to move him to Paradise and to grant you patience and solace. I will never forget what I experienced as a mother, the humanity I understood the day I was allowed to set my son down on beloved Egyptian soil, the land of love, the land of peace, the land that this hero, martyr of peace and love, watered with his pure blood. Peace and the mercy and blessings of God be upon you.

I was touched as well by a beautiful cable from the Prince and Princess of Jedda in Saudi Arabia and by a lovely letter from King Hussein of Jordan. Though he had broken off Jordan's political relations with Egypt, he alone among the Arab leaders had the integrity to personally mourn the passing of his friend. Just as I had gone to Jordan to pay my heartfelt condolences to him after the tragic death of his wife Alia, now the King, in the true spirit of Islam, paid his condolences to me:

> I send to you, and my family shares with me, feelings of sadness at the passing of your husband, God rest his soul, into the company of his Lord whom we look to. We look to Him, praise be upon Him, to protect and care for you and your family. I and my family offer you the same human feelings and emotions you consoled me with personally the day the will of the Almighty was carried out and He chose to move close to Him one from my own family. Please accept from us our feelings of sorrow. We call upon the Almighty to grant you the strength and the power to bear His will and plan. To God we belong, and to Him we return.

The letter was signed "Your brother, Hussein."

I hoped that others among the Arab leaders would find it in

their hearts to honor Anwar, but they did not. Their wives and the women I had befriended in the Arab countries showed more compassion. Madame Wassila of Tunisia sent her sister Naila to pay condolences because for political reasons she couldn't come herself. Sheikha Fatima of Abu Dhabi sent a delegation to Cairo to pay their respects. A group of women came, too, from Qatar. The concern and courage of these women touched me deeply. The actions of many other Muslims did not, deepening my sorrow.

In Baghdad, people danced in the street with joy, as did flag-waving crowds in Libya after Radio Tripoli made their announcement of my husband's death. For a week the hateful Libyan propaganda continued, Qadaffi urging the people of Egypt to overthrow their new government and even to march on Cairo and dismember Anwar's body. In Iran, the Ayatollah Khomeini too called for the people to overthrow "the dead Pharaoh's successors" and to install an Islamic republic. In Lebanon, militant Palestinians celebrated, too, with dancing, singing and *sharbat,* the drink we reserve for our most joyous occasions. "We shake the hand that pulled the trigger," said one PLO commander.

I felt so sad as I watched the demonstrations of those misguided people. When the time comes for those who hurt us to die, my anger toward them will be finished. Rather than rejoicing, I will offer my condolences. That is the true message of Islam. But after Anwar's death some were so bitter that they betrayed their religion. How shameful their actions were, especially the disrespect shown by some Palestinians. No one had tried to do more for the Palestinians than had my husband. In all his negotiations with Israel, Anwar had remained firm in his demands for their right to autonomy and self-determination. Anwar had made the first courageous step toward solving our problems by making peace. Now he had been killed for it.

Martial law was declared in Egypt, no groups larger than five allowed to gather on the streets. Anwar's village of Mit Abul-Kum was cordoned off and travel there forbidden. Over a thousand religious fanatics were detained for questioning and their houses searched. Unbelievably, the police found not only huge caches of weapons, but a detailed plan for the takeover of the country. Why had our security forces not known this and acted sooner? In less than forty-eight hours the fever of violence spread to Assiut, where militant fundamentalists battled the police in two days of rioting which left sixty-six policemen and twenty-one religious fanatics dead.

Tension spread across the country, no one knowing whether a coup was under way or even who would lead it. Anwar's assassination was being claimed by a group called Jihad, the same terrorist cell that had bombed the churches in Alexandria in 1980. No one knew how many of them there were or how deeply they had infiltrated Egyptian society. In Cairo I did not know what to expect, did not know whether my children and I were in danger. Out of earshot of everyone, we went out into our garden in Giza to discuss in whispers whether to flee Egypt or to stay. All of us were of the same mind. Regardless of what danger we might be in, we agreed as one to stay in Egypt to honor Anwar.

As it became clear that my husband's death was the work of a few madmen and not a national conspiracy, business tentatively went back to normal. Unlike the chaos that had followed Nasser's death, the transition of the presidency from my husband to Mubarak went very smoothly, a testimony to the strong democratic institutions Anwar had established in Egypt. But the country was in shock. We had one of the lowest crime rates in the world. We were not used to killings and violence in Egypt. Only the fundamentalists, still a tiny minority of our population, considered violence as a legitimate means to their supposedly religious but actually political ends.

"Glory for Egypt! Attack!" one of the four assassins was reported to have shouted as he rushed toward the military reviewing stands, spraying gunfire. In the investigation that followed, their twenty-four-year-old leader, First Lieutenant Khaled Ahmed Shawki el-Islambouli, was found to have been acting under the orders of Colonel el-Zoumar, the intelligence officer whom Anwar had been warned about and who had eluded arrest in the September roundup of political and religious subversives.

I was disgusted as I watched the trial proceedings on television in December descend into chaos. Constantly the four assassins and their twenty accused accomplices shouted insults and interrupted the legal proceedings. As Chairman of the People's Council in Munufiyya I had allowed argument, even encouraged argument, but I had controlled it when it went too far. Now in the courtroom in Cairo the judge was doing nothing. I knew he had to be impartial, but he didn't have to be that weak. Unchecked, the conspirators shouted insults about Anwar and his whole regime. It was as if Sadat had committed the crime instead of they, as if Sadat had done the killing rather than been the one killed. It was not the assassins who were on trial, but Sadat.

Islambouli and the others showed no remorse or regret, bragging instead that they had fulfilled their sacred mission. It was God's plan, Islambouli claimed, to replace civil law with Islamic law, to undo the peace with Israel and, by killing Anwar, to avenge the September arrests of fundamentalist Muslim leaders and followers, among them his older brother, Muhammad. They seemed to be looking for congratulations, not punishment, for having killed my husband.

The chaos grew even worse in March when the assassins and Abd el-Salam Farag, the coordinator of the attack and the author of *The Hidden Imperative,* which advocated jihad against unpious leaders, were condemned to death, most of the others to prison terms. "Do not be sad, because I will be joining my God," Islambouli shouted to his heavily veiled wife and mother. "We are free and you are the prisoners." It was terrifying, really, to see such obsession. How could anyone defend oneself from such a cult whose suicidal followers shoot or bomb the innocent without even thinking of their own safety or escape? "O Jerusalem, Caliphate of Death, the Muslims are coming!" shouted another of the convicted when the sentences were handed down. "Begin will die at the hands of the Muslims!" shouted another, waving the Quran and a banner of the Star of David dripping blood. "Sadat was the biggest Zionist agent!"

Inflamed by the fundamentalists, the anti-Sadat fever spread. Now all those who had been opposed to Anwar banded together to destroy his image. "The Prophet's wives stayed in the sanctuary of their home, cleaning and cooking. The widow of our leader sent helicopters to bring her fresh vegetables and fruits," claimed one fundamentalist sheikh in his Friday *khutba.* Rumors were bannered in the opposition newspapers that after Anwar's funeral I had been stopped at the airport trying to flee with suitcases filled with gold, that I had stolen works of Egyptian art from a museum, that my teaching position at the university had been gained illegally, even that my children were not qualified to be students.

Every morning I woke up to headlines in the newspapers leveling some new charge at us which was 100 percent false. Anwar had owned twelve houses in Egypt, one rumor went, while I myself owned properties all over the world. How ridiculous. We didn't even own our home in Giza. The only property we owned was in Mit Abul-Kum. The presidential rest houses where Anwar stayed for security reasons when he visited the governorates were all owned by the government and now were to be used by Mubarak. "If they could produce just one deed to one property, one bit of proof, then I would believe them," I said to my friends. It was a terrible time for us. A terrible time.

No one knew whom to believe. Not even our new President. Shortly after Anwar died, Husni Mubarak called me to say that he wanted to treat me exactly the way my husband had treated Mrs. Nasser, by giving me a government pension to live on and housing for my family. But even he didn't know the facts. "Do you own your house in Giza?" he asked me.

I was in such terrible condition that I could not even laugh. "Even you, Mr. President, think this house belongs to me? Where would Anwar or I have gotten the money to buy this house? No. It's a rental."

"I just wanted to be sure," he said. And he deeded me the Giza house and the one in Alexandria for my lifetime as well as that of my children.

I was grateful, of course. But I was chilled when I hung up the phone. If a man as close to us as Mubarak did not know what we owned and what we didn't, what were the people who were much farther removed thinking?

"How did the Sadats grow so rich?" ran the new rumors in the newspapers, along with pictures of me and the children. "Just see how they are dressed." I felt both helpless and furious. I had always spent the barest amount of money on clothes, buying only three or four good dresses a year which then lasted me as long as ten years. The suits I bought for Anwar were, again, just a few good ones. And I made many of my own clothes as well as clothes for the children for Shamm el-Nessim and other holidays. At the university I was mercilessly teased by my students for my frugality—constantly turning off the lights in classrooms not being used, and teaching my own classes without any electric light at all. "Do you want us to be blind?" my students used to joke. "Daylight is free and electricity is not," I would reply. But after Anwar's death the false accusations went on and on.

The situation was impossible. If I started answering even one of these charges, I would never be able to stop. What was the use? I decided to let the people say whatever they wanted until they calmed down and could listen to reason. But finally I could remain silent no longer.

Two months after my husband died I was summoned to court by a member of Parliament in Alexandria who accused me of not depositing a contribution he had made years before to the SOS Village. Immediately I called the SOS, got the dated deposit receipt, and published it in the newspaper. The case was thrown out of court. I began to receive weekly court summonses from another man, a lawyer who claimed that I didn't have the credentials to be legally enrolled at the university. The president of the university answered him, publishing my marks and my degrees. But the court summonses continued, as if I and not Anwar's assassins should now be the one on trial. "Islambouli wants to hear your defense," the lawyer even said publicly. Islambouli? What was I supposed to say to him—that he was right to kill my husband? I refused to answer the summons.

Most of the lies I could ignore. But some hurt me deeply, especially new rumors concerning the Wafa' wal Amal. To discredit me as a woman, to show that whatever influence I had had was due only to my husband, two disabled veterans at the Wafa' circulated a petition among the Cabinet ministers and, of course, the newspapers, accusing me of providing the veterans with inferior food and cheating them by not giving them cars. Cars!

Day after day the newspapers carried their lies. "Please, Mummy, just resign from the Wafa'," my children begged me. "After all your efforts for the disabled, you do not deserve all this trouble." But I have never been one to walk away from a fight. "The Wafa' is not for these two only," I told my children and my friends too who were urging me to resign. "I am serving the majority of the disabled, and if two are displeased it does not mean that everything I have done is in vain." In my defense, sympathetic letters started pouring in to the news-papers from the other veterans the Wafa' was serving. And at a board meeting which I didn't attend but which all the other board of directors did, a vote was taken to expel the two trou-blemakers.

I was sick, sick for myself, for my children, for the honor of Anwar's name. I kept waiting for someone to put a stop to these unfounded attacks, but no one did. Perhaps such dissen-sion was a part of our new democracy. But I was suffering terribly. And so were my children, whose grief over their fa-ther's death was being compounded by these slurs against his name. "Do not be bitter. Be proud," I kept telling them. "Your father is being criticized because he was the first to bring de-mocracy to Egypt, the first to allow those who disagreed with him to speak out. Remember, too, what he has done for Egypt, bringing peace to our country. This is what he wanted. Let it pass. Your father is satisfied. Even his soul is satisfied."

Still my children remained bitter, not understanding why the papers and my husband's critics were allowed to speak so harshly against him. "If this is a democracy, then why didn't they criticize him just as severely when he was alive?" my children persisted. "*Inna allathee a'malu kabira, lahu a'da' kathira.* Whoever achieves great things has great numbers of enemies," I told them. "Those against him are lying, and they waited until he died and couldn't answer them back."

The slander in the newspapers went on for three years before it finally began to fade. But at least when Muhammad Heikal, the former editor of *el-Ahram,* published books recreating these lies, they were banned in Egypt for their disrespect. Still, much damage had been done. Some continued to think I was a wealthy woman when in fact all that I had was my pension from the government.

Gamal tried to help me from the moment his father died, having been charged by his father to look after me and his sisters. But he was only twenty-five and had just started work-ing as a petrochemical engineer for his brother-in-law. A few months after his father's death, Gamal came to me with an envelope.

"What is this?" I asked him.

"It is for you," he said.

"But where did it come from?" I pressed him.

Finally he confessed that it was his salary, which he had divided between me and his wife.

"Gamal, I have my pension. Keep this for your wife and daughter," I said to him.

But he refused. "It is my duty, Mummy," he said. "I must do what my father asked."

Gamal felt just as responsible for his sisters. After Anwar died, one of my husband's daughters from his first marriage was fired by the newspaper she was working for in America. Deciding to go to university, she asked her brother, as was her right, for the tuition money. Immediately Gamal went to the bank to borrow what it would take for her to complete her studies, and together with his brother-in-law Mahmoud Osman he paid for his sister's expenses. I felt sorry that he should carry such a burden. But Anwar had been right during our last walk in the garden. Gamal had become a responsible young man, of whom I was very proud.

As the months passed, I could not shed my own depression. I resigned as chairman of the Munufiyya People's Council, withdrew also from the university. I had no heart even for my charity work, visiting the Talla Cooperative only twice in the first year, the Wafa' wal Amal and the SOS Village only four or five times. I knew, of course, that Anwar's death was God's will, and that what happened to him was not only his fate but mine as well. But always nagging at me was the feeling of guilt that I could somehow have prevented his death, that at least I could have arranged quietly for more security for him. For a year I blamed everything and everyone, including myself.

I wore only black, and when the traditional period of mourning ended, after a year, I continued to wear black. Every morning when I opened my closet I saw nothing but black and felt nothing but black. I had no desire to put on colors, to wear jewelry or makeup. Some women can just snap their fingers and say that their period of mourning is finished. But I could not. Something inside of me had died.

My children grew very worried. "Mummy, you must lighten yourself," they begged, bringing me new blouses or skirts that were at least gray. But I was overtaken with sadness. I still rose at 6 A.M. and, after praying, read the newspapers, answered my mail and checked the daily menus with the cook, but for the rest of the day I would wander restlessly around the house, not having the energy to go out, not having the concentration to make good use of my time staying in. The scene of Anwar's death kept replaying itself in my mind. As in a nightmare, I wanted to escape from it, but I kept hearing the sound of jet planes flying overhead, the sound of the bullets, the screaming . . .

"Boom! Boom!" For months my grandchildren relived their terror in the reviewing stands, playing a morbid game they called "Parade." "Boom! Boom!" one of them would cry out, prompting the others to cover their heads and fall to the ground. Every time Gamal's two-and-a-half-year-old daughter Yasmin saw a picture of her grandfather, she would point her hand at it like a pistol. They missed their grandfather terribly, remembering how soft the expression on his face had become when he looked at them, how he had allowed them to climb all over him and play with his mustache. "I am going to tell my grandfather that you are being mean to me," four-year-old Laila, Loubna's daughter, told me once when I disciplined her. But then her face fell. "Where is he?" she asked. "Where can I find him? I need to speak to him."

Of all the grandchildren, six-year-old Sherif took Anwar's death the hardest. As the oldest, Sherif had been particularly close to his grandfather. It was Anwar who had taken Sherif to his first day at school, Anwar who had listened to Sherif's lessons when he came home. Now Sherif lost all interest in schoolwork, putting down his pencil in class and refusing to write anything at all. The other children, his teacher explained to us, kept talking to him about his grandfather, not letting him forget.

"You are lying to me," Sherif said to me one day in a rage. "You say that Geddo is in heaven, but my friends say he is buried in the ground. They saw it on television."

"They are right and I am right," I explained gently to the little boy. "Your grandfather's body is buried in the tomb, but his soul, which is more important, is with God in heaven."

When after a month Sherif refused to go to school altogether, claiming that all the other children were smarter than he was because they had grandfathers and he had none, we transferred him to another school.

Anwar's murderers were executed on April 15, 1982, a day which brought me even more pain. Instead of going to their deaths like the martyrs they had professed to be, suddenly they were not so sure they had pleased God. My heart filled with bitterness when an officer who attended the execution told me that one of the assassins had had to be carried to his execution and that Islambouli himself had repeatedly asked the sheikh there to hear his last words, "Was I right in what I did? Was I right?"

I was filled with disgust for them. I could understand such a crime being committed out of firm but misguided religious conviction, but to have my husband's murderers suddenly question their actions made it seem as if Anwar's death had been merely a prank. Belal, a muezzin close to the Prophet, had been tortured by the Quraish tribe to make him deny Islam and the Prophet, but Belal had never given up his faith. Nor had Joan of Arc, even as she stood in the flames of her own funeral pyre. These cowards had robbed me of my husband, my children of their father, my country of its leader. And none of their last minute doubts would bring him back.

A year after Anwar's death, I traveled abroad for the first time, going to America to accept from Nancy Reagan the Friendship Medal awarded posthumously to my husband, to England, where the Greater London Fund for the Blind named me "Woman of the Year," then on to Paris, where Patrick Wasjmann, editor of *Politique International,* named my husband "Personalité de l'Année." I was honored by the respect being paid to me and my husband, but I felt that half of me was missing. Back in Cairo, I resumed my studies at the university and began working toward my Ph.D. on the influence of English criticism on Egyptian Romantic critics between the two World Wars. I also started rereading my diaries and collecting papers and photographs in preparation for writing a book about my husband, about our life together, and about Egypt.

Many have said he was a man ahead of his time. But I do not agree. How can the idea of peace, of ending war, be ahead of its time? No. My husband represented the majority of opinion in Egypt. With the help of God, he lived his life as a mission, devoting himself and finally sacrificing himself for his country. Anwar lived his ideals every moment, never losing his vision. He liberated our land and brought peace to our country. He introduced the permanent constitution of 1971, establishing the supremacy of law, and laid the economic framework for prosperity. He abolished press censorship and gave our people freedoms they had never known before. "Freedom is the most beautiful, holy and precious fruit of our culture," he often said. That some abused these freedoms was inevitable. It takes time to learn the self-discipline of democracy.

Others have charged that I too was ahead of my time. But I do not agree with that either. Muslim women have just as much right as any other women to take an active role in society, to work side by side with each other and with men to better their lives and the lives of those around them. That I joined the fight to break through the traditional barriers that had kept Muslim women silent was my fate and God's will. I suffered for it, yes. But both Anwar and I knew and accepted that for any progress, for any change, there would be a price to pay. And, willingly, we paid it.

Looking back, I would not change a moment of my life. I only regret that Anwar did not live long enough so that we could have retired together. It would have seemed like Paradise to share together a peaceful atmosphere without responsibility, without pressure. Both of us had been looking forward so much to a new life, to watching our grandchildren grow up, to relaxing in our home in Mit Abul-Kum, where Anwar planned to write. "I am dreaming of the day when you will take me to Europe or to America without bodyguards, without protocol, to live a real life," I often said to him as the time for the return of the Sinai neared. "Don't worry. We'll go, Jehan," he would reply. But that was a dream that didn't happen.

I continue now to live my life as though he is still alive, not like some other widows who stay at home and cry, giving in to their loss. I work still for peace, to raise the standard of the poor, to train the disabled to care for themselves, to create a loving atmosphere for orphans, to fight for the rights of women. The real serenity we feel as individuals, I believe, comes in our efforts to help others. I like to think that Anwar is seeing what I am doing and is proud.

Never will I remarry, never even consider changing my name. All I ever wanted was to be Anwar's wife and to stand by his side. Yet I do not live in the past or in illusion. Anwar is gone and I must go on. I believe in today and tomorrow and I live today and tomorrow. Perfection is for God only, but as a human being I try to do as much as possible to be the best person I can while I am on this earth. And after death, I know I will meet my husband again.

Someday, Egyptians will recognize what Anwar did for our country and give him his rightful place in history. With patience, I wait. His papers have been collected, as have tape recordings of all his speeches and his correspondence with leaders all over the world. Someday, I am sure, a museum will be built to honor him.

At our home in Giza, I keep his personal belongings for this museum yet to be built. Sometimes I go to his bedroom and unlock the closet to look at the military uniform he was wearing on the last day of his life. I refused to have it cleaned or altered when I took it from the hospital. It hangs there with the bullet holes in the shoulder and in the brown leather belt, the right sleeve still slashed where the doctors gave the blood transfusions. On the closet shelf is Anwar's military hat, streaked with blood which may be not his, as he was not wearing it when he was shot.

In the closet also hangs the blood-drenched undershirt he was wearing, now turned stiff and brown. Even this I save for the day when Egypt will be ready to honor my husband, to recognize and respect not only what one man gave for his country, but what he gave for all of us.

Epilogue

he six years since my husband's death have been difficult ones for me. What was I going to do? How was I
going to support myself? As promised, the Egyptian government gave me a small pension, and I continued to lecture on
Arabic literature at Cairo University. But I felt increasingly
restless. One day in 1984, the president of the University of
South Carolina, Dr. James Holderman, came to visit me. I had
been given an honorary doctorate at that university in 1979 and
had become a friend of Dr. Holderman and his family. He had
even come to Egypt with his wife and daughter to pay condolences after my husband's death. Now, sitting in my living
room in Giza, Dr. Holderman suggested I make a change and
come teach in the United States. After talking to my children,
I decided to accept his advice. I have not regretted it.

I spent the winter of 1985 in Washington in a house gra-
ciously loaned to me by Sophie Engelhard. Once a week, I
commuted to the University of South Carolina where I lectured
on the status of women in developing nations; in Washington,

461

I put together a symposium for the American University, where I had been invited to be the Distinguished Professor in Residence for the spring semester. The symposium, entitled "Women in the Changing World," was a great success, due entirely to the participation of my dear friends Rosalynn Carter, Betty Ford, Jeane Kirkpatrick, Coretta King, Barbara Bush and Barbara Walters. Dr. Holderman had been right. I loved the change and the challenge of living and teaching in America. My students both in Washington and in South Carolina were open and frank, wanting to know even the smallest details of my life in Egypt. I'm sure I learned more from them than they did from me. And when I was asked to return in 1986 to lecture once more at the University of South Carolina and to be a visiting professor at Radford University in Radford, Virginia, as well, I readily accepted.

I was very, very busy during my first two winters in America, preparing for my lectures and flying back and forth not only between Virginia and South Carolina, but all over the country to deliver lectures on the status of women and on the need for world peace. I exhausted myself, but at first I was quite insecure. I had never had to support myself before, had in fact never even been paid a salary save for a small amount as the Chair of the Munufiyya Council which I had donated to the Talla Cooperative.

At the same time I was also preparing to take my doctorate in literary criticism at Cairo University. My presentation had to be perfect, for I knew that my work would be highly scrutinized by those in Egypt still opposed to me and, more specifically, to my husband. My heart raced when I entered the examination hall at the university in the summer of '86. To give me support and encouragement, friends had sent hundreds of flower arrangements to the university. I felt as if I were in a beautiful garden while the examining committee questioned me, at times severely, during my three-hour examination. Afterwards, my daughter Jehan objected to one of the professors about the harshness of his questions. "I had no choice," Dr. Ibrahim Abdel Rahman explained to her. "I did not want there to be the slightest suspicion in anyone's mind that your mother was being favored. She had to be more knowledgeable and more articulate than ordinary doctoral candidates to prove she had truly earned her degree." I was most gratified when my degree was awarded, with honors.

I divide my time now between Giza and Virginia, where I bought a small house in 1985 after discovering that the mortgage payments were almost the same as paying rent. I live very quietly, accompanied by one of two military aides who had served my husband. In the fall of '86, I took a leave from both universities to work on my book and found that after moving around the country so frenetically I was quite content to relax at home. I especially enjoy the luxury of watching my favorite programs on television: *The MacNeil-Lehrer Newshour,* the wonderful National Geographic nature films on Public Television, sports contests like tennis, ice skating or my new favorite, basketball. In Egypt, Anwar and I were great soccer fans, as was the rest of my family, and we tried to watch every game we could, though we had to act impartially in public. Now I can show my favoritism, and I root always for the local basketball team from Georgetown University.

My friends in Egypt and my new American friends ask me often if I am unhappy living so simply now after the more luxurious life I enjoyed as the wife of the President of Egypt. But I miss none of the pomp. Instead I am proud of my independence and my self-reliance. I take my exercise now mowing my lawn in the summer and, during this past winter, shoveling too much snow.

My neighbors in Virginia have been wonderful to me, inviting me to share in their traditions like Thanksgiving and Christmas and coming to my home in the afternoons to take a cup of tea and chat. When Noha, her husband Hassan and their four children visited me in June of '86 along with Gamal, Dina and their daughter Yasmin, the neighbors lent me cribs, playpens and bicycles and invited the older children to go on trips to the beach. Together we all went to the King's Dominion Theme Park and to visit the National Zoo, exciting visits that my grandchildren are still talking about. This June my daughter Loubna, her husband Abdel Khalek, and their two daughters will come to visit, as will Nana and Noha and their families.

The friends that Anwar and I made here during his presidency have remained loyal and extremely thoughtful, especially Nancy Reagan, whom I have visited several times at the White House. Henry Kissinger calls me often to see how I am doing, as does my dear friend Barbara Walters. David Rockefeller has been particularly gracious to my family, arranging for my son Gamal to enter the Chase Training Program at Chase Manhattan Bank in New York during this past winter. I have loved having my son and his family close to me in America; though they live in New York and I am in Virginia, we talk often and the airplane flight is only one hour instead of the ten hours that separates me from the rest of my family in Cairo. In March of '87, Gamal and Dina had their second daughter, whom they named Nur.

Still, it is not that easy for me to be so far from Egypt, and I am often homesick. I miss the tiniest things, even the sand. I have video cassettes of Egyptian plays which I watch often, and tapes of Um Kalthum which I listen to in the car. And there is always the telephone. My friends call me often from Egypt, and other friends keep in touch as well. Princess Fawzia, the Princess of Jedda, calls occasionally from Saudi Arabia, as does Sheikha Fatima from Abu Dhabi, and Farah Diba from her home in the States. At least once a week my daughters call from Cairo, but talking to them over the phone sometimes makes me feel even farther away. I want to see them, to hug my grandchildren, to make sure with my own eyes that everyone is all right. But that is not the way life has turned out for me.

I invite the new friends I meet here to visit me in Egypt, knowing they will be pleased. Egyptians are the most welcoming and friendly people in the world. Our ancient temples and wonders are the most beautiful. The sun shines on the Nile. "Welcome in Egypt," the people in the streets cry out to strangers. "Welcome in our home." Anyone considering a vacation in Egypt should not postpone it. We are a country of peace, the proudest legacy of my husband.

I return home to Egypt every summer and, when I can, for our religious holidays and feasts. And, of course, I return always on October 6 to honor my husband. I count the days until I can be in Egypt. Always I visit the Wafa' and the Talla Cooperative, though I have resigned as chairman of all my social organizations. I did not feel that it was fair or productive to stay on as chairperson when I was travelling so much.

The fight for women's rights continues in Egypt. In 1985 the Egyptian Supreme Court struck down the amendments we had won in the Personal Status Laws. The repeal of the laws was a great victory for the fundamentalists who had claimed all along that the laws protecting women in marriage and divorce were not in accord with Shar'ia. The women's groups, of course, hotly contested the abolition of the laws and demanded they be reintroduced into Parliament. We were all extremly gratified when, a few months after their repeal, the 1979 laws were once more passed by Parliament, having been scrutinized again by the courts and found to be consistent with Islamic law. Twice now we have won the battle on the Status Laws, but the opposition to women is still deep-seated. In the summer of '87, the election law proposed by my husband earmarking a number of seats in Parliament for women was overturned. The struggle never ends.

Writing this book has been very difficult for me, bringing back memories I wished to forget, bringing back moments of peace and happiness that I will never know again. I have many photos of my children and Anwar hanging on my walls in Virginia so that I can see them every day: all of us in Isma'iliyya just before Anwar left for Jerusalem; a photo of Anwar and me with the Carters at Camp David where we had a snowmobile race; Anwar and Yasmin in the garden the day before he died. I also have the last photo ever taken of Anwar, looking up at the sky and smiling during the air show at the military review on October 6, 1981. Seconds later he was dead.

Because of his strength and his confidence in me, I have been able to go on. After all the difficulties, with all that I have seen, I have remained strong. I have had to stand on my own feet and to start a new life without my husband. I have neither asked for nor received any favors. I am making my way alone and with dignity. I am very proud as an Egyptian woman to do this.

Index

Abu Bakr, 43
Abu Dhabi, 303, 348–52
Abu Dhabi Society for the
    Awakening of Women, 350
Abu Wafia, 216–17
Adawiyya, Rabi'a el-, 68
Afaf, Dr., 362–63
Agency for International
    Development, 320
Agrarian Reform Law, 134
Ahidjo, Mrs. Ahmadou, 323
Ahram, el-, 220, 231, 263, 369
'Aida (Jehan Sadat's cousin), 36, 110–
    111, 146
'Aid el-Adha (Feast of the Sacrifice),
    280–82
'Aid el-Saghir, 50
Air Force, Egyptian, 224–26, 291
Akhar, Abdel Akhar Muhammad
    Abdel, 356
Ahkbar, el-, 437
Alexander the Great, 174
Alexandria, Egypt, 55, 174, 209
Algeria, 295, 384
Ali, 43
Ali, Kamal Hassan, 234
Alia, Queen of Jordan, 323–25, 370
Álvarez, Gregorio, 446
Amer, Abdel Hakim, 115, 139, 211,
    218, 220, 225–26, 231
    insurrection mounted by, 239–41
    Liquidation Committee headed
    by, 211–13
Amer, Hussein Sirry, 126
American University (Cairo), 425
American University (Washington,
    D.C.), 462
Anaizi, Mrs., 332
Anglo-Egyptian Treaty of 1936, 79,
    120

Ansariyya, Nusiba Bint Ka'ab el-,
    261
Arab League, 176, 417
Arab Socialist Union, 253, 255, 265
Arafat, Ena'am, 431
Arafat, Fathi, 431
Arafat, Yasir, 243, 372, 385
Army, Egyptian, 79, 114, 211
    Sadat in, 79–80, 113–15
    Sadat supported by, 226
Asian-African Conference on Non-
    aligned Nations, 155
Assad, Hafez el-, 296, 373, 394
assassination trials, 451–52, 457–58
Assiut University, 24, 401, 409, 434
Aswan High Dam, 52, 242
    bilharzia and, 192
    foreign aid for, 155–56
Atherton, Alfred L., 19
Atrash, Farid el-, 81
Attasi, Nur el-Din, 218
Avneri, Uri, 395–96
'Awatif (Jehan Sadat's cousin), 58
Azhar, el-, 36–37
Aziz, Fawwaz ibn Abdel, Prince of
    Jedda, 344–45
'Aziza ("Zouzou") (Jehan Sadat's
    aunt), 36, 53, 58, 67–70, 146,
    193

Badawi, Ahmad, 296
Baghdad Conference (1979), 417
Baghdad Pact, 154
Bakr, 'Aisha Bint Abi, 67–68, 261
Bandaranaika, Sirimavo Ratwatte
    Dias, 429
Banna, Hassan el-, 64, 97, 98, 99
Barrein, Sitt el-, 78, 95, 125, 163
Baudouin I, King of the Belgians,
    30

Bedouins, 174–75
in Iran, 340
In 1967 War, 233
Begin, Aliza, 391, 404–5, 408, 447
Begin, Hasya, 405, 447
Begin, Menachem, 30, 401–6, 444–445
in Camp David peace talks, 388, 389, 393, 395
In Jerusalem peace talks, 372, 374, 382, 384
Belal (muezzin), 460
Beni Suef cooperative, 209
Bery, Siad el-, 30
Bhutto, Nusrat, 429
bilharzia, 191–92, 193
birth celebration, 146–47
birth control, 315–22
Bisar, Muhammad Abdel Rahman, 356, 359
Black Saturday, 121
Bou'hered, Gamila, 261
Boumédiene, Houari, 295, 426
Bourguiba, Habib Ben Ali, 338, 426
Bourguiba, Mme. Wassila, 380, 394, 451
Brezhnev, Leonid, 283–84
bukhur, 198
Bulgaria, 166
Bush, Barbara, 462

Cairo, 42, 46–47, 97, 98, 120–22, 316
Cairo Central Prison, 84–85
Cairo Opera House, 99
Cairo Radio, 228
Cairo Spring, 253
Cairo University, 144, 262, 308–9, 315–16, 400–401, 411–14, 434, 461
Cairo Women's Union, 334, 352
Call, The, 416, 422
Call of the Wild, The (London), 86
Camp David peace talks, 388–96
accords signed in, 189, 404–6
Arab reaction to, 31, 393–95, 407, 417–18
Carter's Middle East tour and, 401–6
Israeli violations of, 395–96, 433
negotiations in, 391–92
Sinai occupation and, 407
Canal Company, 156–57

Canal Zone, Suez, 120, 235, 242
cancer prevention project, 304–5
Carter, Jimmy, 24, 30, 388, 389, 391, 401–6, 409
Carter, Rosalynn, 30, 391, 401–4, 462
Centers of Power, 214
Chamoun, Camille, 154
Charles, Prince of Wales, 30, 448
China, 320
Chinmoy, Sri, 446
cholera, 191
Christians, 40–41
see also Coptic Christians
Churchill, Winston, 66, 91, 92–93, 447
City of the Dead, 170, 316
civil liberties, 252–53, 270–71, 418
class divisions, 97
Cleopatra, 174
Committee for the Liquidation of Feudalism, 211–18, 240, 252
Committee to Preserve Egyptian Antiquities, 304, 422
commodities subsidies, 369–70, 429
Commonwealth of Nations, 446
Communists, 122, 370, 418
Congress, U.S., 365
Constantine, King of Greece, 432
Constitution, Egyptian, 155
Coptic Christians, 18, 231, 260
fundamentalists and, 416, 425, 426–28, 436–38
Corrective Revolution, 270–71
Country Pioneers, 318
Cromer, Lord, 38
Czechoslovakia, 155, 166, 385

Dar el-Hilal publishing house, 100
Dayan, Moshe, 223, 294, 377, 382, 389, 391, 405, 406
dayas, 318
day-care centers, 315
Debakey, Michael, 425
Deeb, Emtethal el-, 362
defense spending, 368
detente, 283–84
Dhu el-Hijja, 273, 279
Diana, Princess of Wales, 448–49
divorce, 108–10, 353–54
birthrate and, 357
reformed laws on, 358, 365
Dorjee, Tsering, 446

Douglas, Lloyd, 86
Dulles, John Foster, 154–55

Eban, Abba, 381
economy:
   commodities subsidies in, 369–70, 428
   inequalities in, 97
   1967 War and, 231
   open door policy in, 300–301, 368
   after Palestine War, 96–97
   after Suez War, 166
Eden, Anthony, 154–55
education 135, 300, 301, 305–6, 412
Egyptian Women's Organization, 356
Egyptian Women's Union, 352–53
Eisenhower, Dwight D., 165
Elizabeth II, Queen of England, 448
Engelhard, Sophie, 461
Erfan, Dina, 386–88, 390–93
Erfan, Nicole, *see* Sheeha, Nicole
Eshkol, Levi, 218
evil eye, 146, 183, 196–98

Fahd, King of Saudi Arabia, 393
Fahmy, 'Affaf, 373–74
Fahmy, Isma'il, 373
Faisal, King of Saudi Arabia, 273, 295, 345, 352
family planning, 315–22
family structure, 411–12
Farag, Abd el-Salam, 452
Farah Diba, 30, 339–43, 352, 370, 389–90, 396–400, 422–24, 431–32
Farida, Queen of Egypt, 119
Farouk, King of Egypt, 35, 46, 65, 118–19, 155
   American protection for, 130
   Army officers and, 79
   in auto accident, 114
   cabinet of, 124, 126
   during Cairo riots, 121, 122
   in exile, 130–31
   fellaheen and, 97
   Muslim Brotherhood and, 99
   palaces of, 135–36
   Revolution against, 126, 128, 129–131
   as womanizer, 123–24, 136

Fatima, 196–97
Fatima, Sheikha of Abu Dhabi, 348–352, 450, 464
Fatimids, 36, 42–43, 129
Fawzi, Muhammad, 239, 252, 266
Fayek, Muhammad, 252
fedayeen, 120
fellaheen, 46–47
   land reform and, 134–35, 217
   poverty of, 97
feminists, 330
Ferengia, Iris, 352
feudalists, 211, 217
food shortages, 316
Ford, Betty, 462
Ford, Gerald, 30
foreign investors, 301, 368
France, 158, 160, 165, 365
Fraser, Malcolm, 446
Free Officers' Organization, 119, 122, 126, 128, 153, 286–87
Fu'ad, Fadila Ahmad, 449
Fuad, King of Egypt, 79, 121, 130
fundamentalists, 356–61, 364–66, 409, 413–14
   in anti-Shah protests, 425
   at Cairo University, 400–401, 411–414, 434
   Copts and, 416, 425, 426–28, 435–438
   Sadat's death and, 451–53
   Sadat's policies on, 415–16, 438–439
   sexual segregation demanded by, 414–15
   see also Muslim Brotherhood

Gabr, Mamdouh, 318
Ga'far, Nefisa Abdel, 215
Galloud, Muhammad, 336
Gamasi, Gen. Mohamed Abdul Ghani al-, 17
Gameiner Mr., 306–7
Gandi, Indira, 320, 377–78
Gaza, 116–18
Germany, East, 166, 385
Germany, West, 329–30
Ghali, Butros, 375
Ghali, Fuad Aziz, 293
Giscard d'Estaing, Valéry, 30
Gom'a, Sha'arawi, 252, 266
government employees, 45–46

Great Britain:
    anti-British sentiment and, 119–120
    arms sales refused by, 154–55
    Aswan High Dam project and, 155–56
    Baghdad Pact and, 154
    Egypt as protectorate of, 37–38, 46, 64–65, 69–70
    1951–1952 revolt against, 120–22
    Palestine policy of, 66
    Sadat imprisoned by, 73
    in Tri-Partite Aggression, 157–160, 165
Great Contemporaries (Churchill), 447
Greater London Fund for the Blind, 458
Greece, 382
Greeks, 128–29
Green Book (Qadaffi), 330
Gumhuriyya, el-, 139, 159, 183–84, 403
Gur, Mordechai, 377

Hadith, 63, 413
Hafez, Fawzi Abdel, 19, 32, 170, 258, 262, 263–65, 268, 369
Hagar (Mother of the Muslims), 277–278
Haidar Pasha, el-Farik Muhammad, 114
Hajj, 273, 279, 282
    see also hujjaj
Hakim, el-, 42–43
Haqq, Gad el-, 356
Haqq, Zia el-, 446
Haram, 274–75
Hatshepsut, Queen of Egypt, 256–257
hegab, 192
Heikal, Muhammad, 263, 265–66, 455
helba, 147
henna, 195
Herod, King, 28
Hidden Imperative, The (Farag), 452
Hikmat Abu Zeid, Dr., 259
Holderman, James, 461, 462
Hosny, Gawad, 244
House of Obedience Law, 354
housing shortage, 411–12
Howeidi, Amin, 252
Hudaybi, Hassan el-, 64

hujjaj, 278–82
Hungary, 166, 385
Hussein, 43–44, 400
Hussein, Aziza, 357
Hussein, Taha, 309
Hussein ibn Talal, King of Jordan, 154, 218, 286, 325, 407, 449
Hyksos, 128–29

Ibn Tulun Mosque, 304
Ibrahim, 275, 277, 280
Ibrahim Khayri Pasha, 142
Idris I, King of Libya, 426
Ihram, 273–74
illiteracy, 300, 328
Indonesia, 154
infitah policy, 18, 300–301, 368
inflation, 368
International Monetary Fund, 369
Iran, 339–43, 366, 389–90, 396–400
    Shah of, 295, 339–43, 385, 396–400, 423–27, 432–33
Iranian hostage crisis, 423, 427
Iran-Iraq War, 400
Iraq, 154, 190, 384, 433
Isaac, 277
Islambouli, Khaled Ahmed Sawki el-, 451, 452, 454
Islambouli, Muhammad el-, 452
Islamic Congress, 154
Islamic law, see Shari'a
Isma'il, 277
Isma'il, Khedive, 38, 167
Isma'ilis, 399
Israel, 66
    Iraqi reactor bombed by, 433
    Jerusalem claimed by, 433–34
    1955 attacks by, 154
    in 1967 War, 218–21, 223–25, 230
    in October War, 289, 291–98
    propaganda issued by, 219, 226–227
    in Tri-Partite Aggression of 1956, 157–60, 165
    UN Resolution 242 and, 243
    in War of Attrition, 241–43
    see also Camp David peace talks; Jerusalem visit
Italy, 303, 304
Izzat, Ali, 77
Izzat, Hassan, 69–77, 80, 82, 85–90, 109–11

Jerusalem, 433
Jerusalem visit, 367–86
 Arab reaction to, 372, 373, 382,
  384–86
 economic pressures and, 369–70
 Egyptian reaction to, 373–74,
  383
 Israeli reaction to, 378, 384
 Knesset address in, 380–83
Jerusalem Post, 378
Jews, 98, 165–66, 416
Jihad, 426, 451
Jihaz el-Sirri, 98
John Paul II, Pope, 446
Jordan, 66, 218, 230

Kaaba, 275–77
Kalamawi, Suheir el-, 309
Kamel, Muhammad Ibrahim, 389
Kamel, Saleh, 303
Karim, Abdel, 265
Katzir, Ephraim, 376
Kaunda, Kenneth, 446
Khadija, 67
Khaldun, Ibn el-, 36
Khalek, Abdel, 463
Khalek, Loubna Abdel, *see* Sadat,
  Loubna
Khalid, Laila, 429
Khalid Ibn Abdul Aziz, King of
  Saudi Arabia, 343–44, 348
Khalil, Mustafa, 375
Khan, Aga, 399
Khansa, el-, 67
Khatib, Ahmad el-, 394
Khomeini, Ayatollah Ruhollah, 390,
  400–401, 422–24, 425, 427,
  428, 450
Khrushchev, Nikita, 165
King, Coretta, 462
Kirkpatrick, Jeane, 30, 462
Kissinger, Henry, 297, 303, 463
Kosygin, Alexei, 218
Kreisky, Bruno, 438
Kuwait, 231
Kuwatli, Shukri el-, 165

landowners, 97, 134–35, 211, 217
land reform, 134–35, 211, 217
Lebanon, 304
L'Égyptienne, 68
Lesseps, Ferdinand de, 157
Lev, Bar, 381

Libya, 231, 286–88, 382, 384
 in October War, 295–96
 women in, 330–39
 see also Qadaffi, Col. Muammar
  el-
Look Around You, 321
Loutfi, Ibrahim, 418
Lys, Ruth, 297–98

Madi, Ekbal (first wife of Anwar
  Sadat), 83–85
Madinat el-Wafa' wal Amal, 302–4
Mahroussa, 130
majlis, 351–52
Malaysia, 154
Mansour, Anis, 21
Marakiz el-Quwwa, 214
 see also Committee for the
  Liquidation of Feudalism
Marawan, Ashraf, 267–68
Mare'i, Hassan, 20, 22, 31, 379
Mare'i, Jehan, 197, 379
Mare'i, Sayyid, 395
Mare'i, Sherif, 15, 341, 374–75, 459
Mare'i, Suad, 334
marriage, 101, 104–5, 194–96, 329
 see also Personal Status Laws
martial law, 450–51
masir, 150
Mecca, 59, 272–82
medical clinics, 135, 191, 192
Mehashi, Omar, 336
Meir, Golda, 197, 377–78, 396
 Arabs as viewed by, 219
 Palestinians dismissed by, 230
Mena House, 51
Menkar, Abu, *see* Nasser, Gamal
  Abdel
Mexico, 423, 424
middle class, 45–46, 47
midwives, 318
Milhan, Um Muslim el-, 261
misaharati, 49
Mit Abul-Kum village, 28, 310–13
 diseases in, 191–92
 financial cooperative in, 186
 housing in, 182–83
 sheikh in, 192–93
 superstititions and rituals in, 196–
  198
 trickery in, 194
 women in, 181, 182, 184–87
Mitterrand, François, 446

Mohammed Reza Shah Pahlavi,
295, 339–43, 385, 396–400, 422–
427, 431–32
Moses, 28, 51
Muallaqa Church, 304
Mubarak, Lt.-Gen. Muhammad
Husni:
in October War, 294
as President, 451, 453
Sadat's death and, 17, 19–23, 25,
27, 29–30, 31
as Vice-President, 441
Mubarak, Suzanne, 17
mughat, 147
Muhammad Ali (boxer), 275
Muhammad Ali (Egyptian ruler),
34, 36, 65, 119
Muhammad V, King, 154
Muhammad the Prophet, 43, 59–60,
62
Muhi el-Din, Fuad, 26
mulid celebrations, 43–44
Munufiyya cooperative, 209
Munufiyya People's Council, 310–
315
Munufiyya University, 314
Muslim Brotherhood, 63–64, 66
anti-Jewish sentiment in, 416
arms held by, 98
Committee for the Liquidation of
Feudalism and, 211–12
Nasser assassination attempt and,
148
after Palestine War, 97–98
Revolutionary Command Council
and, 144
social services provided by, 63,
412–13
violence used by, 98–100
Muslims, *see* Shiite Muslims; Sunni
Muslims
Muslim Sisters, 63

Nabarawi, Siza, 68
Naguib, Muhammad, 130, 136–38,
155
Nahhas Pasha, Mustafa el-, 119,
120
Naieri, Abbas, 397
Najjar, Su'ad el-, 311–12
Narayan, 177
Nariman, Queen of Egypt, 130

Nasser, Gamal Abdel, 56, 79, 152–
153, 418
Amer's attempted insurrection
against, 239–41
Anwar Sadat's relationship with,
152–53, 156, 168, 177, 252
armaments purchased by, 154–55
arrests under, 153
assassination attempt against, 148
Cabinet under, 252
death of, 244–50
in Free Officers' Organization,
119
illness of, 178, 179, 241–42
Naguib and, 136–37
nationalization under, 166
in 1967 War, 218–21, 228–31
nonaligned status announced by,
155
in Palestine War, 118
popular style of, 153–54
purge under, 211, 214, 217
on Revolutionary Command
Council, 139
in Revolution of 1952, 126
Suez Canal nationalized by, 156–
157
Tri-Partite Aggression and, 157–
161, 165, 166
United Arab Republic founded
by, 167–68
War of Attrition and, 241–43
Nasser, Khalid, 247
Nasser, Mona, 394
Nasser, Tahia, 152, 168, 249, 256,
257, 258
Nasser Bank of Egypt, 418
Nassif, el-Leithy, 266–67, 268, 270,
271
National Assembly, Egyptian, 173
Nationalist Union Party, 422, 428
nationalization, 166–67
Navon, Yitzhak, 447–48
Nimr, Muhammad Abdel Mun'em
el-, 356, 359
1967 War:
blame for defeat in, 231
casualties in, 230, 232–34, 236–37
Egyptian Air Force destroyed in,
225–26
Israeli propaganda in, 219, 226–
227
social consequences of, 231–32

territories occupied in, 230, 243
War of Attrition after, 241–43
Nixon, Richard, 30, 243, 253, 283, 432, 447
Nkruma, Kwame, 426
Nobel Peace Prize, 189, 393, 395
Nukrashi Pasha, 98, 99
Numeiry, Bouthaina, el-, 30, 352
Numeiry, Gaafar el-, 30, 31, 399
Nyerere, Mrs. Julius, 323

October, 21
October War:
  casualties in, 297
  cease-fire in, 296–97
  Egypt's position of strength in, 294–95
  oil embargo in, 295
  preparations for, 288–91
  Qadaffi, in, 295–96
  soldiers' attitudes in, 292–93
  Suez Canal crossed in, 291–92
  U.S. in, 295, 296–97
oil embargo, 295
Oman, 31, 304
Onassis, Jacqueline Kennedy, 448
open door policy, 18, 300–301, 368
Operation Badr, 291–93
orphans, 94, 306–8
Osman, Amin, 72, 74
Osman, Mahmoud, 456
Osman, Osman Ahmad, 179
Ottomans, 129

Pahlavi, Shah Reza, *see* Iran, Shah of
Pahlavi, Rida, 496
Pakistan, 154
Palestine, 66
Palestine Liberation Organization (PLO), 218, 219, 243, 372, 384
Palestine War (1948), 66, 96, 116, 118, 154, 165
Palestinians, 176, 407, 451
  in Gaza refugee camps, 116–118
  Jerusalem peace talks rejected by, 372, 382, 385
  Nasser and, 243
  in 1967 War, 230
  at UN Womens' Conference, 429–431
Panama, 422, 423, 424
Paris Group, 320
Parliament, Egyptian, 363–65, 372

peace talks, *see* Camp David peace talks, Jerusalem visit
pension program, 321–22
People's Court, 148
Persians, 128–29, 132
Personal Status Laws, 352–66, 464–465
  committee for reform of, 356–360
  divorce under, 353–54, 357
  fundamentalists and, 356–61, 364–366, 464
  polygamy under, 354–56
Poland, 385
political prisoners, 262, 270
Politique International, 458
polygamy, 329, 354–56, 360–61
population growth, 97, 315–22
Port Sa'id, 55
poverty, 97, 300, 311
prayers, 59–62
Presidential Guard, 19, 25–26, 266
press, freedom of, 97

Qadaffi, Col. Muammar el-, 243–244, 249, 382, 409, 450
  Camp David peace talks rejected by, 394–95, 407
  Egyptian/Libyan union proposed by, 286
  Nasser and, 243–44, 249
  in October War, 295–96
  women as viewed by, 330–39
Qadaffi, Fathiyya, 244
Qadaffi, Hanah, 333
Qadaffi, Safiyya el-, 331–32, 333, 334, 335, 337
Qatar, 303, 450
qollah, 146
Qubbah Palace, 136, 425
Queen Elizabeth II, 287
Quran, 58–59, 61, 62–63, 259–60, 327–29, 353, 358

Rabin, Leah, 408, 429
Radford University, 462
Radio Cairo, 153
Radio Damascus, 373
Radio Jordan, 218
Rahman, Ibrahim Abdel, 462
Ramadan celebration, 47–50
Raouf, Abdel Mun'em, 148
Raouf, Ali, 35, 53

Raouf, 'Aziza ("Zouzou"), *see*
'Aziza
Raouf, Fatima ("Batta"), *see* Zaid,
Fatima Abu
Raouf, Gladys Charles Cotrell, 34,
35, 37–43, 51, 66–67, 103, 164,
166
Jehan's marriage plans considered
by, 88–94
Raouf, Magdi, 35, 53
Raouf, Mustafa, 36, 58
Raouf, Nini, 58
Raouf, Safwat, 35, 37–43, 51, 66, 76–
77, 111–12
Anwar Sadat's relationship with,
102–3
death of, 170–71
Jehan's marriage plans considered
by, 88–90
during Revolution of 1952, 128,
131
Rashad, Yussef, 113–14, 122–23
Rateb, 'Aisha el-, 315, 356, 360, 364–
65
Reagan, Nancy, 437, 438, 447, 458,
463
Reagan, Ronald, 437, 438, 447
Red Crescent, 222, 224, 234–35,
291, 301
rehabilitation centers, 302–4
Revlon, 420, 421
Revolutionary Command Council,
79, 133, 134, 136, 137, 144
Revolution of 1952:
agrarian reform in, 134–35, 211,
217
armaments and, 154
coup in, 126–32
egalitarian message of, 139–40
patronage system and, 141
purge in, 211–18
royal palaces confiscated in, 135–
136
second phase of, 155
social reforms in, 135
Riad, Muhammad, 375
Rockefeller, David, 463
Roda Island, 35, 36–37
Rogers, William, 243
Rogers Plan, 243, 254
Romans, 128–29
Rommel, Erwin, 73, 91
Royal Guard, 130

Royal Intelligence Service, 122
Royal Military Academy, 79
Ruelle, Ambassador, 20
Rumania, 166
rural cooperatives, 135
rural migrations, 316

Sabah, 390
Sabour, Salah Abdul, 175
Sabri, Ali, 252, 263
Sabri, Mousa, 437
Sa'dani, Mahmoud el-, 265
Sadat, Amina, 95
Sadat, Anwar el-:
in Army, 79–80, 113–15
birth control programs and, 316–
317, 319–21
Cabinet under, 252, 263–70
in Camp David peace talks, 388–
396, 401–6
celebrities and, 419–22
childhood of, 78–79
in construction job, 109, 110–11
Coptic/Muslim violence and, 435–
439
Corrective Revolution under, 270–
271
coup attempt against, 253–56, 262–
271
courtship of, 82–83, 85–94
death of, 13–33
death premonitions of, 441–42
democratic freedoms under, 252–
253, 270–71, 418
economic policies of, 300–301
engagement party for, 94–96
family of, 95
first marriage of, 80, 83–85
in Free Officers' Organization,
119
fundamentalists and, 415–16, 435–
439
as heart attack victim, 178–80
infitah policy of, 18, 300–301,
368
Islamic Congress headed by, 154
Jehan's marriage to, 100–107
in Jerusalem peace talks, 367–88
Mit Abul-Kum village and, 188–
189
Naguib and, 137–38
Nasser's relationship with, 152–
153, 156, 168, 177, 252

as National Assembly speaker,
173–74
newspaper founded by, 139
in 1967 War, 218, 221, 223, 224,
232–34, 238–39
in October War, 288–98
in Osman assassination trial, 72–
74
peace initiative announced by, 253–
254
political subversives held by, 439–
441
presidency assumed by, 250–56
in prison, 73, 81–86
Qadaffi and, 286–88
as religious man, 426–27
resignation offered by, 428–29
in Revolution of 1952, 126–32
Sadat, Ekbal, *see* Madi, Ekbal
Shah of Iran and, 339–43, 385,
397–400, 423–27, 432–33
Soviet relations under, 250, 252–
253, 254, 262–63, 283–86, 289,
384–85
threats against, 148–51
as Vice President, 242
women's rights and, 364–66
Year of Decision proclaimed by,
282–83
Sadat, 'Atif, 293–94
Sadat, Camelia, 172
Sadat, Dina, *see* Erfan, Dina
Sadat, Esmat, 95
Sadat Gamal, 383, 406, 440, 442–43,
445, 463–64
in 'Aid celebration, 281
Anwar Sadat's death and, 14, 20,
23–28, 31, 32, 446, 455–56
birth of, 163–65
childhood of, 15, 169, 170, 173
in engineering school, 142
injury of, 207–8
during insurrection, 269–70
marriage of, 386–88, 390–93
Sadat, Jehan el-:
in Abu Dhabi, 348–52
African and Arab women's
conference convened by, 323–
324
during assassination attack, 13–33
birth control programs promoted
by, 315–22
British background of, 39–42

cancer prevention project
launched by, 304–5
charitable organizations headed
by, 301
childhood of, 34–37, 39–42, 47–
57
childrearing practices of, 169–73
condolence messages to, 446–50
corruption accusations against,
418–19, 452–56
courtship of, 82–83, 85–94
daily schedule of, 322
day-care centers expanded by, 315
degrees completed by, 308–9, 462
as doctoral candidate, 462
early married life of, 108–18
early political interests of, 64–69
engagement party for, 94–96
financial hardship and, 111–13
First Lady role changed by, 256–
262
fundamentalist opposition to, 356–
361, 364–66, 412–15
Gamal born to, 161–65
government wives' meetings
organized by, 175–77
in Iran, 339–43
Loubna born to, 144–48
marriage of, 100–107
marriage prospects for, 77–78
in Mecca, 272–82
in mourning, 444–60
in Munufiyya People's Council,
310–15
Muslim Brotherhood and, 63–64
Nasserists and, 256–59, 262
Nasser's relationship with, 152,
243–44
1967 War work by, 221–23, 224,
232–39
Noha born to, 168
in October War work, 291–94
in Personal Status Laws reform,
352–59, 364–66
petitioners and, 141–44
preservation projects initiated by,
304
prisoners' petitions to, 262
Qadaffi and, 330–39
rehabilitation center established
by, 302–4
religious instruction for, 58–63
as returning student, 139

Sadat, Jehan el- (*cont.*)
  in Saudi Arabia, 343–48
  in secondary school, 57
  social position of, 140–44
  SOS Villages established by, 306–308
  staff of, 302
  student housing project initiated by, 305–6
  Talla cooperative founded by, 201–209
  at UN Conferences, 327, 408, 429–431
  as university lecturer, 461–62
  Virginia home of, 463–64
  in Zagazig, 108–10
Sadat, Jehan ("Nana"), 168, 173, 181, 227, 245, 337–38, 370–71, 408–9, 445–46, 462, 463
Sadat, Jehan Talaat, 419
Sadat, Loubna, 144–48, 167, 225, 440, 463
  childhood of, 172
  during insurrection, 268–69, 270
  during Suez War, 159–60
Sadat, Muhammad, 78, 95
Sadat, Noha, 168, 266, 371, 379, 463
Sadat, Nur, 464
Sadat, Rawia, 172
Sadat, Rokaya, 172
Sadat, Talaat, 31, 419
Sadat, Yasmin, 15, 16, 442, 457, 463
Sadat, Zainab Esmat, 95
Sadat Pension, 321–22
Safer, Morley, 319
Saghira, Nagat el-, 246–47
Sa'id, Ahmad, 228
Sa'id, Amina el-, 175–76, 335, 357, 360, 361, 365, 415
Sa'id, Karima el-, 356
Salal, Marshal Abdullah as-, 426
Salem, Gamal, 130
Sattar, Abdus, 446
Sa'ud, King of Saudi Arabia, 426
Sa'ud, Muhammad Ibn el-, 345–46
Saudi Arabia, 154, 328–29, 344–48
Savak, 389–90, 399
Schmidt, Hannelore, 446
Schmidt, Helmut, 30, 446
Seba'i, Yusif el-, 385
sebu'a, 146
Seda, Hassan Abu, 20–21

Sekou-Toure, Ahmed, 323
sequestration decrees, 252
Sha'arawi, Huda, 68–69, 176, 339
Shaf'ei, Magda el-, 327
Shamm el-Nessim celebration, 50–51
Sharaf, Sami, 252, 258–59, 267
Shari'a, 327–28, 427–28
Sharon, Ariel, 377, 405
Sheeha, Nicole, 387
sheikhs and sheikhas, 192–93
Shenouda, Patriarch, 426–27, 428, 437–438, 439
Shepheard's Hotel, 121
Shiite Muslims, 43–44, 399, 400
Shirin, Isma'il, 124, 126
Shukeiri, Ahmad el-, 219
siga, 117
Sinatra, Frank, 420–21
Six Day War, *see* 1967 War
60 Minutes, 319–20
Sobky, Zeinab el-, 16, 20
Social Affairs, Ministry of, 209, 302, 306–7, 315
Socialist Labour Party, 422
Society for Social Development, 208–209
Soeharto, General, 446
Somalia, 30, 31
SOS Villages, 306–8
Soubky, Zenaib el-, 335
Soursuk, Gladys, 215–16
South Carolina, University of, 461–462
Soviet Union, 155, 165
  Anwar Sadat and, 250, 252–53, 254, 262–63, 283–86, 289, 384–385
  Aswan High Dam funding from, 156
  expulsion of, 283–86
  1967 War and, 223
Spain, 382
State Department, U.S., 223
Sudan, 30, 31, 363
Suez Canal, 29, 38, 155
  nationalization of, 156–57
  in October War, 291–92, 297
Suez Canal Zone, 120, 235, 242
Suez War, *see* Tri-Partite Aggression
Sufis, 44, 442
Sunni Muslims, 43–44, 400–401
Supreme Court, Egyptian, 466–67

Supreme Family Planning Council, 301, 317–21
Syria, 66, 373, 382, 393–94
    Egypt's union with, 167–68
    in 1967 War, 218–20, 230
    in October War, 294

Talla cooperative, 201–9, 313, 352
Tarabulsi, I'timad el-, 216
Tawfiq, Khedive, 79
Taylor, Elizabeth, 419–20
Thant, U, 220
Thatcher, Margaret, 448
Time, 384
titles, Turkish, 135, 142
Tito, Marshal (Josip Broz), 295, 369–370
Tito, Mrs., 344
Traore, Mrs. Moussa, 323
Tri-Partite Aggression, 157–61, 165–166
Tunisia, 329
Turkey, 154

ulema, 327, 353
Um Kalthum, 56–57, 81, 153, 221, 464
Um Muammar, 332–33
Um Muhammad, 78, 187–88
Umrah, 273–78
    Kaaba visited in, 275–77
    prayers in, 275
    purity rituals in, 273
    ritual sites in, 277–78
United Arab Republic, 168
United Nations, 66, 160, 165, 254, 446
    1967 War and, 218–19, 220
    Resolution 242 in, 243
    Sinai peacekeeping force of, 218–219, 220
United Nations Conference for Women, Copenhagen (1980), 429–31
United Nations International Women's Year Conference (1975), 327, 408
United Nations Relief Fund, 116
United States, 155–56, 223, 231–32, 294–95, 296–97
    see also Carter, Jimmy
United States Information Library, 231–32

Vance, Cyrus, 385, 388, 389
village life, *see* Mit Abul-Kum village
visitors of the Dawn, 212–13
Voice of the Arabs, 224

Wafa' el-Nil, 51–52
Wafa' wal Amal, *see* Madinat el-Wafa'wal Amal
Wafd nationalist party, 36, 119
Wafia, Dalia, 35, 52–53, 146, 167
Wafia, Mahmoud Abu, 161, 167, 170
Wahhab, Abdel, 290
Wahhab, Muhammad Ibn Abdel, 345–46
Wahhab, Nahla, 290
Wallace, Edgar, 81
Walters, Barbara, 462
War of Attrition, 241–43, 252
Wasjmann, Patrick, 458
Weizman, Ezer, 381, 382, 409
Who's Who of Egypt, 165
women:
    in Abu Dhabi, 348–52
    divorce laws and, 108–10, 353–354, 357, 358, 365
    fundamentalists' views of, 356–358
    in grieving rituals, 187–88
    in Iran, 339–40
    Islam and, 328–30
    marriage as central to, 194
    in 1967 War effort, 222–23, 235
    in peasant vs. middle-class settings, 185–87
    under Personal Status Laws, 352–366, 464–65
    political rights of, 310–12, 363–365
    presidential decrees on, 364
    Quran on, 259–60
    in Saudi Arabia, 328–29, 344–348
    Shari'a and, 327–28
World War I, 79, 174
World War II, 46, 64, 66, 98
wudu', 60

Yacoub, Magdi, 21, 23,
Year of Decision, 282–83
Yemen, 226
Yemen, South, 384

Yom Kippur War, *see* October War
Yugoslavia, 295

zaffa, 105
zaghreet, 16, 104, 105
Zaid, Ahmed Abu, 77
Zaid, Fatima Abu ("Batta"), 36, 58, 93
Zaid, Husni Abu, 36
Zainab, Sayyida, 68
Zamalek Island, 35

Zamzam, Well of, 277–78
Zaytun Detention Center, 81
Zayyid, Sheikh, 348–49, 352
zikr, 44
Zion, Ben, 166
Zog, King of Albania, 426
Zoumor, Abboud el-, 439, 451
Zuwwar el-Fagr, 212, 214, 215–218

Printed in the United States
895000002B